Praise for The *Last Day of Oppression, and t*

"At a time when most scholars of contentious po...... ..a.. abandoned political economy, Jeffery Webber's latest book is a breath of fresh air. He shows how the rise of the new Latin American left was linked to a regional crisis of neoliberal capitalism at the turn of the millennium. And he shows how the delayed effects of the global economic crisis of 2007–2008 pushed left and center-left governments to adopt a politics of austerity, creating new opportunities for the right. Webber's analysis is also sensitive to the class and other struggles within and between left parties and movements, struggles which shaped how these formations would react to changing material circumstances. In all, this is simply the best book we have on the rise and current crisis of the new Latin American left. It's also a model for how to analyze contentious politics."
— Jeff Goodwin, New York University

"If you have ever wondered what happened to the beacon of hope that was, until recently, Latin America, this is the book to turn to. With supreme grasp of the continent's politics, Jeffrey R. Webber unpacks the contradictions of the left governments that once inspired dreams of a twenty-first-century socialism. Most importantly, he shows how they banked on extracting natural resources for the global market and then distributing the crumbs to the masses—and how dismally that strategy failed. Weaving together GDP data and traditions of anticolonial resistance, individual biographies, and debates in Marxist theory, always with a pulse of street movements running through the text, this is concrete analysis of the conjuncture as it should be done."
— Andreas Malm, author of *Fossil Capital: The Rise of Steam Power and the Roots of Global Warming*

"Combining Marxist and decolonial theoretical frameworks, Webber brings us much more than a study on economic policies: an insightful assessment of class struggles against the capitalist oligarchies and the market dictatorship in Latin America. In a brilliant discussion of José Carlos Mariátegui, he brings to the fore the relevance, for the present popular, peasant, and indigenous rebellions, of a utopian-revolutionary dialectic between the precapitalist past and the socialist future."
—Michael Löwy, author of *Ecosocialism: A Radical Alternative to Capitalist Catastrophe*

"A lucid, incisive and indispensable contribution for understanding the rise and fall of left and center-left governments associated with Latin America's 'pink tide.' Webber validates the superiority of a critical Marxian and decolonial approach for slicing through the thick layers of the center-left's self-serving rhetoric and for clearly identifying the tactical and strategic tasks popular movements have confronted in recent years. In the context of a fleeting commodities boom, the center-left's embrace of extractivism and compensatory state politics, as well as its penchant for servicing the interests of domestic and foreign capital while demobilizing social movements, lie at the core of its ultimate defeat. His meticulously crafted analysis examines the ebb and flow of social movements in diverse Latin American countries and spans the critical years that opened up with Venezuela's 1989 Caracazo and are seemingly being brought to a close by right-wing resurgence, evidenced most clearly in the 2016 institutional coup against Brazil's Dilma Rousseff. The end of the cycle of progressive governments poses new historical challenges. If they are to be successfully navigated, Latin American scholars (and societies) must overcome the stultifying effects of prevailing liberal conceptions about democracy, markets, capitalism, and the root causes of inequality; Jeffery Webber's book unflinchingly and brilliantly shows us 'why' but also 'how' to begin doing so."
—Fernando Leiva, author of *Latin American Neostructuralism:*
The Contradictions of Post-Neoliberal Development

The Last Day of Oppression, and the First Day of the Same

The Politics and Economics of the New Latin American Left

Jeffery R. Webber

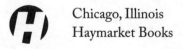

Chicago, Illinois
Haymarket Books

© 2017 Jeffery R. Webber

Published in 2017 by
Haymarket Books
P.O. Box 180165
Chicago, IL 60618
773-583-7884
www.haymarketbooks.org
info@haymarketbooks.org

ISBN: 978-1-60846-715-0

Trade distribution:
In the US, Consortium Book Sales and Distribution, www.cbsd.com
In Canada, Publishers Group Canada, www.pgcbooks.ca
All other countries, Publishers Group Worldwide, www.pgw.com

This book was published with the generous support of Lannan Foundation and Wallace Action Fund.

Cover design by Dan Tesser. Cover photo of a woman participating in massive government protests in Quito, Ecuador on August 13, 2015 © Amazon Watch.

Printed in Canada by union labor.

Library of Congress Cataloging-in-Publication data is available.

10 9 8 7 6 5 4 3 2 1

For Tieneke

Contents

ONE

Latin America's Second Independence

Ecuador's independence from Spain in the early nineteenth century did not bring with it a social revolution. The racist and unequal pyramidal hierarchy of colonial society was not turned on its head. Instead, the elite descendants of Spanish *conquistadores* now ruled on their own behalf, rather than in the service of the Spanish crown. For those beneath them, much remained as it had been. Thus a popular slogan of the postindependence period emerged: the last day of oppression, and the first day of the same.[1]

The expression, if in a novel form, captures something essential of the first decade and a half of twenty-first-century Latin American politics. The early 2000s saw a remarkable political and economic crisis of neoliberalism facilitate an explosive reawakening of extraparliamentary social movements throughout Latin America, but particularly in South America—strikes, land occupations, unemployed workers' roadblocks and factory takeovers, and indigenous uprisings. By the mid-2000s, this effervescence translated in a muted style into the parliamentary halls and presidential palaces of many South American countries as center-left and left parties were elected to office.

Parallel to these political dynamics, the economic crisis of neoliberalism

---

1 "Oppression" in this phrase is translated as "despotism" in Agustín Cueva's famous text *El proceso de dominación política del Ecuador* (Quito: Ediciones Crítica, 1972). I prefer "oppression" in this book, following common use of the slogan today, as described to me in a 2010 interview by indigenous activist Luis Macas in Quito, Ecuador.

in the region was eclipsed by the rising tide of a China-driven boom in international commodity prices. With minimal changes to the tax regimes and royalty rates on resource commodities—mining minerals, natural gas and oil, and agro-industrial products—left governments witnessed massive revenue increases in the state treasuries, even as multinational and domestic capitalists enjoyed soaring net profits. Targeted distribution through cash-transfer programs and other social welfare initiatives, along with higher employment rates, led to falling poverty rates, and even some falls in income inequality in parts of Latin America ruled by the various shades of the left.

Still, even taking into account variability across cases, the new Latin American left did not challenge the underlying class structures of its societies or the systems of capitalist accumulation that fundamentally reproduce the basic patterns of simultaneous wealth and poverty, of luxury alongside misery. The facility with which center-left and left governments were able to skim a portion of the rent generated by the commodities boom and redirect it to the popular classes helped for a time to conceal underlying structures of continuity. Politically, social movements were channeled into the labyrinth of state apparatuses and significantly disarmed in the process.

Then global capitalism entered its latest severe crisis in 2007–2008. The impact on Latin America was not immediate. Indeed, after a dip in growth in 2009, the next two years seemed to suggest the region had somehow escaped world dynamics. By 2012, however, China had dramatically slowed down, the Eurozone and the United States were sputtering, and the commodity prices that had done much to hold South America aloft started their swift descent. The politics of austerity already introduced with such rabidity in North America and Europe (especially southern Europe and particularly Greece) were now dictating the winds of Latin American political economies once again.

This time, however, it was center-left and left governments that began to make the class decisions of austerity politics. With declining state revenues, they began—again with variation across cases—to socialize the costs of declines in state treasuries onto the vast majority, rather than turning on the rich. They sided with the surplus appropriators rather than the direct producers of Latin American wealth. These class decisions often took the form of cuts to social programs that had been primed during the era of commodity booms. As opposed to radicalizing the left turn in the context of the emerging crisis, center-left and left governments increasingly adapted to the imperatives of capital. But while capital had flourished under many of these governments, the new left had never been the first choice of private investors. They have sensed blood, and are now going for the kill—new right politics are on the ascent in extraparliamentary and parliamentary forms throughout the region.

Thus, while left governments bend over backward to capitulate to capital and ensure market confidence, capital has left them to flounder in the political darkness, preferring a return to traditional and new rights, or sometimes a novel symbiosis of the two. Meanwhile, the austerity drives of left governments have alienated much of their popular bases, who show up in meager numbers when they are finally called upon to defend left administrations against right-wing belligerence in the streets, as in Congress.

The last day of oppression, and the first day of the same.

But this phrase should not be understood in fatalistic terms of predestined outcomes. The end of the cycle of progressive governments should not be equated straightforwardly with the end of the Latin American left. The latter's social movement and trade union modalities are unlikely to suffer quietly the counteroffensive of the right. The future is still in play. The outcome is undecided. And we will need to turn our eyes below and to the left to register the pulse of political developments in the years ahead—to the evolving ideological, organizational, and political balance of forces outside the institutional halls of formal professional politics and leaderships, as much as to what is happening inside those visible corridors of power. This book raises some of the questions that are important to keep in mind and provides some preliminary outlines of responses to these questions.

The Architecture of the Book

Chapter 2 examines the political and economic dynamics of the Latin American left from the early 1990s to the present. It measures the shifting balance of forces—ideological, social, economic, and military—between the rural and urban popular classes and oppressed groups, the domestic ruling classes, and imperialism across the different phases of the period in question. It maps the 1990s as a period of neoliberal hegemony and left-wing disarticulation before shifting to the economic crisis of neoliberalism between 1998 and 2002. It shows how this economic crisis transformed into a political crisis through the rise of extraparliamentary social movements and left-wing rearticulation in the early 2000s. From here it charts the movement of the left from the extraparliamentary terrain to the corridors of state power through the election of center-left and left governments in the mid-2000s in the context of a commodities boom. In this context, it explores the rise of compensatory states as the dominant left form of rule during the boom period. Next, the chapter maps the delayed reverberation of the global economic crisis of 2007–2008 into the region and its political consequences. It provides in-depth case studies of the present conjuncture in Argentina, Venezuela, Brazil, and Ecuador. The predominant themes in the case studies are declining forms of left hegemony and the various modalities of right-wing rearticulation.

Chapter 3 interrogates contemporary theoretical debates around enduring patterns of inequality in contemporary Latin America. It argues that the dominant streams of academic and policy writing on the topic are limited by their acknowledged or unacknowledged adherence to Weberian historical sociology and/or neostructuralist economics. These theoretical limitations mean that most writing on inequality in contemporary Latin America is flawed by a thin conception of democracy and a misconceptualization of capitalism, class, and other social relations of oppression. Much of this scholarship and policy literature is underpinned by a liberal ideology incapable of conceiving the constitutive coercive features of the capitalist market. Instead, the market is understood to require regulation at the margins, but it is ultimately understood to be a sphere of opportunities either to be seized or missed. Starting with the axiom of the market as the preeminent domain of freedom itself, liberal ideology cannot grasp struggles for *freedom from* the market. It thus misses most of what has been important about popular struggles in recent decades in Latin America. The chapter suggests as an alternative a combined Marxist and decolonial theoretical framework to approach inequality, one that attempts to encompass the totalizing power of capital and the complexity of class relations and other internally related social oppressions—gender, sexuality, race, and nation—in contemporary Latin American capitalism. The chapter grounds these theoretical discussions in concrete investigations of extractive capitalism and the militant biography of Luis Macas, an indigenous-Marxist dissident in contemporary Ecuador.

Chapter 4 explores the complex relationship between Marxism and Romanticism in the work of early twentieth-century Peruvian Marxist José Carlos Mariátegui. Following Michael Löwy, it argues that there is a utopian-revolutionary dialectic of the precapitalist past and socialist future running through Mariátegui's core works. The romantic thread of Mariátegui's thought was in many ways a response to the prevalent evolutionist and economistic Marxist orthodoxies of his time. An argument is made that the fruitful heresy embedded in the Mariáteguist framework might suggest the outlines for a theoretical research agenda to counter a novel orthodoxy emerging out of the state ideologies of the Andean new left in an era of intensifying extractive capitalism. Deploying a certain Marxist idiom, figures such as Bolivian vice president Álvaro García Linera defend as progressive the extension of large-scale mining, natural gas and oil extraction, and agro-industrial mono-cropping in alliance with multinational capital. Left and indigenous critics of this latest iteration of extractive capitalism in Latin America are condemned in this worldview as naive romantics, or worse, the useful idiots of imperialism. A creative return to Mariátegui allows us to read the opposition of left and indigenous critique and activism in a different light. What is more, we can see in the biographies of activists such as Felipe Quispe in Bolivia a concrete realization of the Romantic Marxist critique of evolutionism and economism being discussed theoretically in our exploration of Mariátegui.

Chapter 5 investigates the origins and outcomes of the student-worker rebellions of 2011–2012 in Chile. It argues that these remarkable mobilizations marked a before-and-after break in contemporary Chilean history. They introduced new elements into the common sense of Chilean society that broke with the neoliberal paradigm introduced under the dictatorship of Augusto Pinochet and consolidated under the post-authoritarian governments of the center-left Concertación coalitions. The 2011–2012 revolts were not reducible to student rebellion, although this obviously played a key part in the events. There were also various interconnections established in this period between the student movement and the revitalization of parts of the labor movement, Mapuche indigenous struggles, and socio-ecological resistance. Although the rebellions as a whole introduced a significant rupture in Chilean politics, the model of accumulation and political domination persisted in many respects. While the conservative government of Sebastián Piñera (2010–2014) provided a common enemy around which popular forces could easily cohere, the new center-left administration of Michelle Bachelet and her Nueva Mayoría (New Majority, NM) coalition, in office since 2014, has proved a more complicated antagonist. Bachelet ran on a platform to the left of her earlier presidency (2006–2010), absorbing key elements of the popular demands coming from below, even while consolidating relations with the dominant sections of capital in the country. The NM government has incorporated the Partido Comunista de Chile (Chilean Communist Party, PCC) and, crucially, many of its leading youth, who played such an important role in the rebellions of 2011–2012. In office, the overarching logic of the administration has been to introduce reforms at the margins, stabilizing political life and protecting the underlying fundamentals of the system of accumulation and the mode of political domination consolidated in the 1990s under the Concertación governments. It has sought to channel and disarm pressures from below, while surviving economic and political pressures from the hard right. Bachelet appeared to be eminently capable of such a dance for the first year in office, but 2015 has seen renewed instability, with charges of corruption coming from the right and a rebirth of the student-worker movement in the streets.

Chapter 6 examines the dynamics of the urban labor markets of Bolivia under Evo Morales (2006–2016) as a prism through which to characterize the class character of that administration. While the government of Morales rules in the name of indigenous workers and peasants, the chapter shows how in fact the country's political economy since 2006 has witnessed the ongoing subjugation of these classes. If the logic of large capital persists, it is legitimated in and through petty indigenous capitalists. The chapter argues that Antonio Gramsci's conceptualization of passive revolution offers a superior analytical point of departure for understanding contemporary Bolivian politics than Álvaro García Linera's more widely accepted theory of creative tensions. However, the dominant manner in which passive revolution has been employed in contemporary Latin American debates has treated the sociopolitical and the ideological as relatively autonomous from the process of capital accumulation. What is necessary, instead, is a sharper appreciation of the base/superstructure metaphor as expressing a dialectical unity of internal relations between "the economic" and "the political," thus avoiding one determinism or another. Through a reading of Gramsci that emphasizes such unity, chapter 6 interrogates the dynamics of "extractive distribution," class contradictions of the "plural economy," and transformations in the urban labor market that have characterized Bolivia's passive revolution under Evo Morales between 2006 and 2016.

Chapter 7 also deals with Bolivia, but this time from the vantage point of the countryside. It begins with a survey of Bolivia's rural sociospatial dynamics. From this point of departure it then explores the historical development of agrarian capitalism across three historical phases: 1) the 1952–1985 period of nationalist import-substitution industrialization; 2) the period of orthodox neoliberal restructuring between 1985 and 2000; and 3) the period of contested neodevelopmentalism under Evo Morales between 2006 and 2016.

The chapter challenges the notion that there has been extensive, egalitarian reform in Bolivia since Morales assumed the presidency in 2006. Its argument hinges on the changing balance of agrarian class forces in Bolivian society and the related changes in the class composition of the ruling MAS (Movimiento al Socialismo) bloc over time. Initially, there was a period under Morales's rule, between 2006 and 2009, in which the indigenous peasant social movement alliance, the Unity Pact, fought from below for a genuine transformation of the Bolivian rural class structure, and in which the agro-industrial elite fought openly against the central government through an autonomist and regionalist destabilization campaign, headquartered in Santa Cruz and radiating outward through the rest of the lowland departments of the country. The main institutional terrain of struggle in these opening years of the Morales regime was the Constituent Assembly process, and there was a possibility during this period of deep structural reform to the countryside. However, by 2010 the Morales government had defeated the political project of autonomy in the lowlands, and this laid the basis for a class realignment in the ruling bloc. Between 2010 and 2016, a novel agro-capital-state alliance emerged, with subordinate support from rich peasants in the coca, soy, and quinoa commercial export sectors, among others. The Unity Pact fragmented, and the lowland indigenous movements were expelled from their earlier participation in the governing alliance.

Chapter 8 shifts our attention to Venezuela. It offers an analysis of the Bolivarian process under Hugo Chávez (1999–2013) through an extended interrogation of George Ciccariello-Maher's influential *We Created Chávez*. The chapter argues that *We Created Chávez* is the most important book available in English proposing an anticapitalist framework for understanding the Bolivarian process in contemporary Venezuela, as well as its historical backdrop dating back to 1958. The book contains within it a laudable critique of Eurocentrism and a masterful combination of oral history, ethnography, and theoretical sophistication. It reveals with unusual clarity and insight the multiplicity of popular movements that allowed for Hugo Chávez's eventual ascension to presidential office in the late 1990s. *We Created Chávez* has set a new scholarly bar for social histories of the Bolivarian process and demands serious engagement by Marxists. As a first attempt at such engagement, this chapter reveals some critical theoretical and sociological flaws in the text and other areas of analytical imprecision. Divided into theoretical and historical parts, it unpacks some of the strengths and weaknesses by moving from the abstract to the concrete. The intervention begins with concepts—the mutually determining dialectic between Chávez and social movements; "the people"; and "dual power." From here, it grounds these concepts, and Ciccariello-Maher's use of them, in various themes and movements across specific historical periods of Venezuelan political development—the rural guerrillas of the 1960s, the urban guerrillas of the 1970s, the new urban sociopolitical formations of the 1980s, Afro-indigenous struggles in the Bolivarian process, and formal and informal working-class transformations since the onset of neoliberalism and its present contestation in the Venezuelan context.

TWO

Global Crisis and Latin American Tendencies: The Political Economy of the New Latin American Left

This chapter assesses the political and economic dynamics of the Latin American left in the lead-up to, and fallout from, the ongoing global economic crisis that began in 2007–2008. Claudio Katz, a leading Argentine Marxist, argues persuasively that for anyone interested in making sense of the modern Latin American left in any period over the last century or so, it is necessary to establish some measure of the balance and movement in power relations (ideological, social, economic, political, and military) between at least three social forces with distinct interests and capacities: the rural and urban popular classes and oppressed groups, the domestic ruling classes, and imperialism—particularly, but not exclusively, that of the United States.[1] The strength of the left—understood in all its complex social movement, party, and regime modalities—simultaneously flows out of and reinforces dialectically the objective organizational strengths of the popular classes and oppressed groups within this overarching balance of forces at any given time.[2]

---

1 Claudio Katz, "Socialist Strategies in Latin America," *Monthly Review* 59, no. 4 (2007).
2 Jeffery R. Webber and Barry Carr, "Introduction: The Latin American Left in Theory and Practice," in *The New Latin American Left: Cracks in the Empire*, eds. Jeffery R. Webber and Barry Carr (Lanham, MD: Rowman and Littlefield, 2013).

In tracing the trajectory of the left within this wider balance of forces, the chapter is divided into various parts. It begins by exploring the parameters of the left's weakness in the 1990s and the associated consolidation of the neoliberal economic model. It then turns to an analysis of how neoliberal consolidation turned into neoliberal crisis through the vector of the 1998–2002 regional recession. From here, it charts the rise of extraparliamentary and parliamentary left rearticulation out of the wake of the neoliberal crisis at the turn of the century. The chapter then explains how the initial radicalism associated with the extraparliamentary left was increasingly moderated through a combination of the structural stresses of electoral participation and a worldwide commodity boom driven by China's dynamic accumulation within the world market over this period. Next, the chapter attempts to provide a brief portrait of both the early aggregate economic fallout in Latin America from the global crisis beginning in 2007, and the heterogeneity of its initial effects across different subregions and countries. The following section then points toward the early political repercussions of the dynamics of the global crisis and world political conjuncture throughout Latin America. From here, the chapter looks at the delayed and deep economic reverberation of the global crisis into Latin America, which began in earnest in 2012, and shows how this has provided new opportunities for the right, as in the cases of Argentina and Venezuela. The last two sections explore the paradigmatic cases of declining left hegemony and the complexities of political impasse that have emerged in these settings, first in Brazil and then in Ecuador.

The Nadir of the Left in the 1990s

The Latin American left reached its lowest point in living memory in the early 1990s. From that vantage point, it would have been very difficult to foresee that in less than a decade the region would transform itself into the leading edge of antineoliberal resistance in the world. There had been a fierce physical and military annihilation of large swathes of the organized left and the leadership of its associated social and trade union organizations in the preceding decades. In Brazil and the Southern Cone of South America—Argentina, Chile, Paraguay, and Uruguay—a series of right-wing military dictatorships established over the 1960s, 1970s, and 1980s targeted leading individuals and rank-and-file activists in the organized left, trade union and peasant movements, and human rights organizations. A trail of death was left in the wake of these regimes, and the sociopolitical—not to mention psychological—destruction wrought on these societies as a result meant that the rearticulation of the left in its various forms would be halting and hesitant in the decades to follow.[3]

In Central America, a not dissimilar military attack was launched against the left in the 1970s and 1980s, this time in the form of counterrevolutionary authoritarian regimes facing off against mass guerrilla organizations such as the Frente Farabundo Martí para la Liberación Nacional (Farabundo Martí National Liberation Front, FMLN) in El Salvador, and the Unidad Revolucionaria Nacional Guatemalteca (Guatemalan National Revolutionary Unity, URNG) in Guatemala. The peace processes and accords that closed those civil wars in the 1990s were hardly a compromise between two equal sides. Rather, they left behind them hundreds of thousands killed at the hands of military and paramilitary forces, and an utterly routed left. Of course, both the military dictatorships of the Southern Cone and the right-wing regimes and death squads of Central America were systematically supported by the US Empire. These levels of sheer violence on the part of the domestic ruling classes and imperialism are absolutely central to the subsequent rolling out of neoliberal economic restructuring in the 1980s and 1990s. In order for that political project to come to fruition, the organized capacities of the popular classes and oppressed first had to be defeated.[4]

If that was the political and military balance of forces in the early 1990s, the ideological scene likewise showed little remorse to the left. The Soviet Union and its client states in Eastern Europe had collapsed. Cuba's regime, so inextricably bound up in the bipolarity of the Cold War, entered into immediate economic crisis as its principal sugar exports to the Soviet Union plummeted while the economic embargo from the United States continued in place. A "special period" of austerity was introduced on the island at the same time as the rest of the region was moving toward a full embrace of the market. The revolutionary regime of the Frente Sandinista de Liberación Nacional (Sandinista National Liberation Front, FSLN), first established in 1979, was defeated in elections in 1990 by a conservative candidate after a decade of violent destabilization on the part of the Contras, a right-wing paramilitary force backed by the United States.[5]

---

3 One of the best texts on these matters is Greg Grandin, ed., *A Century of Revolution: Insurgent and Counterinsurgent Violence in Latin America's Long Cold War* (Durham, NC: Duke University Press, 2010).

4 Greg Grandin, *The Last Colonial Massacre: Latin America in the Cold War*, 2nd ed. (Chicago: University of Chicago Press, 2011).

5 See Barry Carr and Steve Ellner, eds., *The Latin American Left: From the Fall of Allende*

Even for those sections of the Latin American left that had never been enamored with the bureaucratic authoritarianism of the Stalinist model, the collapse of the Soviet Union nonetheless marked a turning point after which great confusion and fatalism entered the ideological landscape with a vengeance. Left and center-left parties moved dramatically to the right, as the whole political spectrum narrowed. Electoral debates between the mainstream political parties in the 1990s turned on technical issues regarding how fast to roll out austerity, privatization, and liberalization, with very few significant forces calling into question the logic of the neoliberal model of accumulation in its entirety. Social movements retreated in large numbers to localized, community-based projects, where their reliance on internationally financed nongovernmental organizations (NGOs) tended to increase; this was a context that fed into their already accelerating depoliticization. Strategic aims of power at the level of the state began to recede from the left's purview.

Economically, this was the season of neoliberal ascent. Behind an ideological guise of the free market, strong and coercive states throughout the region rammed through policy agendas of free trade, austerity, financial liberalization, privatization of state-owned enterprises, and the retrenchment of welfare and developmental programs.[6] Disarticulated organizations of the social and political left were unable to mount much of a defensive struggle. In the early 1990s, the major exceptions to these trends were the Landless Rural Workers Movement (MST) in Brazil, the Zapatistas in southern Mexico, and the indigenous movement in Ecuador.[7]

The uneven international process of neoliberalization led to a series of worsening social conditions in Latin America and a difficult terrain for left recomposition. The old organizations and associational forms of urban working classes were decomposing as trade union power declined. In most countries, there was a dramatic informalization of the world of work, with insecure environments and

---

to Perestroika (Boulder, CO: Westview Press, 1993).

6 Alfredo Saad-Filho, "The Political Economy of Neoliberalism in Latin America," in *Neoliberalism: A Critical Reader*, eds. Alfredo Saad-Filho and Deborah Johnston (London: Pluto Press, 2005).

7 Leandro Vergara-Camus, *Land and Freedom: The MST, the Zapatistas, and Peasant Alternatives to Neoliberalism* (London: Zed, 2014); Marc Becker, *Indians and Leftists in the Making of Ecuador's Modern Indigenous Movements* (Durham, NC: Duke University Press, 2008). The popular anti-austerity revolt in Venezuela in 1989 known as the Caracazo is also a partial exception. See Margarita López-Maya, "The Venezuelan *Caracazo* of 1989: Popular Protest and Institutional Weakness," *Journal of Latin American Studies* 35, no. 1 (2003): 117–137.

no contracts.[8] In the countryside, peasants and indigenous communities were dispossessed of their land through processes of liberalization in the agrarian economies.[9] Their numbers swelled the ranks of the urban informal proletariat now populating the shantytowns on the edges of major cities.[10] Growing social inequality and poverty marked the condition of the region as a whole by the end of the 1990s, after the two-decade experiment with orthodox neoliberalism. While the military hand of US imperialism was perhaps less evident in the 1990s than it had been in previous decades in the region, its economic might was exercised without precedent through the mediating channels of the World Bank, International Monetary Fund, and Inter-American Development Bank.

The Crisis of Neoliberalism in Latin America

The ideological promise of neoliberal advocates in Latin America, as elsewhere, hinged on the promise of a rising tide that would lift all boats. The pain of austerity in the short term would be transcended over the medium and long run, as private investment flooded the market and sparked job growth, and as bloated state-owned enterprises were replaced with free competition and the dynamism of the market. Rising rates of employment would also lower rates of poverty, even as the system allowed the rich to get richer as an incentive mechanism. By the close of the 1990s, however, it was all too evident that even this minimal justification for the immediate social devastation of neoliberal structural adjustment could not hold up under scrutiny.

Economic growth over the course of the 1980s and 1990s—the core neoliberal epoch of Latin America's "silent revolution"—included a modest boom (1991–1997) positioned between "the lost decade" of the 1980s and the "lost half-decade" between 1997 and 2002. The neoliberal policy era in

---

8 Alejandro Portes and Kelly Hoffman, "Latin American Class Structures: Their Composition and Change during the Neoliberal Era," *Latin American Research Review* 38, no. 1 (2003): 41–82; Amy Bellone Hite and Jocelyn S. Viterna, "Gendering Class in Latin America: How Women Effect and Experience Change in the Class Structure," *Latin American Research Review* 40, no. 2 (2005): 50–82; Susan Spronk, "Neoliberal Class Formation(s): The Informal Proletariat and 'New' Workers' Organizations in Latin America," in Jeffery R. Webber and Barry Carr, eds., *The New Latin American Left: Cracks in the Empire* (Lanham, MD: Rowman and Littlefield, 2013).
9 William I. Robinson, *Latin America and Global Capitalism: A Critical Globalization Perspective* (Baltimore, MD: Johns Hopkins University Press, 2008).
10 Brodwyn Fischer, Bryan McCann, and Javier Auyero, eds., *Cities from Scratch: Poverty and Informality in Urban Latin America* (Durham, NC: Duke University Press, 2014).

Latin America progressed through the "deep recession" of 1982–1983, the "false dawn" of a temporary and meager recovery in positive per capita growth from 1984 to 1987, the increasing depth and breadth of neoliberal policy implementation between 1988 and 1991, and a thorough attempt to consolidate the model throughout the 1990s and early 2000s in the midst of increasing contradictions and crises—the Mexican Peso Crisis in 1994, Brazil's financial breakdown in 1998 in the wake of the Asian and Russian crises, and, most dramatically, the Argentine collapse, which reached its apogee in December 2001.[11] Following twenty years of debt rescheduling, the region's total debt was approximately $US 725 billion by 2002, twice the figure at the onset of the debt crisis in the early 1980s. Poverty rates between 1980 and 2002 increased from 40.5 percent of the population in 1980 to 44 percent in 2002.[12] In absolute figures, this translated into an increase of 84 million poor people across the region, from 136 million in 1980 to 220 million in 2002. Latin America continued to be the most unequal part of the world, such that, in 2003, the top 10 percent of the population earned 48 percent of all income.[13]

The recession between 1998 and 2002 was the worst to have struck Latin America since the early years of the debt crisis. Poverty and inequality shot up across the region, after two decades of declining social conditions and empty promises. The chasm between the ideology of neoliberalism and the material reality facing the rural and urban popular classes became unsustainable.[14] The answer from the great bulk of the conservative regimes in power at that moment, however, was simply an acceleration of neoliberal policies. The problem, as they assessed it, was one of consistent and widespread bureaucratic failure to fully implement initial structural adjustment programs, rather than being an issue inherent to the neoliberal paradigm itself. But if this agenda had been possible to sell to significant parts of the Latin American public at the outset of the debt crisis, after two decades of failed experimentation, in a period of

11 Duncan Green, *Silent Revolution: The Rise and Crisis of Market Economics in Latin America*, 2nd ed. (New York: Monthly Review Press, 2003), 72–118.

12 Araceli Damián and Julio Boltvinik, "A Table to Eat On: The Meaning and Measurement of Poverty in Latin America," in *Latin America after Neoliberalism: Turning the Tide in the 21st Century?*, eds. Eric Hersberg and Fred Rosen (New York: New Press, 2006), 145.

13 Luis Reygadas, "Latin America: Persistent Inequality and Recent Transformations," in *Latin America after Neoliberalism*, 122.

14 Susan Spronk and Jeffery R. Webber, "Introduction—System Logics and Historical Specificity: Renewing Historical Materialism in Latin American Political Economy," in *Crisis and Contradiction: Marxist Perspectives on Latin America in the Global Political Economy*, eds. Susan Spronk and Jeffery R. Webber (Chicago: Haymarket Books, 2015).

left defeat and panic over hyperinflation, ending in a massive recession, the bitter pill became increasingly difficult to swallow.

Latin America's Left Resurgence

A new recomposition of the social and political left emerged out of this conjuncture.[15] Its first expression was perhaps the 1998 election of Hugo Chávez on a moderately left ticket in Venezuela. But the larger part of this story in the early twenty-first century was an explosion of extraparliamentary forms of social struggle—road blockades, strikes, land occupations, worker takeovers of abandoned factories, protests, and even quasi-insurrectionary waves of mass action that toppled neoliberal governments in Argentina, Bolivia, and Ecuador.[16] A diversity of social subjects were involved in this rearticulation of popular movements, with unemployed workers leading unrest in Argentina, indigenous urban informal proletarians and peasants at the helm in Bolivia, and the Confederation of Indigenous Nationalities of Ecuador (CONAIE) playing a vanguard role in Ecuador. The demands of these movements between 2000 and 2003 shifted in some cases from defensive struggles against neoliberal continuation in a context of recession toward offensive anticapitalist struggles that sought a strategy of socialist transition in the novel setting of the twenty-first century.[17]

However, a recovery in growth levels across South America by 2003, and a concomitant turn away from extraparliamentary revolt and toward electoral politics, witnessed a moderation of strategic horizons and the rise to office of left and center-left governments throughout most of South America and parts of Central America in the mid- to late 2000s. If these areas had been controlled almost exclusively by parties committed to neoliberal orthodoxy in the 1980s and 1990s, it was by the mid-2000s impossible to run openly on a neoliberal ticket and succeed in electoral politics in most of Latin America. The ideological sea change ushered forth by the recession of 1998–2002 and the rearticulation of the militant social left in the early years of the century was remarkable. Argentina, Bolivia, Brazil, Chile, Ecuador, El Salvador, Guatemala, Nicaragua, Paraguay, Peru, Uruguay, and Venezuela were among the countries in the region that

---

15 Claudio Katz, *Las disyuntivas de la izquierda en América Latina* (Buenos Aires: Ediciones Luxemburg, 2008).

16 Franck Gaudichaud, ed., *El volcán latinoamericano: Izquierdas, movimientos sociales y neoliberalismo al sur del Río Bravo* (Madrid: Editorial Otramérica, 2010).

17 Massimo Modonesi and Julián Rebón, eds., *Una década en movimiento: Luchas populares en América Latina (2000–2009)* (Buenos Aires: CLACSO, 2011).

witnessed electoral victories of self-described left or center-left parties in the first decade of the twenty-first century.[18] This political reorientation of the Latin American scenario was occurring, of course, alongside shifts in the region's political economy and its relationship to the world market. Commodity prices stalled in 2011 and then began a precipitous and ongoing decline to the present. This, as will be discussed, has been the principal mechanism through which the global economic crisis has made its delayed impact on Latin America. Center-left and left governments in South America have suffered the political brunt of these dynamics, declining in popularity as they rule over economies in descent. The right has a new lease on life in the region, even if it is too early to declare unequivocally the end of the current cycle of Latin American left politics.

Latin America's Commodities Boom and the Compensatory State

A set of unique regional dynamics in South America between 2003 and 2011, related to patterns of accumulation elsewhere in the world market (notably high rates of growth in China), kicked off a concerted shift towards the acceleration of mining, oil and gas extraction, and agro-industrial mono-crop cultivation throughout the continent.[19] Similar to the period normally described as "neoliberal," massive multinational corporations were deeply imbricated in the extension of extraction at the heart of this primary commodity–led growth everywhere in the region.[20] Those cases in which center-left regimes entered into joint contracts between state-owned enterprises and multinationals, and negotiated relatively higher royalties and taxes on these extractive activities, were no exception.[21]

---

18 Franck Gaudichaud, ed., *América Latina: Emancipaciones en construcción* (Santiago: Editorial América en Movimiento y Tiempo robado editoras, 2015); Massimo Modonesi, ed., *Movimientos subalternos, antagonistas y autónomos en México y América Latina* (Mexico: CLACSO y FCPyS-UNAM, 2015).

19 José Seoane, Emilio Taddei, and Clara Algranati, *Extractivismo, despojo y crisis climática: Desafíos para los movimientos sociales y los proyectos emancipatorios de Nuestra América* (Buenos Aires: Herramienta editores, 2013).

20 Todd Gordon and Jeffery R. Webber, *Blood of Extraction: Canadian Imperialism in Latin America* (Halifax: Fernwood, 2016).

21 Anthony Bebbington and Jeffrey Bury, eds., *Subterranean Struggles: New Dynamics of Mining, Oil, and Gas in Latin America* (Austin: University of Texas Press, 2014); Nicolás Grinberg and Guido Starosta, "From Global Capital Accumulation to Varieties of Centre Leftism in South America: The Cases of Brazil and Argentina," in Spronk and Webber, eds., *Crisis and Contradiction*.

Skimming from the rent generated, many South American governments have established what Uruguayan political economist Eduardo Gudynas terms "compensatory states," whose legitimacy rests on the modest redistribution achieved through the priming of often already existing cash-transfer programs to the extremely poor, without touching the underlying class structure of society.[22] Other political economists prefer the term "neodevelopmental" states, but this conceptualization sometimes exaggerates the heightened role of the state and the weakened role of multinational capital in the most recent period of Latin American development.[23] Indeed, the very reproduction of these political economies depends upon states prioritizing the maintenance and security of private property rights and juridical environments in which multinationals can profit. But there was a set of contradictions that impeded the easy reproduction of South American compensatory states, even in a period of booming commodity prices.

Because the legitimacy function of relatively petty handouts ran on the blood of extraction, the compensatory state increasingly became a repressive state on behalf of capital, as the expansion of extraction necessarily accelerated what David Harvey called accumulation by dispossession, and the variegated forms of resistance it regularly spawns.[24] In the representative and ongoing case of the Territorio Indígena del Parque Nacional Isiboro-Sécure (Isiboro Sécure National Park and Indigenous Territory, TIPNIS) in Bolivia, the steamrolling of the rights to self-governance of indigenous communities resisting highway construction through their territory illustrates the coercive wing of the compensatory state in action.[25] Indigenous self-government in Bolivia is to be defended by president Evo Morales, it would seem, only when

22 Eduardo Gudynas, "Estado compensador y nuevos extractivismos: Las ambivalencias del progresismo sudamericano," *Nueva Sociedad*, 237 (January–February 2012): 128–146. See also Eduardo Gudynas, *Extractivismos: Ecología, economía y política de un modo de entender el desarrollo la Naturaleza* (Cochabamba: CEDIB, 2015).

23 For a critique of the neo-structuralist economics which underpins much of the work on "neo-developmentalism" see Juan Grigera, "Conspicuous Silences: State and Class in Structuralist and Neo-Structuralist Thought," in Spronk and Webber, eds., *Crisis and Contradiction*.

24 David Harvey, *The New Imperialism* (Oxford: Oxford University Press, 2003), 144. It should be obvious that while accumulation by dispossession and state repression occur under compensatory states in the region, and should be analyzed in all the necessary depth and detail, the point here is not to suggest any equivalence in levels or character of repression between these regimes and the kind of state and paramilitary terror carried out in recent years under far-right regimes in the region, such as Mexico, Colombia, Peru, and Honduras.

25 The TIPNIS conflict is discussed in more detail in chapter 7.

the claims are to territories marginal to the state's development project.[26]

The compensatory state in Latin America co-opted and coerced in response to such signs of opposition and built an accompanying ideological apparatus to defend multinationals—an ideology in which communities of resistance were vilified as internal enemies acting in concert with the interests of, or even in the pay of, various instruments of imperialism. The discursive gestures of state officials, of course, safely set to one side the obvious imperial character of the dispossessing activities of multinational corporations—now called "partners" rather than "bosses" in development—within the matrix of the new extractivism. Whatever the ecological and social contradictions of this development strategy over time, however, its fairly impressive capacities for reproduction in the short term were demonstrated in the Bolivian case.

In the midst of the commodities boom driven by China's dynamism, aggregate economic growth was steady in Bolivia, averaging 4.8 percent between 2006 and 2012, with an apex of 6.1 percent in 2008 and a low of 3.4 percent in 2009, in the immediate fallout from the world crisis.[27] Bolivian growth did not suffer in the immediate wake of the global crisis because regional demand for natural gas persisted, and there were locked-in deals as set prices with Brazil and Argentina. The export of natural gas to Brazilian and Argentine markets continued to outpace all other national exports in the immediate aftermath of the crisis in the United States and Europe. Between January and May 2013, for example, the value of external sales of natural gas reached $US 5 billion, up 15.6 percent relative to the same period in 2012. According to figures from the National Statistics Institute of Bolivia, gas exports constituted 52.8 percent of total exports in the first trimester of 2014, followed by industrial manufacturing (24.2 percent), mining (17.2 percent), and agriculture (4.5 percent). In 2013, the country logged a record peak of foreign direct investment, again mostly in gas. The Morales era has witnessed an unprecedented accumulation of international reserves, and inflation rates have been clamped at levels that keep Milton Friedman satisfied from the grave.

The general development strategy, according to Marianela Prada Tejada, executive of the cabinet that runs the Ministry of Finance, is to "take advantage of the possibility of growth through the exploitation of natural resources, with the state capturing the surplus and redistributing it to social programs and to other

26 Silvia Rivera Cusicanqui et al., eds., *TIPNIS: Amazonia en resistencia contra el Estado colonial en Bolivia* (Madrid: Editorial Otramérica, 2013).
27 Jeffery R. Webber, "Managing Bolivian Capitalism," *Jacobin* 13 (2014): 45–55.

economic sectors that generate employment."[28] Indeed, Morales was able to capture a bigger share of the rent generated from the commodities boom than did orthodox neoliberal regimes of the past due to moderate increases in the taxes and royalties exacted from multinational petroleum companies, even if this did not warrant the label "nationalization." As a result, there were notable declines in poverty and extreme poverty, and improvements in health and education.

One redistributive channel of rent to the poorest sectors has been a series of targeted cash-transfer programs, which now reach roughly 33 percent of the population—Bono Juancito Pinto (funds to encourage children to attend school), Renta Dignidad (a small monthly payment to the elderly poor), and Bono Juana Azurduy (funds to improve healthcare for expectant mothers, as well as postnatal medical care). Official government figures suggest an impressive fall in poverty from 60.6 percent in 2005 to 45 percent in 2011, and extreme poverty from 38.2 percent to 20.9 percent over the same period. Rural areas have been most affected, with extreme poverty falling from 62.9 percent in 2005 to 41.3 percent in 2011.[29]

Unsurprisingly in this context, the government was popular for the duration of the commodities boom. In a poll of the major cities conducted in June 2014, the administration's nationwide approval rating was 54 percent. In El Alto, the indigenous shantytown that borders the capital city of La Paz, support for the government sat at 66 percent. And, for the first time, just under half the population of Santa Cruz—historically the national heartland of reaction and white supremacy—approved of the government, even though it is led by the country's first indigenous president. Indeed, Morales as a personal figure was more popular than the government as a whole, enjoying an extraordinary 73 percent approval rating in El Alto and 51 percent in Santa Cruz.

In Venezuela, too, high rates of growth and redistribution efforts helped to secure a high level of popularity for Chávez, and, for a brief period and to a lesser extent, his successor, Nicolás Maduro.[30] After recovering from the steep collapse in 2002 and 2003—gross domestic product (GDP) declined to 8.9 percent and 7.8 percent, respectively, as a consequence of political crisis spurred by an unsuccessful coup attempt and business-led oil lockout—GDP soared on high petroleum prices to 18.3, 10.3, 9.9, and 8.2 percent in the years 2004–2007. There was a drop to 4.8 percent in 2008, as the international oil

---

28 Interview with the author, June 28, 2013, La Paz.
29 Jeffery R. Webber, "Managing Bolivian Capitalism," 47.
30 Susan Spronk and Jeffery R. Webber, "Sabaneta to Miraflores: Afterlives of Hugo Chávez in Venezuela," *New Politics* 14, no. 4 (Summer 2014).

price took a fourth-quarter plunge from $US 118 to $US 58 a barrel due to centrifugal waves of the global crisis spreading out from its epicenters in the United States and the Eurozone. Within six months, however, world oil prices recovered, and countercyclical spending brought the Venezuelan economy up to 4.2 percent growth in 2011 and 5.6 percent in 2012.[31]

A significant cut of oil revenue captured by the state over this period was directed toward social programs—known as missions—in health, education, and housing.[32] According to official national statistics, the cash income poverty level fell 37.6 percent under Chávez, from 42.8 percent of households in 1999 to 26.7 percent in 2012. Extreme poverty dropped 57.8 percent, from 16.6 percent to 7 percent between 1999 and 2011. If these income poverty measures are expanded to include welfare improvements such as the doubling in college enrollment since 2004, access to free health care for millions of new users, and extensive housing subsidies for the poor, it is easy to see how there have been very real material reasons for the popular classes to continue supporting the government.

Early Attenuation

The impact of the ongoing global crisis of capitalism that began in 2007–2008 was relatively muted in Latin America until 2012. Aggregate growth in Latin America and the Caribbean as a whole was comparatively high at 4.8 percent in 2008. The first fallout of the crisis struck by way of momentary deceleration to -1.9 percent in 2009, but this was followed by rates of 5.9 percent and 4.3 percent growth in 2010 and 2011, respectively.[33] Relatively steady commodity prices on the international market, sustained by what was still only a modest slowdown in China, were crucial in explaining these trends. In addition, there was an increase in foreign direct investment (FDI) into the region and countercyclical spending on the part of most governments since 2009, drawing on an unprecedented accumulation of foreign reserves as a result of the commodities boom since 2003.[34]

31 Mark Weisbrot and Jake Johnston, *Venezuela's Economic Recovery: Is It Sustainable?* (Washington, DC: Center for Economic and Policy Research, September 2012), 7, 10; EIU, *Venezuela: Country Report* (London: Economist Intelligence Unit, March 2013), 8.

32 The missions are discussed in Gregory Wilpert, *Changing Venezuela by Taking Power: The History and Policies of the Chávez Government* (London: Verso Books, 2006); and Iain Bruce, *The Real Venezuela* (London: Pluto Press, 2009).

33 CEPAL, *Anuario Estadístico de América Latina y el Caribe, 2012* (Santiago, Chile: Comisión Económica para América Latina y el Caribe, 2012), 77.

34 Claudio Katz, "Los atolladeros de la economía latinoamericana," *Herramienta Web* 10

But this overarching picture concealed considerable heterogeneity across different subregions and particular countries. Notably, South America, with the exception of Venezuela, was the least affected in the early years of the crisis, mostly due to the fact that trade patterns in South America shifted away from the United States in the first decade of the twenty-first century and toward the Chinese market and, to a lesser extent, Europe. Mexico, Central America, and the Caribbean, in contrast, were struck much more severely early on by the crisis, given their deep integration with the US economy. The crisis in the United States meant for these areas the collapse of their principal export market, in one direction, and, in the other, a slowdown in remittances returning from migrant laborers based in the United States, as well as the temporary or permanent return of many laborers from the United States as they lost their jobs, applying added pressure on labor markets at home.

Initial Politics of Crisis

The initial political repercussions of the current world conjuncture in Latin America proved to be as diverse as the economic dynamics. In the early years of the global crisis, and as an expression of its attenuated introduction to the Latin American setting, there was as much continuity as rupture in the region's political landscape. At the level of governmental forms, there was a consolidation of the center-left regimes in South America, with electoral continuity of moderately reformist parties in power in Brazil, Argentina, Uruguay, and Paraguay, among other cases. These regimes benefited from being able to manage modest redistribution policies in a context of continuing high commodity prices while appeasing, and in many cases further enriching, their domestic capitalist classes. The geopolitical pull of these regimes in South America in this setting, particularly that of Brazil under Luiz Inácio Lula da Silva ("Lula") and then under Dilma Rousseff, has been a factor in attracting the regimes that have typically been considered to be more radical in character—Bolivia under Evo Morales, Venezuela under Hugo Chávez (and now Nicolás Maduro), and Ecuador under Rafael Correa—increasingly into the center-left orbit. The fact that the language of "neodevelopmentalism" promoted by center-left regimes had considerably more cachet in the region as a whole by 2013 than that of "twen-

(December 2011); Claudio Katz, "The Singularities of Latin America," in *Socialist Register 2012: The Crisis and the Left*, eds. Leo Panitch, Gregory Albo, and Vivek Chibber (New York: Monthly Review Press, 2011); Claudio Katz, "The Three Dimensions of the Crisis," in Spronk and Webber, eds., *Crisis and Contradiction*.

ty-first century socialism" is one basic indication of the ideological shifts under way since the decline of the extraparliamentary radicalism of the early 2000s.

Meanwhile, the early years of the global crisis saw orthodox neoliberalism consolidate itself at the government level in Mexico under Enrique Peña Nieto, in Chile under Sebastián Piñera (the furthest right government in Chile since the dictatorship of Augusto Pinochet), in Guatemala under Otto Pérez Molina (linked to scorched-earth campaigns and other human rights abuses during his time as a military commander under the dictatorship of Efraín Ríos Montt), and in the conservative legacy of Álvaro Uribe in Colombia, fundamentally living on, albeit in a different surface mode, under his successor Juan Manuel Santos.[35]

In extraparliamentary terms, the far right was equally active, seeking to counter the leftward trajectory of politics in the region in the preceding fifteen years. Successful coups d'état were carried out in Honduras in 2009, against democratically elected center-leftist Manuel Zelaya, and in Paraguay in 2012, against the reformist priest Fernando Lugo.[36] The latter took the form of a "parliamentary coup," whereby Congress illegally forced the president to resign, without needing the military to expressly intervene, as was the case in Honduras.[37] A failed coup attempt, mimicking in some ways the one of April 2002 in Venezuela, was carried out in Bolivia in 2008.[38] Paramilitary goons and private security companies operated in the interests of extractive multinational capital in the mining and oil and natural gas industries throughout much of the region, intimidating and assassinating social movement activists who got in the way.

The extraparliamentary left, meanwhile, took on distinct forms in different country contexts. In ostensibly conservative Chile, the incredible student-worker uprisings of 2011–2013 shook to the core the stability of the Piñera govern-

---

35 As the balance of forces shifted decisively against the principal guerrilla group, the Fuerzas Armadas Revolucionarias de Colombia (Revolutionary Armed Forces of Colombia, FARC) in Colombia over the course of the 2000s, and as the benefits of continuing war to the Colombian state and various sections of foreign and domestic capital deteriorated, Santos began in 2012 a two-pronged strategy of peace negotiations with the FARC (hosted by the Cuban government in Havana and enraging Uribe), on the one hand, and ongoing military assault against the guerrillas within Colombia, on the other. The peace process continues as this book goes to press.

36 Todd Gordon and Jeffery R. Webber, "Post-Coup Honduras: Latin America's Corridor of Reaction," *Historical Materialism* 21, no. 3 (2013): 16–56.

37 Lorena Soler, "Golpe de Estado y derechas en Paraguay: Transiciones circulares y restauración conservadora," *Nueva Sociedad* 254 (November–December 2014): 73–83.

38 I discuss this at length in Webber, *From Rebellion to Reform in Bolivia: Class Struggle, Indigenous Liberation, and the Politics of Evo Morales* (Chicago: Haymarket Books, 2011).

ment. In Colombia, a nationwide rural strike in August and September 2013 crippled the Santos government and sparked major sympathy demonstrations by students and workers in the major cities. In Mexico, a defensive strike by teachers against the restructuring of public education in 2013 was the biggest workers' demonstration in the country for several decades. In Honduras, a national movement of resistance rose up in impressive unity against the consolidation of the coup regime under president Porfirio "Pepe" Lobo.

At the same time, self-styled radical regimes rooted in the accumulation model of extractive capitalism also faced increasing opposition from the social left. In Bolivia, protesters engaged in demonstrations and strikes against the end of subsidies to domestic natural gas consumption, and the extension of a highway through the TIPNIS, among other major conflicts during the second administration of Morales (2010–2014). In Ecuador, anti-mining activism pitted a new left opposition against Correa's government, with CONAIE playing a leading role.[39] In Venezuela, far left forces within Chavismo struggled against conservative, bureaucratic layers within their own movement at the same time as they faced off against imperialism and the recalcitrant Venezuelan right in the wake of Chávez's death in March 2013.[40]

Delayed Reverberation

By 2012, it was patently clear that Latin America, whatever the hopes and illusions of some analysts, would not be shielded from the effects of the global crisis. While in 2011 aggregate growth in Latin America and the Caribbean reached 4.7 percent, this was followed by a downturn to 2.9 percent growth in 2012 and 2013 alike, with further drops to follow. In 2014, the world economy picked up slightly from 2013, with aggregate growth moving from 2.4 percent to 2.6 percent.[41] The growth of "developing countries" continued to decelerate, however, even if growth levels in the developing world continued to be superior to growth of the developed world. On average, developing countries grew at 4.4 percent in 2014. China's growth continued to slow in 2014 to 7.3 percent, down

39 Jeffery R. Webber, "A New Indigenous-Left in Ecuador?" *NACLA Report on the Americas* (September–October 2011): 9–13; Marc Becker, *Pachakutik: Indigenous Movements and Electoral Politics in Ecuador* (Lanham, MD: Rowman and Littlefield, 2012).

40 Susan Spronk and Jeffery R. Webber, "Sabaneta to Miraflores: The Afterlives of Hugo Chávez in Venezuela," *New Politics* 14, no. 4 (2014): 97–109.

41 CEPAL, *Balance Preliminar de las Economías de América Latina y el Caribe 2014* (Santiago: CEPAL, 2013), 7.

from 7.7 percent in 2013, which was the slowest rate of growth the country had experienced in over two decades. Aggregate external demand for Latin America and the Caribbean weakened, both because of the continued low growth of the core countries and the slowdown of developing countries—above all China, which had become the principal trading partner of various countries in the region, particularly those that were primary exporters. The prices of primary materials in this context have continued on a downward trend. Overall prices of primary materials fell 10.5 percent in 2014, on the back of a fall of 5.2 percent in 2013.[42] This helps to explain why Latin America and the Caribbean witnessed a decline in FDI of 25 percent to 30 percent in 2014, corresponding with the end of the cycle of investments into mining in particular.[43]

In this worsening global context, the overall GDP of Latin America and the Caribbean reached only 1.1 percent growth in 2014, the lowest since 2009. But there were important differences in the rhythm of growth in different countries. Most significantly, there was a lack of dynamism and even contraction in some of the region's major economies: Argentina (-0.2 percent), Brazil (0.2 percent), Mexico (2.1 percent), and Venezuela (-3.1 percent).[44] By contrast, the fastest growing countries were Panama and the Dominican Republic (both 6.0 percent), followed by Bolivia (5.2 percent), Colombia (4.8 percent), and Guyana and Nicaragua (both at 4.5 percent). In a reversal of earlier trends in the fallout from the global crisis, Mexico, Central America, and the Caribbean benefited from the return of modest growth in the United States, the principal destination for many of these countries' exports, as well as the source of remittances. South America, in contrast, experienced a drop in demand for goods because of lower growth in Europe and China.[45]

In 2015, the world economy grew 2.4 percent, down slightly from 2014. Global patterns were conditioned by further slowdown in developing countries, from 4.3 percent to 3.8 percent growth between 2014 and 2015. Again, China's pace of growth continued its slumping trajectory, in 2015 slowing to 6.8 percent, the first time the country's economy had expanded at less than 7 percent since 1990.[46] This dynamic helped to extend the fall of raw material prices. Metal and agricultural product prices began their downward trend in the first quarter of 2011. Between then and April 2015, the respective decline in prices in these

42 Ibid., 7.
43 Ibid., 9.
44 Ibid., 8.
45 Ibid., 9.
46 ECLAC, *Preliminary Overview of the Economies of Latin America and the Caribbean 2015* (Santiago: ECLAC, 2015), 7.

sectors was 41 percent and 29 percent.[47] Energy prices (crude oil, natural gas, and coal), meanwhile, dropped sharply by 52 percent between July 2014 and January 2015, after an extended period of stagnation and slow decline. Crude oil, the most significant component of this price index, fell by almost 60 percent in that period.[48] The nosedive in energy continued in 2015, with prices falling a further 24 percent between January and October 2015, while metals dropped 21 percent and agricultural commodities by 10 percent over the same period.[49] This is part of the explanation for the 22 percent decline of inward flowing FDI into the region in 2015, relative to its already low level in 2014.[50]

Across Latin America and the Caribbean as a whole, terms of trade worsened by 9 percent in 2015. But there was considerable subregional variation. In Central America and the Caribbean (excluding Trinidad and Tobago), terms of trade actually improved by 5 percent and 2 percent, respectively. South America, by contrast, witnessed a deterioration of 13 percent. This, predictably, hit countries that export hydrocarbons (natural gas and oil) the hardest, where terms of trade fell by 27 percent.[51] In this scenario, aggregate GDP in Latin America and the Caribbean contracted by 0.4 percent in 2015, recording the worst year since 2009. But subregional variation was once again notable. South American economies were hit most severely, falling from 0.6 percent growth in 2014 to -1.6 percent in 2015. Of these, the economies of Brazil and Venezuela were the most gravely injured.[52] Central American economies, meanwhile, grew at 4.4 percent overall.[53]

While the external context of falling commodity prices severely affected South American economies, domestic consumption was also a serious problem. In Latin America and the Caribbean as a whole, domestic demand fell by 0.7 percent. Private consumption contracted at a rate of -0.3 percent, as did gross fixed capital formation (which declined at a rate of -4.2 percent). Public consumption picked up meagerly at 0.7 percent. These figures, as in the other economic indicators, were worse in South America and Mexico than in Central America and the Caribbean.[54]

---

47 ECLAC, *Economic Survey of Latin America and the Caribbean 2015* (Santiago: ECLAC, 2015), 15.
48 Ibid.
49 ECLAC, *Preliminary Overview*, 7.
50 Ibid., 8.
51 Ibid.
52 Ibid.
53 Ibid., 9.
54 Ibid.

New Right Revival in Argentina

On the surface of formal politics there are many regional continuities, despite the trenchant economic reversals. Peña Nieto and Santos continue their conservative reign over Mexico and Colombia, respectively. The horrific terror of the post-coup regime in Honduras persists, with the murder in early March 2016 of Berta Cáceres, a leading activist in Consejo Cívico de Organizaciones Populares e Indígenas de Honduras (Civic Council of Popular and Indigenous Organizations of Honduras, COPINH), an emblematic indicator of the obstacles facing social movements in that country. In contrast, Michelle Bachelet, of the Chilean Socialist Party, succeeded Piñera as president in 2014, and on an electoral platform that was further left than her earlier presidency (2006–2010), thanks in no small part to the impact of the student-worker rebellions that precipitated her rise. At the time of writing (mid-April 2016), it also seems likely that Keiko Fujimori, daughter of ex-dictator Alberto Fujimori, will become the next president of Peru, replacing Ollanta Humala, in office since 2011. Fujimori is running on the far-right legacy of her father. Humala, for his part, ran on a moderate left platform, but has governed from the right, aligning with multinational mining capital and fiercely repressing socioecological and indigenous resistance to capitalist extractivism in that country.

The most important sea change of the conjuncture is still in motion, however, and the results have in no way stabilized. The key phenomenon in flux is a rejuvenating new right in settings of center-left and left hegemonic erosion. We see this happening, at different speeds and with specific national characteristics, in various countries of South America where the economic crisis has become a political one. It has crystallized in the formal field of politics in Argentina and Venezuela, and is driving part of the extraparliamentary struggles in Brazil and Ecuador, as will be explained in more detail below.

In Argentina, there was an unexpected second-round runoff in the presidential election on November 22, 2015, pitting Daniel Scioli—the continuity candidate to succeed Cristina Fernández de Kirchner for the Peronist party, but decisively on the right wing of Peronism—against Mauricio Macri, a prominent businessperson, mayor of Buenos Aires, and candidate for Propuesta Republicana (Republican Proposal, PRO), a center-right outfit.[55] Scioli had been expected to win in the first round but ended up losing in the second. Macri won by a slight margin, ran on a vague platform of empty platitudes, and faces growing resistance to his austerity agenda. But his zeal in carrying

---

55 Juan Grigera, "The Argentine Challenge," *Jacobin*, November 1, 2015.

out an orthodox neoliberal restoration has surprised many. The Macri project is to fundamentally uproot the heterodox neoliberal/neodevelopmental legacy of Kirchnerism—Néstor Kirchner (2003–2007), Cristina Fernández de Kirchner (2007–2015)—and to restore, in many ways, the earlier legacy of right-wing Peronist Carlos Menem (1989–1999).[56]

Within the first three months in office, Macri laid off 20,000 public sector workers and facilitated the sacking of another 30,000 in the private sector. Tariff hikes to basic services have been introduced, acting as a flat tax increase with the sharpest repercussions for the poorest consumers, a number of whom have had their electricity cut. Macri has gifted agribusiness with a simultaneous devaluation of the currency and a cut in their taxes. Mining companies, similarly, have seen reductions in their corporate tax rates, while oil companies—which accumulated massive profits in the years of high prices—have been compensated by the state for the recent crash in the price per barrel of petroleum. Banks, too, are enjoying a spike in profitability under the Macri presidency, as regulations and controls introduced during the Kirchner era have been discarded.[57]

Under the guise of combatting narcotrafficking, Macri has reintroduced a role for the military in domestic policing, an imminent threat to criminalize popular urban neighborhoods and social movements more generally. Rule by decree has been normalized, with parliamentary checks on the president's power set aside with gusto. Functionaries of the new government are attempting to rewrite history, calling into question the fact that 30,000 people were disappeared during the dictatorship of 1976–1983 and breathing new life into the discredited "two demons" thesis of the Cold War—that is, that there was somehow a symmetry of blame for the violence of the dictatorship, between a provocative radical left and a reactionary radical right.[58]

Geopolitically, Macri's early rule has been stamped by unhesitating sub-

---

56 For probing political and economic assessments of the Kirchner era, see Juan Grigera, ed., *Argentina despúes de la convertabilidad (2002–2011)* (Buenos Aires: Imago Mundi, 2013); Mariano Féliz, "The Neo-Developmentalist Alternative: Capitalist Crisis, Popular Movements, and Economic Development in Argentina since the 1990s," in Spronk and Webber, eds., *Crisis and Contradiction*; Emilia Castorina, "The Reproduction of Democratic Neoliberalism in Argentina: Kirchner's 'Solution' to the Crisis of 2001," in Spronk and Webber, eds., *Crisis and Contradiction*; Alberto Bonnet, *La insurrección como restauración: El Kirchnerismo, 2002–2015* (Buenos Aires: Promoteo, 2015); Adrián Piva, *Economía y política en la Argentina Kirchnerista* (Buenos Aires: Batalla de ideas, 2015); Maristella Svampa, "The End of Kirchnerism," *New Left Review* 53 (2008): 79–95.

57 Claudio Katz, "Noventa días de Macri," electronic bulletin, March 5, 2016, www.lahaine.org/mundo.php/noventa-dias-de-macri.

58 Ibid.

mission to empire. At the World Economic Forum in Davos, Switzerland, he met with conservative British prime minister David Cameron without mentioning the British government's recent provocations over the fate of the Malvinas/Falklands islands. He has assured Benjamin Netanyahu that securing contracts for Israeli firms will be forthcoming. March 24, 2016, the fortieth anniversary of the military coup that was backed by the US government, was scheduled by Macri's handlers, whether out of stupidity or arrogance, as the day to receive US president Barack Obama in Buenos Aires.[59] The new Argentine president has also promised that Argentina will join the US-led regional integration project, Trans-Pacific Alliance, alongside Chile, Colombia, Mexico, and Peru; is seeking a bilateral free trade agreement with the European Union; is open to signing onto the Transatlantic Trade and Investment Partnership (TTIP); and has severed ties with the subsidized Latin American alternative television channel, Telesur.[60]

All the same, there are severe constraints standing in the way of the full realization of Macri's aspirations. Inflation is increasing. Domestic consumption is falling. Investment is stagnating. Exports have stalled. Although the right has momentum regionally, unlike the period under Menem, neighboring countries are not governed by hegemonic neoliberal regimes. Most importantly, there are early signs of enlivened popular antagonism, with repeated strikes by public sector workers and neighborhood demonstrations against tariff increases leading the way.[61]

Venezuela at a Crossroads

In Venezuela, the stakes are that much higher. Unlike in Argentina, where the popularity of Kirchnerism was rooted in expanding the consumption capacity of the popular classes while continuing to line the pockets of domestic and multinational capitalists, redistribution in Venezuela was also accompanied by a much more deeply rooted process of politicization and organization of the popular classes, and consequently much fiercer and repeated confrontations with the country's old elite and US interests.

---

59 Ibid.
60 Carlos E. Cué, "Argentina sale de Telesur, la cadena latinoamericana creada por Chávez," *El País*, March 28, 2016; Jason Marczak and Peter S. Rashish, "Argentina's New President Wants to Change the Way Latin America Does Business," *Foreign Policy*, December 10, 2015.
61 Katz, "Noventa días de Macri."

On live television in early March 2013, Venezuelan vice president Nicolás Maduro choked on his words. Hugo Chávez, the improbable president, born in the rural poverty of Sabaneta in the state of Barinas in 1954, had died of cancer.[62] To his wealthy and light-skinned enemies he was evil incarnate. To many impoverished Venezuelans, his contradictory and eclectic ideology—a labyrinthine blend drawing on the thought of nineteenth-century Simón Bolívar and Ezequiel Zamora; twentieth-century left-military nationalism and anti-imperialism; Soviet-inflected, bureaucratic Cuban socialism; social Christianity; pragmatic neostructuralist economics; and currents of socialism-from-below—made a good deal of sense at least insofar as he had come from origins like theirs and had made the right sort of enemies. For sound reasons, the international legacy of the Venezuelan president for sections of the left has been tarnished by his appalling support of Gadhafi, al-Assad, Ahmadinejad, and the Chinese state. But to begin there for an understanding of the profound resonance of his death for the millions upon millions of Venezuelan and Latin American victims of colonial rule, capitalist exploitation, and imperial humiliation would be to resolutely miss the point.

Hysterical Venezuelans

There's something about Chávez that encourages a starker than usual embrace of mediocrity in the quarters of the establishment press. How else to explain the appeal of Rory Carroll, whose dystopic fantasies about the life and times of Venezuela since 1999 have found their unmitigated expression in the pages of the *Guardian, New York Times,* and *New Statesman,* among others.[63] For Carroll, the Venezuelan popular classes have been the mute and manipulable playthings of the "elected autocrat," whose life in turn is reducible to one part clown, one part monster.

If we once imagined that Chávez emerged out of the debauched embrace of neoliberalism by an old rotating political elite ensconced in the traditional Acción Democrática (Democratic Action, AD) and Comité de Organización Política Electoral Independiente (Committee for Independent Electoral Political Organization, COPEI) parties in the late 1980s and early 1990s, the concomitant sociopolitical fissures created by the popular explosion of anti-neoliberal sentiment during the Caracazo riots of 1989, and the folkloric rise

---

62 Adolfo Sánchez Rebolledo, "Hugo Chávez: el torbellino," *La Jornada,* March 7, 2013.
63 Rory Carroll is the former Caracas-based Latin American correspondent for the *Guardian.* He is the author of *Comandante: Hugo Chávez's Venezuela* (London: Penguin Books, 2013).

of a dissident military man to the status of popular hero though a failed coup attempt of 1992 (targeting the status quo), we now stand corrected. The idea that Chávez is the *result* of Chavismo—a pervasive groundswell of demands for social change, national liberation and deeper democracy—becomes a fraud,[64] "We Created Chávez!" a popular delusion.[65]

"His dramatic sense of his own significance," we learn from Carroll, is rather what "helped bring him to power as the reincarnation of the liberator Simón Bolívar"—the trope of autocratic caudillo and crocodile charisma. It was this very same "dramatic flair" that "deeply divided Venezuelans" rather than, say, the uneven and combined development of neoliberal capitalism in a dependent country of the Global South—the trope of manufactured polarization. "He spent extravagantly on health clinics, schools, subsidies and giveaways"—the trope of populist clientelism and the undeserving poor. "His elections were not fair"—the trope of creeping authoritarianism. He "dominate[d] airwaves"—the trope of media monopolization. Ultimately, though, his evil was banal; his rule was, "in the final analysis," that of "an awful manager."[66]

"As Venezuela begins a new chapter in its history," US president Barack Obama said in response to the death of Chávez, "the United States remains committed to policies that promote democratic principles, the rule of law, and respect for human rights," all implicitly absent in the South American country.[67] "At this key juncture," then Canadian prime minister Stephen Harper noted in the same register, "I hope the people of Venezuela can now build for themselves a better, brighter future based on the principles of freedom, democracy, the rule of law and respect for human rights." Although disingenuous in the extreme, this was still more measured than Harper's comments in 2009, just prior to a Summit of the Americas meeting. There he noted that Chávez was representative of certain leftist leaders in the Western Hemisphere who were "opposed to basically sound economic policies, want to go back to Cold War socialism… want to turn back the clock on the democratic progress that's been made in the hemisphere."[68]

We are to understand from this that contemporary liberal democracy is the selection of good managers. A proper manager for the twenty-first century is presumably something closer to the pliant figure of unelected free-market

---

64 Guillermo Almeyra, "El papel irrepetible de Hugo Chávez," *La Jornada*, March 7, 2013.
65 George Ciccariello-Maher, *We Created Chávez* (Durham: Duke University Press, 2013).
66 Rory Carroll, "In the End, an Awful Manager," *New York Times*, March 5, 2013.
67 Keith Johnson, "Obama Reacts to Chávez Death," *Wall Street Journal*, March 5, 2013.
68 Mike Blanchfield, "Venezuela Slams Harper for 'Blunt, Insensitive, Impertinent' Remarks on Hugo Chávez's Death," *National Post*, March 7, 2013.

Italian technocrat Mario Monti, whose loss in the recent Italian elections was mourned by the same media outlets demonizing Chávez. The *Economist* spoke of the stubborn Italian electorate's "refusal to recognise the underlying causes of Italy's plight" achieving its full expression in "their refusal to back Mr Monti."[69] The tidal wave of anti-Chávez vitriol on behalf of the world's rulers is rooted in the refusal he represents for the poor and dispossessed, for the exploited and oppressed—a refusal to go on as before, to submit to neoliberal capitalism, and to get on one's knees before imperialism. It's true, in other words, that he made an awful manager.

On March 7, 2013, the conservative opposition media reported "hundreds of thousands" in the streets of Caracas mourning their manager's demise.[70] An editorial in the Mexican daily *La Jornada* speaks of "millions."[71] A quick search of Google images and YouTube produces a veritable red tide of mourners. Through Carroll's prism these multitudes must radically misunderstand the legacy of fourteen years of Chávez: "the decay, dysfunction and blight that afflict the economy and every state institution." They must misconceive the "profound uncertainty" the late president has thrust them into. They must be blind to the "bureaucratic malaise and corruption" surrounding them.[72]

Charges of Autocracy, Clientelism, and Decay

Mark Weisbrot, a social democratic economist based in the United States, once complained that Venezuela "is probably the most lied-about country in the world."[73] In fourteen years Chávez won fourteen national electoral contests of different varieties, coming out securely on top of thirteen of them. According to Jimmy Carter, former US president, Nobel Prize winner, and monitor of ninety-two elections worldwide in his capacity as director of the Carter Center, these Venezuelan contests were the "best in the world." In the 2006 presidential race, it was opposition candidate Manuel Rosales who engaged in petty bids of clientelism aimed at securing the votes of the poor. Most notoriously, he offered $US 450 per month to 3 million impoverished Venezuelans on personal black credit cards as part of a plan called *Mi Negra*.

69 "Italy's Election: Ungovernability Wins," *Economist*, March 2, 2013.
70 "El cuerpo de Chávez tras el cristal del féretro," *El Universal*, March 7, 2013,
   www.eluniversal.com/nacional-y-politica/hugo-chavez-1954-2013/130307/el-cuerpo
   -de-chavez-tras-el-cristal-del-feretro.
71 "Venezuela: Duelo y perspectivas," *La Jornada*, March 7, 2013.
72 Carroll, "In the End, an Awful Manager."
73 Mark Weisbrot, "Why the U.S. Demonises Venezuela's Democracy," *Guardian*, October 3, 2012.

In what his right-wing critics could only understand as a rare act of agency, the ungrateful would-be recipients apparently aligned themselves on the other side of history, backing Chávez with 62 percent of the vote.[74]

The "suppressed media" mantra is another favorite go-to card of the opposition. In one representative report, the US-based Committee to Protect Journalists claimed that the heavy hand of the Chávez government wielded control over a "media empire." In actual fact, Venezuelan state TV reaches "only about 5–8% of the country's audience. Of course, Chávez [could] interrupt normal programming with his speeches (under a law that predates his administration), and regularly [did] so. But the opposition still [had] most of the media, including radio and print media—not to mention most of the wealth and income of the country."[75] Walking the downtown streets of the capital in the lead-up to the presidential election of October 2012, with billboards of right-wing candidate Henrique Capriles Radonski hanging from the lampposts, and kiosks overflowing with newspapers beaming headlines on the latest disaster induced by the Chávez regime, even the most spiritual of journalists would strain in vain to find a ghost of Stalin in Caracas.

Back to Some Basics

At its root, explaining support for Chávez among the lower orders involves neither the complexity of quantum mechanics nor the pop-psychological theory of masses entranced by a charismatic leader. Venezuela sits on oil. Other petrostates, such as those in the Gulf, have funneled the rent into a grotesque pageantry of the rich—skyscrapers, theme parks, and artificial archipelagos—built on the backs of indentured South Asian migrant laborers. They've done so, moreover, while aligning geopolitically with the US Empire—backing the wars and containing the Arab uprisings.[76] Much to the bizarre dismay of journalists like Ian James, the Venezuelan state in the last fourteen years has been forced into embracing different priorities.[77]

From above, more state resources consequently began to flow, feeding an

74 Carter quote and figures for the black credit card plan from Greg Grandin, "On the Legacy of Hugo Chávez," *Nation*, March 5, 2013.

75 Mark Weisbrot, "Why the U.S. Demonises Venezuela's Democracy."

76 Mike Davis, "Fear and Money in Dubai," *New Left Review* 41 (September–October 2006); see also Adam Hanieh, *Capital and Class in the Gulf Arab States* (New York: Palgrave Macmillan, 2011).

77 Ian James, "Venezuela Oil Production Growth: Chávez Presidency May Have Squandered Oil Riches," *Huffington Post*, September 23, 2012, www.huffingtonpost.com/2012/09/23/venezuela-oil-production_n_1907170.html.

expanding array of parallel health and education systems for the poor.[78] As was indicated above, according to official national statistics, cash income poverty fell significantly under Chávez, and this was accompanied by effective literacy campaigns, the extension of health care, expansion of entry into university, housing subsidies for low-income groups, low unemployment, and an increasing proportion of formal compared to informal jobs in the labor market. Social investment, by some estimates, amounted to $US 650 billion between 1999 and 2013. The poor were better fed and more politically active. The country climbed the categories of the Human Development Index of the United Nations Development Program (UNDP) from "medium" to "high" and, at the end of Chávez's rule, was tied with Uruguay as the most equal country in the region.[79] This backdrop in its entirety provides a reasoned explanation for the red tide of mourners commemorating Chávez's death. But it cannot explain the challenges that the Bolivarian process faced in its immediate future, following the death of its most emblematic leader.

With Nicolás Maduro's narrow victory over the right in the April 2013 elections, the pragmatic balancing of contradictory elements within the Bolivarian process that Chávez managed to sustain became that much more difficult. The game, ultimately, was not a virtuous circle of mutuality, but a zero-sum competition of classes with opposing interests. The lubricant of oil had blurred this reality temporarily, but different developmental exits in which distinct classes win and lose came to the fore as quickly as the price of oil plummeted. The conservative Chavista right within the state apparatus, the currents of reaction inside the military, the red bureaucrats enriching themselves through manipulation of markets, and the union bureaucrats aligned against working-class self-organization and emancipation were the preeminent obstacles of immediate concern. At the same time, the experiences of workers' control, communal councils, communes, and popular assemblies had raised the consciousness and capacities of millions. A dire turn, therefore, was not a fait accompli.

---

78 The social programs are discussed in Gregory Wilpert, *Changing Venezuela by Taking Power: The History and Policies of the Chávez Government* (London: Verso Books, 2006); and Iain Bruce, *The Real Venezuela* (London: Pluto Press, 2009). On the variegated forms of popular power in the urban peripheries of Caracas see Sujatha Fernandes, *Who Can Stop the Drums? Urban Social Movements in Chávez's Venezuela* (Durham, NC: Duke University Press, 2010); George Ciccariello-Maher, *We Created Chávez* (Durham, NC: Duke University Press, 2013); and Dario Azzellini, "Constituent Power in Motion: Ten Years of Transformation in Venezuela," *Socialism and Democracy* 24, no. 2 (2010): 8–31.

79 Edgardo Lander, *Venezuela: Terminal Crisis of the Rentier Petro-State Model?* (Amsterdam: Transnational Institute, 2014).

Faces of the Right

The April elections following the death of Chávez saw Maduro best Henrique Capriles, the right-wing candidate for the Mesa Unida Democrática (Round-table for Democratic Unity, MUD), albeit by a narrow margin of less than one percent of the vote. Capriles and his supporters refused to recognize the veracity of the results and then staged violent protests causing the death of a dozen Bolivarian activists, while leaving another hundred or so injured. The violent vandals of April 2013 also committed extensive property damage to public buildings and institutions. It is worth noting, furthermore, that unlike in the case of the November 2013 Honduran elections—widely recognized by mainstream human rights organizations to have been fraudulent, and which further consolidated right-wing strong man Porfirio "Pepe" Lobo's grip on that country—the United States never formally recognized the legitimacy of Maduro's presidency.[80]

Once it was evident that provocation in the streets following the April elections was failing to destabilize the regime or to rally new social sectors to the side of the opposition, the latter regrouped and reconsidered its tactics.[81] The MUD held internal elections to establish a new mandate for its leadership. Capriles came out on top once again, beating Leopoldo López and María Corina Machado, two personalities running even further to the right of Capriles. The revised agenda for the right was to frame the December 2013 municipal elections as a plebiscite on the legitimacy of the Maduro administration.

In the municipal elections, Chavismo won the popular vote decisively, regaining some of the political ground lost in the presidential elections eight months earlier. In spite of a voluntary voting regime and a historical tendency of abstention in local elections, there was a turnout of 60 percent. Chavismo won by approximately 10 percent, capturing 242 mayoralties to MUD's 75. Crucially, though, Chavismo lost in the major cities, including Caracas—the center of Venezuelan politics. This unanticipated, weaker-than-expected outcome for the opposition signified its failure since April 2013 to undermine the legitimacy of the Maduro presidency.[82] MUD proved itself incapable of

---

80 Atilio Borón, "La amenaza fascista," *Rebelión*, February 19, 2014, www.rebelion.org /noticia.php?id=181044&titular=la-amenaza-fascista-.

81 See the illuminating discussion of these matters by Gregory Wilpert on *The Real News Network*, February 22, 2014, http://therealnews.com/t2/index.php?option=com_content &task=view&id=31&Itemid=74&jumival=11517.

82 Pedro Santander, "Diálogo o golpismo: Lo que está en juego en Venezuela," *Rebelión*, February 19, 2014, www.rebelion.org/noticia.php?id=181024&titular=di%E1logo-o -golpismo-.

disputing the hegemony of Chavismo in the electoral field, even during a year in which inflation rose very sharply to 56 percent and shortages of foodstuffs and other basic commodities began to proliferate.[83]

Surface Divisions, Integral Unities

Shortly after the results were in, Capriles, now acting as governor of the state of Miranda, changed gears and responded to the second call in the post–municipal election period by President Maduro for opposition mayors and governors to meet with him in the presidential palace and work out a plan of peace and national reconciliation. A photo of Capriles and Maduro shaking hands in the palace was circulated widely in the media, ostensibly ending the right's strategy of openly questioning the legitimacy of the constitutional president.

Alongside Capriles, the majority of oppositional mayors and governors also attended the dialogues with the president, and agreed to participate in a new program designed to reduce crime and enhance citizen security. The move toward moderation and dialogue was unpersuasive to the hardest elements of the ultra-right within the MUD coalition, as expressed publicly and vociferously by López and Machado.[84]

For many on the left of Chavismo, however, it is easy to exaggerate the divisions within the counterrevolutionary bloc and, in so doing, to dangerously obscure their basic unity of purpose.[85] "We are facing the classic counter-revolutionary schema," reads a recent communiqué of the revolutionary socialist current Marea Socialista (Socialist Tide, MS), which operates within the governing United Socialist Party of Venezuela (PSUV).

> It consists of applying pressure on the government to implement anti-popular measures and in so doing completely lose its social base, deepen its exhausted image in front of the Bolivarian people. As a result, they will be more open to the ousting of the government, whether that ousting is violent or soft. The government of Maduro is committing a grave error insofar as it believes that there is a "violent" Right and another one that's "peaceful," with which the

---

83 See Andrés Schipani, "Venezuela: Amid Unrest, Another Forex Mechanism," *Financial Times*, February 20, 2014, http://blogs.ft.com/beyond-brics/2014/02/20/venezuela-amid-unrest-another-foreign-exchange-mechanism/#axzz2u4V0vinF. The figure of 56 percent inflation cited in this chapter is also the standard figure reported in sources close to the government.

84 Santander, "Diálogo o golpismo."

85 Nicmer N. Evans, "Oposición dividida pero no desunida y 'la salida,'" *Rebelión*, February 6, 2014, www.rebelion.org/noticia.php?id=180472&titular=oposici%F3n-dividida-pero-no-desunida-y-%93la-salida%94-.

government can negotiate and which will respect the Constitution. As in the old combination of the "carrot and the stick" these sectors converge among themselves around a common objective, the defeat of the Bolivarian Process.[86]

"These days, fascist violence and the potential of a coup are taking place in a very distinct situation," to the one of that coup attempt in April 2002, notes Roland Denis.[87] His reservations on the depth of division of purpose in the camp of the right are of the same register as the Marea Socialista communiqué.

> That fascist subjectivity planted in 2002 has always remained, diminished but consolidated. In fact, López and Capriles, as the personalities most representative of this "citizen" movement, have never separated themselves from it, albeit starting from their individually distinct hysterical psychologies and pathologies, and the divisions between them in their original party Primero Justicia. Today they appear as the leaders of the opposition, competing between each other for its singular leadership.[88]

López, together with Machado, called for the initial demonstration on Youth Day, February 12, 2014, that kicked off a string of violent events in February 2014, under the slogan "La Salida," or "exit," unambiguously signifying their intention to overthrow the democratically elected government. "Opposition leader Leopoldo López—competing with Capriles for leadership—has portrayed the current demonstrations as something that could force Maduro from office," the American economist Mark Weisbrot reports. "It was obvious that there was, and remains, no peaceful way that this could happen."[89]

The cartography of protest in Caracas in February 2014 closely mirrored the sociogeographic divisions of the capital, featuring as it does a lighter-skinned and richer east, and a darker-skinned and poorer west. Middle-class barricades were erected in the east, populated by the students of elite private universities, alongside students of the main state university—historically, a cordoned-off stomping ground for kids of the rich.[90]

---

86 Marea Socialista, "Rectificar y avanzar hacia la revolución económica: Para frenar la ofensiva de la derecha," *Rebelión*, February 15, 2014, www.rebelion.org/noticia.php?id =180860&titular=rectificar-y-avanzar-hacia-la-revoluci%F3n-econ%F3mica-.

87 Roland Denis, "Desactivar el fascismo," *Aporrea*, February 19, 2014.

88 Denis, "Desactivar el fascismo."

89 Mark Weisbrot, "US Support for Regime Change in Venezuela is a Mistake," *Guardian*, February 18, 2014, www.theguardian.com/commentisfree/2014/feb/18/venezuela -protests-us-support-regime-change-mistake.

90 Although it is also true that the student movement has always been divided, and its left wing has had at different historical moments a presence within the elite state universities as well.

The west, in contrast, was relatively free of unrest. In the days following the initial explosion of activity, the "peaceful" protests of the right included attacks on fifty of the public buses from a new system that acts as affordable transportation for the poor. The Bolivarian University, a new institutional network designed to incorporate the lower orders into the higher education system, was also besieged. And Cuban medical personnel working for the Barrio Adentro health program were the targets of fierce physical offensives. According to numerous observers, paramilitary shock troops operated behind the cannon fodder of right-wing students in the streets. In protests that were supposedly driven in part by the scarcity of foodstuffs and other basic commodities available to the population, rightist militants had the audacity to attack government vehicles delivering precisely such products.[91]

Capriles, meanwhile, was reluctant to join the call for demonstrations in the streets, and indeed piously condemned excessive violence by protesters while hoping that popular memory had faded of his leading role in calling out protests that led to a dozen deaths in April 2013. With Capriles there is always one hand discreetly, cautiously maintaining its measure of the pulse of insurgent conspiracy. If that pulse grows sufficiently strong, he'll abandon the path of negotiation. In a sign that the effects of aggressive student protests alienated moderate sections of the reactionary bloc, it seems that few political leaders on the right of any importance—beyond López and Machado—lent their formal backing to the violent posturing of student and paramilitary demonstrations.

Edgardo Lander captures some of the core features of the February 2014 dynamic:

> The more radical sectors who justified the violence made it quite clear what the objective of these actions was: "la salida" or exit, meaning the overthrow of Nicolás Maduro's government. These are the same groups who have received the most systematic political and financial support over the years from the US State Department, mainly—but not solely—through USAID. These actions are likely to have been planned with the aim of creating a Ukraine-style "orange revolution" scenario. In this they had the unconditional support of the global corporate media, especially those based in the United States, Spain and Colombia…. Information on the military dimension of these movements remains shrouded in secrecy. The government announced the arrest of three air force generals, followed by other members of the armed forces, who were accused of

---

91 Mike González, "Is Venezuela Burning? A Letter from Caracas," *Revolutionary Socialism*, http://revolutionarysocialism.tumblr.com/post/77478189373/is-venezuela-burning -a-letter-from-caracas.

fomenting a coup, but several months later there has been little further information on the matter. In two months of street barricades, marches both peaceful and armed, and violent clashes with the police and the army, 41 people died, many were wounded and hundreds were arrested, while the material damage will cost millions. The dead and wounded included opposition activists, members of the security forces, and citizens who had nothing to do with the clashes. It is difficult to determine who is responsible with any degree of accuracy.[92]

In the wake of crisis and dozens of deaths of February 2014, López was arrested and eventually sentenced to just under fourteen years in prison for public incitement to violence and criminal association.[93] Ensuring his freedom has since become a rallying cry for the opposition. Who is López, then?

López used to be the mayor of wealthy Chacao. After finishing prep school in the United States, he studied at the Kennedy School of Government at Harvard University in the 1990s, where he made contact with US establishment figures such as David Petraeus, ex-chief of the Central Intelligence Agency and confidant of Barack Obama in all matters connected to national security. After the stint at Harvard, López returned to Venezuela, where he established relations with the Caracas offices of the International Republican Institute, an entity of the US Republican Party—the institute lent López strategic and financial support. Beginning in 2002, the Republican Party, then in office under George W. Bush, flew López to Washington on multiple occasions to meet with functionaries of the Bush administration. That same year, López led the opposition march on the Miraflores Presidential Palace in the capital, which resulted in dozens of deaths and precipitated the short-lived coup and kidnapping of then President Chávez. López is also a longstanding associate of ex–Colombian president Álvaro Uribe (2002–2010), with whom he met on numerous occasions over the last decade. Uribe was well known for his hard line against the Chávez regime, which corresponded with his domestic war of terror against large sections of the civilian population in Colombia under the banner of "democratic security."[94]

The Student Connection

Back in 2002–2003, during the April 2002 coup attempt and a 2002–2003 destabilizing oil lockout, the core rightist bloc consisted mainly of the US em-

---

92 Lander, *Venezuela: Terminal Crisis*, 9–10.

93 Andrés Schipani, "Venezuela's Leopoldo López Sentenced to Jail for Nearly 14 Years," *Financial Times*, September 11, 2015.

94 Ana Esther Ceceña, "Leopoldo López: Agente de la CIA, el golpe, guarimbas, Uribe y el fascism," *Herramienta*, www.herramienta.com.ar/content/leopoldo-lopez-agente-de-la -cia-el-golpe-guarimbas-uribe-y-el-fascismo.

bassy in Caracas, the highest echelons of management of the state oil company Petróleos de Venezuela, S.A. (PDVSA), the business confederation Fedecámaras, the Confederación de Trabajadores de Venezuela (Workers' Confederation of Venezuela, CTV), the domestic hierarchy of the Catholic Church, and a variety of other oligarchic and conservative cross sections of political society. This ugly melange was prettified through the lens of private media empires, both national and international, transforming the coup attempt into a struggle of democracy against tyranny.[95]

Beginning in roughly 2008, the right wing of the perennially divided student movement was sought out as a new vanguard through which to advance the opposition agenda. The counterrevolution had not enjoyed significant successes in linking organically to any other social subject that might otherwise have flagshipped their enterprise.[96] In 2008, the US-based Cato Institute awarded the $US 500,000 Milton Friedman Prize for Advancing Liberty to student leader Yon Goicoechea for his role in mobilizing protests against the government's suspension of private broadcaster RCTV's license. Subsequently, a considerable chunk of the $US 45 million in annual funding from US institutions to the Venezuelan opposition was directed toward "youth outreach" programs. As an outcome of such financial backing and logistical training in media campaigns, the right-wing Juventud Activa Venezuela Unida (United Venezuelan Active Youth, JAVU) became an increasingly active organization. In 2010, for example, JAVU led protests against ostensible state censorship of private broadcasters, as well as struggles framed as defending the "autonomy" of universities from state intrusion. Inside the heat of the internal divisions of the right today, the students have openly aligned with the López–Machado faction, transforming themselves into the cannon fodder serving the ultra-right.[97] "Students as the new social subject of the counterrevolutionary right is something distinct from 2002," Denis observes. "They are favoured for their capacity to engage in permanent activism, above all students who do not work and who do not have any social responsibilities."[98]

95 Luciano Wexell Severo, "Golpe de Estado suave," *Rebelión*, February 21, 2014, www.rebelion.org/noticia.php?id=181112.
96 Corriente Revolucionario Bolívar y Zamora—Poder Popular Socialista, "Momento y perspectivas: la nueva asonada contrarrevolucionaria," *Rebelión*, February 19, 2014, www.rebelion.org/noticia.php?id=181029.
97 This paragraph draws on Julia Buxton, "The Real Significance of the Student Protests." See also Ana Navea, "Mentiras de la derecha para impulsar un golpe de Estado," *AVN*, February 20, 2014, www.avn.info.ve/contenido/mentiras-derecha-para-impulsar -golpe-estado.
98 Denis, "Desactivar el fascismo."

If the students are the visible brigades tearing up the cityscapes, a complex configuration of national and transnational networks forms the counterrevolutionary bloc of the present. Fedecámaras remains active, as do the major players in private media, national and international. Political parties, NGOs, and churches are all articulated under the umbrella of MUD. In terms of parties, this fragile unity contains AD; Primero Justicia (First Justice, PJ); COPEI; La Causa Radical (Radical Cause, LCR); Voluntad Popular (Popular Will, VP); Proyecto Venezuela (Project Venezuela, PV), and a series of other smaller entities of the right.

Parliamentary Elections of December 2015

The Venezuelan economy has been in bad shape for a longer time than other South American economies in the wake of the crisis. In 2009 and 2010 the country's GDP contracted by 3.2 and 1.5 percent, respectively. It then recovered to growth rates of 4.2 percent, 5.6 percent, and 1.3 percent in 2011, 2012, and 2013, respectively, after which it plummeted to -4.0 percent and -7.1 percent in 2014 and 2015, with an expected further contraction of 7.0 percent in 2016.[99] International reserves have been falling dramatically, as the government uses them to stoke countercyclical spending. Meanwhile, loans from China, to be paid back mainly in oil extraction, have accelerated dramatically. Alternative lines of credit are becoming increasingly impossible to obtain, with demands for ever higher interest on repayment.[100] Taking advantage of collapsing oil revenue and a deepening economic crisis in Venezuela, the MUD struck a serious blow to Maduro's government on December 6, 2015, winning a "supermajority" of two-thirds of the seats in the National Assembly. The next presidential elections are scheduled for 2018, but the emboldened MUD is hoping to oust Maduro early through a recall referendum, something newly permitted in the 1999 Venezuelan constitution.[101]

The Regular Misery of Capital

The right's extraparliamentary and parliamentary advances in recent years are taking place both within a steep and enduring economic crisis, and a real set of political contradictions and crises internal to Chavismo. The eruptions of the right in the streets and parliament have coincided with heightened expres-

---

99 ECLAC, *Preliminary Overview*, 59.
100 Lander, *Venezuela: Terminal Crisis*, 12–13.
101 "Venezuela's Election: A Democratic Counter-Revolution," *Economist*, December 12, 2015.

sions of structural weaknesses in the economic development strategy of the government. Underlying problems have come much more boldly to the fore, not least in the shape of inflation and shortages.[102]

Perhaps the most severe paradox facing the Bolivarian process is that the social and participatory achievements highlighted above were not accompanied by equivalent structural transformations of the underlying economic structure or insertion of the country into the international division of labor. Indeed, oil dependency and the rentier-capitalist state have become still more entrenched under Chávez and Maduro. In 1998, oil's share of total export value was 68.7 percent, whereas in the last several years this has risen to 96 percent. Industrial manufacturing was at 17 percent of export value in 2000, compared to 13 percent in 2013. There was a dramatic reorientation under Chávez of the distribution of a greater share of the oil rent to the popular classes, but the underlying model of accumulation was not altered, and thus the social gains of the Bolivarian process were always intensely vulnerable to fluctuations in the price of oil.[103]

The concomitant overvaluation of the currency made imports of most goods cheaper than domestically producing them. Whenever the government faces the prospect of devaluing the currency, it must contend with the fact that this would cause an even greater surge in inflation. The petro-economy has led to major structural distortions. It has meant, first, the undermining of "efforts to promote domestic production, whether in the public, private or social economic sector." Second, it has meant "a permanent and unsustainable haemorrhaging of highly subsidized foreign currency to pay for imports of food and other basic consumer goods, intermediate inputs and supplies, as well as luxury items and tourism abroad." Finally, the consolidation of rentier-capitalism has led to "successive bureaucratic-administrative mechanisms" that were "created to control the use of subsidized foreign exchange" but "have led to severe bottlenecks in imports, with a significant impact on prices and the availability of products as well as massive levels of corruption."[104] Indeed, the corruption reached unfathomable levels. For example, the former president of the Central Bank said that in 2012, when he still held that position, of an allotted $US 59 billion in subsidized foreign exchange, roughly $20 billion was siphoned into "shell com-

---

102 Susan Spronk and Jeffery R. Webber, "Sabaneta to Miraflores: The Afterlives of Hugo Chávez in Venezuela," *New Politics*, Winter 2014, http://newpol.org/content/sabaneta -miraflores-afterlives-hugo-ch%C3%A1vez-venezuela.
103 Lander, *Venezuela: Terminal Crisis*, 2.
104 Lander, *Venezuela: Terminal Crisis*, 5.

panies" completely "unrelated to productive activities," and thus into the pockets of well-placed civilian and military bureaucrats and connected capitalists—the trifecta of the so-called *bolibourgeoisie*.[105]

Discontent among layers of the Chavista grassroots has deepened with time, as electoral and extra-electoral support for the government has been in steady decline.[106] High inflation is destroying workers' purchasing power and makes virtually meaningless various increases in salaries. The social base of Bolivarianism has long been calling for an iron fist in dealings with the bourgeoisie, but the Maduro government has restricted itself to ad hoc and ineffective controls, laws, sanctions, and a series of other measures that do not cohere into an economic strategy.[107]

Government officials and loyalists tend to minimize the structural obstacles facing the economy, ritually blaming the capitalist class for waging "economic warfare," by which they mean speculating, hoarding, and engaging in cross-border contraband. These accusations are substantiated,[108] but they tend to downplay the absolutely routine problems created by capitalist activity in the normal process of capital accumulation in Venezuela. Manuel Sutherland, one of the boldest Marxist economists writing on the Venezuelan process at present, is worth quoting at length on this topic:

> The government continues to believe in the fantasy of a patriotic bourgeoisie that will renounce the extraordinary profits it can capture through illegal imports and currency speculation. Unfortunately, the government cannot imagine a country in which capitalists don't appropriate 70 percent of the private sector GDP and massively exploit the workforce.... In sum, Chavismo dreams of a reasonable and loving capitalist who obviously does not exist. With him it wants to negotiate, even though the normal action of these capitalists, that is to say the process of the accumulation of capital, is the cause of the country's misery.[109]

It is very difficult to sustain the process even in its current state, never mind deepening and extending any long transition toward socialism, given the weight that private capital still enjoys in the economy. According to Suther-

---

105 Lander, *Venezuela: Terminal Crisis*, 5.

106 Andrés Schipani, "Venezuela: Amid Unrest, Another Forex Mechanism," *Financial Times*, February 20, 2014, http://blogs.ft.com/beyond-brics/2014/02/20/venezuela -amid-unrest-another-foreign-exchange-mechanism/#axzz2u4V0vinF.

107 Manuel Sutherland, "Siete apuntes sobre las protestas en Venezuela," *Aporrea*, February 17, 2014, www.aporrea.org/ideologia/a182254.html.

108 George Ciccariello-Maher, "#LaSalida? Venezuela at a Crossroads," *Nation*, February 21, 2014, www.thenation.com/article/178496/lasalida-venezuela-crossroads#.

109 Sutherland, "Siete apuntes sobre las protestas en Venezuela."

land, Venezuela experienced capital flight during the period of fixed exchange rates of around $US 150 billion, the equivalent to approximately 43 percent of GDP in 2010. This looting of capital is part of what is driving the devaluation of the local currency and strengthening speculation in the parallel black market in dollars (in which dollars are sold for fifteen times the official exchange rate).

The black market rate is the rate used by commercial vendors to set their prices, with the exception of the few products subject to regulation. So escalating prices, even setting aside the issue of hoarding, would still be a major issue requiring resolution. Those commercial actors who legally obtain dollars through official channels in order ostensibly to purchase imports of goods from abroad have no incentive to actually use the dollars obtained to this end; rather, they have every incentive to divert those dollars illegally onto the black market in order to make extraordinary profits. This causes further scarcity of goods, increases in prices, and a fall in the quality of goods and services—in other words, it is less a conspiracy of capital through economic warfare than its regular behavior, given the incentive structures that are at the root of the present economic crisis.[110]

According to the communiqué of Marea Socialista—a group that has repeatedly declared its decisive commitment to defending against any and all rightist conspiracies against the Maduro administration—the principal error of the government consists of its vacillation in economic policy since April 2013. The intervening period has witnessed the introduction of certain measures that can only be read as adaptations to demands from the right.[111] An appropriate redirection of economic policy from the defensive to the offensive, according to Marea Socialista, would include the immediate escalation of anticapitalist measures, such as the establishment of a state monopoly under social control of all external commerce, and the assurance that the state be the only importer of essential goods for Venezuelan people; national centralization under social control of all dollars available in the country, whether they are dollars that enter through the oil trade or those that are deposited in foreign accounts; massive intervention and state and social control over the entirety of the private banking system that presently operates in the country, in order both to finance economic planning and to simultaneously centralize control of all funds presently managed by the public banking system; the urgent recovery of state production of basic subsistence products to respond to the authentic shortage crisis; expropriation under workers' and popular control of the largest corporations involved in the biggest operations of hoarding, speculation, and contraband; and a call for the peoples

---

110 Sutherland, "Siete apuntes sobre las protestas en Venezuela."
111 Marea Socialista, "Rectificar y avanzar hacia la revolución económica."

and governments of Latin America to lend support and solidarity through the supply of basic goods and medicines to confront the problems of the immediate moment and of the transition to the implementation of such measures.[112]

Processes of bureaucratization, according to Roland Denis, longtime revolutionary and vice minister of planning during part of Chávez's first administration, are also responsible for the loss of an original vitality on the part of the grassroots organizations of the Bolivarian process that have been transformed, · to an ever deepening degree, into mere clients of the state—made to respond to the incentive structures of a state-capitalist model of development in an oil-rich country, and too often mobilized in the interests of the bureaucrats of that structure rather than being the self-determining subjects of a revolutionary potential which at one time seemed more clearly present on the horizon: "The rentist, parasitic model of state capitalism… delivers a politics of control, concentration of power and the substitution of social control with technocratic and bureaucratic functionaries.… This is a model which if it is not called fundamentally into question, with measures to transform it radically in the short term, will lead to the continuation of out of control shortages and inflation.…"[113]

Nowhere has this been truer than in the top-down antidemocratic functioning of the governing party, the Partido Socialista Unido de Venezuela (United Socialist Party of Venezuela, PSUV). But it is also visible in more celebrated components of the Bolivarian process, such as the communal councils and communes. According to Lander, as a result of the

> reaffirmation of the historical state-centered logic of the rentier petro-economy, the grassroots organizations tend to depend directly on transfers of state funds. Thus, the possibilities for these grassroots community arrangements to become consolidated and autonomous, as an alternative to state structures, has been blocked. In addition, through this same channel, the corruption associated with the power struggles over the distribution of oil proceeds has also reached society's grassroots. After 15 years, the weight of the so-called social economy continues to be insignificant.[114]

Few empty slogans capture the extent of bureaucratization in the Bolivarian process as the thus far merely discursive commitment to the construction of a "communal state"—an impossibility, so long as specific plans to confront the right, to rebuild popular support through the democratization and decen-

---

112 Marea Socialista, "Rectificar y avanzar hacia la revolución económica."
113 Denis, "Desactivar el fascismo."
114 Lander, *Venezuela: Terminal Crisis*, 4.

tralization of power, and to resolutely confront the *structural*—rather than merely superficial—problems of the economy through a transitionary socialist program remain absent from the agenda. Indeed, the direction of Maduro's government has been in the opposite direction—that is, concessions to the right, which will further alienate the social base of the Bolivarian process by transferring more of the costs of austerity onto them while emboldening an already rising right. Comparable processes are afoot in Brazil, the region's biggest country, with the most significant economy, largest population, and most important geopolitical position within the region and the world.

Brazil's Impasse

Millions of Brazilians were glued to their televisions on April 17, 2016, waiting for the results of the Congress's impeachment vote. They came through late: the 513-seat lower house of Congress voted 367 to 137 in favor of impeachment charges against president Dilma Rousseff.[115] The Senate was then expected to vote to formally open the impeachment trial and prompt Rousseff's suspension as president on May 11.[116]

For a moment it seemed the vote in the Senate might be canceled. On May 9, seemingly out of nowhere, Waldir Maranhão, a member of Congress for the center-right Partido Progressista (Progressive Party, PP), and interim president of the lower house since May 5, suspended the impeachment process, citing at least four procedural irregularities in the voting process of April 17. Maranhão insisted that the Senate cease its proceedings on the matter and send it back to the lower house for further deliberations.

Having none of this, the president of the Senate, Renán Calheiro, called Maranhão's decision an "anti-democratic idiocy" and announced that the process would proceed in the Senate as scheduled. Calheiro is a member of the Partido do Movimento Democrático (Brazilian Democratic Movement Party, PMDB)—once an ally of the government but now its leading nemesis. On the day of the reckoning in the Senate, and in lieu of action by the Supreme Tribunal, Rousseff's presidency was indeed suspended.[117]

115 *Economist*, "The Darkest Hour: Brazil's Political Crisis," April 23, 2016.
116 Joe Leahy, "Faint Economic Pulse Detected through Brazil's Political Turmoil," *Financial Times*, May 2, 2010.
117 María Martín and Antonio Jiménez Barca, "Una Guerra institucional deja el proceso de 'impeachment' de Rousseff en el aire," *El País*, May 10, 2016.

Coup in Congress

The spectacle of the lower-house proceedings was as ugly as it was farcical. Speaking for ten seconds each before they voted, the vast majority of the opposition members failed to invoke the actual charges underlying the impeachment proceedings—Rousseff's ostensible tinkering of government accounts to conceal the true size of the deficit. Instead, the rallying cries were a potent mix of god and country, alongside a string of fringe irrelevancies.[118]

No doubt the darkest harbinger of things to come was Jair Bolsonaro's intervention. "Father Bolsonaro"—he's the head of a dynastic family, with many of them in public office—dedicated his vote to Carlos Alberto Brilhante Ustra, who had been chief of secret police during the twenty-one-year military dictatorship that began in 1964. Bolsonaro, in obvious reference to the torture Rousseff personally endured as a guerrilla during the authoritarian period, praised Brilhante Ustra as "the terror of Dilma Rousseff." Bolsonaro's son Eduardo then used his seconds in the spotlight to note that "they lost in '64 and they lost in 2016."[119] By some distance, the most honorable remarks that day were made by Jean Wyllys, a representative for the Partido Socialismo e Liberdade (Socialism and Freedom Party, PSOL), and one of the few openly gay members of Congress. In the face of homophobic epithets launched by right-wing opposition members, he denounced the proceeding as a "farce" and spat in the direction of Bolsonaro.

Unlike in the lower house, where a super-majority of two-thirds was necessary for the impeachment process to move forward, in the Senate only a simple majority was required for the next step. As a result, even though the Senate's electoral structure was slightly more favorable to the Partido dos Trabalhadores (Workers' Party, PT) than the lower house—with the more densely populated, richer, and intensely antigovernment states of the south and southeast relatively underrepresented—impeachment was a foregone conclusion.

How did Latin America's biggest economy and most important political power come to this point?

Economic Slump

The global crisis reached Brazil in 2011, and the political consequences have been dramatic. The renowned "realism" of the PT functioned well enough in a period of high growth and strong external drivers in the international econ-

---

118 *Economist*, "Dilma, Out! Brazil's Terrible Politics," April 23, 2016.
119 Joe Leahy, "Brazil's Crisis Takes on Carnival Atmosphere," *Financial Times*, April 18, 2016.

omy, when the rich could get exponentially richer but the poor could also become less poor. Those pillars faltered in 2011, and the entire edifice has since come crashing to the ground. Political momentum has shifted to a new right-wing, antiparty populism, the PT is increasingly bereft of a social base, and the far-left and popular social movements remain fragmented and disoriented in the new terrain. In an unusually atomized field of political contestation, no alternative sociopolitical force is yet capable of replacing the hegemony that has slipped from the hands of the governing party.

In 2010, after the introduction of a countercyclical stimulus package, Brazil reached a high of 7.6 percent growth, seemingly extracting itself from the global downturn. But that illusion was quickly shattered. Between 2011 and 2014, economic growth averaged 2.1 percent annually, compared to 4.4 percent over the 2004–2010 period.[120] Brazil's economy then shrank by 3.8 percent in 2015, transforming the country long touted in the financial press as one of the fastest growing in emerging markets, rooted in reliable macroeconomic management, into one suffering its sharpest contraction of GDP in a quarter century and deepest recession since official records began. Projections of a further 3 percent fall in 2016 are similarly dour.[121] Once the darling of international and domestic markets, the PT has suddenly become a liability.

Breaking between 2014 and 2016, a massive corruption scandal, involving the state oil company Petrobras, as well as most major political parties in the country, proved to be the principal vector through which subterranean right-wing sentiment was slowly articulated above ground. The demand to impeach president Dilma Rousseff fifteen months into her second term became the adhesive glue holding together disparate right-wing currents. Operation Lava Jato, or "car wash," was initiated on a small scale in 2014 by a then little-known judge, Sergio Moro, from the southern state capital of Curitiba. It began as an investigation into a currency dealer suspected of tax evasion. The scope of the operation widened with time, eventually revealing "an extraordinary tale of large-scale bribery, plunder of public assets, and funding for all major political parties, centered on the relationship between Petrobras and some of its main suppliers—precisely the stalwarts of the PT in the oil, shipbuilding, and construction industries."[122]

---

120 Franklin Serrano and Ricardo Summa, *Aggregate Demand and the Slowdown of Brazilian Economic Growth from 2011–2014* (Washington, DC: Center for Economic and Policy Research, August 2015).
121 Joe Leahy, "Brazil's GDP Shrinks 3.8%," *Financial Times*, March 3, 2016.
122 Alfredo Saad-Filho, "A Coup in Brazil?" *Jacobin*, March 23, 2016.

Petrobras Corruption Scandal

As of March 2016, Operation Lava Jato had led to the arrest of 133 people, as well as the incarceration of some of the richest business figures in the country, from 16 different companies—among them Camargo Correa, OAS, UTC, Odebrecht, Mendes Junior, Engevix, and Queiroz Glavão Engenharia. Politicians of every stripe—those in opposition and those aligned with the government—have been embroiled in the affair, including members of the PT, the PP, the PMDB, the Partido da Social Democracia Brasileira (Brazilian Social Democratic Party, PSDB), and the Partido Trabalhista Brasileiro (Brazilian Labour Party, PTB).[123]

The mainstream newspapers and TV channels, however, have focused their scrutiny, and thus the public's ire, almost exclusively on the PT's involvement—ironic in itself, "since the major media outlets have received billions in financial licenses and publicity contracts from federal government coffers since the PT was first elected in 2002."[124] Luiz Inácio Lula da Silva, the historic former leader of the PT and president of Brazil for two terms (2003–2006, 2007–2010), has also been ensnared in the anticorruption campaign, with claims that he acquired a beachside apartment and a rural getaway through illegal kickbacks. With widescale publicity, he was briefly detained at the São Paulo airport for questioning on March 4, 2016, before being released. Rousseff then attempted to appoint Lula as her chief of staff, which would have made him immune from prosecution from any judicial body below the Supreme Court. Federal Judge Catta Preta Neto blocked the investiture, however, and subsequently posted pictures on his Facebook wall of himself and his family participating in demonstrations against the government on March 7, 2016. Reflecting the crass politicization of sections of the judicial apparatus, Preta Neto wrote beneath the photos: "Help topple Dilma and be able to fly to Miami and Orlando. If she falls, the dollar will drop."[125]

In an attempt to seal the fate of the government, Moro then illegally made public an illegal recording of a conversation between Rousseff and Lula, which the opposition claims demonstrates irrefutably that his brief appointment as chief of staff was made so that he could escape inevitable jail time stemming from prosecution for corruption in the near future.[126] Slaying Lula, who had 80 percent approval ratings at the close of his second term and remains in-

---

123 Raúl Zibechi, "Impasse, antes del diluvio," *Brecha*, March 26, 2016.
124 Sean Purdy, "Rousseff and the Right," *Jacobin*, October 5, 2015.
125 Zibechi, "Impasse, antes del diluvio."
126 Saad-Filho, "A Coup in Brazil?"

tensely popular, would be to slay the PT itself. It would also redirect attention from the imbrication of many of the opposition's leading figures in the Lava Jato scandal, as well as their ties to many other corruption rings. "For most of the political class," writes political analyst Rodrigo Nunes, "toppling the government quickly and using the PT as a scapegoat seems like the surest way to emerge unscathed."[127]

Impeachment Drive

Despite every effort by the opposition to uncover evidence of Rousseff's entanglement with the distended rot of her party and much of the rest of the political elite, they have found nothing implicating her in illegal activity. Insofar as this remains true, the impending impeachment by Congress will constitute a "parliamentary coup" of the variety that toppled center-left Paraguayan President Fernando Lugo in 2012 (the frequent analogies made with Honduras, where a straightforwardly military coup took place in June 2009, are unhelpful). Since no dirt on Rousseff was forthcoming from the Lava Jato operation, her impeachment process has officially proceeded through the charge that she cooked government books to conceal the size of the budget deficit. She is accused of having made budgetary payments—using funds from public banks to cover budget gaps—that were not authorized by Congress, to minimize the appearance of the size of the deficit. This is a common practice in Brazilian history, for which no president has ever been impeached. A post on the presidential blog in early April 2016 noted that the budgetary payments, commonly known as *pedaladas*, did not constitute "a crime of responsibility," the sort of breach of personal conduct by a president required for an impeachment under the constitution. The blog stressed that, "Big or small, pedaladas are not a crime."[128] There were also alternative—albeit even weaker—grounds floated for impeachment. These claims centered on the idea that Rousseff accepted campaign finances from corrupt sources in 2014. But isolating the PT's role in such activity, without implicating all the other major parties simultaneously and thus challenging the legality of the 2014 elections altogether, was recognized by many in the opposition to be farfetched. Most of their money in this game, therefore, remained on the pedalada card.

127 Rodrigo Nunes, "The Realist's Dilemma," *Jacobin*, March 28, 2016.
128 Simon Romero, "Brazil's President Rousseff, Facing Impeachment Effort, Is Delayed by More Bad News," *New York Times*, March 3, 2016. The presidential blog is quoted in Joe Leahy, "Rousseff Report Adds to Impeachment Pressure," *Financial Times*, April 7, 2016; John Paul Rathbone, "Rousseff Presses Her Case in Brazil Drama," *Financial Times*, April 24, 2016.

Rousseff's most important coalition partner, the PMDB, led by vice president Michel Temer, abandoned the government in late March.[129] Eduardo Cunha, the right-wing evangelical speaker of the lower house and ally of Temer, has also been a central protagonist in the drive to unseat the president.[130] Revealingly, Cunha has continued his virtuous campaign despite facing separate corruption charges of his own, mainly involving secret bank accounts in Switzerland, holding sums which total roughly thirty-seven times his declared wealth at home.[131] Indeed, this surrealist avenger has already been indicted by the Supreme Court for corruption and money laundering.[132]

Financial markets have reveled in Rousseff's downfall. "If there is one thing that Brazil's left-leaning president, Dilma Rousseff, probably will not miss when she leaves office," Joe Leahy writes in the *Financial Times*, "it is the tendency of markets to loudly applaud her every misfortune." Leahy notes that Rousseff's worsening prospects "have helped turn Brazilian assets into among the best performers in the emerging world. This year, the Brazilian real has gained 9 percent against the dollar while the benchmark stock index, the Ibovespa, has returned 18.2 per cent gain since the end December. In March alone, Brazilian stocks have soared 20 per cent—their biggest one-month gain in 16 years, according to Bloomberg data."[133] Dan Bogler, in a separate opinion piece for the same newspaper, notes that Rousseff's impeachment could prove a godsend for investors in Latin America more generally, by setting a precedent for the early removal of unwanted left-leaning leaders. "In Venezuela," Bogler writes, "the likelihood of a change of government is rising, as the opposition moves from consolidating its hold on congress to launching a formal recall referendum to cut short Mr. Maduro's term. If Ms. Rousseff falls, by the by, that could end support from one of Venezuela's few remaining allies and further isolate the regime in Caracas. So far, so good for investors, who tend to prefer the economic orthodoxy associated with right-leaning administrations."[134] The will of finance here is axiomatically more important than democratic niceties.

---

129 Joe Leahy, "Rousseff Blow as Coalition Partner Quits," *Financial Times*, March 29, 2016.
130 Joe Leahy, "Brazil's Vice President Faces Prospect of Impeachment," *Financial Times*, April 5, 2016.
131 Jonathan Watts, "Brazilian Police Raid Home of Speaker Cunha and Other Senior Politicians," *Guardian*, December 16, 2015; Perry Anderson, "Crisis in Brazil," *London Review of Books*, April 21, 2016.
132 *Economist*, "The Darkest Hour."
133 Joe Leahy, "Real and Ibovespa Shine as President's Prospects Darken," *Financial Times*, March 31, 2016.
134 Dan Bogler, "Brazil's Lessons for Latin America," *Financial Times*, April 5, 2016.

As political economist Alfredo Saad-Filho observes, Lava Jato has unfolded within an all-encompassing perfect storm. "The Right simultaneously started impeachment procedures in Congress," he notes. "The media has attacked the government viciously, neoliberal economists 'impartially' beg for a new administration 'to restore market confidence,' and the Right will resort to street violence as necessary. Finally, the judicial charade against the PT has broken all the rules of legality, yet it is cheered on by the media, the Right, and even by the Supreme Court justices."[135]

Yet it is easy to forget in present circumstances how the PT arrived at this juncture. The party's precipitous decline cannot be reduced to the machinations and scheming of an authoritarian political right and its allies within elements of the state apparatus. The ugly departure of the PT in the 2000s from the working-class base it enjoyed in the 1980s and 1990s, and its concomitant embrace of capital, was already evident at the outset of Lula's first administration.

Lula's First Term

The political economy of Lula's first term largely preserved the neoliberal parameters introduced by his predecessors Fernando Henrique Cardoso of the PSDB (1995–2003) and Fernando Collor de Mello (1990–1992). In the words of Ricardo Antunes, one of Brazil's most astute political observers, the first Lula administration left "unaltered the constitutive structural features of Brazil's perversely exclusionary bourgeois social formation."[136] The limits of policy were set by a threefold commitment to low inflation and central bank independence, the liberalization of capital flows and floating exchange rates, and fiscal austerity.[137] Within these strictures, distribution to the popular classes was confined to some formalization of labor contracts, small raises in the minimum wage, injections into targeted cash transfer programs, and the extension of the role of development finance by way of the Banco Nacional de Desenvolvimento Econômico e Social (Brazilian Development Bank, BNDES).[138] In essence, however, Lula's first term was dogged by low growth rates and minimal distribution.

---

135 Saad-Filho, "A Coup in Brazil?"
136 Ricardo Antunes, "Brasil: El colapso del Gobierno Dilma y el PT," *Herramienta*, no. 57 (Spring 2015), www.herramienta.com.ar/revista-herramienta-n-57/brasil-el-colapso-del-gobierno-dilma-y-el-pt.
137 Alfredo Saad-Filho and Armando Boito, "Brazil: The Failure of the PT and the Rise of the 'New Right,'" in Leo Panitch and Greg Albo, eds., *Socialist Register 2016: The Politics of the Right* (New York: Monthly Review Press, 2015), 214.
138 Saad-Filho and Botio, "Brazil: The Failure of the PT," 216.

On the political and ideological fronts, the class content of the state appeared to change. Longstanding activists with progressive political alignments, trade unionists, and NGO advocates were incorporated into important positions within the federal administration. "This does not imply that the class character of the state had changed, or that public policies would necessarily shift to the left," write Alfredo Saad-Filho and Armando Boito, "but it changed the *appearance* of the state: millions of workers could recognize themselves in the bureaucracy, which increased hugely the legitimacy of the state among the poor and spread further a feeling of shared citizenship in Brazil."[139]

Then, in 2005, the first harbinger of the series of corruption scandals to haunt the government presented itself in the form of the *mensalão* (monthly payoff) turpitude. Perry Anderson, writing in the *London Review of Books*, captures the scene well:

> In the spring of 2005, the leader of one of the smaller parties in Congress (there were more than a dozen of these), coming under pressure after one of his henchmen was videotaped pocketing a bribe, hit back with the revelation that the government had been systematically buying the votes of deputies, to the tune of $7000 a month each, to secure majorities in the legislature. In charge of the operation was the head of Lula's cabinet in the presidential palace, José Dirceu, the money coming from illegal funds controlled by the PT and distributed by its treasurer, Delúbio Soares. Within weeks of this bombshell, an aide to the brother of the chairman of the PT, José Genoino, was arrested boarding a flight with 200,000 reais in a suitcase and $100,000 in his underpants. A month later, the manager of Lula's bid for the presidency, Duda Mendonça—a notoriety in the PR world—confessed that the campaign had been financed by slush funds extracted from interested banks and enterprises, in violation of electoral law, and that he himself had been rewarded for his services with secret deposits in an account in the Bahamas. Next it was one of Lula's closest political confidants, the former trade-union leader Luiz Gushiken, under fire for siphoning pension funds for political ends, who was forced to step down as secretary of communications. In a yet darker background lay the unsolved murder in early 2002 of Celso Daniel, mayor of the PT stronghold of Santo André, widely suspected of being a contract killing to do with bribes collected from local bus companies.[140]

In historical perspective, as loyalists of the PT were quick to point out, Lula was merely perfecting a longstanding art of Brazil's political elite. But

---

139 Saad-Filho and Boito, "Brazil: The Failure of the PT," 215.
140 Perry Anderson, "Lula's Brazil," *London Review of Books*, March 31, 2011.

while this behavior was almost to be expected of traditional politicians, it was a blow to the credibility of a party whose origins had been rooted in a project of working-class emancipation and whose leader was a former trade union militant. "In 2002," Anderson points out,

> Lula had been elected with 61 per cent of the popular vote, but the PT got less than a fifth of the seats in Congress, where allies had to be found for the government to command a legislative majority. Dirceu had wanted to make a deal with the largest party of the centre, the PMDB, but this would have meant conceding important ministries. Lula preferred to stitch together a patchwork of smaller parties, whose bargaining power was weaker. But they naturally expected a share of the spoils too, if a lower grade one, and so the *mensalão*—the monthly backhander—was devised for them.[141]

Lula's Second Term

The 2006 elections found the PT in internal turmoil, and the party was nearly defeated at the polls. Out of political necessity, and buoyed by the international context of a commodity boom, Lula introduced more distributive elements to his mode of rule in the second term, while maintaining the government's broad allegiance to the various sections of capital—agribusiness, finance, industrial, and the frequent symbiosis of the latter two. Honing a regime of multiclass conciliation, he conceded enormously to the demands of capital while offering targeted welfare to pauperized strata dependent on the state for survival, most famously through the World Bank–lauded *bolsa família*—a conditional cash transfer program that reached millions.[142] Higher education was expanded and university quotas were introduced for Black students.[143] Millions of jobs were created, although these were mainly low-paid, unskilled, and precarious. The state invested in state-owned enterprises, particularly through the expansion of Petrobras activities in 2009, following the company's discovery of deep-sea reserves in the Atlantic.[144] Expansionary policies were introduced in 2009–2010 in the wake of the global crisis, drawing on foreign reserves that had been accumulated at high rates during the commodities boom.

There was much celebration at home and abroad of Lula's statesmanship and of the country's proud membership in the BRICS group of emerging countries, alongside Russia, India, China, and South Africa. Lula become

---

141 Anderson, "Lula's Brazil."
142 Antunes, "Brasil: El Colapso."
143 Saad-Filho, "A Coup in Brazil?"
144 Saad-Filho and Boito, "Brazil: The Failure of the PT," 217–218.

something of an ambassador for Brazilian capital abroad. Between 2011 and 2012, he visited thirty countries, of which twenty were in Africa and Latin America. Construction firms, including the later disgraced Odebrecht, OAS, and Camargo Correa, paid for thirteen of these trips.[145] During the boom years, the PT was capable of lubricating its multiclass alliance, targeting modest social reforms at the poorest, providing employment, and raising the minimum wage and living standards, all the while allowing the rich to capture a vastly disproportionate share of the wealth being accumulated. At the same time, under the second Lula administration there was no diversification of exports, the technological content of manufacturing production remained the same, and infrastructural investment, including basic urban services of transport and water—flashpoints in coming protests—was severely neglected.[146]

Lula's unprecedented popularity at the close of his second term in 2010 allowed him to anoint Dilma Rousseff as his successor and virtually guarantee her election to the presidency by association. Rousseff had been a Marxist guerrilla during the dictatorship and was Lula's first Minister of Energy and Mines (2003–2005), and then his Chief of Staff (2005–2010). Her bureaucratic experience did not translate into political acumen, however, as would become clear in the coming years. Prior to becoming president she had never campaigned or been elected to any office.

Dilma's First Term

The new president inherited a roaring economy. As the continuity candidate, she gathered around her the various bourgeois fractions that had supported Lula. In its broad contours, Rousseff's initial political-economic program reproduced that of Lula's second government. There was an effort to stoke growth in the internal market, there were incentives for the production of commodities for export—particularly in the agribusiness sector—and there was a reduction in taxes for large capitals (in the industrial and construction sectors, among others). Meanwhile, extraordinarily high interest rates were maintained, guaranteeing the support of the financial sector.[147]

Between 2005 and 2011, the country's terms of trade improved dramatically. Primary commodities as a share of total exports rose from 28 percent

---

145 Raúl Zibechi, "Sin izquierda y sin rumbo," *La Jornada*, March 19, 2016. See also Patrick Bond and Ana Garcia, eds., *BRICS: An Anti-Capitalist Critique* (Chicago: Haymarket Books, 2015).

146 Saad-Filho and Boito, "Brazil: The Failure of the PT," 218.

147 Antunes, "Brasil: El colapso."

to 41 percent, while manufacturing fell from 55 percent to 44 percent. This trend continued under Rousseff, with primary materials accounting for over half the value of total exports by the end of her first term. However, from 2011 forward, the international price of Brazil's raw material exports spiraled downward, with iron ore plunging from $US 180 to $US 55 a ton, soy from $US 18 to $US 8 a bushel, and crude oil from $US 140 to $US 50 a barrel.[148]

Despite early appearances, Brazil had not escaped the global crisis but only delayed its arrival. Rousseff's political misfortune was to have risen to head of state just as the hurricane reached the doorstep. The slump was prolonged in the United States and the Eurozone, and China's expansion cooled. Commodity prices fell. Quantitative easing in the United States, UK, Japan, and the Eurozone, meanwhile, ignited capital outflow to Brazil, overvaluing the currency, stoking deindustrialization, and helping sustain a long fall for the country's GDP.[149] In a misguided attempt to restore "market confidence," Rousseff's administration abandoned all deviations from neoliberal orthodoxy and enthusiastically embraced structural adjustment and austerity measures, including severe cuts to social programs and attacks on labor rights. Unemployment rose and wages fell. But the cost of austerity was not distributed equally. In 2013, the profits of Brazil's four largest banks continued to exceed the GDP of 83 countries.[150]

But even the most submissive overtures to big businesses could not lure them back. Alongside plummeting commodity prices, there were problems with domestic consumption. The PT had long relied on stoking the purchasing power of the popular classes through the minimum wage and cash transfers, but also through a breathtaking surge in consumer credit. Between 2005 and 2015, "total debt owned by the private sector increased from 43 to 93 percent of GDP," Anderson points out, "with consumer loans running at double the level of neighbouring countries. By the time Dilma was reelected in late 2014, interest payments on household credit were absorbing more than a fifth of average disposable income. Along with the exhaustion of the commodity boom, the consumer spree was no longer sustainable. The two motors of growth had stalled."[151] Intra-capital feuds began to intensify and confidence in Rousseff's government wavered.

The PT's move to the right did not satisfy capital even as the party alienated the organized working class and informal proletarian layers that had long lent

---

148 Anderson, "Crisis in Brazil."
149 Saad-Filho, "A Coup in Brazil?"
150 Purdy, "Rousseff and the Right."
151 Anderson, "Crisis in Brazil."

the government their support. The first explosive signal of discontent from below arrived with a wave of urban rebellions in June 2013, which eventually involved more than 2 million people countrywide.[152] These were initially organized by the Movimento Passe Livre (Free Fare Movement, MPL), a social movement of the radical left, based principally in São Paulo and rooted in the struggle for free mass transit in urban Brazil. Working-class youth, angered by privatized and unreliable transit and the more general marketization of the public sphere under PT governments, constituted much of the initial base of the demonstrations.[153] Pervasive indignation at public money being wasted on building football stadiums for the 2014 World Cup, rather than being spent on health care, education, and basic infrastructure, was also channeled in these days of rage.[154]

Private consumption had been opened up to the lower orders in Brazilian society under the PT to an unprecedented degree. New forms of credit at high interest rates could be deducted in advance from wages, and aggregate domestic consumption accelerated for much of the Lula era. But the temporary satiation of consumer desire came, "at the expense of public services, whose improvement would have been a more expensive way of stimulating the economy. Purchase of electronics, white goods and vehicles was fanned (cars through tax incitements), while the water supply, paved roads, efficient buses, acceptable sewage disposal, decent schools and hospitals were neglected."[155]

The June mobilizations involved popular sectors appropriating public space, occupying streets and plazas, questioning the existing forms of institutional representation in Brazil's capitalist democracy, and demanding and practicing new forms of direct democracy with mass participation. The pervasive Brazilian myth of a middle-class country, fostered by the PT since 2003, in which a virtuous circle of capitalist development could allow all classes to prosper, was coming apart at the seams.[156]

But incongruity marked the June 2013 demonstrations, characterized as they were by multiclass participation and ideological eclecticism. There was a

---

152 Raúl Zibechi, "Debajo y detrás de las grandes movilizaciones," *OSAL* 34 (November 2013); Ricardo Antunes, "As rebeliões de junho de 2013," *OSAL*, 34 (November 2013); Ruy Braga, "As jornadas de junho no Brasil: Crônica de um mês inesquecível," *OSAL*, 34 (November 2013); and José Mauricio Domingues, "Las movilizaciones de junio de 2013: ¿Explosión fugaz o novísima historia de Brasil?" *OSAL* 34 (November 2013).
153 Antunes, "Brasil: El colapso."
154 Dave Zirin, *Brazil's Dance with the Devil: The World Cup, the Olympics, and the Struggle for Democracy* (Chicago: Haymarket Books, 2014).
155 Anderson, "Crisis in Brazil."
156 Antunes, "Brasil: El colapso."

consistently strong presence of popular social layers, of precarious youth, of working-class university students, and of youth from poor neighborhoods in the suburbs of the major cities. But there were also sectors of the conservative middle class, who with time grew in number and cohered in political clarity. The small but important far-left political groups and social organizations present in the streets—the PSOL, the Partido Socialista dos Trabalhadores Unificado (United Socialist Workers Party, PSTU), the Partido Comunista Brasileiro (Brazilian Communist Party, PCB), the MPL, the Movimento dos Trabalhadores Sem Teto (Homeless Workers Movement, MTST), and the Movimento Periferia Ativa (Movement of the Urban Periphery, MPA)—were unable to achieve hegemony in the boulevards and avenues, the plaza occupations, and the street assemblies. This was in part a reflection—particularly in the case of the expressly political formations—of the difficulties they have encountered in widening their social bases in recent years, despite the declining popularity of the PT. Instead, toward the end of June 2013, as we will see below, a new antiparty, populist right was able to capture extraparliamentary momentum. Protofascist and fascist groups were emboldened and physically attacked and expelled from marches those carrying left-wing banners.[157]

Such was the backdrop to Rousseff's presidential campaign of 2014. She campaigned on an antineoliberal ticket, promising to reject the fiscal adjustments being demanded by the various sections of capital, and to defend the social rights won by Brazilian workers through decades of struggle. This electoral platform, together with fear of the fierce neoliberal restructuring to be endured were Rousseff's conservative opponent Aécio Neves to win, mobilized enough of the traditional popular base of the PT to win the elections, even if by a narrow margin.

Dilma's Second Term

Once elected, Rousseff made an about-face, appointing Joaquim Levy as finance minister. Levy was an unambiguous representative of international financial capital, trained in economics at the University of Chicago and based at Bradesco, one of the largest private banks in the country.[158] Levy was given the task of carrying out a severe austerity package, signaling once again the priority of the PT to present itself as credible before the market. "The imperatives now," Anderson notes, "were to cut social spending, curtail credit from public banks, auction state property and raise taxes to bring the budget back into pri-

---

157 Ibid.
158 Saad-Filho and Boito, "Brazil: The Failure of the PT," 222.

mary surplus."[159] This was all too little, too late for the representatives of capital, while it was seen as a brazen betrayal by workers and the poor. Rousseff's popularity had thus already begun to sink when Operation Lava Jato flooded the political scene. Her approval ratings subsequently dove to single digits.

The political coalition in the Chamber of Deputies and the Senate that had supported the Rousseff government became unhinged. The call for impeachment grew louder. Space opened up for an antiparty, right-wing populism with the authentic capacity to organize mass demonstrations—something not witnessed since the mobilization of hundreds of thousands of right-wing protesters in the lead-up to the coup d'état that overthrew progressive president João Goulart in 1964. Given the hard tack to the right by Rousseff, there were also self-imposed limits to mobilizing popular classes to defend the government against the new right.

Repeated demonstrations of hundreds of thousands of upper-middle-class protesters, backed by the mainstream media, took to the streets in Brazil in 2015 and 2016. By March 2016, demonstrations reached an apotheosis of more than 3 million participants countrywide, according to police. A poll carried out among demonstrators in São Paulo on March 13, 2016, revealed that 77 percent had postsecondary degrees and the same percentage were white, in a country in which 50 percent of the population is Black or mixed-race; 63 percent earned salaries equivalent to at least 5 times the minimal salary; and the average age among protesters was forty-five.[160] The protests of 2015–2016 were distinct from those of 2013. They were unambiguously right-wing, organized under the banner of anticorruption, and called for the downfall of Rousseff's government.

New Right

Where did the new right come from? How did it emerge? Is it the spontaneous creation of mainstream TV and newspapers and right-wing social media groups, as some learned commentary suggests? Or does it have a more complicated organizational, ideological, and political history? What are its strengths but also its weaknesses?

The new right first gained visibility on a large scale on June 20, 2013, the day of the so-called Revolt of the *Coxinhas* (a pejorative term used to refer to pampered, white, upper class men).[161] That day, tens of thousands of coxinhas, carrying green-and-yellow Brazilian national flags, joined the massive

159 Anderson, "Crisis in Brazil."
160 Zibechi, "Impasse, antes del deluvio."
161 Raúl Zibechi, "La nueva derecha en Brasil," *La Jornada*, April 2, 2016.

demonstrations organized by the MPL against bus tariffs and began attacking and expelling protesters carrying symbols of the left. They seized control of the demonstrations.[162] The facility with which they did so suggests something other than social-media spontaneity. The new right is best understood, rather, as militantly organized, with politicized cadres, coherent strategy, tactical experience, and political education through years of work in the public and private university systems.[163]

Raúl Zibechi dates the first action of this new right in formation to August 17, 2007. On that day demonstrations were called under the banner Civic Movement for the Rights of Brazilians, better known as Cansei ("I'm tired of it"). Five thousand people were mobilized in response to the mensalão corruption scandal. The repertoire of the demonstrators foreshadowed what we witness in today's marches, with chants of "Out with Lula!" Then, as today, popular telenovela actors were mobilized to the cause, and mobilizers had the support of the Federação das Indústrias do Estado de São Paulo (Industrial Federation of the State of São Paulo, FIESP), the most powerful manufacturing sector organization in Brazil, as well as the Ordem dos Advogados do Brasil (Brazilian Order of Lawyers, OAB).[164]

Between 2007 and 2013, the new right took formation organizationally through the capture of student federations in the public universities that had historically been bastions of the left. The most significant initial victory occurred at the National University of Brazil (UNB). In 2009, the new right formed a group called Alliance for Freedom, which won the leadership of the UNB student federation in 2011 with 22 percent of the vote, due to the fragmentation of its left opposition. In 2015, this group was reelected for the fourth time with 60 percent of the vote. Under the leadership of the new right, the student federation has engaged in important direct actions, such as the occupation of the rector's office, calling on the rector to resign for acts of corruption.

Alliance for Freedom also has ties to another group, with the moniker Students for Freedom. The latter is financed by neoliberal and Cold Warrior think tanks based in the United States. Also in the network is the Liberal Institute, which takes as its primary focus the quotidian necessities of university students, like clean bathrooms and security on campus. This linkage between everyday student needs and farther-reaching political objectives has been very effective organizationally. Using this strategy, the new right won in other state

---

162 Zibechi, "La nueva derecha."
163 Ibid.
164 Ibid.

universities over the 2007–2013 period, such as Minas Gerais and Rio Grande do Sul, among others. Their support draws mainly on the departments of economics, law, and engineering. Key to their successes has been an ostensibly antipolitical predisposition, always eschewing public association with extant conservative parties in the country.[165]

Parallel to university organizing, this new right has participated in demonstrations and marches. Already in 2011, there were mobilizations of twenty thousand people nationwide, covering twenty-five cities and enjoying the backing of the OAB. Protestors sang the national anthem and carried the national flag. When the rebellions of June 2013 arrived, the new right was well positioned to intervene. Their cadres had experience in extraparliamentary, social-movement leadership, and the left's experience in the streets had simultaneously declined, as core organizers were incorporated into the lower echelons of the state apparatus under successive PT governments. The new right was able to intervene and redirect major left-wing demonstrations of the popular classes against transit fees toward the new right's agenda. On this basis new groups were forged, such as Movimento Brasil Livre (Free Brazil Movement, MBL), Vem Pra Rua (Come to the Streets), and Revoltados On Line (Revolted On Line).[166] These three have become the most important vessels for channelling mobilization against corruption and for impeachment in 2015 and 2016.

Ideologically, this phenomenon does not involve any simple reproduction of old-school Catholicism and right-wing militarism in the authoritarian mold of the 1960s and 1970s, but rather accepts abortion, gay marriage, the decriminalization of marijuana, and free public services, even while opposing quotas for black students in universities, glorifying the free market, and framing bolsa família as a program that takes from the pockets of the deserving upper middle classes and distributes it to the undeserving poor.[167] The upper middle class also resents the fact that, under the PT governments, the darker-skinned popular classes were able to "occupy spaces, literally, previously the preserve of the upper-middle class: airports, shopping malls, banks, private health facilities, and roads, with the latter clogged up by cheap cars purchased

---

165 Ibid.
166 Ibid.
167 Ibid. See also the detailed survey of attitudes conducted by political scientists at an April 2015 demonstration. Pablo Ortellado, Esther Solano, and Lucia Nader, "Um desacordo entre manifestantes e os convocantes dos protestos?" *El País* (Brazil), August 19, 2015.

on seventy-two easy payments."[168] The recent fervor of Brazil's evangelical Protestantism constitutes a final ideological tributary feeding into the river of the right. Teaching a "theology of prosperity," the dominant currents of evangelicalism—now with the allegiance of roughly a fifth of the Brazilian population—share an elective affinity with neoliberalism's idolatry of the market. The new religion promises "material success on earth rather than mere relief in heaven."[169] Among the ranks of the new evangelicals are billionaire media magnates and growing numbers of politicians.

The core groups organizing the protests combine their funding from think tanks, lawyers, and industrial capitalists with small contributions from grassroots supporters as well as proceeds from the sale of T-shirts and protest paraphernalia. While the antipolitics profile is key to the credibility of the main organizations with their support base, many of the leading campaigners in fact have longstanding ties to traditional political parties. right-wing politicians who have served time in prison for corruption, or presently face corruption charges, have played important roles in the demonstrations. The leader of the leading opposition party, the PSDB, was a keynote speaker at an anticorruption mobilization in Belo Horizonte, and ex-president Fernando Henrique Cardoso, also a PSDB member, has joined the growing chorus calling for Rousseff to step down.[170]

The new right mobilizations have been embraced by the police and the media rather than being met with the standard repression and demonization meted out when the left mobilizes. Those in the streets are the shock troops for the politicians waging the technical impeachment proceedings in Congress and the judges and prosecuting teams laying the legal pretexts for Rousseff's removal from office. "The Brazilian judiciary," Anderson observes, "like its colleagues in the apparatus of prosecutors and federal police, can be assumed to share much the same outlook as the country's middle class, to whose better-off layers they belong, with that class's typical preferences and prejudices."[171] But while it may be possible to remove Rousseff from office, the new right still lacks any credible political vehicle with which to fill the power vacuum. As a consequence, Brazil is in an incredible impasse. Competing forces vie for the hegemony that the PT has evidently lost without any obvious alternative presenting itself in organized form.

---

168 Saad-Filho, "A Coup in Brazil?"
169 Anderson, "Crisis in Brazil."
170 This paragraph draws on Purdy, "Rousseff and the Right."
171 Anderson, "Crisis in Brazil."

Fragmented Political Field

To recap, this explosive situation grew out of a confluence of intermingling crisis tendencies. The global economic crisis unleashed its turmoil on Brazil in a delayed but fierce manner. Rousseff won the 2014 elections, but she campaigned on a lie and won with the narrowest margin in recent Brazilian history. She was unable to win back the confidence of the markets even as she alienated the popular classes. In December 2015, fiscal hawk Levy resigned from his position as Minister of Finance and was replaced by Nelson Barbosa, the Minister of Planning, seen as a dove in fiscal matters. Still, this feigned tack to the moderate left only fueled the campaign for impeachment while returning few from the left back to the government's fold.[172] Denunciations of corruption have now entangled virtually the entire leadership of the PT dating back to 2002, with leading figures such as Dirceu and Vaccari now in prison. Rousseff lost all semblance of political authority, as the alliances holding her government aloft unraveled at an alarming speed. Workers and the poor continued to reject the austerity packages of the PT government, and the new right gained confidence and capacities, even if it still lacked an alternative project for power.[173]

Much of Brazil's fragmentary left fears the consequences of a parliamentary coup. But they also rightly persist in their opposition to the PT's abandonment of the interests of the popular classes in Brazil, and its strategic alliances with capital. Many on the social and political left are attempting to mobilize in the streets against the new right and the potentialities of impeachment, while retaining their independence from the PT. They are committed to a strategy of building an alternative sociopolitical pole for a new left in Brazil. The present impasse, then, is both wrought with danger and opportunity. To be "against impeachment today," Ricardo Antunes rightly argues, "cannot mean any complacency with regard to the tragedy of the PT in power, in all of its dimensions."[174]

The challenge, according to Antunes, "is to build a social and political alternative of a new kind," a new left authentically aligned with the best of the popular movements. From where might this emerge? He points to the land struggles and occupations of the Movimento dos Trabalhadores Rurais Sem Terra (Landless Rural Workers Movement, MST); the struggle for housing

---

172 Joe Leahy, "Brazil's Finance Chief Joaquim Levy Resigns," *Financial Times*, December 18, 2015.
173 Antunes, "Brasil: El colapso."
174 Ibid.

of the MTST; the free transit mobilizations of the MPL; the ongoing rebellions in the poor peripheries for housing and against the racist brutality of the military police; recent strikes by metallurgical workers, bank workers, teachers, doctors, and other public employees; and the possibilities of class-struggle union federations such as Conlutas and Intersindical. "It will be the conjunction of these molecular movements with the best of the lefts (social and political) of a new type, rooted in concrete experiences of the social struggles of our time, out of which something new can emerge." For Antunes, the corruption scandal has produced a false polarization in Brazil between the new right and the PSDB, on the one hand, and the PT, on the other. These two camps have more in common than is commonly recognized. Provocation of an authentic sociopolitical polarization, in this view, becomes the order of the day. This requires a new sociopolitical basis of the left and the popular movements, capable of rejecting both of the reigning mirror images of capital.

There is certainly a political coup in motion via the institutions, but an analysis of the longer durée reveals that none of this would have been possible without the internal debacles of the PT and its abandonment of working-class emancipation. The Rousseff government repressed protests, explicitly allied itself with industrial, financial, and agribusiness capital, flexibilized labor legislation, covered for the multinational mining company that committed the environmental crime of Mariana, and applied multiple rounds of austerity with sharp impacts on the country's popular classes.[175] The ruling party now mourns the absence of its own moral capacity to mobilize the poor against the right-wing offensive. But this was foreseeable. The party never defended the rights of the poor against capital when it had the chance to do so, from 2003 to the present.[176] "There was no redistribution of wealth or income," Anderson stresses: "the infamously regressive tax structure bequeathed by Cardoso to Lula, penalising the poor to pamper the rich, was left untouched. Distribution there was, appreciably raising the living standards of the least well-off, but it was individualized in form."[177]

Maintenance of the basic logics of neoliberal rule diminished the government's support base, as has its continuance of the routine corruption expected of parties of the right. The officialist argument that the corruption of other

---

175 Salvador Schavelzon, "La destitución de Dilma y el debate que se abre en las calles," *Asuntos del Sur*, March 31, 2016.

176 Raúl Zibechi, "Golpe al corazón de la izquierda latinoamericana: Fin del ciclo del Partido de los Trabajadores," *Brecha*, March 14, 2016.

177 Anderson, "Crisis in Brazil."

parties is not receiving the same attention in the mainstream media is real, but is a characteristically depressing defense by a party with origins in a project of liberation. The political vacuum of the present is a product, fundamentally, of its own trajectory.[178] "The party's so-called realism, in short," Nunes writes, "prevented it from defining a new reality. There was a price to pay for that. If one lives by realism only, one may very well end up dying by realism too."[179]

Rather than "centering debate on the government and leaders who do not have anything to offer," the anthropologist Salvador Schavelzon suggests, it is necessary to return to the popular left-wing potential of the early days in June 2013. "Neither support for a government who cannot defend any just cause," he writes, nor "any room for fascism and racist hate under a liberal banner."[180] For Schavelzon, the best of June 2013 represents "the possibility to resist, to create and to disarm the coup that began as a result of measures taken by the government of the PT. This is the dispute that will play itself out in the streets and in the challenge to invent new political spaces."[181]

The PT, as is its instinct, will continue to try to forge a negotiated, elite-driven pact with the centrist parties in the lower house and the Senate in order to hold on to power. As historian and PSOL activist Sean Purdy notes, "The anti-government left must organize opposition to the deal between the PT and the centrist parties, which will only bring more austerity." There are already actions in this direction. "The MTST has promised to launch massive demonstrations if the government defaults on its promises to boost public housing programs," Purdy writes. "And the two left-wing trade union centrals—Conlutas and Intersindical—are stepping up their support from the public- and private-sector strike actions that are multiplying across the country."[182] Thus navigation of the complicated terrain of the moment will fundamentally involve strategically mapping the balance of forces in the extra-institutional and institutional arenas alike, plotting interventions, and hoping to turn the tide. Fragmented left political groupings and social movements are struggling to oppose all austerity, and to keep their independence from the PT, while combating the new right through a renewal of the early days of June 2013. But prospects are dim, at least for the early days ahead.

---

178 Schavelzon, "La destitución de Dilma."
179 Nunes, "The Realist's Dilemma."
180 Schavelzon, "La destitución de Dilma."
181 Ibid.
182 Purdy, "Rousseff and the Right."

Ecuador's Impasse

An indigenous march and people's strike converged on Quito on August 13, 2015, the Andean city still Ecuador's political center despite the fact that the coastal metropolis of Guayaquil is now bigger in number. Coordinated principally by the CONAIE, the march began on August 2 in Zamora Chinchipe, passing through Loja, Azuay, Cañar, Chimborazo, Tungurahua, Cotopaxi, and Salcedo before arriving in the capital. Demands emanating from the different sectors of urban and rural groups supporting the initiative were diverse and sometimes contradictory.

But Alberto Acosta, at least, saw a certain clarity in the morass. Acosta was the presidential candidate for the Plurinational Unity of Lefts in the 2013 general elections. An economist by profession, he was the Minister of Mines and Energy and the president of the Constituent Assembly in the opening years of the government under Rafael Correa. After the assembly ended, he and Correa parted ways. Acosta remains an important shaper of opinion in the country. In the lead-up to August 13, he maintained that there was a discernible core to the protesters' demands.[183]

Those in the streets, according to Acosta, were opposed to any constitutional changes that would allow indefinite reelection of the president. They were opposed to the ongoing criminalization of social protest. They were outraged by a new agrarian reform initiative that would work to displace peasants in order to advance the interests of agribusiness. They were lined up against the expansion of mega-mines, with all their nightmarish socioecological implications. They were defending workers' rights to organize and strike, elemental freedoms limited in the labor code introduced in April 2015. They were also aligned against oil exploitation in Yasuní, one of the most biodiverse areas in the world and a zone that Correa had once committed himself to protecting if international actors would pay for the lost revenues nondevelopment implied—they didn't, and so Correa didn't, as was predictable. And, finally, the popular organizations were opposed to the free trade agreement Ecuador signed with the EU, because of its neoliberal character and its negative implications for national sovereignty. These were some of the overlapping areas that, according to Acosta, stood above other divisions in the left opposition to the Correa administration.

A Day in the Streets of Quito

And yet walking through the different sections of the march on August 13,

---

183 "'Molesta e indigna el estilo autoritario y caudillesco de Correa': Entrevista con Alberto Acosta," *Montecristi Vive*, August 12, 2015.

it was difficult to miss the fact that a contest for hegemony within the opposition was unfolding. There were left-wing unions calling for dignified wages and the right to strike, socialist feminists chanting slogans against Correa's Opus Dei–inflected "family plan." Anticapitalist environmentalist groups were there to oppose extractivism—the expansion of the mining, oil, and agro-industrial frontiers especially. Alongside them were social democratic and revolutionary socialist and anarchist collectives, some of significant strength and long organizational histories, others little more than affinity groups. Together, these eclectic expressions of a left—broadly conceived—seemed to dominate the streets in numerical terms as well as in political sophistication. But they have yet to cohere into any unified left bloc, independent of Correa.

CONAIE's demands were made public in a manifesto, and they are clearly distinguishable from the politics of the right—whatever officials of the state might suggest to the contrary. Many of the points on CONAIE's platform reiterate longstanding aims of the indigenous movement. Nonetheless, the social bases, potential or realized, of the myriad faces of the right-wing opposition—Guillermo Lasso, the largest shareholder in the Bank of Guayaquil and presidential candidate for the right in 2013, Jaime Nebot, the conservative mayor of Guayaquil, and Mauricio Rodas, the mayor of Quito—were also visible in the avenues and byways of Quito. This politics found material expression in middle-class banners defending families and freedom and audible resonance in the chanted echoes of "Down with the dictator!" President Correa points to the large demonstrations of last June against taxes on inheritance and capital gains as evidence that this right is a real and imminent threat to stability.

The immediate battle lines of August 13 were delineated by the various participants' desires to demonstrate social power in the extraparliamentary domain, but anxious anticipation of the 2017 general elections weighed on every element of the day's events. No one knows if Correa will amend the constitution and run a third time as candidate for Alianza País (Country Alliance, AP), the party in power since 2007, and under Correa's leadership since its inception.

Golpe Blando?

The Correa administration, suffering significant recent declines in popularity in the midst of an extended rut in oil prices and looming austerity measures, framed the demonstrations as either intentionally, or naively, playing into the hands of the domestic right and imperialism. On this view, they are reinforcing the destabilization of the country and laying the groundwork for the right's sought-after *golpe blando*, or soft coup. One AP Congressperson, María

Augusta, told the media casually that the CIA has been financing the indigenous march, although she offered no evidence. Correa also placed the strategic blame for organizing the demonstration on indigenous and labor "elites"
who were supposed to have no sense of the interests and sentiments of their
rank-and-file bases. In many ways, activism has become sedition and left-wing
dissent betrayal of the country, in the current conjuncture.

During the commodities boom, Correa could depend on a fluctuating
amalgam of co-optive measures and targeted retaliation vis-à-vis the principal
social movements—above all the indigenous movement, often rooted simultaneously in socioecological conflicts around mining and the integrity of indigenous territories. Under charges of "terrorism and sabotage" several nonviolent
indigenous leaders are serving punitive sentences in prison for activities like
blocking roads, or preventing mining capitalists from gaining access to their
(ever-expanding) concessions throughout the country. At the end of the day
on August 13, two prominent indigenous leaders were arrested and roughed
up by police: Carlos Pérez Guartambel of the Andean indigenous organization
ECUARUNARI and Salvador Quishpe, the prefect of Zamora Chinchipe.

Exhaustion of Redistributive Boom

According to official figures—which take $US 2.63 per day as the baseline—pov-
erty had been reduced from 37.6 percent in 2006 to 22.5 percent in 2014. Income
inequality, as measured by the Gini index, also improved. These important gains
go some distance in helping to understand Correa's relative popularity, at least
until recently. According to the indispensable conjunctural reports regularly published by sociologist Pablo Ospina Peralta, however, polling data show the president lost between ten and twenty points in popularity in the summer of 2015.[184]

Just as the right-wing antitax protests in June 2015 were a sign of the
fragile political reproducibility of Correísmo in the medium term, the weighty
presence of the left in the protests of August 2015 suggests that the popular
sectors have an inkling of a change in the balance of forces as well. "What is at
the centre of the national debate is the exit from *Correísmo*," Acosta explains.
"How, with whom, towards what, and on what terms."

Yet, as Alejandra Santillana Ortíz notes, it can be misleading to trace this
change back only to its proximate catalysts—particularly the fall in the price
of oil.[185] Ruptures between social movements and the state began to surface

184 Pablo Ospina Peralta, *Protesta social, crisis económica y escenario politico* (Informe de
   Coyuntura. Quito: CEP, July 2015).
185 Interview with the author, August 12, 2015, Quito.

in earnest as far back as 2009, intensifying measurably over the last four years. Their culmination in the march on Quito was at least as much a question of this medium durée as it was the response to political-economic developments of the summer of 2015.

Vying for Hegemony

Such a perspective finds an echo in sociologist Mario Unda's recent snapshot comparison of the country's principal sociopolitical lines of demarcation across two years: 2007 and 2013, the first year of the first and second administrations of Correa, respectively. For Unda, at the outset of the first Correa administration conflict was overdetermined in many ways by the right's fear of Correa's potential radicalism and the left's hope for the same.[186]

Conflict gravitated around the political-institutional terrain of the state, with the right still retaining control of the National Assembly and the Supreme Electoral Tribunal. Alongside this institutional competition with the right, big private media corporations lined up against Correa, increasingly playing the role of conservative opposition, as the traditional parties of the right imploded into irrelevance. The principal business confederations in the country also adopted an extremely confrontational stance in the face of the new government.

Yet, even in 2007 it was possible to identify certain lines of conflict between the AP government and popular movements and sectors. Some of these were marginal and localized—disputes over rural and urban service provision, labour disputes, pension disputes, and so on. However, in the countryside the indigenous movement was already being drawn into battles with the state and multinational capital on the extractive fronts of mining, oil, water, hydroelectricity, and agro-industry. Far from marginalia, these issues proved to be central to Correa's development model in the years to come.

A Dispute Internal to the Bourgeoisie

By comparison, the divisions were distinct in 2013. The scene was overdetermined not by the axis of right-wing contestation with the government but rather the government's growing disputes with popular movements and their historic allies. There were also conflicts within *sections* of the bourgeoisie, but face-offs with capital no longer accurately captured the determining dynamics of the terrain. This far into ruling the country, the Correa government had determined that its principal enemy was the indigenous movement and what

---

186 Mario Unda, "La trayectoria del correísmo a la luz de los conflictos (2007–2013)," *La Linea del Fuego*, July 1, 2013.

it conceived of as infantile environmentalists. Consequently, the government threw all the coercive and co-optive powers of the state in their direction.[187] At the same time, Correa sharpened its relations with public sector workers, most notoriously laying off thousands through obligatory redundancies. High schools—students and teachers—were another live field of contention at this moment, as the government sought to ram through its "meritocratic" reforms in the educational sector. All the while, criminalization and control of social protest and independent organizing were primary concerns of the regime.

Ideologically, the right had taken on novel forms in 2013 as well, relative to their collective demeanor in 2007. Sections of the traditional right continued to do battle for a purist retention of neoliberal axioms, but there were also new right experiments—such as Creating Opportunities (Creando Oportunidades, CREO) and United Society in Action (Sociedad Unida Más Acción, SUMA)—that sought to present to the public a face of moderation and modernity; in other words, appropriating much of the language of the Correa administration for itself.[188]

If that was the political tenor of the right, the economic organizations of the bourgeoisie were also developing in interesting directions. The confrontational disposition of business confederations was largely eclipsed by 2013, as most federations had elected new leaderships whose mandates were to negotiate and reach agreement with a regime seen to be far more flexible than originally anticipated. The negotiation hypothesis of the right paid dividends in the creation of a new Ministry of Foreign Trade and the signing of the Ecuador-EU free trade agreement, which had the enthusiastic backing of all the big capitals.[189]

For Unda, then, the dispute between the government and the bourgeoisie had metamorphosed into one of an internal type. That is, control of the state apparatus was still a domain of contestation, but the field of consensus on capitalist modernization defined the entire backdrop—a fundamentally shared vision of society and development. Of course, this did not mean the obsolescence of sectional and conjunctural conflict, but it did mean the bourgeois–state axis of conflict had been eclipsed by that of the state–popular movement. The disputes with business and the right were disputes over control of the same societal project, whereas battle lines between popular movements and the state were drawn over distinct visions of society, development, and the future.[190]

---

187 Unda, "La trayectoria del correísmo."
188 Ibid.
189 Ibid.
190 Ibid.

Passive Revolution Slows Down

Massimo Modonesi's reading of Antonio Gramsci's "passive revolution" can help us to understand the trajectory of progressive governments in South America over the last ten to fifteen years.[191] In Modonesi's reading of Gramsci, passive revolution encompasses an unequal and dialectical combination of two tendencies simultaneously present in a single epoch—one of restoration and the other of revolution, one of preservation and the other of transformation. The two tendencies coexist in tandem, but it is possible to decipher one tendency that ultimately determines or characterizes the process or cycle of a given epoch. The transformative features of a passive revolution mark a set of changes distinct from the preceding period, but those changes ultimately guarantee the stability of the fundamental relations of domination, even while these assume novel political forms.

At the same time, the specific class content of passive revolutions can vary within certain limits—that is to say, the different degrees to which particular components of popular demands are incorporated (the transformative tendency) within a matrix that ultimately sustains the fundamental relations of domination (the restorative tendency). Passive revolutions involve neither total restoration of the old order, the full reenactment of the status quo ante, nor radical revolution. Instead they involve a dialectic of revolution/restoration, transformation/preservation. Capacities for social mobilization from below in early stages are contained or co-opted—or selectively repressed—while the political initiative of sections of the dominant classes is restored. A form of domination is established, capable of enacting conservative reforms masked in the language of earlier impulses emerging from below, achieving in this way a passive consensus of the dominated classes. Rather than an instantaneous restoration there is a molecular change in the balance of forces under passive revolution, gradually draining the capacities for self-organization and self-activity from below through co-optation, guaranteeing passivity to the new order and encouraging demobilization, or at least controlling what mobilization of the popular classes does occur.

In the idiom of Ecuadorian Marxism, Agustin Cueva's theorization of *impasse* in the 1970s most closely parallels that of Modonesi's passive revolution today.[192] There have been recurring moments in Ecuadorian history in which the

---

191 Massimo Modonesi, "Revoluciones pasivas en América Latina: Una aproximación gramsciana a la caracterización de los gobiernos progresistas," in *El Estado en América Latina: Continuidades y rupturas*, ed. Mabel Thwaites (Buenos Aires: CLACSO, 2012).
192 Agustín Cueva, *El proceso de dominación política en Ecuador* (Mexico: Editorial Diogenes, 1974).

intensity of the horizontal conflicts internal to capital, and simultaneously vertical contests between the ruling and popular classes, were simply too much for the existing form of domination to bear. Its reproducibility was put into jeopardy. Politicians sought new and more stable forms of domination. Instability reigned in the interregnum—an *impasse* was reached. Overcoming such impasses has been the work of populists in Ecuadorian history, of Caesars and Bonapartes.

Between 1982 and 2006 the dominant classes of the country attempted to introduce neoliberal restructuring through a variety of different channels. It was a deeply unstable period, reaching an apex in the 1999 financial crisis, followed by a series of mobilizations that threw out various heads of state in succession before their mandate was completed. Correa has calmed the storm. Profits have been high—in banking, mining, oil, agro-industry, and so on. Correa has co-opted or crushed most independent social movement activity.

Rhetorically, the regime has employed vague ideologies, from *buen vivir* (an indigenous conception of "living well") in the beginning of the administration to the techno-fetishism that has dominated the last several years (best exemplified, perhaps, by a dystopic model cities project in the Amazon).[193]

Correa has, in the main, been functional to capital, which isn't the same as saying he is capital's first choice. He is as expendable, ultimately, as all the populists in the past. With the price of oil falling, capitals are scrambling to collect what's available and regain a more direct control of the state. It's an uncertain period ahead, and the sentiment on the right is that Correa should go. A recent piece in the *Economist* captures this nicely, essentially thanking him for his service while showing him the door. "Mr. Correa faces a choice," the *Economist* suggests. "He could persist in his bid for permanent power and risk being kicked out by the street, like his predecessors. Or he could swallow his pride, stabilise the economy and drop his re-election bid. He would then go down in history as one of Ecuador's most successful presidents."[194]

The various forces of the left, broadly defined, are meanwhile trying to rebuild and regain initiative, to forge the bases of a societal project that is genuinely an alternative to Correa and the right. But the left is starting from a point of weakness and disarticulation, and the present ideological and political landscape could scarcely be more complicated.

---

193 For discussion of the model cities, see Japhy Wilson and Manuel Bayón, "Concrete Jungle: The Planetary Urbanization of the Ecuadorian Amazon," *Human Geography* 8, no. 3 (2015): 1–23.

194 *Economist*, "Scraping the Barrel: Will Ecuador Turn into Latin America's Greece?" August 1, 2015.

Conclusion

As this chapter has tried to show, since 1998 the Latin American social and political left experienced a dramatic rearticulation relative to its nadir of the early 1990s. Out of the crisis of neoliberal legitimacy during the recession of 1998–2002, extraparliamentary movements rose up in a series of defensive actions that eventually shifted to offensive anticapitalist struggles in a number of cases. The recovery of economic growth across much of South America in the context of an extraordinary China-led commodities boom, however, provided the material context for the consolidation of center-left regimes through electoral victories and the advance of the compensatory state in several countries. This relatively easy international environment for the reproduction of the compensatory state was confronted with a rougher terrain as aggregate growth in the region stumbled in 2009. However, as this chapter has shown, the global crisis was initially attenuated in the Latin American scene by the relative continuity in commodity prices, foreign direct investment, and the capacity for countercyclical spending through the tapping of unprecedented foreign reserves accumulated by many states since 2003. That all changed by 2012, as the delayed reverberation of the crisis struck South American economies viciously, laying the basis for simultaneous economic and political crises of center-left and left administrations and creating material conditions ripe for right-wing rearticulation. We examined such processes in detail across the cases of Argentina, Venezuela, Brazil, and Ecuador.

While there are no simple roadmaps—tactical or strategic—for building anticapitalist alternatives in contemporary Latin America, the historical record since the early 1990s suggests that building capacities for organization and activity of the popular classes and oppressed as against ruling classes and imperialism is a necessary first step in what will necessarily be an extended struggle. Recognizing the structural limitations of the developmental strategies of compensatory states to facilitate the further development of such capacities is a prerequisite for building both country-specific and region-wide movements oriented toward a more profound, structural transformation of extant forms of domination and exploitation.

THREE

Contemporary Latin American Inequality: Class Struggle, Decolonization, and the Limits of Liberal Citizenship

Recent decades have witnessed a welcome flourishing of social-scientific literature on the enduring problems of inequality in Latin America.[1] However, this chapter argues that the dominant trends in this new season of academic and policy attention to inequality are limited by a strict adherence to Weberian historical sociology, a thin conception of democracy, and a partial and flawed understanding of capitalism, class, and other social relations of oppression. The liberal ideology underpinning much of the current investigation of inequality in the region is incapable of understanding the capitalist market as a field characterized by coercion and imperatives. Rather, the market, albeit in need of taming and regulation, is ultimately understood to be an arena of opportunities, which can be seized or missed. Because markets are the domain of freedom, movements for freedom from the market become impossible to understand. The empirical separation of the economic from the political under capitalism is celebrated as a normative ideal upon which liberal democracy

1 Many thanks to Phil Oxhorn and José Jouve Martín for their probing comments on an earlier draft of this chapter.

rests. The invulnerability to democratic power of the coercive and imperative economic sphere is therefore a sacrosanct feature of liberal democracy, one with important consequences for the horizons of human emancipation.

An alternative Marxian and decolonial framework is proposed as a better way of conceiving inequality and analyzing the totalizing power of capital and the complexity of class relations and other internally related social oppressions—gender, sexuality, and race—in the current moment of Latin American capitalism. Class is understood in this framework as a living, relational phenomenon rather than an empty abstraction. It is, therefore, conceptualized as being multiply determined in and through gender, race, and sexuality in contemporary Latin American societies. These latter social oppressions are not mere epiphenomena of class structure, nor are they reducible to class exploitation. However, the way in which they constitute capitalist society alongside class can only be properly understood when we think of them as being internally related to class. Relations of class, gender, and race are a dialectical unity of multiple determinations rather than independent spheres, separate from one another. They are discrete phenomena but only fully comprehensible as they relate to one another. Class exploitation under capitalism operates nationally, regionally, and internationally at the point of production, in the sphere of circulation, within the private sphere of gendered reproductive labor, through race and racism, and upon the basis of nature.[2] This totalizing complexity exceeds the boundaries of the Weberian sociological imagination and the confines of liberal democratic theory that inform most studies of inequality in contemporary Latin America. Such complexity is central to the theoretical alternative advanced in this chapter.

Empirically, we use two areas of inquiry to substantiate our claims. The first is the lens of extractive capitalism in twenty-first-century Latin America. The multiple constitutive moments of capitalist exploitation are visible here through Latin America's subordinate repositioning as primary commodity producer in the international division of labor, as novel forms of class struggle emerge through peasant contestation against the dispossession of their land, as racism is used against indigenous communities resisting incursions into their territories for the extraction of natural resources, and, finally, as capitalism's interface with the substratum of nature is revealed through the centrality of mining minerals, oil, gas, and agricultural products to the latest rounds of capitalist accumulation in much of the region. If these are some of the structural

2 Benjamin Selwyn, *The Global Development Crisis* (Cambridge: Polity Press, 2014).

nodes through which extractive capitalism operates in the current period in Latin America, our second area of empirical inquiry brings to the surface the political subjectivities informing particular patterns of resistance. Specifically, we focus on the life story and activism of Luis Macas, an indigenous dissident in Ecuador who develops, in theory and praxis, a combined and totalizing critique of colonialism and capitalism. We show how Macas's political subjectivity is informed by a utopian–revolutionary dialectic, through which he draws on elements of a precapitalist past in looking forward to an anticolonial and socialist future.

Departing from this theoretical backdrop, the chapter is organized into five sections, each relating back in complex ways to the experience of Latin America's recent trends in inequality and the region's uneven and contradictory left turn in the political sphere since the late 1990s. First, it looks in detail at the empirics of recent improvements in income inequality set against a long historical regional trajectory. Second, and more importantly, it explores the ways in which renewed scholarly attention to themes of inequality in Latin America in the last decade has been dominated in North American social sciences by the uneasy pairing of a) an historical sociological explanatory framework drawing on Max Weber, Barrington Moore, and Karl Polanyi, and b) an ideological prism of truncated, twenty-first-century social democracy.[3] Drawing on recent Marxist scholarship, a third section suggests that, on the one hand, the historical sociological framing of much of the recent mainstream literature has offered important contributions to our knowledge of the origins and patterns of trends in inequality, while, on the other, its conceptualization of thin social democracy as the appropriate limit on the region's reformist horizon reflects a failure of sociological imagination, with important implications for our understanding of capitalism, citizenship, and class. A fourth section examines recent developments in Latin America's new extractivism, which offer a rich, dynamic, and totalizing perspective on the rhythms of capitalist accumulation, old and emerging axes of inequality, and forms of contestation in the twenty-first century. Finally, these widespread Latin American political and economic developments are put into conversation with a biographical portrait of the decolonial and anticapitalist Ecuadorian activist Luis Macas.

---

3 Max Weber, *Economy and Society: An Outline of Interpretive Sociology* (Berkeley and Los Angeles: University of California Press, 1978); Barrington Moore, *Social Origins of Dictatorship and Democracy: Lord and Peasant in the Making of the Modern World* (New York: Beacon Press, 1993); Karl Polanyi, *The Great Transformation: The Political and Economic Origins of Our Time*, 2nd ed. (New York: Beacon Press, 2001).

Latin American Trends in Inequality

Whatever its wider theoretical and political shortcomings, the English translation of Thomas Piketty's *Capital in the Twenty-First Century* in 2015 provoked a welcome international stir in popular political debate by showing—with an enormous historical database—that inequality in income and wealth is both inherent to capitalism and becoming alarmingly worse of late.[4] Ironically, within this wider global discussion, Latin America, long recognized as the world's most unequal region,[5] was being touted in scholarly and policy circles alike as an anomalous zone of hope, where income inequality in the twenty-first century was moving in the opposite direction.[6] The worst crisis in global capitalism since the Great Depression, beginning in 2007–2008,[7] seemed to have had only a minimal and temporary dampening effect on relatively high rates of growth in Latin America, in part due to initial continuities in a Chinese-driven commodities boom that began in 2003.[8] The uptick in the international commodities market coincided with the rearticulation of the extraparliamentary and electoral Latin American left[9]—a tidal wave of

4 Thomas Piketty, *Capital in the Twenty-First Century* (Cambridge, MA: Harvard University Press, 2014). On the shortcomings see Alberto Toscano, "Capital (It Fails Us Now)," *Historical Materialism* 23, no. 1 (2015): 53–69; Michel Husson, "Capital in the Twenty-First Century by Thomas Piketty," *Historical Materialism* 23, no. 1 (2015): 70–85; Michael Roberts, "Thomas Piketty and the Search for R," *Historical Materialism* 23, no. 1 (2015): 86–105.

5 Paul Gootenberg, "Latin American Inequalities: New Perspectives from History, Politics, and Culture," in *Indelible Inequalities in Latin America: Insights from History, Politics, and Culture*, eds. Paul Gootenberg and Luis Reygadas (Durham: Duke University Press, 2010); Stanley L. Engerman and Kenneth L. Sokoloff, "Colonialism, Inequality and Long Run Paths of Development," NBER Working Paper 11057 (Cambridge, MA: National Bureau of Economic Research, 2005); Merike Blofield, *The Great Gap: Inequality and the Politics of Redistribution in Latin America* (University Park, PA: Pennsylvania State University Press, 2011).

6 Luis Felipe López-Calva and Nora Claudia Lustig, *Declining Inequality in Latin America: A Decade of Progress?* (Washington, DC: Brookings Institution, 2010).

7 David McNally, *Global Slump: The Economics and Politics of Crisis and Resistance* (Oakland, CA: PM Press, 2011).

8 Jeffery R. Webber, "Crisis and Class, Advance and Retreat: The Political Economy of the New Latin American Left," in *Polarizing Development: Alternatives to Neoliberalism and the Crisis*, eds. Lucia Pradella and Thomas Marois (London: Pluto Press, 2015); Claudio Katz, "The Singularities of Latin America," in *Socialist Register 2012: The Crisis and the Left*, eds. Leo Panitch, Gregory Albo, and Vivek Chibber (New York: Monthly Review Press, 2011).

9 Jeffery R. Webber and Barry Carr, "The Latin American Left in Theory and Practice," in *The New Latin American Left: Cracks in the Empire*, eds. Jeffery R. Webber and Barry

presidential victories for left and center-left candidates in elections between 1998 and 2011 put eleven countries, and two-thirds of the region's population, under their rule.[10] A combination of auspicious external circumstances and renewed attention to redistributive policies by these governments resulted in the first sustained declines in income inequality in the region in many decades.[11]

It may be, however, that the bright light of Latin America is beginning to fade in some respects, as the mutations of the ongoing global crisis begin to wreak their havoc on the region's economic trends. Slowing growth has very recently coincided with a diminution in the pace of income leveling, for example.[12] In 2014, the world economy picked up slightly from 2013, with aggregate growth moving from 2.4 percent to 2.6 percent.[13] The growth of developing countries continued to decelerate, however, even if growth levels in the developing world continued to be superior to growth in the developed world.

In this worsening global context, the overall GDP of Latin America and the Caribbean reached only 1.1 percent growth in 2014, the lowest since 2009. But there were important differences in the rhythm of growth in different countries. Most significantly, there was a lack of dynamism and even contraction in some of the region's major economies: Argentina (-0.2 percent), Brazil (0.2 percent), Mexico (2.1 percent), and Venezuela (-3.1 percent).[14] By contrast, the fastest growing countries were Panama and the Dominican Republic (both 6.0 percent), followed by Bolivia (5.2 percent), Colombia (4.8 percent), and Guyana and Nicaragua (both 4.5 percent). In a reversal of earlier trends in the fallout from the global crisis, Mexico, Central America, and the Caribbean

Carr (Lanham, MD: Rowman and Littlefield, 2013); Claudio Katz, *Disyuntivas de la izquierda en América Latina* (Buenos Aires: Ediciones Luxemburg, 2008); Steven Levitsky and Kenneth M. Roberts, "Introduction—Latin America's 'Left Turn': A Framework for Analysis," in *The Resurgence of the Latin American Left*, eds. Steven Levitsky and Kenneth M. Roberts (Baltimore, MD: Johns Hopkins University Press, 2011).

10 Kenneth M. Roberts, "The Politics of Inequality and Redistribution in Latin America's Post-Adjustment Era," in *Falling Inequality in Latin America: Policy Changes and Lessons*, ed. Giovanni Andrea Cornia (Oxford: Oxford University Press, 2014), 50.

11 Giovanni Andrea Cornia, "Recent Distributive Changes in Latin America: An Overview," in *Falling Inequality in Latin America*, ed. Cornia.

12 Jeffrey G. Williamson, "Latin American Inequality: Colonial Origins, Commodity Booms, or a Missed 20th Century Leveling?" NBER Working Paper 20915 (Cambridge, MA: National Bureau of Economic Research, 2015); World Bank, *Inequality in Lower Growth Latin America*. LAC Semiannual Report, October (Washington, DC: World Bank LAC Region, 2014).

13 CEPAL, *Balance Preliminar de las Economías de América Latina y el Caribe 2014* (Santiago: CEPAL, 2014), 7.

14 Ibid., 8.

are benefiting from the return of modest growth in the United States, the principal destination for many of these countries' exports, as well as the source of remittances. South America, in contrast, is experiencing a drop in demand for goods because of lower growth in Europe and China.[15] "The recent Latin American experience demonstrates that equity gains can be made in a context of steady economic growth," Kenneth M. Roberts points out; "whether such gains can be sustained in a period of austerity is yet to be determined."[16]

Although not the poorest region in the world, Latin America has a long history of entrenched inequalities, flowing in the first instance out of the colonial legacies of highly concentrated landholdings, means of production, credit, and political power.[17] The classical liberal period of export-oriented mining and agriculture in the late nineteenth and early twentieth centuries deepened and extended extant patterns of accumulation that benefited large landowners and industrial and financial elite. Despite important increases in economic growth and industrialization during the import-substitution in-dustrialization (ISI) era that followed, inequality became even worse.[18] By the 1950s and 1960s the distribution of income per capita as measured by the Gini coefficient was the worst in the world, ranging from 0.47 to 0.65.[19] Such measures of income, which exclude wealth, underestimate the multidimen-sionality of inequality. "In a vivid daily sense," Paul Gootenberg notes, "Latin Americans live and see these disparities in how they do politics, build urban spaces, work the land, join new and older social movements, experience crime and environmental stress, and access educational, nutritional, healthcare, le-gal, cultural, and media resources."[20]

Beginning in the 1970s and accelerating through the 1980s and 1990s, neoliberal restructuring spanned the breadth of the region in the midst of hy-perinflation and debt crises, liberalizing international trade and investment,

---

15 Ibid., 9.

16 Roberts, "The Politics of Inequality and Redistribution," 57.

17 On the additional role of patrimonial institutions of ethnic stratification see James Mahoney, "Explaining the Great Continuity: Ethnic Institutions, Colonialism, and Social Development in Spanish America," in *Political Power and Social Theory* 28, eds. Mounira M. Charrad and Julia Adams (Bingley, UK: Emerald Group Publishing Limited, 2015).

18 Rosemary Thorp, *Progress, Poverty, and Exclusion: An Economic History of Latin America in the Twentieth Century* (Washington, DC: Inter-American Development Bank, 1998).

19 Cornia, "Recent Distributive Changes in Latin America," 5.

20 Gootenberg, "Latin American Inequalities," 1.

privatizing public enterprises, and retrenching social spending.[21] This was, particularly in its initial stages, a violent, authoritarian transition away from an exhausted model of ISI. "With a few important exceptions," historian Greg Grandin points out, throughout Latin America "state- and elite-orchestrated preventive and punitive terror was key to ushering in neoliberalism."[22] The cataclysm of neoliberal counterreform in the 1980s, Grandin rightly stresses, "had as much to do with the destruction of mass movements as it did with the rise of new financial elites invested in global markets."[23] These economic policies had negative consequences for poverty and inequality, making the most unequal region of the world worse still on every measure. As discussed in chapter 2, the Latin American poverty rate increased in the 1980s and 1990s, reaching 44 percent in 2002, and the region continued to be the most unequal part of the world.[24] The average regional Gini index rose skywards throughout these decades, increasing by 2.2 points from the early 1980s to 1990, 1.7 points over the 1990s, and a further 1.2 points during the regional recession of 2001–2002, to a total of 5.1 points over the orthodox neoliberal period.[25] Real industrial wages declined, the informalization of the world of work expanded, and already insufficient social security programs from the ISI period were cut back drastically.[26]

The recession between 1998 and 2002 was severe, the sharpest in Latin America since the early years of the debt crisis in the 1980s. Poverty and inequality spiked on the heels of two decades of declining social conditions. The chasm between the ideological promises of neoliberalism and the material reality facing the rural and urban popular classes became unsustainable. A novel recomposition of the social and political left emerged, first in the form

---

21 Duncan Green, *Silent Revolution: The Rise and Crisis of Market Economics in Latin America* (New York: Monthly Review Press, 2003); Victor Bulmer-Thomas, *The Economic History of Latin America since Independence* (Cambridge: Cambridge University Press, 2014), 391–435; Susan Spronk and Jeffery R. Webber, "Systemic Logics and Historical Specificity: Renewing Historical Materialism in Latin American Political Economy," in *Crisis and Contradiction*, eds. Spronk and Webber, 9–10.

22 Grandin, *The Last Colonial Massacre*, 14.

23 Ibid., 14.

24 Luis Reygadas, "Latin America: Persistent Inequality and Recent Transformations," in *Latin America After Neoliberalism*, eds. Hershberg and Rosen, 122.

25 Giovanni Andrea Cornia, "Inequality Trends and Their Determinants: Latin America Over the Period 1990–2010," in *Falling Inequality in Latin America*, ed. Cornia, 25.

26 Roberts, "The Politics of Inequality and Redistribution," 56; Alejandro Portes and Kelly Hoffman, "Latin American Class Structures: Their Composition and Change During the Neoliberal Era," *Latin American Research Review* 38, no. 1 (2003): 41–82; William I. Robinson, *Latin America and Global Capitalism* (Baltimore, MD: John Hopkins University Press, 2008).

of militant extraparliamentary social movements in countries such as Argentina, Bolivia, and Ecuador, and then electorally across huge swathes of Latin American territory.

As Latin American growth rates recovered in the wake of the early twenty-first-century recession and the onset of the commodities boom, the drastic worsening of inequality in the 1980s and 1990s began to trend in the opposite direction. In one of the more comprehensive recent studies,[27] eighteen countries were analyzed, excluding the Caribbean (except the Dominican Republic), and including all South American countries (excepting the Guyanas) and the entirety of Central America. In sixteen of the eighteen countries, inequality declined between 2002 and 2010, the exceptions being Nicaragua and Costa Rica. While a third of the decline in inequality is attributable to the 2003–2004 period, following its intense surge during the 2001–2002 crisis, inequality nonetheless continued to decline during the subsequent period, including during the regional downturn of 2009.[28] Inequality declined even in regimes governed by the right in this period—Colombia, Mexico, Panama, and Honduras after the 2009 military coup[29]—but "the steepest and most consistent reductions were recorded under left-of-center governments—in particular, Argentina, Venezuela, Brazil, and Ecuador."[30]

Inequality and Sociological Imagination

How should we understand these recent transformations theoretically, and where might they point us politically and ideologically in terms of imagining still more far-reaching transformations of the colonial and capitalist legacies of unequal development in Latin America? There are severe limitations, I want to argue, built into the most influential social scientific modes of inquiry at the moment. The dominant trend in recent North American studies of the region has been a combination of Weberian historical sociology and social democratic policy advocacy.[31] Such a union can be found, for example, in one

27 Cornia, "Recent Distributive Changes in Latin America."
28 Ibid., 26.
29 Ibid., 34.
30 Roberts, "The Politics of Inequality and Redistribution," 63.
31 Here I limit myself mainly to political scientists and sociologists. The closest equivalent turn among political economists is probably toward neostructuralism, following closely the intellectual production of the United Nations Economic Commission for Latin America and the Caribbean. For distinct but complementary Marxian critiques of the neostructuralist turn, see Fernando Leiva, *Latin American Neostructuralism: The*

of the most important recent works on social democracy in the global periphery (with Costa Rica and Chile as Latin American case studies).[32] The argument here is for a pragmatic version of social democracy in which integration into competitive global markets is wedded with genuine democracy and social equity, thereby avoiding the unrealizable utopias of socialism or delinked antiglobalization, on the one hand, and unfettered neoliberal markets on the other. Key to this general perspective is an emphasis on class compromise within the parameters of the capitalist system, whereby the contending classes of capital and labor, or wider social forces, seek a "redistributive societal compromise," rooted in "an agreement in which the contending sides... make real concessions with the objective of avoiding mutual damage and achieving social peace."[33] The sanctity of private property must be guaranteed, lest the middle classes be frightened into an alliance with the capitalist class, bent on the overturning of liberal democratic rule.[34] Likewise, while it is understood that only mobilization from the popular classes can force a compromise on the part of the propertied classes, it is also stressed that their collective action, rhetoric, and strategic aims must be sufficiently moderate so as not to spark fear and authoritarian reaction from above.[35]

The vision of social democracy on offer in such a framework often draws on a "soft" reading of Karl Polanyi's famous articulation of a societal countermovement against totalizing market domination.[36] Markets, in this soft Polanyian reading, remain the motive force allocating most resources in society, but through government intervention and regulation they are subject to social

Contradictions of Post-Neoliberal Development (Minneapolis: University of Minnesota Press, 2008); Jeffery R. Webber, "Neostructuralism, Neoliberalism, and Latin America's Resurgent Left," *Historical Materialism* 18, no. 3 (2010): 208–229; Juan Grigera, "Conspicuous Silences: State and Class in Structuralist and Neostructuralist Thought," in *Crisis and Contradiction*, eds. Spronk and Webber.

32 Richard Sandbrook, Marc Edelman, Patrick Heller and Judith Teichman, "Can Social Democracies Survive in the Global South," *Dissent* 53, no. 2 (2006): 76–83; Richard Sandbrook, Marc Edelman, Patrick Heller, and Judith Teichman, *Social Democracy in the Global Periphery: Origins, Challenges, Prospects* (Cambridge: Cambridge University Press, 2007).

33 Judith Teichman, "Redistributive Conflict and Social Policy in Latin America," *World Development* 36, no. 3 (2008): 446–460.

34 Judith Teichman, "The Role of the Middle Class in Distributional Outcomes: Chile and South Korea." *Studies in Comparative International Development* 50, no. 1 (2015): 17–18.

35 Judith Teichman, *Social Forces and States: Poverty and Distributional Outcomes in South Korea, Chile, and Mexico* (Stanford, CA: Stanford University Press, 2012).

36 Eduardo Silva, *Challenging Neoliberalism in Latin America* (Cambridge: Cambridge University Press, 2009).

and ecological limits. Taxation mechanisms concentrate substantial resources in the central authority of the state, allowing it to meet the social and economic rights of citizens in accordance with the law. Meanwhile, an ethos of reciprocity underlines the citizenry in such societies, allowing for social democratic reproduction on the basis of empathy.[37] Some of the more influential interventions in debates on the rise of the new left in Latin America offer a variation on these themes.[38] Kurt Weyland, for example, suggests that because of Latin America's unfavorable insertion into the global economy, its underdeveloped productive apparatus, its polarized societies and segmented labor markets, denuded trade unions, and weak party systems—both the more radical left of the sort in Venezuela under Hugo Chávez, and the moderate left, as exemplified by Luiz Inácio Lula da Silva in Brazil or Michelle Bachelet in Chile—are under severe constraints in terms of the depth of sustainable redistributive programs they can offer to their societies.[39] However, because the moderate left avoids entering into acrimonious relations with domestic and foreign capital, accepting the basic parameters of the region's new market model, it has "achieved better, more solid economic results and has charted a more promising course for the long run."[40] In any case, even the radicals have abandoned any fundamental confrontation with capitalism: "Who still believes that socialism as a truly new mode of production is an attainable and desirable goal"?[41]

The intellectual production of Dietrich Rueschemeyer, Evelyne Huber Stephens, and John D. Stephens over the last two decades,[42] with its para-

---

37 Richard Sandbrook, "Polanyi and Post-Neoliberalism in the Global South: Dilemmas of Re-Embedding the Economy," *New Political Economy* 16, no. 4 (2011): 429–430.

38 Steven Levitsky and Kenneth M. Roberts, "Introduction—Latin America's 'Left Turn'"; Kurt Weyland, "The Left: Destroyer or Savior of the Market Model?" in *The Resurgence of the Latin American Left*, eds. Steven Levitsky and Kenneth M. Roberts (Baltimore, MD: Johns Hopkins University Press, 2011); Robert Kaufman, "The Political Left, the Export Boom, and the Populist Temptation," in *The Resurgence of the Latin American Left*, eds. Levitsky and Roberts.

39 Kurt Weyland, "The Performance of Leftist Governments in Latin America: Conceptual and Theoretical Issues," in *Leftist Governments in Latin America: Successes and Failures*, eds. Kurt Weyland, Raúl Madrid, and Wendy Hunter (Cambridge: Cambridge University Press, 2010), 6–9.

40 Ibid., 12.

41 Ibid., 8.

42 Dietrich Rueschemeyer, Evelyne Huber Stephens, and John D. Stephens, *Capitalist Development and Democracy* (Chicago: University of Chicago Press, 1992); Evelyne Huber and John D. Stephens, *Development and Crisis of the Welfare State: Parties and Policies in Global Markets* (Chicago: University of Chicago Press, 2001); Evelyne Huber and John D. Stephens, *Democracy and the Left: Social Policy and Inequality in Latin America* (Chicago: University of Chicago Press, 2012).

doxical coalescence of rich historical-sociological insight and impoverished political imagination, has had an important impact on research agendas pertaining to different facets of inequality in Latin America, and captures nicely some of the intellectual tensions of contemporary Weberian sociology and social democratic advocacy I am trying to draw to the surface in this chapter. In the magisterial historical sweep of their classic *Capitalist Development and Democracy*,[43] they laid out the core theoretical foundations of the class-analytic model they have followed ever since, turning on the domestic balance of class forces in societies; the structure, autonomy, and capacity of states; and transnational configurations of power. They showed convincingly how it has been precisely the historical contradictions of capitalist development that have lent that mode of production its common association with democracy in the modern world—in transforming the class structure of society, capitalism strengthened the class most consistently supportive of democracy (the working class) and weakened the class most consistently pitted against it (the landed upper class). Historically, the bourgeoisie has been generally supportive of constitutional and representational government but opposed to incorporation of subordinate classes. This class has sometimes forged alliances with large working classes against especially intransigent landed interests, but once democracy has been installed bourgeois support for constitutional rule has been contingent on the reproduction of its fundamental interests—property, above all. When these interests come under threat at the hands of insurgent popular classes, the bourgeoisie can be counted on to turn to authoritarian solutions. The peasantry plays a complex and variegated role inside these shifting class coalitions. Those peasants lacking autonomous organizational capacity and beholden to their lords often fell under the political sway of dominant rural configurations of power, but rural wage workers on plantations frequently sought to join pro-democratic urban working-class coalitions if they did not face unrelenting repression.[44] This is a fundamentally convincing argument and, in many respects, a pathbreaking contribution to historical sociology.[45]

Nonetheless, in the same book, the strict policing of the constitutive parameters of democracy marks a preemptive foreclosing on more far-reaching emancipatory conceptualizations, an early narrowing of horizons that would

---

43 Dietrich Rueschemeyer, Evelyne Huber Stephens, and John D. Stephens, *Capitalist Development and Democracy* (Chicago: University of Chicago Press, 1992).
44 Ibid., 8–10.
45 For recent work lending further support to working-class centrality in the extension of formal democracy in Europe, see Vivek Chibber, *Postcolonial Theory and the Specter of Capital* (London: Verso Books, 2013).

find heightened expression in Huber and Stephens's subsequent works. Relaxing the otherwise rigorous formality of their investigation in *Capitalist Development and Democracy*, Rueschemeyer, Huber Stephens, and Stephens fail to identify specific authors in their often caricatural portrayal of the Marxist tradition when they begin their discussion of the conceptualization of democracy by noting that the "Marxist critique of 'bourgeois democracy' [a position from which they correctly distance Marx himself] raises perhaps the most central issue: is the claim of democracy to constitute the rule of the many real, or is this claim a sham that makes the de facto rule of the few more effective and secure behind a screen of formally democratic institutions?"[46] They respond decisively that "no actually existing democracy can claim to constitute in a realistic sense the rule of the many; but 'bourgeois' or formal democracy does make a difference for the process of political decision-making and for the outcomes of that process."[47] Thus far, this is a rather banal argument with which many Marxist theorists and actually existing radical anticapitalist movements would agree.

Their next definitional move is more dramatic, in which they make a plea for the abandonment of "the most far-reaching ideals of democratic thought" in favor of "the more modest forms of popular participation in government through representative parliaments that appear as realistic possibilities in the complex societies of today."[48] The realism of this position is not defended theoretically but is rather assumed to be a commonsense formulation. In the formal democracy of this type—the only realistic mode of democratic rule in modern societies—states are responsible to parliament, possibly with the complement of an elected executive, there are regular free and fair elections, freedoms of expression and association, and universal suffrage. We should care about formal democracy, they argue, because "it tends to be more than merely formal. It tends to be real to some extent. Giving the many a real voice in the formal collective decision-making of a country is the most promising basis for further progress in the distribution of power and other forms of substantive equality."[49] Again, there is much in this specific passage with which many Marxists would agree. More controversially, however, they "see in democracy—even in its modest and largely formal contemporary realizations—the beginning of the self-transformation of capitalism."[50] In light

---

46 Rueschemeyer, Huber Stephens, and Stephens, *Capitalist Development and Democracy*, 10.
47 Ibid., 10.
48 Ibid.
49 Ibid.
50 Ibid., 11.

of world historical patterns since the early 1990s, this view is so optimistic, not to say complacent, that even many social democratic observers of contemporary North American, European, and Latin American societies would presumably disagree quite vociferously.[51] It simply does not follow that because there are often more possibilities for popular influence on political life in formal democracies than under historical varieties of authoritarian rule, and that because formal democracies have been established historically out of the contradictions of capitalist development and associated transformations of class structures, we therefore ought to accept the profound limitations on human freedom that this mode of production and this form of political rule entail as the parameters of the possible. The operative conflation here is one of *democracy as liberalism*, in which, ironically, capitalism is taken for granted, naturalized, and thereby rendered outside the remit of further interrogation.

In *Democracy and the Left*,[52] Huber and Stephens employ the class-analytic theoretical model involving domestic, state, and transnational clusters of power—now called "power constellations theory"—that they first established in *Capitalist Development and Democracy*[53] and *Development and Crisis of the Welfare State*.[54] In their latest book, the framework is adapted to the study of redistributive outcomes in various historical periods of twentieth- and twenty-first-century Latin American development. Again, crucial elements of the explanatory framework are compelling, if not as theoretically significant as the findings of their earlier investigation into the relationship between capitalism and democracy in the advanced capitalist countries, Latin America, Central America, and the Caribbean. In *Democracy and the Left* Huber and Stephens argue that politics matters quite fundamentally for inequality outcomes in Latin America, and that therefore the long-term structural trends of inequality in the region may be less immutable than often assumed. "Democracy and the rise of left parties," they argue more specifically, "reduce the degree to which political power distributions are skewed and thus open the possibility for a greater range of policy options to be perceived, for demands for new policies to be articulated, and for those demands to

51 Philip Oxhorn, *Sustaining Civil Society: Economic Change, Democracy, and the Social Construction of Citizenship in Latin America* (University Park, PA: Pennsylvania State University Press, 2010); Wolfgang Streeck, *Buying Time: The Delayed Crisis of Democratic Capitalism* (London: Verso Books, 2014); Peter Mair, *Ruling the Void: The Hollowing of Western Democracy* (London: Verso Books, 2013).
52 Huber and Stephens, *Democracy and the Left*.
53 Rueschemeyer, Huber Stephens, and Stephens, *Capitalist Development and Democracy*.
54 Huber and Stephens, *Development and Crisis of the Welfare State*.

be met."[55] Democracy "makes the rise of actors committed to redistribution and the pursuit of actions aimed at redistribution possible."[56]

Argentina, Brazil, Chile, Costa Rica, and Uruguay are identified as Latin America's welfare state leaders over the course of the twentieth century, while all of them, except Costa Rica, are also highlighted for praise with regard to the contemporary era of the region's latest left turn. Specific policy praise is directed at Lula's increases in the conditional cash-transfer programs first instituted under Fernando Henrique Cardoso in Brazil; health care and pension reforms under the Concertación governments of Ricardo Lagos and Michelle Bachelet in Chile; access to basic medicine, conditional cash transfers, and labor market reforms in Argentina under the presidencies of Néstor Kirchner and Cristina Fernández de Kirchner; and tax, labor market, and health care reforms, as well as family allowances under Tabaré Vázquez in Uruguay.[57] While the commodities boom "made major amounts of resources available to governments" of various political stripes, "the benefits from this growth could have accrued mainly to upper income earners, as they did under Pinochet from 1985 to 1989 or during the Brazilian economic miracle of 1968–73."[58] Unlike these earlier periods, however, "pressures from left-of-center parties, first in opposition and then in government, managed to shape social policy increasingly according to the principles of basic universalism."[59]

From this often persuasive analytical basis, Huber and Stephens shift to more spurious prescriptive terrain. They advocate, first, incremental change and a narrow range of social pursuits, what they call "basic universalism."[60] Incremental change is said to avoid destabilizing political polarization and allow for efficient management of new social initiatives, both of which benefit macroeconomic performance and democratic sustainability.[61] Working with the assumption of scarce resources—or, austerity—classical universalism is rejected in favor of a basic universalism that broadly targets transfers to those most in need.[62] Alongside incrementalism and basic univeralism, investment in human capital plays a major role in their prescriptive conclusions for the Latin American welfare state. In part, this is because human capital is seen to

---

55 Huber and Stephens, *Democracy and the Left*, 11.
56 Ibid.
57 Ibid., 9.
58 Ibid., 248.
59 Ibid., 248.
60 Ibid., 257.
61 Ibid.
62 Ibid.

be "the most essential measure in a strategy to put Latin American countries on a development path that results in moving up the product cycle through industrial upgrading."[63] Higher average years of education and better skills training will facilitate further transition to a value-added, export-oriented economic model with good jobs and better wages, what they take to be an innovation on the "developmental state" for the Latin American region.[64] They accept the institutionalist and neoliberal consensus that the exhaustion of ISI in the 1970s meant that a turn to open trade markets was the only reasonable alternative. More than reasonable, in fact, open trade markets are to be celebrated because they are "compatible with low levels of inequality and poverty, as the examples of the Nordic countries and Taiwan and Korea show."[65] Together with incrementalism, basic universalism, investment in human capital, and open trade markets, the best-practice model of social policymaking according to Huber and Stephens also includes higher taxes in the Latin American context, a pragmatic approach to privatization of public enterprises, and a balanced budget across economic cycles. This vision is broadly in alignment with the post–Washington Consensus view of the international financial institutions, and particularly that of the World Bank, which is understood to have transcended the neoliberal paradigm.[66]

Unsurprisingly, given these prescriptive premises, Huber and Stephens single out for criticism the ostensibly more radical political and social orientation of the governments of Hugo Chávez in Venezuela, Evo Morales in Bolivia, and Rafael Correa in Ecuador.[67] One problem is their distance from incrementalism, including in their agendas as they do "a broader program of

---

63 Ibid., 259.

64 Ibid., 260–261.

65 Huber and Stephens, *Democracy and the Left*, 261–262. For an early persuasive critique of both the institutionalist and neoliberal assumptions regarding the "flying geese" model of development derived from East Asian experiences, and echoed by Evelyne Huber and John D. Stephens in *Democracy and the Left*, see Martin Hart-Landsberg and Paul Burkett, "Contradictions of Capitalist Industrialization in East Asia: A Critique of 'Flying Geese' Theories of Development." *Economic Geography* 74, no. 2 (2008): 87–110.

66 Huber and Stephens, *Democracy and the Left*, 261–263.

67 Huber and Stephens, *Democracy and the Left*, 263–266. For a perspective on the Morales and Correa governments that sees them as much less radical in their political-economic orientation and social policy regimes, see Jeffery R. Webber, "A New Indigenous-Left in Ecuador?" *NACLA Report on the Americas* 44, no. 5 (2011): 9–13; Jeffery R. Webber, *From Rebellion to Reform in Bolivia: Class Struggle, Indigenous Liberation and the Politics of Evo Morales* (Chicago: Haymarket, 2011); Jeffery R. Webber, "Managing Bolivian Capitalism," *Jacobin* 13 (2014): 45–55; Jeffery R. Webber, "Teatro Político en Bolivia." *Herramienta* 56 (2015): 41–51.

transformation, extending to the economic model and political institutions" through such mechanisms as state ownership, increased regulation of private markets, and constituent assemblies to establish new constitutions and reconfigured state-society relations.[68] While Huber and Stephens worry of centralizing power in the hands of the executive across all three cases, the now common trope of Chávez's authoritarianism is highlighted specifically: "In the case of Venezuela, the reforms arguably went so far as to undermine democracy."[69] Perhaps the most crucial error of these Andean administrations, however, has been their "militant rhetoric, promising to move toward socialism and attacking capitalism as a system and capitalists as enemies of the people, which is counterproductive in a mixed economy that depends on private investment to generate growth and employment."[70] The potent combination of wide ranging sociopolitical aims and militant rhetoric has unhelpfully alienated foreign and domestic capital and radicalized opposition forces.[71]

To sum up, the dominant social scientific framing of inequality in contemporary Latin America is a pairing of Weberian historical sociology and tepid social-democratic policy advocacy. The historical sociological angle of analysis has led at times to powerful historical findings, such as in the broad conclusions on the class contradictions of capitalist development and the associated rise of liberal democratic rule advanced in *Capitalist Development and Democracy*. Such a theoretical framework, however, is unable to build on these findings to investigate fully the consequences for democracy once capitalism is established. Indeed, it offers only the most limited tools for understanding the severe limits on human freedom under liberal democracy precisely because it does not theorize explicitly the novel scope of market domination and coercion that the rise of capitalism implied historically, nor its implications for class rule under societies in which liberal citizenship is predominant. The root of the failure of sociological imagination in much of this tradition of inquiry is not contingent on, but rather necessary to, the commitment to liberalism ultimately underpinning it. In the early twenty-first-century scholarship on Latin America outlined above, modest possibilities for redistribution are outlined in the social-democratic policy recommendations, but empirical investigation into class exploitation, rather than merely income distribution outcomes, is

---

68 Huber and Stephens, *Democracy and the Left*, 264.
69 Ibid. For a critique of this line of argument concerning the Chávez government, see Susan Spronk and Jeffery R. Webber, "Sabaneta to Miraflores: The Afterlives of Hugo Chávez in Venezuela." *New Politics* 14, no. 4 (2014): 97–109.
70 Huber and John D. Stephens, *Democracy and the Left*, 264.
71 Ibid.

absent from the axiomatic starting points of the dominant theoretical framework. The classically liberal work of T. H. Marshall on citizenship is another example of the weaknesses I am identifying here, insofar as Marshall celebrates as a normative ideal the empirical separation of economics from politics under capitalism.[72] In an effort to elaborate a way forward, we turn next to an explicit examination of the limits of contemporary Weberian sociological analysis into Latin American inequality through a close exploration of the relationship between capitalism, class, and citizenship.

Capitalism, Class, and Citizenship

"The critique of capitalism is out of fashion," Ellen Meiksins Wood wrote in 1995, right around the time of the publication of Rueschemeyer, Huber Stephens, and Stephens's magnum opus.[73] "Capitalist triumphalism on the right is mirrored on the left by a sharp contraction of socialist aspirations. Left intellectuals, if not embracing capitalism as the best of all possible worlds, hope for little more than a space in its interstices and look forward to only the most local and particular resistances." She explains in this text that it was the emergence of capitalism itself that made possible the historical redefinition of democracy in such a way that it was reduced to liberalism. In particular, the differentiation of the political and economic spheres that capitalism allowed for the first time in history, whereby "extra-economic" status—whether it be political, juridical, or military—no longer had "direct implications for economic power, the power of appropriation, exploitation and distribution," meant that, by association, "there now existed an economic sphere with its own power relations not dependent on juridical or political privilege."[74] These historical conditions of capitalist development, which made liberal democracy possible, simultaneously circumscribed the parameters of its constitutive domains:

> Liberal democracy leaves untouched the whole new sphere of domination and coercion created by capitalism, its relocation of substantial powers from the state to civil society, to private property and the compulsions of the market. It leaves untouched vast areas of our daily lives—in the workplace, in the distribu-

---

72 T. H. Marshall and Tom Bottomore, *Citizenship and Social Class* (London: Pluto Press, 1992).

73 Ellen Meiksins Wood, *Democracy against Capitalism: Renewing Historical Materialism* (Cambridge: Cambridge University Press, 1995), 1; Rueschemeyer, Huber Stephens, and Stephens, *Capitalist Development and Democracy*.

74 Wood, *Democracy against Capitalism*, 234.

tion of labour and resources—which are not subject to democratic accountability but are governed by the powers of property and the "laws" of the market, the imperatives of profit maximization. This would remain true even in the unlikely event that our "formal democracy" were perfected so that wealth and economic power no longer meant the gross inequality of access to state power which now characterizes the reality, if not the ideal, of modern capitalist democracy.[75]

Part of the problem is that liberalism cannot even recognize the market as an arena of coercion and compulsion. Instead, the market is seen as a sphere of opportunity, freedom, and choice, even if it requires regulation at the margins. The conceptual framework of liberal democracy makes it impossible to "really talk, or even *think*, about freedom *from* the market. We cannot think of freedom from the market as a kind of empowerment, a liberation from compulsion, an emancipation from coercion and domination."[76] Liberal democracy is premised upon the "separation and enclosure of the economic sphere and its invulnerability to democratic power. Protecting that invulnerability has even become an essential criterion of democracy. This definition allows us to invoke democracy *against* the empowerment of the people in the economic sphere."[77]

The separation of the political from the economic under capitalism, and the often historically associated political form of liberal democracy that arose out of capitalist contradictions, situates the problem of class exploitation and the appropriation of surpluses by dominant classes outside the proper remit of formal democratic concern.[78] "This is not to suggest that formal democracy, civil rights and liberties and representative government are not an improvement on less democratic political forms," insists Colin Mooers.[79] "For those who have been denied basic civil rights historically, such as women, racialized groups, indigenous peoples or gays and lesbians, winning full citizenship rights is of great significance. But it is equally true that capitalism has had to limit the substance of these rights in ways which make them compatible with the rule of capital."

Liberal ideology presents the global capitalist system as an arena of free exchange and the source of potential opportunities for the development of less developed countries. The problems of poverty and inequality are generally framed as originating in exclusion from the market. Human development, the amelio-

75 Ibid.
76 Ibid., 235.
77 Ibid.
78 Colin Mooers, *Imperial Subjects: Citizenship in an Age of Crisis and Empire* (London: Bloomsbury, 2014), 4.
79 Ibid., 5.

ration of problems of poverty and inequality, is possible only through proper integration into the world market. This framework explicitly redirects our attention away from the ways in which capitalism as a socioeconomic system, operating across national, regional, and international scales, inherently generates a simultaneity of concentrations of poverty alongside concentrations of wealth, zones of economic dynamism, wealth creation, and technological innovation, alongside and in interaction with zones of immiseration. If inclusion into capitalism is axiomatically taken to be the only solution on offer for the world's poor, capitalism as a social system becomes "a pristine non-object of analysis."[80] It pays, then, in a discussion of inequality, to remind ourselves what capitalism is.

"Capitalism," Wood points out, "is a system in which goods and services, down to the most basic necessities of life, are produced for profitable exchange, where even human labour-power is a commodity for sale in the market, and where all economic actors are dependent on the market."[81] Rather than neutral arenas of benign exchange, capitalist markets are comprised of social relations that "reproduce the subordination of the greater part of society (labourers) to the minority (owners of capital)."[82] Capitalism involves the production of goods and services for exchange on the market under the profit motive. It is founded upon a definitive and exploitative relationship of social classes, principally between the owners of capital and the owners of labor power.[83] Any interrogation of relationships of power in that economic sphere that stands outside formal democratic accountability in liberal conceptions must ask at a minimum: "Who owns what? Who does what? Who gets what? What do they do with it?"[84] Class exploitation is a precondition of capitalist formation and reproduction, and it unfolds nationally, regionally, and internationally.

In offering a Marxist critique of Weberian historical sociology and liberal democratic theory, it is also fundamentally important to avoid any temptation toward abstract and empty counterpositioning of class against differentiated identities of gender, race, or sexuality. Understood concretely as a moving, living, social relationship, class in real-world settings cannot be separated from the ways in which it is multiply determined in and through other social relations

---

80 Selwyn, *The Global Development Crisis*, 2.
81 Ellen Meiksins Wood, *The Origin of Capitalism: A Longer View* (London: Verso Books, 2002), 2.
82 Selwyn, *The Global Development Crisis*, 2.
83 Henry Bernstein, "Colonialism, Capitalism, Development," in *Poverty and Development*, eds. Tim Allen and Alan Thomas, 2nd ed. (Oxford: Oxford University Press, 2000), 242.
84 Henry Bernstein, *Class Dynamics of Agrarian Change* (Halifax: Fernwood, 2010), 22.

of oppression.[85] Contemporary capitalist societies are organized around, and constituted by, social relations of gender, race, and sexuality, just as they are simultaneously constituted by class. Relations of race, gender, and sexuality are not epiphenomena of underlying class structures, and their dynamics are not reducible to class exploitation; nor, however, can they be fully understood except in their internal relations with class.[86] "Too often," David McNally points out, "Marxist critics of the particularism at the heart of personal-identity politics have modelled their notions of working-class unity on the form of unification that characterises capital":[87]

> As a consequence, they offer up an abstracted concept of class that is indif-
> ferent to the diverse forms of experience in capitalist society—and hence one
> whose experiential purchase is minimal. In so doing, they treat class as an es-
> sence-structure, in Hegel's terms, that unifies labouring people *from the out-*
> *side*—an approach that has had multiple political expressions in the practices
> of self-appointed external vanguards of the working class…. In place of the
> "living essence" of social class, we get the "monochromatic" schematism of
> essence-categories and their "lifeless determinations." Dynamic relations of
> becoming are reified in an effort to generate a static taxonomy that captures
> nothing of the rich and diverse life-processes of social class.[88]

In contrast, vibrant working-class movements "draw together the griev-ances and oppositional practices of particular oppressed groups into a dynamic totality that expresses (rather than suppresses) its discrete parts," McNally ar-gues.[89] "A truly comprehensive working-class movement," he writes,

> requires a self-activating "unity of the diverse" in which distinct parts of the
> dominated class, with their specific experiences of oppression, find avenues
> of self-expression and self-organisation within the wider class movement…
> only in such ways can socially differentiated groups of workers come to see
> how their distinct experiences of oppression are in fact internally related,
> discrete but interconnected parts of a totalising system.[90]

---

85 David McNally, "The Dialectics of Unity and Difference in the Constitution of Wage Labour: On Internal Relations and Working Class Formation," *Capital and Class* 39, no. 1 (2015): 133.

86 David Camfield, "Theoretical Foundations of an Anti-Racist Queer Feminist Histori-cal Materialism," *Critical Sociology* 42, no. 2 (March 2016): 289–306.

87 McNally, "The Dialectics of Unity and Difference in the Constitution of Wage La-bour," 139.

88 Ibid.

89 Ibid., 142.

90 Ibid..

Seen from such a vantage point, "the multiple relations of power and domination therefore appear as concrete expressions of the articulated and contradictory unity that is capitalist society."[91] In the case of Latin America, one concrete expression of the unity of the diverse in contemporary capitalist society is the relationship between indigenous oppression and class exploitation. Indeed, as is developed further below in our biographical narrative of the life and struggles of Ecuadorian indigenous activist Luis Macas, Latin American indigenous movements have more often than not been linked extensively and intensively with class conflict. The legacies of formal Spanish colonialism live on in Republican times in many ways. They find expression through contemporary internally colonial race relations, which are imbricated necessarily in the capitalist character of Latin American societies in the twenty-first century.

It is in these broad, encompassing senses, then, that we reintroduce Marxist class analysis as an entry point through which to critique Weberian historical sociology and limited conceptualizations of Latin American democracy. In summary form, class exploitation—operating on national, regional, and international terrains—should be understood expansively, "across five distinct but interconnected and mutually constituting moments"[92]:

1. Within the sphere of production (the workplace) where surplus value is generated by workers and extracted by capital;

2. Within the sphere of exchange (the labor market) where workers' labor power is institutionally organized so that it can be sold to capital for its subsequent exploitation in the workplace, and where workers' wages constitute "effective demand" for capital's products;

3. Within the private sphere (the family) where (mostly) women's unpaid labor contributes to the generational reproduction of the labor force;

4. Through "race" and racism, which facilitates the generation of categories of worker for particular occupations, reproduces cultural "distinctions" and divisions among laboring classes and "justifies" unequal economic rewards;

5. In capitalist society's interface with its substratum (nature) where the latter is commodified and used by capital as an input into production and as a dumping ground for waste production.

These five mutually constituting moments of exploitation are not as immediately visible as noncapitalist forms of surplus extraction, say through the

---

91 Cinzia Arruzza, "Remarks on Gender," *Viewpoint Magazine*, September 2, 2014, https://viewpointmag.com/2014/09/02/remarks-on-gender/.
92 Selwyn, *The Global Development Crisis*, 14–15.

master–slave relation, or the lord–peasant relation. When capitalists purchase labor power and workers sell it in the sphere of exchange, they appear to meet as equals—individuals responding to opportunities as they arise in the marketplace. The coercive element of market dependency and the class inequality of the economic sphere is naturalized and hidden from view due to formal juridical equality of all actors before the law. The basic reality that workers, deprived of access to means of subsistence of their own, have no other choice but to (try to) sell their labor power to capitalists is largely concealed. "Just as the commodity form conceals the human labours which went into its production," Colin Mooers points out, "so too does the form of capitalist citizenship obscure the class antagonisms which lie below its surface. Thus, the systematic distortion of social reality associated by Marx with the fetishism of commodities now encompasses the gamut of social relations under capitalism, from wage relations to its most developed juridical and political forms."[93] Much of the theory and history of liberalism deserves protection and improvement, "not only in parts of the world where it scarcely exists but even in capitalist democracies where it is still imperfect and often under threat. Yet the scope for further historical development may belong to the *other* tradition of democracy, the tradition overshadowed by liberal democracy, the idea of democracy in its literal meaning as popular power."[94] Such popular power in the economic sphere would necessarily entail much more than a passive paternalism of the welfare state (itself under dramatic retrenchment in most of the world in the age of austerity). It would also entail more than merely a moral condemnation of poverty and inequality; rather, a renewal of the other tradition of democracy, as literally popular power, would require a recognition of, and resistance to, the inbuilt exploitative basis of class relations under capitalism and their internal relations with other forms of social oppression.

The next two sections offer empirical examples of the integrated constituent moments of capitalist class relations outlined above, and demonstrate further the ways in which Weberian historical sociology and limited liberal conceptualization of democracy are unable to comprehend the totalizing power of capital and its multifaceted forms of coercion and exploitation. First, the particular rhythms of extractive capitalism in twenty-first-century Latin America are outlined, followed by biographical reflections on the life of Luis Macas, who has been active in indigenous struggles of the sort that are regularly erupting within and against the new extractivism in the region.

---

93 Mooers, *Imperial Subjects*, 32.
94 Wood, *Democracy against Capitalism*, 235.

Extraction, Dispossession, and Value Struggles

If against this backdrop we examine the totalizing dynamics of capitalism in Latin America in the first decade of the twenty-first century, one of the outstanding features has been the so-called "new extractivism."[95] Through the lens of extractivism we can see at work a number of the constitutive moments of capitalist exploitation assume concrete forms: shifts in the international division of labor as Latin America returns to its historic role as primary commodity provider to the world market, novel forms of class struggle in peasant communities as they resist dispossession of their lands and livelihoods, racism as indigenous communities in particular are targeted for displacement, and capitalism's interface with its substratum (nature) in the form of mining minerals, oil, gas, and fertile agricultural land.

Similar to the orthodox neoliberal period (1980–2000), massive multinational corporations in the epoch of the latest commodities boom (2003–2011) were deeply imbricated in the extension of extraction at the heart of this primary-commodity-led growth everywhere in the region.[96] This is true of all extractivist countries, governed by regimes differentially situated across the right-left ideological spectrum. While the extreme violence of paramilitary dispossession associated with intensified extractivism in right-ruled countries like Mexico, Honduras, Guatemala, and Colombia has been avoided by the center-left regimes of South America, the latter have nonetheless entered into joint contracts between state-owned enterprises and multinationals, negotiating relatively higher royalties and taxes on these extractive activities.

The reproduction of these political economies depends upon states prioritizing the maintenance and security of private property rights and juridical environments in which multinationals can profit. But there is a set of contradictions that impede the easy reproduction of South American compensatory states, even in a period of booming commodity prices. Whatever the ecological and social contradictions of this development strategy over time, however, it has shown fairly impressive capacities for reproduction on its own terms in the short term.

---

95 Todd Gordon and Jeffery R. Webber, *Blood of Extraction: Canadian Imperialism in Latin America* (Halifax: Fernwood, forthcoming); Bebbington and Bury, *Subterranean Struggles*; Henry Veltmeyer and James Petras, *The New Extractivism: A Post-Neoliberal Development Model or Imperialism of the Twenty-First Century* (London: Zed, 2014); José Seoane, Emilio Taddei, and Clara Algranati, *Extractivismo, despojo y crisis climática: Desafíos para los movimientos sociales y los proyectos emancipatorios de Nuestra América* (Buenos Aires: Herramienta ediciones, 2013).

96 Webber, "Crisis and Class, Advance and Retreat."

In Benjamin Selwyn's compelling reconceptualization of development as "labour-centred," this kind of state compensation for dispossession falls well short of the possibilities of human emancipation. In Selwyn's concept of labor-centered development,

> Labouring-class struggles are re-interpreted as potentially "developmental" in that they contribute directly to improvements, both materially and in terms of generating more freedoms, of their lives and of their dependants and communities. Unlike state-centred and capital-centred conceptions of development, that variously ignore or subordinate labouring classes to the requirements and actions of states and capital, a labour-centred development studies does not ignore the actions of states and market actors in attempting to foster their own, respective, visions of development. Rather it views these actions from the perspective of labour, and attempts to interpret them as processes and outcomes of complex relations between social classes.... The struggle against exploitation takes myriad forms and has many outcomes. The challenge of a labour-centred development is to conceptually connect these struggles and their potential outcomes to a vision of human development free from exploitation.[97]

Properly enhanced, to better emphasize the always racialized and gendered forms that class struggle concretely assumes,[98] Selwyn's labor-centered vision directs us to focus less, in this particular area, on the compensatory policies to ameliorate inequality coming from above on the part of states, and more on the self-activity and self-organization of myriad forms of resistance from below.

In a reflection of one concrete form that such analysis can assume, the next section focuses on the combined critique of colonialism and capitalism offered by Luis Macas, who lives and struggles in Ecuador, one of the paradigmatic cases of the twenty-first-century compensatory states. Through the method of individual biographical portraiture,[99] the aim here is to map, in cursory and partial form, historical processes of Ecuadorian popular class formation; ideological consciousness; and the interplay between racism and capitalism, indigeneity, and class-based resistance. What comes to the surface in

---

97 Selwyn, *The Global Development Crisis*, 21, 208.

98 McNally, "The Dialectics of Unity and Difference in the Constitution of Wage Labour"; Camfield, "Theoretical Foundations of an Anti-Racist Queer Feminist Historical Materialism"; Arruzza, "Remarks on Gender."

99 C. Wright Mills, *The Sociological Imagination* (Oxford: Oxford University Press, 2000); Javier Auyero, *Contentious Lives: Two Argentine Women, Two Protests, and the Quest for Recognition* (London: Duke University Press, 2003).

Macas's thinking is a utopian-revolutionary dialectic of past and future, where specific values and threads of the precapitalist past social fabric are drawn out and combined with the envisioning of an anticapitalist, anticolonial, and socialist future.[100] This worldview, as we will see in chapter 4, mirrors crucial components of the revolutionary theory of the early twentieth century Peruvian Marxist José Carlos Mariátegui.

Turning Colonial Capitalism Upside Down

I met up with Luis Macas in his office at the Instituto Científico de Culturas Indígenas (Scientific Institute of Indigenous Cultures, ICCI) in Quito, on July 14, 2010. Macas, arguably the most renowned indigenous leader in late twentieth and early twenty-first-century Ecuador, was born in 1951 in Saraguro, in the province of Loja. A lawyer by training, he is currently executive director of ICCI. Macas is an ex-president of CONAIE, the most important nationwide organizational body of the indigenous movement, and former congressional deputy (in the late 1990s) and presidential candidate (2006) for the Movimiento Pachakutik (Pachakutik Movement, MP) party.

"I learned most of what's guided me for the better part of my life in the community where I was born and raised," Macas told me when I asked him if he could describe the long process of his political formation.

> My father was a leader in the community at various points. He participated a great deal in the collective leadership of the community. There was no single leadership in the community, no type of *caudillismo* (big man leadership), but rather collective leadership. There are various people, men and women, who lead a process of organization, of unity in the community. This is what I learned about simply by watching. I was raised with all of these lessons.... So my first steps in learning how to conduct myself were these experiences—in my own community, with the elders.

Macas describes the communitarian traditions and obligations that he was raised with as having "diminished since that time in many communities, even disappearing in some," but he repeatedly returned to them in the interview, marking them off as formative features of his present-day political identity.

For most of his time in elementary school Macas went outside of his ru-

---

100 For theoretical reflection on the utopian-revolutionary dialectic of past and future, see Michael Löwy, "The Romantic and the Marxist Critique of Modern Civilization." *Theory and Society* 16, no. 6 (1987): 891–904; and chapter 4 in this book.

ral community to a small town, where he was first introduced to the Spanish language, having been raised speaking exclusively in Kichwa. "In this new urban school," Macas explained, "I encountered things that were very strange, very distinct from our practices, beginning with the language itself. I had a very generous, very good teacher. She spoke Spanish very slowly. But nonetheless, I couldn't understand. It was quite a dehumanizing experience, as the educational experience has been for indigenous people." After a dispute between his mother and father over whether Macas ought to return to their community after elementary school and take up agricultural work, his mother won, and Macas was sent to Cuenca, Ecuador's third-largest city, to get a high school diploma.

With hindsight, this move reveals itself as a decisive moment in the future indigenous leader's political formation. At high school in Cuenca—the same high school attended by Ecuador's most important Marxist intellectual of the twentieth century, Agustín Cueva—Macas first encountered Marxism, both as theory and praxis. Together with his ongoing ties to the customs, values, and traditions of the indigenous community, Marxism would shape how he came to understand and act in the world from then forward. "In this secondary school," Macas said, "I came into contact with a few interesting teachers. They talked about the community, the system, poverty, how poverty comes about, and so on. And I became friends with some of my teachers."

The teachers in question were heavily involved in land reclamation struggles in neighboring rural indigenous areas. They introduced Macas to the ideas of socialism and communism. "I was a little afraid," Macas said to me, laughing, "because back in my community my parents had been very conservative insofar as their political, ideological orientation. My father always voted for the Conservative Party. But he didn't do it with bad faith. He did it with good faith, saying, 'It seems to us that this man is correct.' The motivation had more to do with the person than conservative ideology. And so I was a little afraid. 'What's going to happen, I'm learning about these types of things,' I asked myself. I'd been told that these things were bad, that socialists and communists go to hell," Macas said, still laughing. "God was going to punish me."

Nonetheless, Macas persevered and became accustomed to navigating the libraries of Cuenca. "Because the teachers had talked to me about socialism, communism, and Marxism," he explained, "I went to the libraries and started making my way through the range of literature associated with these ideas. I read away like that, but I didn't understand anything. I read for hours and hours, but I didn't understand what they were trying to say." Later in life, when studying in Quito at the Central University, he "read historical materialism, dialectical materialism, and so on, and by that point, yeah, I understood. But I had tons of enthusiasm [during the high school period in Cuenca] to know, to study. And at the same time, I was always tightly linked to the community. Every weekend I would return to my community, participate in the collective work, in the meetings, in community decision-making, and so on."

After finishing high school, Macas returned to his community once again. The community reportedly saw him as a "rare bird," someone who had learned things of very little practical application during his high school education. All the same, they needed an elementary school teacher. Overcoming initial trepidation, Macas took up the work and stuck with it for one year. "What I accomplished I don't know. But I learned a lot from the kids. The simplicity and innocence of children is a beautiful world. During this period there was a big gathering in Quito, called the First Educational Gathering of Mother Languages and Bilingual Education. Interesting, I thought. An invitation came to our community, and they said to me, 'Do you want to go?' I said yes, and went."

At the gathering in Quito, Macas met with "indigenous comrades from all over" the country; "it was a discovery" for him to share ideas and learn of the mutual if differentiated experiences of indigenous communities in the rest of Ecuador. The rector of the Catholic University, where the seminar was being held, happened to be a leftist priest influenced by liberation theology, and after talking with Macas the priest offered to try to arrange a full scholarship for him. Macas eventually did attend the university, studying applied anthropology of indigenous languages, the field in which the scholarship was available. Macas "learned a lot about the different indigenous peoples of the country and finished the degree," and stayed on at the university teaching Kichwa for a period, before beginning a law degree at the same university.

The experience was alienating. "I started my law degree at the Catholic University, but the faculty of law at the Catholic University is very elite. The children of ambassadors and government officials go there. I felt more comfortable at the Central University. There were comrades there who spoke my language, who came from the same province, other people from the countryside, and so on. So the Central University was something else from the Catholic University." The Central University was also a center of Marxist studies at the time, and Macas "began to learn a lot about historical materialism and dialectical materialism from the professors," carrying with him until today "the idea that Marxism is helpful as a way of systematizing, interpreting reality. Not to simply apply Marxism as such. But to apply Marxist methodology to understand reality and to apply some of the theory's content."

During this university period in Quito, Macas became more deeply en-meshed in the organized indigenous movement, by far the strongest extra-parliamentary social force in Ecuador at the time.[101] In particular, he was an activist within the Kichwa Confederation of Ecuador (ECUARUNARI), the most important indigenous organization of the Andean highlands in the country, and part of CONAIE at the national level. "The struggle then was the struggle for land," Macas explained, "the defense of indigenous territories in the Andean Sierra—the struggle for identity and education of indigenous peoples, an education that would correspond to the identity and culture of the indigenous peoples."

Returning to themes of the universal and the particular, as well as the utopian-revolutionary dialectic of past and future, what is striking in Macas's recollection of the period and his ongoing commitment to the indigenous movement is the way in which he conceives of it as simultaneously drawing from the communal practices and customs of the past while reaching for-ward in a revolutionary commitment to transform the entirety of structures of domination and oppression in Ecuador as a whole. As an indigenous person coming from an impoverished rural community, Macas notes how his life in Quito was both unique and particularly fruitful for his political development. He was "learning theoretically" on the one hand, while "always [being] in-volved in the communities."

It became evident to Macas that the indigenous resistance he was a part of was "not merely a reformist struggle" but a combination of sociocultural reclamation of indigenous liberation and a simultaneous assault on the wider patterns of capitalist exploitation and oppression in the country.

> The revindication of our identities is important for the reproduction of our historical cultures as peoples—for example the struggle for land is a vital el-ement, because without land there can be neither our culture nor identity, absolutely nothing—but the constant of the indigenous movement has been what I call the global struggle, a proposal of an alternative to the entire system.

For Macas, the indigenous movement was thoroughly and simultaneously interlinked with the class struggle and left rearticulation in Ecuadoran poli-

---

101 See Marc Becker, *Leftists and Indians in the Making of Ecuador's Modern Indige-nous Movements* (Durham: Duke University Press, 2008); Marc Becker, *Pachakutick: Indigenous Movements and Electoral Politics in Ecuador* (Lanham, MD: Rowman and Littlefield, 2011).

tics. "None of us doubt that there were these two joined lines of struggle," he told me, "the struggle for revindication and the strategic struggle for change. The indigenous movement has always balanced these two lines."

Summing up these biographical vignettes and what they have meant for his political consciousness over time, Macas notes again the significance of his introduction to the praxis and theory of Marxism in high school, the university, and city as crucial to his ideological orientation and grounding, but returns, ultimately, to his childhood as the axiomatic point of departure. "The whole process I've described of learning has been important for me... but my formation was in the community." In 2010, at the time of the interview, the priority for Macas was how to reconcile these two traditions in practice: "The main point for me is how to combine two central struggles: the indigenous struggle—the struggle for identity, the historical struggle of the indigenous peoples—and the class struggle. This is what needs to be understood, this is what we need to do so that neither struggle is isolated."

For Macas, there are two conditions of struggle: "One is to make visible and to transcend coloniality. Coloniality is still very much alive in Ecuador, Peru, and Bolivia, and in all parts of Latin America—the coloniality of power, the coloniality of knowledge, the coloniality of being. This is one major component of what has to be overcome through political struggle. But," Macas continues, "there's another arm of struggle, which has to do with the condition of this economic model, the capitalist model. If we don't destroy both, one is going to remain." A combined liberation struggle capable of "the elimination of both these conditions of oppression and exploitation is what has to be done when we're thinking of the transformation of society, of social and political transformation."

Coloniality and capitalism, then, are, in this worldview, intricately intertwined systems of exploitation and oppression in contemporary Ecuador. In describing the theoretical framework emerging out of the Ecuadoran indigenous movement, Macas returns repeatedly both to a total critique of bourgeois civilization and a perennial dialectic between the utopian characteristics of specific precapitalist practices and values of indigenous life, and a future that will abolish capitalism while expropriating and subordinating its technological and productive advancements to human and environmental needs. "There are two civilizational models that are confronting one another in the current moment," Macas stresses, "two distinct paradigms—a Western paradigm and a paradigm from here. But the paradigm from here has everything to lose because no one values it whatsoever. 'It's those Indians again, trying to recover their notion of buen vivir, or living well'…. These paradigms of 'living well,' of harmony between humankind and nature—it's from these indigenous paradigms that, in part, an alternative must emerge. I'm not saying that everything in the Western paradigm is crap. Humanity has evolved and grown. And there are many things worth saving from the Western paradigm."

Conclusion

This chapter has sought to retain the sometimes powerful empirical findings of dominant trends in recent investigations into inequality in contemporary Latin America while challenging their theoretical allegiances to Weberian historical sociology and liberal ideology. An alternative Marxist and decolonial framework has been defended as a better way to fully understand the totalizing complexity of class and other social relations of oppression in contemporary Latin American capitalism. Rather than the capitalist market as an arena of opportunity, it is understood as one of imperatives and often invisible coercion. The invulnerability of the economic realm to democratic power from below in liberal capitalist democracy is exposed as a perversion limiting the possibilities of human emancipation rather than a normative ideal that we should celebrate.

Class exploitation in capitalist society has been shown in this chapter to operate in the workplace, in the labor market, in the household (through gendered reproduction), through race and racism, and on an interface with the substratum of nature. Class, it has been argued, is not an empty abstraction but rather a living and dynamic relationship that is determined concretely in and through gender, race, and sexuality. These latter forms of social oppression are not epiphenomena of the class structure, but are nonetheless fully understandable only as internally related to class, within a dialectical unity of co-constitution.

We have shown that recent studies of inequality in Latin America, informed by Weberian historical sociology and a normative commitment to liberal democratic theory, are incapable of grasping the totalizing power of capital in all its complexity and ferocity. Empirically, we argued, such complexity is expressed in the rhythms of extractive capitalism in twenty-first-century Latin America. The region is regressing, in many ways, to a primary commodity producer within the evolving international division of labor. New forms of class struggle are identifiable even at a glance in the countryside of many countries, as peasants resist processes of dispossession associated with the advancing frontiers of multinational capital in natural resource extraction. Racist ideology is mobilized to demonize and infantilize indigenous resistance to extractive activities. The natural substratum with which capitalism shares an interface is nowhere more visible than in agro-industrial mono-cropping, exploration for oil, extraction of natural gas, and mining minerals.

Finally, this chapter has focused on the life and activism of Luis Macas. His combined critique of colonialism and capitalism, in theory and praxis, reveals the ways in which the objective structural conditions of uneven capitalist development in contemporary Latin America, and their interaction with racist ideologies, can help to shape the political subjectivities of anticapitalist and anticolonial sources of opposition. The preferred theoretical optic of this chapter not only allows us to understand the sources of such opposition but also persuades us to see in them vital potential resources for meaningful human emancipation and ecological sustainability. The traditions of Weberian historical sociology and liberal democratic theory, by contrast, encourage us to see in these struggles sources of instability and democratic regression.

FOUR

The Indigenous Community as "Living Organism": José Carlos Mariátegui, Romantic Marxism, and Extractive Capitalism in the Andes

This chapter is concerned theoretically with the dialectic of Marxism and Romanticism in the work of the most influential Latin American Marxist theorist of the early twentieth century, José Carlos Mariátegui.[1] But the chapter is not

---

1 A new season in the study of Mariátegui has begun in Latin America in recent years, particularly exploring the possibilities opened up by his approach for the theoretical and practical advance of ecological socialism, liberation theology, indigenous liberation, and subaltern struggle, among other themes. See, for example, David Sobrevilla, *El Marxismo de Mariátegui y su aplicación a los 7 ensayos* (Lima: Universidad de Lima, 2012). See also the essays in a recent special issue of the Argentine Marxist journal *Herramienta: debate y crítica marxista*, available online at www.herramienta.com.ar /revista-impresa/revista-herramienta-n-51: Michael Löwy, "Comunismo y religión: la mística revolucionaria de José Carlos Mariátegui," *Herramienta* 51 (October 2012); Deni Ireneu Alfaro Rubbo, "Marxismo política y religión de 'un marxista convicto y confeso': Michael Löwy lector de José Carlos Mariátegui," *Herramienta* 51 (October 2012); Miguel Mazzeo, "Apuntes sobre la hermenéutica mariateguiana," *Herramienta* 51 (October 2012); Noelia Figueroa, "Walter Benjamin y José Carlos Mariátegui: gestos para refundar una teoría crítica subaltern," *Herramienta* 51 (October 2012); Martín Salinas, "José Carlos Mariátegui, la crítica de las vanguardias y la conquista de la realidad," *Herramienta* 51 (October 2012); Fabio Mascaro Querido, "Afinidades electivas:

chiefly interested in an exhaustive exegesis of his collected works or in simply tracing similitudes and differences in the development of his thought over time. Rather, it takes as its principal preoccupation the investigation of some select ideas and patterns in the Mariáteguist framework that might provide a first step in the construction of an analytical counterweight to a rather more concrete and immediate phenomenon in contemporary Andean politics—that is, the development of a new economistic and evolutionist dogma, deployed through a certain Marxist idiom, that seeks to defend as progressive the current intensification of extractive capitalism in the region—mining, natural gas and oil, and agro-industrial mono-cropping. It is possible to grasp the central elements of this ideological perspective, I argue, in the recent writings and speeches of one of the most important South American state ideologues of the new Latin American left, Bolivian vice president Álvaro García Linera.[2] The material expression of this ideology is observable, furthermore, in the general political-economic strategy of development adopted by the government of Evo Morales since he first assumed office in 2006. Exploring the ideas of García Linera and the political economy of Bolivia under Morales, this chapter also traces a connection between Mariátegui, on the one hand, and Felipe Quispe, a contemporary indigenous, anticapitalist activist and movement leader in Bolivia, on the other. Both men, in their different times, similarly develop a revolutionary romanticism that can be read against the Latin American new left's economism and evolutionism of the early twenty-first century.

The central argument here is that a utopian-revolutionary dialectic, looking backward to elements of a precapitalist past and pointing forward simultaneously to a socialist future, constitutes a connecting thread linking the eclectic lines of argument running through many of Mariátegui's writings. Mariátegui's treatments of colonialism and imperialism, uneven and combined development, and racism and indigenous liberation in colonial and early republican Peru, offer a compelling antidote to the sterility of developmental evolutionism in the thinking of many of the regimes of the new Latin American left. We can see these fruitful Mariáteguist combinations in movement in the life and activism of Quispe in the early 2000s.

Benjamin, Mariátegui y los movimientos sociales contemporáneos a contramano de la historia del progreso de los vencedores," *Herramienta* 51 (October 2012). For classical discussion, see José Aricó, ed., *Mariátegui y los orígenes del marxismo latinoamericano* (Mexico: Siglo veintiuno editores, 1978).

2 For a vociferous defence of García Linera's position on extractivism see also the influential latest book of Argentinian Marxist Atilio Borón: Atilio Borón, *América Latina en la geopolítica del imperialismo* (Buenos Aires: Luxemburg ediciones, 2012).

The chapter begins by mapping the broad contours of extractive capitalism in South America in the context of a commodities boom driven by China's dynamism, and situates the recent writings of García Linera in that context. From here the narrative shifts to alternative readings of Marx and Marxism, particularly through dialogues between Marxism and Romanticism in the twentieth century. With this as a backdrop, the chapter then interrogates the oeuvre of Mariátegui, offering his perspective as one starting point for a critique of García Linera. This section also links Mariátegui's intellectual lineage back to Romantic Marxism through a reading of Brazilian-French theorist Michael Löwy. Finally, our attention turns in the last part of the chapter to Felipe Quispe as an embodiment of Mariátegi's return to the concrete political struggles of late twentieth-century and early twenty-first-century Bolivia.

Extractive Capitalism and the Compensatory State

In 2010 and 2011, South America achieved an average growth rate of 6.4 percent, with Paraguay hitting 15 percent, Argentina 9.2 percent, and Uruguay 8 percent. Aggregate economic growth has been steady in Bolivia, averaging 4.8 percent between 2006 and 2012, with an initial apex of 6.1 percent in 2008 and a low of 3.4 percent in 2009, in the immediate fallout from the world crisis. In 2013, the country hit a new recent high of 6.8 percent growth, and GDP was still among the highest of Latin American countries in 2014 and 2015, at 5.5 and 4.5 percent for these respective years.[3] Growth has been maintained in spite of a general and accelerating decline since April 2011 in mining mineral prices at the international level, with prices of lead dropping 10 percent, tin 14 percent, and silver 28 percent in 2013 alone.[4] In other words, the uneven mutations of the ongoing economic crisis on a world scale have not resulted in low growth rates on an aggregate level across South America—at least not yet.[5] Similar to the period in the 1980s and 1990s normally described as neoliberal, massive multinational corporations remain deeply imbricated

---

3 CEPAL, *Blance Preliminar de las Economías de América Latina y el Caribe 2015* (Santiago: Comisión Económica para América Latina y el Caribe, 2016), 28.

4 For a background of the political economy of the Morales administrations from 2006 to 2014, see Webber, *From Rebellion to Reform in Bolivia*; Webber, "Managing Bolivian Capitalism."

5 Claudio Katz, "The Singularities of Latin America"; Jeffery R. Webber, "Crisis and Class, Advance and Retreat: The Political Economy of the New Latin American Left," in *Polarizing Development Alternatives to Neoliberalism and the Crisis*, eds. Lucia Pradella and Thomas Marois (London: Pluto Press, 2015).

in the extension of extraction at the heart of this primary-commodity-led growth everywhere in the region.

The logic of extractive capitalism has its particular expression in the Bolivian case. In terms of natural gas extraction, it pays to remember that in the first administration of orthodox neoliberal Gonzalo Sánchez de Lozada (1993–1997), the Bolivian state attempted to extend the area designated for gas exploration and exploitation to approximately 13 million hectares. When this initiative was defeated through indigenous resistance in different areas of the Amazon, the multinational petroleum corporations were forced to concentrate on their mega-gasfields in the south of the country, above all in the department of Tarija. At the end of 2011, however, Morales had taken up this bit of the defeated mantle of Sánchez de Lozada, and proposed the extension of gas exploration and exploitation to roughly 12 million hectares—an area four times as great as that in 2009. Of this area, close to 50 percent was conceded entirely to multinationals. Government measures introduced in 2012 amplified this area significantly, bringing the level of extraction of gas in the country to unprecedented heights. Likewise, in mining, spokespeople for the Morales government have announced initiatives for the large-scale expansion of mining activities beyond those in the traditional zones of the *altiplano*, or western high plateau, where mining has been underway since the colonial era. Much of this new mining will involve opening new frontiers into the Amazon.[6]

Similar to other cases of dispossession, from Mexico to Chile, the geographies being encroached upon in Bolivia for extending gas and mineral extraction, together with the growth of agro-industrial production (the majority of which is soya production under the control of Brazilian capital), include protected areas of biodiversity and indigenous territories that are currently among the last regions of the country relatively free of industrial and commercial activity, and that are, at the moment, governed by ecologically sustainable economies. It is the logic of accumulation by dispossession at the heart of this tripartite process—mining, gas, and agro-industry—that has generated the TIPNIS conflict, and is likely to generate many more socioecological conflicts into the future.[7]

Drawing on larger shares of the commodity rent than those captured during the orthodox neoliberal period, the Bolivian state under Morales has

---

6 Webber, "Managing Bolivian Capitalism."

7 For general discussion of the conflict-ridden political economy of extraction in Latin America generally, see Bebbington and Bury, *Subterranean Struggles.* On Bolivia specifically, see Nicole Fabricant and Bret Gustafson, eds., *Remapping Bolivia: Resources, Rights and Territory in a Plurinational State* (Santa Fe, NM: School of Advanced Research Press, 2011).

been able to finance redistributive programs such as Bono Juancito Pinto, Renta Dignidad, and Bono Juana Azurduy. These programs have led to improvements in education and healthcare and have diminished impoverishment of the elderly, while contributing to the significant overall decline in poverty registered over much of Morales's time in office.

Álvaro García Linera and the Progress of Extraction

The writings and speeches of Bolivian vice president Álvaro García Linera since he assumed the office in 2006 have made an important contribution to ideological attempts to legitimate such extractive capitalism in contemporary South American countries led by governments describing themselves as left or center-left.[8] As a former guerrilla, political prisoner, and author of a number of books on Marxism, indigenous movements, and social struggle in Bolivia, García Linera is closely associated in the public's eye with the Bolivian radical left, especially as it expressed itself in the massive left–indigenous cycle of revolt between 2000 and 2005. That quasi-insurrectional cycle witnessed the overthrow of two neoliberal presidents and laid the groundwork for Evo Morales's ascension to the presidency in 2006 (after elections in December 2005) as the country's first indigenous head of state.[9] García Linera's leftist pedigree is, in many ways, unassailable.

García Linera took up his role as the preeminent proponent of the state's development model under Morales and his party, shortly after accepting the vice presidential candidacy in the campaign leading up to the 2005 general elections: a light-skinned mestizo intellectual with calming, moderate rhetoric was thought to appeal to the middle- and even upper middle-class sectors, while Morales was expected to continue to bring out the popular indigenous vote.[10] While Morales continued to invoke many of the symbols that conjured

---

8 It is important to emphasize that García Linera wrote a series of highly sophisticated texts prior to his vice presidency, and that the critique offered here is strictly focused on his writings since 2006. For often insightful, sympathetic treatments of his earlier work, see Bruno Bosteels, *The Actuality of Communism* (London: Verso Books, 2011) and Bruno Bosteels, *Marx and Freud in Latin America: Politics, Psychoanalysis, and Religion in Times of Terror* (London: Verso Books, 2012).

9 Jeffery R. Webber, *Red October: Left-Indigenous Struggles in Modern Bolivia* (Chicago: Haymarket Books, 2012); Raquel Gutiérrez Aguilar, *Rhythms of the Pachakuti: Indigenous Uprising and State Power in Bolivia* (Durham: Duke University Press, 2014).

10 García Linera was born in Cochabamba in 1962, and trained as a mathematician while in university in Mexico. Upon returning to Bolivia he participated in the short-lived

up the radical past of the MAS, García Linera became the primary public voice of the MAS's new economic development program during the 2005 campaign. As part of this trajectory he began publishing and speaking in various forums about the impossibility of establishing socialism in Bolivia for at least fifty to one hundred years. Instead, García Linera posited that Bolivia must first build an industrial capitalist base. The capitalist model he envisioned at the time—Andean-Amazonian capitalism—projected a greater role for state intervention in the market. The formula essentially meant capitalist development with a stronger state to support a petit-bourgeoisie that would eventually become a powerful national bourgeoisie to drive Bolivia into successful capitalist development. That national bourgeoisie would be indigenous, or "Andean-Amazonian." Only after this long intermediary phase of industrial capitalism had matured would the fulfilment of socialism be materially plausible.[11] Fernando Molina, a neoliberal critic of the MAS, correctly points out that in many respects Andean-Amazonian capitalism closely resembles the old line of the Stalinist Partido Comunista Boliviana (Bolivian Communist Party, PCB), which stressed the necessity of a "revolution by stages": feudalism to capitalism (bourgeois), and, in the long to very long run, capitalism to communism (communist).[12]

García Linera expounded further on the character of the MAS after the party formed the government in 2006, attempting to define the ideology of "Evismo." The indigenous, democratic, and cultural "revolution," he reminds us in one early text, does not imply "radical" economic change, or even transformative restructuring of political institutions. Rather, "modifications" in the existing political structures of power and elite rule are all that is promised in the current context:

Ejército Guerrillero Túpaj Katari (Túpaj Katari Guerrilla Army, EGTK), as a consequence of which he spent five years in jail, between 1992 and 1997. He was never charged and was tortured while imprisoned. Upon his release he became a sociology professor at the main public university in La Paz, a prolific writer on political affairs and social movements, and one of the most important TV personalities of the 2000s, perpetually making the rounds of the evening news programs and talk shows. Before becoming vice president García Linera was one of the most prominent figures in the multitendency Bolivian Marxist intellectual collective, La Comuna, alongside Luis Tapia, Raquel Gutiérrez Aguilar, Oscar Vega, Raúl Prada Alcoreza, and others.

11 Álvaro García Linera, "El capitalismo andino-amazónico," *Le Monde Diplomatique*, Bolivian edition, January 2006.

12 Fernando Molina, *Evo Morales y el retorno de la izquierda nacionalista: Trayectoria de las ideologías antiliberales a través de la historia contemporánea de Bolivia* (La Paz: Eureka, 2006), 127.

In the case of Evismo, we are before a political revolution that has its impact in the economic realm but not in a strictly radical manner. Evo Morales has himself conceptualized the process that he is leading as a democratic cultural revolution, or a decolonizing democratic revolution, that modifies the structures of power, modifies the composition of the elite, of power and rights, and with this the institutions of the state. It has an effect on the economic structure because all expansion of rights means the distribution of wealth.[13]

Creative Tensions and Useful Idiots

In what is perhaps his most important book since he became vice president, García Linera maps out the five phases of what he understands to be a revolutionary process still unfolding in Bolivia.[14] The first phase of the revolutionary epoch began in 2000 with the Water War, a successful rural–urban uprising against the World Bank–driven privatization of water in the city of Cochabamba. This marked the first reversal of orthodox neoliberal policy since Bolivia became a neoclassical laboratory in the mid-1980s. The example of Cochabamba began to reverberate elsewhere in the country, and a series of left-indigenous movements began to regroup and rearticulate themselves. The pillars of state domination began to unravel—the institutionality of the state, through the decomposition of the principal parties responsible for introducing neoliberalism; the ideological legitimacy of neoliberal ideas, through their steep and irreversible decline; and the correlation of forces, through the fact that the governed and the governing no longer met on terms that had been established in the 1980s and 1990s. Their relationship had shifted such that the governed were no longer willing to accept being governed in the way they had been previously, and the governing could no longer govern in the way they had become accustomed to doing.[15]

The second phase lasts between 2003 and 2008 and is described by García Linera, following Antonio Gramsci, as a catastrophic equilibrium.[16] The equilibrium pertains to the temporary paralysis of state domination.

---

13 Álvaro García Linera, "El Evismo: Lo nacional-popular en acción," *El Juguete Rabioso*, April 2, 2006.

14 Álvaro García Linera, *Las tensiones creativas de la revolución: la quinta fase del Proceso de Cambio* (La Paz: Vicepresidencia del Estado Plurinacional, 2011).

15 Ibid., 13.

16 Ibid., 15.

Two power blocs had emerged in society with two antithetical sociopolitical projects for power, a national-popular bloc of left-indigenous forces, territorially rooted in the western highlands, and a bourgeois bloc, led by right-wing and racist forces in the eastern lowlands, the so-called *media luna* (crescent) departments of Santa Cruz, Tarija, Pando, and Beni. Neither was able to impose its project on society as a whole, and thus Bolivian society was catastrophically unable to move forward.[17] Overlapping with the second phase, the third involves the racialized class struggle between these two blocs entering into the field of the state itself, between 2006 and 2008. Evo Morales was the first indigenous person to be elected to the presidency in the entire history of the republic in December 2005—a particularly salient fact given that 62 percent of the population self-identified as indigenous in the 2001 census. For García Linera, Morales's assumption of the presidency in January 2006 signified the symbolic overturning of the Bolivian universe.[18] The insurrectionists had taken the reins of the state in their hands, but that state's logics of class and race—capitalism and internal colonialism—remained in place. The insurrectionists were in government but this did not mean they had conquered power. The two power blocs continued to face off, although now the terrain of struggle included the apparatuses of the state itself.[19]

A fourth phase begins for García Linera between August and October 2008, a "point of bifurcation."[20] The catastrophic equilibrium, always unstable, could not continue forever. The two irreconcilable projects for power were now forced to measure their capacities in open conflict, a conflict through which one side would necessarily come out on top. The strategy of the autonomist right-wing bloc of the eastern lowlands was a campaign of destabilization through a civic-coup attempt—occupying airports in departments where they had a presence, attacking official government buildings, preventing the landing of government planes in territories under their control, and, ultimately, murdering a group of peasants who were government supporters in the department of Pando on September 11, 2008.[21] The MAS government, for its part, mobilized the peasant unions and popular opinion, which was increasingly hostile to the lowland autonomists once the latter were shown to

---

17 Ibid., 15–16.
18 Ibid., 17–18.
19 Ibid., 18.
20 Ibid.
21 Ibid., 20.

have been implicated in the peasant massacre. The civic-coup attempt failed, the bourgeois bloc retreated and capitulated, and the US ambassador, Philip Goldberg, was expelled, for his alleged participation in the destabilization plot. A new, hotly contested constitution was passed in Congress in October 2008, and Morales won the presidential elections of December 2009 with an impressive 64 percent of the popular vote on a high turnout. The catastrophic equilibrium was over, and the national-popular bloc, expressed in the consolidation of MAS hegemony socially and politically, had been achieved.[22]

Thus the revolutionary process in Bolivia entered a fifth phase, which continues to the present. This time drawing on Mao, García Linera argues that the fundamental domestic contradictions in the revolutionary process have been resolved, and only secondary contradictions, conceived as creative tensions within the national-popular bloc itself, remain.[23] He deals specifically with four of these. First, there is the tension between social movements and the state, where the state is understood to embody the concentration of decision-making power, coercion, administration, and the ideas that articulate society as a whole. Social movement here is the state's antipode, representing the democratization and decentralization of decision-making power and the ongoing socialization of deliberative processes. This tension is productively mobilized for the advance of revolutionary process, in García Linera's view, through the MAS administration, which can be understood as a *government of social movements*—that is, the MAS encompasses within its form a creative tension, or dialectic, between the concentration of decision-making power characteristic of the state and the socialization of power characteristic of the social movement.[24]

A second creative tension centers around the multiclass character of the social bloc supporting the MAS government and the associated populist project of framing the distinct class interests of each component of that bloc as ultimately nonconflictual. The understanding here is that a state apparatus administered by such a national–popular bloc can create a virtuous circle of development for the various class components of the bloc, rather than succumbing to a zero-sum, conflict-ridden development process in which for there to be winners there must also be losers. García Linera explicitly argues that the popular bloc needs to incorporate sectors of the national bourgeoisie, which he takes to be patriotic capitalists, into the bloc on the side of government, while simultaneously ensuring that the hard nucleus of the revolutionary process, its

---

22 Ibid., 22.
23 Ibid., 24.
24 Ibid., 28.

vanguard, remains the popular classes of indigenous workers and peasants.[25]

A third creative tension internal to the national-popular bloc, for García Linera, is that which exists between the general interests of society and those interests of particular individuals, sectors, or groups. Since 2009, there has been a tension between institutionalized consolidation of the universal and general demands of the social-revolutionary bloc and those demands that assume a corporatist, sectional, and fragmented character within the same bloc. The right, García Linera warns, can take advantage of such tensions. A victory of the universalist will of the popular bloc would allow the expansion and hegemonic consolidation of the revolutionary process, with the MAS being the ultimate expression of that will. By contrast, if corporatist and unionist particularisms assume the lead in the actions of the bloc, it would mark the beginning of the bloc's degeneration and thus the degenerative process of the revolution itself. All of this would allow an opportunity for conservative restoration.[26] Through this lens, García Linera facilitates the government critique of a whole series of independent, disparate social movement actions that emerged outside of the control of the MAS, such as strikes organized by the Central Obrera Boliviana (Bolivian Workers' Central, COB), strikes by urban and rural teachers' unions, regional conflicts in the impoverished department of Potosí, and, crucially, as we saw above, the conflict over highway construction through a national park and indigenous territory in the TIPNIS. These are, for García Linera, exemplary cases of sectional interests getting in the way of the universalist will, as expressed in the actions of the MAS government.

The fourth and final creative tension turns on the oppositional necessities of ecological sustainability, on one side, the industrialization of natural resources—particularly natural gas and mining minerals—on the other.[27] García Linera makes the rather extraordinary claim that the state, through the surplus it has begun to generate by way of the industrialization of natural resources, has already begun to remove itself gradually from the capitalist logic of private appropriation as an economic norm. The Bolivian state, under the control of the Morales administration, is expansively introducing the logic of use-value, or the satisfaction of human needs, over the logic of

---

25 Ibid., 38–40.
26 Álvaro García Linera, El "ONGismo," enfermedad infantile del derechismo (O cómo la "reconducción" del Proceso de Cambio es la restauración neoliberal) (La Paz: Vicepresidencia del Estado Plurinacional, 2011), 41–48.
27 Ibid., 62.

exchange-value, or the maximization of profit.[28] It is a process with advances and setbacks, but there is movement in the direction of use-value over exchange-value. The tension arises from the fact that the surpluses extracted, which allow for the extension of the logic of use-value through social programs, are obtained through material processes that undermine the sensitive ecologies at the base of human existence.[29]

To summarize, then, for García Linera, writing in 2011, a revolutionary process opened up in 2000 and proceeded through a series of five phases, the last of which the country continues to navigate. The hegemony of the national-popular bloc, expressed through the MAS, had been achieved by 2010, after which tensions and contradictions of the process of change became creative, internal tensions, operating within the national-popular bloc at the base of the government. The Bolivian people had thus been united around the over-arching project of the Morales administration, part of which entailed the establishment of a plural economic model—with public, social-communitarian, and private property forms—that has been gradually ushering in the dominance of use-value over exchange-value.

More recently, as an increasing number of dissenting voices of a left opposition have emerged and begun to challenge the political economy and governance model of Bolivia under Morales, García Linera has assumed the role of slanderer in a harder form. After a group of left intellectuals and activists who had been a part of, or close to, the government released a joint manifesto in 2011 criticizing the government for abandoning the radical aims of the left-indigenous cycle of revolt between 2000 and 2005,[30] García Linera responded with a lengthy textual diatribe, dismissing the dissidents as "infantile" pawns of foreign NGOs who knowingly or unknowingly were guilty of strengthening counterrevolutionary social forces in Bolivia bent on the restoration of neoliberalism.[31] The sectional interests of certain groups once aligned with the national-popular bloc had apparently become too big for their britches. More recently, García Linera focused squarely on the left-indigenous opposition to the highway development through the TIPNIS, associating them with the side of the domestic right and US imperialism, although

---

28 Ibid., 67.

29 Ibid., 68–71.

30 *Por la recuperación del proceso de cambio para el pueblo y con el pueblo: Manifiesto de la coordinadora plurinacional de la reconducción* (Cochabamba and La Paz, 2011).

31 Álvaro García Linera, *El "ONGismo," enfermedad infantil del derechismo*, 62. Several of the left oppositionists then responded with a second pamphlet, *La MAScarada del poder* (Cochabamba and La Paz, 2011).

1 as to whether this was a case of willing collusion on their part,
merely been unwittingly reduced to useful idiots.[32]

~ this chapter seeks to demonstrate why and how the perspective
⸱⸱⸱⸱⸱⸱⸱⸱ by García Linera is deserving of a critique generated from *within*
Marxism, albeit a Marxism of a romantic kind.

Romanticism, Marx, and Marxism

Among the first critics of bourgeois modernity, of the civilization created by the
development of capitalism and the concomitant onset of the Industrial Revolution, were the Romantic poets, writers, and philosophers of Western Europe
born out of the mechanizing cauldron of the second half of the eighteenth century and the first years of the nineteenth. Looking back nostalgically to a real
or imagined past, Romanticism was constituted by both conservative and revolutionary currents and thinkers.[33] It was a "cultural movement"—cutting across
literature, philosophy, the arts, politics, religion, and history—that emerged as
a "protest against the development of modern capitalist civilization and industrial bourgeois society, which are based on bureaucratic rationality, market rei-
fication, the quantification of social life, and the 'disenchantment of the world'
(in the famous phrase of Max Weber)."[34] Industrial bourgeois civilization was
condemned through myriad appeals to social and cultural values of precapitalist
ways of life.

Romanticism took as its shared basis the fundamental critique of "the
quantification of life, i.e. the total domination of (quantitative) exchange-value,
of the cold calculation of price and profit, and of the laws of the market, over
the whole social fabric." With the quantification of life in bourgeois civilization came the "decline of all *qualitative* values—social, religious, ethical, cultural or aesthetic ones—the dissolution of all *qualitative* human bonds, the
death of imagination and *romance*, the dull uniformization of life, the purely
'utilitarian'—i.e. quantitatively calculable—relation of human beings to one
another, and to nature." This quality of quantification under capitalist social
relations expressed itself in specific ways in the workplace and labor process
of the Industrial Revolution. Precapitalist handicraft, and its association with

---

32 Álvaro García Linera, *Geopolítica de la Amazonía: Poder hacendal-patrimonial y acumu-
lación capitalista* (La Paz: Vicepresidencia del Estado Plurinacional, 2012).
33 Löwy, "The Romantic and the Marxist Critique of Modern Civilization," 891.
34 Michael Löwy, "Marxism and Romanticism in the Work of José Carlos Mariátegui,"
Latin American Perspectives 25, no. 4 (1998): 76.

creativity and imagination, was replaced by an increasingly strict division of labor, and dull and repetitious toil, in which the worker, losing what made her human, became a mere appendage to the machine.[35]

Marx himself drew with gusto from Romantic novelists, economists, and philosophers, even if the pull of the Enlightenment and classical political economy on his thinking would make it erroneous to label him a romantic anticapitalist. "Neither apologetic of bourgeois civilization nor blind to its achievements," Michael Löwy notes of Marx, "he aims at a higher form of social organization, which would integrate both the technical advances of modern society *and* some of the human qualities of pre-capitalist communities—as well as opening a new and boundless field for the development and enrichment of human life. A new conception of labor as a free, non-alienated, and creative activity—as against the dull and narrow toil of mechanical industrial work—is a central feature of his socialist utopia."[36]

The trajectory of Marxism after the death of Marx, according to Löwy, has been dominated by a productivist, economistic, and evolutionist determinism, a "modernist" Marxism that "took over only one side of the Marxian heritage and developed an un-critical cult of technical progress, industrialism, machinism, Fordism, and Taylorism. Stalinism, with its alienated productivism and its obsession with heavy industry is the sad caricature of this kind of 'cold stream' in Marxism (to paraphrase Ernst Bloch)."[37] A Romantic Marxism, a warmer stream that drew both from Marx and the revolutionary Romantic tradition, lived on, however, as a minority presence, insisting "on the essential break and discontinuity between the socialist utopia—as a qualitatively different way of life and work—and the present industrial society... look[ing] with nostalgia toward certain pre-capitalist social or cultural forms."[38] If the cold stream embraced Plekhanov, Kautsky, and the majority of the Second and Third Internationals, the Romantic Marxists included, in all their variety, Luxemburg, Gramsci, Lukács, E. P. Thompson, and Benjamin—and, central for our purposes, José Carlos Mariátegui. Central to the revolutionary Romantic worldview of Mariátegui is a simultaneous critique of "illusions of progress" and a sketch of a "utopian-revolutionary dialectic between the precapitalist past and the socialist future."[39] Mariátegui continues to represent, if you will,

---

35 Löwy, "The Romantic and the Marxist Critique of Modern Civilization," 894.
36 Ibid., 900.
37 Ibid.
38 Ibid., 901.
39 Löwy, "Marxism and Romanticism in the Work of José Carlos Mariátegui," 77–78.

a warm stream running through and against the later García Linera's barren industrial tundra.

The Indigenous Socialism of Mariátegui

It is perhaps Mariátegui's strong emphases on the history of colonialism, the world market and the dynamics of imperialism in an asymmetrically patterned world system of states, the uneven and combined development of capitalism in late-developing societies, and the enduring legacies of racism through slavery and conquest that allow for a fruitful mediation of his framework into the environment of contemporary Andean capitalism. Mariátegui's diverse writings propose a unique balancing of the universal and the particular. Mariátegui was scorned in the 1920s by Peruvian nationalists for his deviations into European Marxism, while the defenders of orthodoxy in the Comintern's Latin American bureau simultaneously condemned him for his romantic nationalism and populism.[40] "In reality," Löwy contends, "his thought was an attempt to move dialectically beyond this type of dualist thinking, caught between the universal and the particular."[41] He defended the universal character of the struggle for socialism, seeing it as a possibility opened up by global capitalist processes. In a 1928 essay, originally appearing in the journal he edited, *Amauta*, for example, we can read the following:

> Socialism is certainly not an Indo-American doctrine. But no doctrine, no contemporary system is or could be. And although socialism, like capitalism, may have been born in Europe it is not specifically or particularly European. It is a worldwide movement in which none of the countries that move within the orbit of Western civilization are excluded. This civilization drives toward universality with the force and means that no other civilization possessed. Indo-America can and should have individuality and style in this new world order, but not its own culture or fate that is unique.[42]

And at the same time, the specificity of socialism in Peru, and Latin America more generally, is repeatedly seized upon in his writings. He warns of the danger

---

40 Michael Löwy, "Introducción: Puntos de referencia para una historia del marxismo en América Latina," in *El marxismo en América Latina: Antología, desde 1909 hasta nuestros días*, ed. Michael Löwy (Santiago, Chile: LOM ediciones, 2007), 10–12.

41 Löwy, "Marxism and Romanticism in the Work of José Carlos Mariátegui," 86.

42 José Carlos Mariátegui, "Anniversary and Balance Sheet," in *José Carlos Mariátegui: An Anthology*, eds. Harry Vanden and Marc Becker (New York: Monthly Review Press, 2011), 129.

of mimicry: "We certainly do not want socialism in Latin America to be a copy or imitation. It should be a heroic creation. We have to give life to Indo-American socialism with our own reality, in our own language."[43] A year earlier, in 1927, in an address to the Peruvian Workers' Congress, Mariátegui stresses the Marxist method's attention to concrete variability across different national realities:

> Marxism, of which all speak but few know or above all comprehend, is a fundamentally dialectic method. It is a method that is completely based in reality, on facts. It is not, as some erroneously suppose, a body of principles of rigid consequences, the same for all historical climates and all social latitudes. Marx extracted his method from history's guts. Marxism, in every country, in every people, operates and acts on the environment, on the medium, without neglecting any of its modalities.[44]

The universal and the particular are also forged in complex unison in Mariátegui's repeated references to the necessity of studying Peru's "deep history" or "deep reality," and his insistence that such an acquaintance with the particularities of the national setting actually enables a thoroughgoing internationalism, and vice versa. "The internationalist feels, more than many nationalists," Mariátegui argues, "the Indigenous, the Peruvian; that the things Indigenous, Peruvian are not the *esprit* of the Jirón de la Unión or the Lima soireés, rather something much deeper and more transcendent."[45] A similar bridge across the divide appears in the "Programmatic Principles of the Socialist Party," drafted by Mariátegui in the same period. "The international character of the contemporary economy," he writes, "does not allow any country to escape the transformations flowing from the current conditions of production."[46] Out of this emerges the material basis for the "international character of the revolutionary proletarian movement." The document insists that the party "adapts its practice to the country's specific circumstances, but it follows a broad class

---

43 Mariátegui, "Anniversary and Balance Sheet," 130.
44 José Carlos Mariátegui, "Message to the Workers' Congress," in *José Carlos Mariátegui*. Relatedly, in a provocative recent cartography of Latin American Marxist theory, Omar Acha and Débora D'Antonio call for renewed sensitivity to the dialectical relation between national experiences and Latin American tendencies more generally: Omar Acha and Débora D'Antonio, "Cartografía y perspectivas del 'marxismo latinoamericano,'" *A Contra Corriente* 7, no. 2 (2010): 225.
45 José Carlos Mariátegui, "Toward a Study of Peruvian Problems," in *José Carlos Mariátegui*, 67–78.
46 José Carlos Mariátegui, "Programmatic Principles of the Socialist Party," in *José Carlos Mariátegui*, 237.

vision and its national context is subordinated to the rhythm of world history."[47] A final example can be found in one of Mariátegui's lectures, "The World Crisis and the Peruvian Proletariat," delivered as part of a series at the González Prada Popular University in Lima in 1923 and 1924, after Mariátegui had returned from several years in Europe. "Above all, capitalist civilization has internationalized the life of humanity," Mariátegui explains. "It has created the material connections among all peoples that establish an inevitable solidarity among them. Internationalism is not only an idea, it is a historical reality. Progress makes interests, ideas, customs, the peoples' regimes unify and merge. Peru, like the other peoples of the Americas, is not, then, outside the crisis, it is inside it."[48]

A second set of themes running throughout Mariátegui's writings turns on the history of colonialism and the subsequent dynamics of economic imperialism and the asymmetries of the world market. He begins from the premise that the Spanish conquest of Peru "destroyed economic and social forms that were born spontaneously from the Peruvian land and people," forms which were "nourished by an indigenous sense of life."[49] The conquest was, above all, "a terrible carnage," after which the "political and economic organization of the colony… continued the extermination of the Indigenous race. The viceroyalty established a system of brutal exploitation."[50] In what is probably his most famous essay, "The Land Problem," Mariátegui distinguishes between the feudal economy introduced to Peru through Spanish colonization and the later capitalist colonization of North America by the British. "Whereas in North America," Mariátegui explains, "colonization planted the seeds of a spirit and an economy then growing in Europe and to which the future belonged, the Spanish brought to America the effects and methods of a declining spirit and economy that belonged to the past."[51] Despite the way in which this concern with colonialism and the subsequent role of imperialism in the world system has been understood in recent commentary to be an anticipation of "much of the subsequent neo-Marxist and dependency literature,"[52] in fact, I would

---

47 Ibid.

48 José Carlos Mariátegui, "The World Crisis and the Peruvian Proletariat," in *José Carlos Mariátegui*, 297.

49 José Carlos Mariátegui, "The Economic Factor in Peruvian History," in *José Carlos Mariátegui*, 118.

50 José Carlos Mariátegui, "On the Indigenous Problem: A Brief Historical Overview," in *José Carlos Mariátegui*, 145.

51 José Carlos Mariátegui, "The Land Problem," in *José Carlos Mariátegui*, 76–77.

52 Harry Vanden and Marc Becker, "Amauta: An Introduction to the Life and Works of José Carlos Mariátegui," in *José Carlos Mariátegui*, 41.

argue, Mariátegui's analysis of the uneven combinations of precapitalist indigenous communal production, feudalism, and capitalism in Peru is much more refined and sophisticated than much of subsequent dependency theory, particularly its crudest versions, which date the origin of capitalism in Latin America as far back as the sixteenth century.[53]

At one point in the same essay, Mariátegui describes Peru's economy in the early twentieth century as "colonial," in the sense that its "movement, its development, are subordinated to the interests and the necessities of the markets in London and New York."[54] Peru is reduced to supplying the primary products to the dominant imperial powers, as well as serving as a market for their manufactured goods. Elsewhere he charts a large part of the flow of profits from mining, commerce, and transportation leaving Peru for capitals based in the imperial countries, forcing the South American country into a position of requesting them back through loans and the acquisition of debt.[55] Elsewhere, Mariátegui notes the way in which imperialism "does not allow any of these semicolonial peoples, whom it exploits as a market for capital and goods and as a source for raw materials, to have an economic program of nationalization and industrialization." The recurring crisis of the Peruvian economy "arises from this rigid determination of national production created by forces of the world capitalist market."[56]

His analytical conclusions on the history of colonialism and the ongoing imperialist character of the global capitalist system in the early twentieth century led Mariátegui logically to develop an associated strategy of anti-imperialism, laid out most fully in the document "Anti-Imperialist Point of View," submitted to the First Conference of Latin American Communist Parties in Buenos Aires in June 1929. The most notable aspect of this document is its condemnation of the complicit role played by Latin American national bourgeoisies in the perpetuation of imperialism, which they saw as "the best source" of their own profits and the continuity of their own political power.[57] As a result, any ostensible anti-imperialist alliance led by bourgeois or petit-bourgeois forces under the banner of nationalism could never successfully break with imperialism. What was needed instead was an alliance between workers and peasants, in a movement that combined the

---

53 Andre Gunder Frank, "The Development of Underdevelopment," *Monthly Review* 18, no. 4 (1966): 17–31.
54 Mariátegui, "The Land Problem," 111.
55 José Carlos Mariátegui, "Colonial Economy," in *José Carlos Mariátegui*, 134.
56 Mariátegui, "Programmatic Principles of the Socialist Party," 238.
57 José Carlos Mariátegui, "An Anti-Imperialist Point of View," in *José Carlos Mariátegui*, 265–266.

perspective of anti-imperialism with a commitment to socialist revolution at home. "We are anti-imperialists," Mariátegui insists, "because we are revolutionaries, because we oppose capitalism with socialism as an adversarial system called to succeed it. In the struggle against foreign imperialism we are fulfilling our duties of solidarity with the revolutionary masses of Europe."[58]

There is a consistency here as well between Mariátegui's reflections on twentieth century anti-imperialist strategy, and his reading of the limited social achievements flowing out of the War of Independence between 1811 and 1821. While formal independence from Spain was achieved, the internal hierarchies of class and racial stratification remained intact, and new forms of economic subordination to different dominant powers emerged on an international scale as Peru was inserted ever more thoroughly into the machinations of the world market. The independence revolution, Mariátegui is at pains to point out, was carried forward for the benefit of creoles (descendents of Spanish colonialists born in Peru) and expressly against the indigenous peasant majority, even if the indigenous masses were enlisted in the battles. The Peruvian independence revolution "did not bring in a new ruling class.... The colony's landholding aristocracy, the owner of power, retained their feudal rights over land and, therefore, over the Indians. All provisions apparently designed to protect them have not been able to do anything against feudalism even today."[59]

The intricate portrayal of postindependence economic development in Peru, which one finds throughout Mariátegui's work, closely parallels what Leon Trotsky later theorized as uneven and combined development, most extensively in his *History of the Russian Revolution*.[60] In place of a sterile advance through the various stages prescribed by the texts of cold stream Marxist orthodoxy, we discover the complicated intertwining and combining of different modes of production within the Peruvian social formation. The existing communal property of indigenous communities in the highlands is not replaced instantly through Spanish colonialism by the succession of individual property rights and onset of capitalism, rather these communities are "stripped of their land" in the postindependence period "for the benefit of the feudal or semi-feudal landholdings that are constitutionally incapable of technical progress." Meanwhile, on the Pacific coast, large landholdings break the "feudal routine" and commence before anywhere else in the country "a capitalist technique" under the influence of foreign capital, uprooting indigenous communities

---

58 Ibid., 272.
59 Mariátegui, "On the Indigenous Problem," 147.
60 Leon Trotsky, *History of the Russian Revolution* (New York: Pathfinder Press, 1980).

from the land and employing former African slaves as agrarian proletarians in the new agricultural industries of cotton and sugarcane.[61]

For Trotsky, arriving at an understanding of uneven and combined development analytically had significance politically in his formulation of a theory of permanent revolution, whereby the necessary evolution through discrete stages of development, advocated by the Marxism of the Second International, was countered with the possibility of "leaping" stages and fomenting socialist revolution in "backward" countries, such as Russia in the early twentieth century.[62] Similarly, in the case of Mariátegui, the care with which he examined the Peruvian social formation and its development, and the disregard he exhibited for established orthodoxies, led him on a path against the rigid determinism of evolutionism, which finds a strong contemporary echo, as we have seen, in the work of García Linera since 2006. "The political advent of socialism," he suggests, "does not presuppose the perfect or exact accomplishment of the liberal economic stage, according to a universal itinerary. Elsewhere, I have already said it is very possible that the destiny of socialism in Peru might be in part achieving certain tasks that are theoretically capitalist in accordance with the rhythm of history that guides us."[63]

Unique to Mariátegui's work in this period is the systematic treatment of the racialized character that uneven and combined development assumed in republican Peru. The colonial origins of the feudal mode of production in Peru gave rise to this specificity. "In Europe," Mariátegui writes, "the feudal lord embodied, to some extent, the primitive patriarchal tradition, so that in respect to his servants he naturally felt higher, but not ethnically or nationally different from them." As a result the European aristocracy "found it possible to accept a new concept and a new practice in their dealings with the agricultural worker. In colonial America, meanwhile, the white person's arrogant and deep-rooted belief in the inferiority of people of color has stood in the way of this development."[64] If that was the form of racial oppression that characterized the feudal system in the highlands, the capitalist coast offered no reprieve on this score. Mariátegui notes of the Peruvian Pacific coastline of the period, "when the agricultural worker has not been an Indian he has been an African

61 Mariátegui, "The Land Problem," 99.

62 Leon Trotsky, *The Permanent Revolution and Results and Prospects* (New York: IMG Publications, 2007).

63 José Carlos Mariátegui, "On the Character of Peruvian Society," in *José Carlos Mariátegui*, 252.

64 Ibid., 103.

slave or Chinese coolie who is, if possible, held in more contempt."[65]

"Feudal and bourgeois elements in our countries have the same contempt for the Indians, as well as for the blacks and mulattos, as do the white imperialists," Mariátegui stresses again in his dissident address (read in his absence) to the First Conference of Latin American Communist Parties in Buenos Aires in 1929:

> The ruling class's racist sentiment acts in a manner totally favorable to imperialist penetration. The native [Peruvian, not indigenous] lord or bourgeois has nothing in common with their pawns of color. Class solidarity is added to racial solidarity or prejudice to make the national bourgeoisie docile instruments of Yankee or British imperialism. And that feeling extends to much of the middle class, who imitate the aristocracy and the bourgeoisie in their disdain for the plebeian of color, even when it is quite obvious that they come from a mixed background.[66]

"The republic has the responsibility to raise the status of the Indian," Mariátegui notes in the essay "Peru's Principal Problem": "And contrary to this duty, the republic has impoverished the Indians. It has compounded their depression and exacerbated their misery. The republic has meant for the Indians the ascent of a new ruling class that has systematically taken their lands."[67]

Considering the centrality to Mariátegui's framework of the racialized character of economic and political development in Peru, it is not surprising that a politics of antiracism, and especially of indigenous liberation, proliferates throughout his discussions of emancipatory strategy and the potential sources of liberation. In Mariátegui's engagement with indigenous liberation we find our link back to Löwy's utopian-revolutionary dialectic of the precapitalist past and socialist future—a dialectic that, if taken seriously, necessitates quite a different reading of contemporary Bolivian conflicts, such as the TIPNIS, than the one on offer in the writings of García Linera. This is particularly evident in Mariátegui's interrogation of the Andean *ayllu* (independent indigenous community) and, more problematically, "Inca communism." The residual customs, values, and institutional forms of indigenous communities are mobilized in Mariátegui's thinking as a *transitional* conflict against both feudalism and capitalism in Peru, in a manner that overlaps with the depiction of the Luddites in the work of British social historian E. P. Thompson—as a heroic, quasi-insurrectional

---

65 Ibid.
66 José Carlos Mariátegui, "The Problems of Race in Latin America," in *José Carlos Mariátegui*, 310.
67 José Carlos Mariátegui, "Peru's Principle Problem," in *José Carlos Mariátegui*, 140.

force against the imposition of the factory system in eighteenth and nineteenth century England.[68] It is through Mariátegui's exploration of indigenous sources for socialist revolution in Peru, furthermore, that we encounter an emphasis on the self-activity, self-organization, and self-emancipation of the oppressed that finds its echo, if in a distinct idiom, throughout much of Thompson's writing.

We need not accept the entirety of Mariátegui's more or less blanket defense of "Inca communism" in his essay "The Land Problem" to draw out from the surrounding discussion some essential kernels of insight into the way he conceptualized the utopian-socialist dialectic of past and future. As important as is the discussion of the greater yields achieved by the Inca's agrarian economy compared to that of the colonial one which replaced it, more crucial are Mariátegui's repeated invocations of the lasting institutional forms, values, and customs of the ayllu that survived, if only partially and in distorted form, the onslaught of feudalism and later capitalist development in highland Peru.[69] "I believe that our agrarian problem has a fundamental indisputable and concrete factor that gives it a special character," Mariategui notes, "the survival of the community and elements of practical socialism in Indigenous agricultural life."[70]

Writing of early twentieth-century Peru, Mariátegui refers to the "vitality of Indigenous communism that invariably promotes various forms of cooperation and association for the aboriginals. Indians, despite the laws of one hundred years of the republican regime, have not become individualistic."[71] The indigenous community is "still a living organism," Mariátegui argues, "despite the hostile environment that suffocates and deforms it." But more than merely persisting, it helps point the way to a socialist future, insofar as the indigenous community "spontaneously manifests obvious possibilities for evolution and development."[72] In one evocative passage, Mariátegui explains how, "in indigenous villages where families are grouped and bonds of heritage and communal work have been extinguished, strong and tenacious habits of cooperation and solidarity that are the empirical expression of a communist spirit still exist. The community draws on this spirit. It is their body. When expropriation and redivision seem about to liquidate the community, Indigenous

---

68 E. P. Thompson, *The Making of the English Working Class* (New York: Vintage, 1963), 553.
69 Mariátegui, "The Land Problem," 95.
70 Ibid., 71. The similarities here with Marx's late engagement with Russian populism are interesting to note, but a proper discussion of them is beyond the scope of this inquiry. See, among others, Kevin B. Anderson, *Marx at the Margins: On Nationalism, Ethnicity, and Non-Western Societies* (Chicago: University of Chicago Press, 2010).
71 Mariátegui, "The Land Problem," 98.
72 Ibid., 97.

socialism always finds a way to reject, resist, or evade it."[73] For Mariátegui, "the communities that have demonstrated a truly amazing persistence and resistance under the harshest conditions of oppression represent in Peru a natural factor for the socialization of the land."[74]

The persistence of cooperative bonds and customs of solidarity in the indigenous community are the building blocks of Mariátegui's utopian-socialist dialectic of drawing selectively on the precapitalist past in order to forge new values and social forms in the future.[75] Any return to the Inca period, even if that empire is valorized as against the regime of Spanish colonial conquest that replaced it, is explicitly and emphatically rejected on a number of occasions by Mariátegui. "But this," he writes for example,

> like the stimulation that freely provides for the resurgence of Indigenous peoples, the creative manifestation of its forces and native spirit, does not mean at all a romantic and anti-historical trend of reconstructing or resurrecting Inca socialism, which corresponded to historical conditions completely bypassed, and which remains only as a favorable factor in a perfectly scientific production technique, that is, the habits of cooperation and socialism of Indigenous peasants. Socialism presupposes the technique, the science, the capitalist stage. It cannot permit any setbacks in the realization of the achievements of modern civilization, but on the contrary it must methodically accelerate the incorporations of these achievements into national life.[76]

---

73 Ibid., 98.
74 Mariátegui, "The Problems of Race in Latin America," 322.
75 Mariátegui, "Programmatic Principles of the Socialist Party," 239. If one were registering any doubt that Mariátegui's view is overly one-sided in its backward-looking character, this error of interpretation ought to be disabused with a close reading of the following passage: "These people are surprised that the most advanced ideas in Europe make their way to Peru; but they are not surprised, on the other hand, at the airplane, the transatlantic ocean liner, the wireless telegraph, the radio—in sum, all the most advanced expressions of material progress in Europe. The same kind of thinking that would ignore the socialist movement would have to ignore Einstein's theory of relativity. And I am sure that it does not occur to the most reactionary of our intellectuals—almost all of them are galvanized reactionaries—that there should be a ban on studying and popularizing the new physics of which Einstein is the greatest and most eminent representative." Mariátegui, "The World Crisis and the Peruvian Proletariat," 297.
76 Mariátegui, "Programmatic Principles of the Socialist Party," 239. See also Mariátegui, "The Land Problem," 93, where he notes: "Modern communism is different from Inca communism. This is the first thing that a scholarly man who explores Tawantinsuyu needs to learn and understand. The two kinds of communism are products of different human experiences. They belong to different historical eras."

Mariátegui envisions the emancipation of the indigenous Peruvian majority flowing out of their own initiative. "The solution to the problem of the Indian must be a social solution. It must be worked out by the Indians themselves," he writes in a passage addressing the organization of the first nationwide congresses of the indigenous movement in Peru:

> This concept leads to seeing the meeting of Indigenous congresses as a historical fact. The Indigenous congresses have not yet formed a program, but they do represent a movement. They indicate that the Indians are beginning to gain a collective consciousness of their situation. The least important aspect of the Indian Congress is its deliberations and its votes. The transcendent, historic aspect is the congress itself. The congress is an affirmation of the will of the race to make their own claims.[77]

More emphatically, in his address to the Conference of Latin American Communist Parties in Buenos Aires, Mariátegui blithely dismisses the view that lingers in the Peruvian imagination of the passive and servile indigenous communities, in which "degraded and oppressed Indians are incapable of any form of struggle or resistance. The long history of Indigenous insurrections and mutinies, and the resulting massacres and repression, is sufficient in itself to dispel this impression."[78] A similar sentiment expresses itself in a brief preface elsewhere: "The Indian, so easily accused of cowardice and submission, has not ceased to rebel against the semi-feudal regime that continues to oppress under the republic, the same as it did during the colonial period."[79]

A research program into the dynamics of contemporary extractive capitalism and the Andean compensatory state that drew explicitly on this heritage, I want to argue, could expose a range of contradictions that the reigning evolutionism of García Linera hopes to conceal. More than merely a theoretical paradigm or analytical research agenda, however, the thematics of Romantic Marxism running through Mariátegui can be found as an already existing, living praxis in the left-indigenous opposition to extractivism in the Andes. A brief portrayal of the life and activism of Felipe Quispe might provide an initial insight into how this operates concretely.

---

77 Mariátegui, "Peru's Principle Problem," 142.
78 Mariátegui, "The Problems of Race in Latin America," 320.
79 José Carlos Mariátegui, "Preface to *The Amauta Atusparia*," in *José Carlos Mariátegui*, 329.

An Aymara Condor

There is little doubt that Felipe Quispe has been one of the most prominent and important leaders of indigenous struggle in the last two decades of Bolivian history, even if he more or less receded from the political scene once Evo Morales assumed office in January 2006.[80] During the mobilizations of the Aymara peasantry in 2000 and 2001—against the commodification of communal lands and the privatization of water resources—Quispe was the focal point of popular struggle, more or less embodying and personifying the revolutionary sentiments of those blocking the roads and bringing the country to a standstill.[81] Quispe articulated this collective voice audaciously and confrontationally in full view of the media and the Bolivian citizenry and in the face of racist Bolivian elites. For Aymara and other indigenous radicals Quispe's public expressions provoked and inspired indigenous pride and solidified a consciousness around the necessity of popular struggle. For the *q'aras*, or nonindigenous white and mestizo élites, the same expressions from Quispe elicited reactions of fear, hatred, and racism. His personal political trajectory sheds at least partial light on the collective history of indigenous movements over the last few decades in Bolivia, their ideological transitions, infrastructures of struggle, and important contribution to the cycle of combined liberation across the country.[82]

By all accounts, Quispe has led a seditious life, one that embodies Mariátegui's utopian-revolutionary dialectic of the precapitalist past and socialist future.

---

80 On a national scale, only Evo Morales has enjoyed a parallel status to Quispe in contemporary indigenous politics, as measured by the intensity of sentiments coming from various sectors of the population. Quispe was perhaps the figure most reviled and feared by the Bolivian ruling class in the early 2000s. By contrast, in the Aymara indigenous countryside of La Paz and Oruro, he received enthusiastic respect from the peasantry for his militant defense of indigenous self–determination and dignity in the face of racism and neoliberal capitalism.

81 For my account of the left-indigenous insurrectionary cycle between 2000 and 2005, as well as its long historical backdrop, see Webber, *Red October*. For a brilliant history of the same period, written in a distinctly Thompsonian register, see Forrest Hylton and Sinclair Thomson, *Revolutionary Horizons: Past and Present in Bolivian Politics* (London: Verso Books, 2007).

82 For the argument that the left-indigenous cycle of revolt constituted a combined liberation struggle, see Webber, *Red October*. The struggle for combined liberation refers to the integral unity of the simultaneous opposition to racial oppression and class exploitation in the Bolivian context between 2000 and 2005. Emancipation in one domain was seen by many activists to require emancipation in both. Because of the specific racialized form that capitalism assumed in Bolivia, combined liberation for the indigenous majority meant a united emancipation from class and ethnic domination.

He was born in the community of Jisk'a Axariya, outside Achacachi.[83] After having been educated politically in revolutionary Marxist organizations in the 1970s, he gravitated later in that decade to the small political party Movimiento Indio Tupaj Katari (Tupaj Katari Indian Movement, MITKA).[84] MITKA was situated in the *indianista* wing of the broader *katarista* movement. MITKA was therefore distinct from the katarista currents closer to the Confederación Sindical Única de Trabajadores Campesinos de Bolivia (Bolivian Peasant Trade Union Confederation, CSUTCB) of the time, and the Movimiento Revolucionario Tupaj Katari (de liberación) (Tupaj Katari Revolutionary Liberation Movement, MRTK[L]). The latter currents maintained some residual peasantist, or *campesinista*, class-based ideological characteristics, alongside the elements of ethnic revindication common throughout katarismo.[85]

Quispe was an important player in semiclandestine indigenous popular politics in the 1970s and early 1980s. But his real ascent probably began with the Extraordinary Congress of the CSUTCB in Potosí in 1988, where he was a representative for a new militant organization, Ofensiva Roja de Ayllus Kataristas (Red Offensive of Katarista Ayllus, also known as Ayllus Rojos, Red Ayllus). The Ayllus Rojos were an eclectic amalgamation of Marxist-indigenous activists, bringing together *indígenista* Aymaras, miners, and urban Marxists.[86] As noted, in 1991–1992 an armed wing of the Ayllus Rojos, the Ejército Guerrillero Tupaj Katari (Tupaj Katari Guerrilla Army, EGTK), emerged and Quispe was a leading figure alongside García Linera and Raquél Gutiérrez Aguilar. Although EGTK never matured into a successful or large guerrilla army, it did develop a popular base of sympathizers among the Aymara peasantry in Achacachi and the surrounding area, influenced some of the internal politics of the CSUTCB, and deposited ideological seeds

---

83 Many of the basic biographical details of Quispe's life narrated here are drawn from Xavier Albó, *Pueblos indios en la política* (La Paz: Plural editores, 2002).

84 Tupaj Katari was one of the leaders of the indigenous anti-colonial rebellions that constituted the Great Andean Civil War—in what is today Bolivia and Peru—of 1780–1782. When the rebellion was defeated by the Spanish, Katari was drawn and quartered by the colonialists.

85 Albó, *Pueblos indios en la política*, 9; Felipe Quispe, Interview, La Paz, Bolivia, May 12, 2005.

86 Quispe once remarked: "When we speak about the indigenous, Aymara or Quechua, revindicating our ancestral culture, at the same time we are automatically embracing our brothers who work in the cities as workers or proletarians." Felipe Quispe, "Organización y proyecto politico: Entrevista a Felipe Quispe," in *Tiempos de rebelión*, eds. Álvaro García Linera, Raquel Gutiérrez, Raúl Prada, Felipe Quispe and Luis Tapia (La Paz: Muela del Diablo, 2001), 189.

of Aymara nationalism, the fruits of which were seen in the mobilizations of 2000 and 2001 in the altiplano.[87] In jail, Quispe gained popular credibility and respect among Aymara and other indigenous peasants for his guerrilla past and his fervent denunciations of the neocolonial nature of the Bolivian state.[88]

Already in the 1980s Quispe had evoked the heroic collective memory of Tupaj Katari and the 1781 anticolonial rebellion he led. This was evident in Quispe's book, *Tupaj Katari vive y vuelve, carajo* (Tupaj Katari Is Alive and Returning), published in that period. However, as a result of his devotion to political study in jail, when Quispe was released, his political oratory was notably replete with historical references. Moreover, his credibility, gained through years of activism, guerrilla struggle, and, now, incarceration, remained intact—indeed strengthened.[89]

In the Extraordinary Congress of the CSUTCB, between November 26 and 28, 1998, Quispe was elected executive secretary, essentially because he was seen as the consensus candidate between the internally feuding factions of the CSUTCB aligned behind either Evo Morales or Alejo Véliz.[90] By this stage, Quispe had already become known in popular parlance by the moniker "el Mallku," "leader" or "condor" in Aymara.[91] The CSUTCB developed a radical indigenous politics once again under the leadership of Quispe. From 1998 to 2000 the organizational groundwork was laid for the 2000–2001 uprisings. A process emerged through which the very state institutions of the Bolivian republic were called into question for their failure to reflect the multinational character

---

87 At the same time, Quispe is not prone to romanticizing the historical impact of the EGTK: "… in the 1990s we had a revolutionary organization called Tupaj Katari Guerrilla Army (EGTK). It was a political-military organization that we thought would arrive in power through armed struggle and by being the vanguard of the people. It turns out that, with time, we saw that there wasn't support from the population. So, we ended up in jail for five years. I was captured on August 19, 1992, and remained in jail until 1997. When I left I returned to my community, like any other *comunario*, like any other peasant. From there the people chose me and told me that I had to be leader of the CSUTCB." Quispe, Interview.

88 While incarcerated, Quispe read and studied, completing his high school diploma. He was granted provisional freedom to attend classes in history at the Universidad Mayor de San Andres (UMSA) in La Paz, eventually completing his bachelor's degree.

89 Albó, *Pueblos indios en la política*, 81.

90 Álvaro García Linera, Marxa Chávez, and Patricia Costas Monjes, *Sociología de los movimientos sociales en Bolivia: Estructuras de movilización, repertorios culturales y acción política*, 2nd ed. (La Paz: Oxfam and Diakonia, 2005), 121.

91 The name refers to a principal title of authority in traditional Aymara organizational structures. Albó, *Pueblos indios en la política*, 81.

of Bolivian society and the basic oppression of the indigenous majority.[92]

Building on longstanding, historical, collective memories of indigenous rebellion was a key facet of organizing the capacity for mobilization and the political consciousness of the movement's rank and file. Just as Mariátegui sought to recover selective features of "Inca communism"—the values of co-operation and solidarity of the independent indigenous community—Quispe returned to the deep legacies of indigenous insurrection:

> So, we knew of the uprising of Manco II of 1536–1544. We knew of the up-rising of Juan Santos Atahuallpa from 1742–1755. We also knew about the uprisings of Túpac Amaru, Túpac Katari of 1780–1783, and Zárate Willca in 1899... we see Katari as an example, as a model. He spent ten years prepar-ing the Indian rebellion, and like that, successively, with other men, rose up against colonial power, and against the republic.[93]

Quispe's writings and interviews highlight both the role of a militant layer of CSUTCB organizers traveling to different rural communities, politicizing and raising the consciousness of the bases over months and years. At the same time, again an echo of Mariátegui, Quispe emphasizes the radicalization of the grassroots themselves, their capacity to self-organize and mobilize and ultimately to disobey the high command of the CSUTCB when it refused at times to sanction radical action against the state.[94] Quispe reflects in one interview on his own political and ideological trajectory away from isolated guerrilla action and toward the power of mass mobilization as a basis for in-digenous liberation. Originally he put his faith in the possibility of forming a small vanguard of armed revolutionaries within the indigenous communities. "But, you know what, it turned out that the mobilisations of April and Sep-tember [2000] have clarified things for us," Quispe points out. "In rebellion, I have learned that the true struggle has not been of a few people, but has been taken up by millions and millions" of indigenous people.[95] He calls for an insurrection "supported by our own resources from the communities and the unions," a rebellion of a "communal and indigenous" character, which employs "our own philosophical thought" and traditions.[96] Quispe points to the au-

---

92 Pablo Mamani Ramírez, *El rugir de las multitudes: La fuerza de los levantamientos indí-genas en Bolivia/Qullasuyu* (La Paz: Aruwiyiri, 2004), 24.
93 Quispe, "Organización y proyecto político," 165. Note Tupaj and Tupac are both cor-rect spellings of the same name.
94 Ibid., 166–167.
95 Ibid., 174.
96 Ibid., 174.

thentic protagonists of the uprisings in April and September 2000:

> The true actors of the indigenous uprising have been the communities them-
> selves.... The cause was not only water, coca, territory, land. Rather, the cause
> already has sown the seeds to take over political power, to govern ourselves
> with a communitarian socialist system based in our ayllus and communities.[97]

The Aymara struggle for communitarian collective sovereignty and
self-governance, on the one hand, was increasingly pitted against the capitalist,
white-mestizo state, on the other.[98] In the regions of northern La Paz and central and southern altiplano, the *wiphala*—the multicolored, checkered Aymara
flag—is probably the most important political symbol of this struggle. It differ-
entiates collective Aymara identity from the Bolivian identity promoted by the
state and represented by the Bolivian flag. Further, the wiphala was understood
over the course of the 2000–2005 left-indigenous cycle of revolt as a symbol of
war and social struggle, as well as a commitment to communitarian social life
and the ayllus.[99]

The more radical sectors of the rebellions of 2000 and 2001 were ideologically oriented toward a fundamental, revolutionary challenge to the neoliberal
capitalist model in place since 1985. Large sections of the Aymara altiplano,
aligned with Quispe in these contentious moments of confrontation with the
state, were building the incipient ideological and organizational foundations
for an alternative revolutionary and democratic state.[100] This alternative democracy envisioned by the indigenous activists on the road blockades has been
expressed intellectually by scholars working in the Bolivian context as ayllu
or communal democracy versus liberal-capitalist representative democracy.[101]
Quispe, as we have seen, conceives of the rebellions as a communitarian socialist challenge to the neocolonial capitalist Bolivian state. Recalling Mariátegui's

---

97 Ibid., 178.
98 Felix Patzi, "Rebelión indígena contra la colonialidad y la transnacionalización de la
   economía: Triunfos y vicisitudes del movimiento indígena desde 2000 a 2003," in *Ya es
   otro tiempo el presente: Cuatro momentos de insurgencia indígena*, eds. Forrest Hylton, Felix
   Patzi, Sergio Serulnikov, and Sinclair Thomson (La Paz: Muela del Diablo, 2005), 217.
99 Ramírez, *El rugir de las multitudes*, 35. At the same time, it ought to be noted that the
   wiphala is a paradigmatic case of invented tradition. See Eric Hobsbawm and Terence
   Ranger, eds., *The Invention of Tradition* (Cambridge: Cambridge University Press,
   1983). The flag was not used by indigenous radicals in 1899, 1927, or 1946–47, for
   example. Thanks to Forrest Hylton for drawing my attention to this point.
100 Patzi, "Rebelión indígena contra la colonialidad y la transnacionalización de la
   economía," 66.
101 Silvia Rivera Cusicanqui, "Liberal Democracy and *Ayllu* Democracy in Bolivia: The
   Case of Northern Potosí," *Journal of Development Studies* 26, no. 4 (1990): 97–121.

dialectic, he speaks of the reassertion of the communal system of the ayllu, adapted to the twenty-first-century context, as a way of replacing the colonial institutions and practices inherited by the republicans at Bolivian independence in 1825.[102] In many respects, this notion of communitarian socialism in the countryside was the rural counterpart to the revolutionary, assemblist forms of urban democracy experienced during the other explosive moments in the nationwide cycle of uprisings, such as the Water War in Cochabamba in 2000 and the so-called Gas Wars in La Paz and El Alto in 2003 and 2005, with their mass meetings in the streets and plazas.

Conclusion

In light of the intensification of extractive capitalism in the Andes, and the role of leftist figures of state appropriating a language of Marxism to defend the "progressive" character of the new model of accumulation, this chapter has called for a return and reappraisal of Romantic Marxism through a close study of José Carlos Mariátegui. Against the seductive and determinist rhetoric of progress and the evolutionism of stages, it has suggested instead a reconsideration of the total critique of bourgeois civilization in a revolutionary mode. The utopian-revolutionary dialectic of seizing upon selective values and practices of the precapitalist past while struggling for a socialist future is an element common across the long arc of Mariátegui's writings, and increasingly alien to the extractivist ideology of figures such as Álvaro García Linera. Quispe's resurrection of the indigenous casualties of history and his agency-centered narrative of insurrectional legacies represent a sort of reincarnation of Mariátegui's spirit and a celebration of heroic forms of transitional resistance. All of this resonates powerfully in the contemporary reality of Bolivia, where left–indigenous movements increasingly come into confrontation with the compensatory state and the extractive model of accumulation, even as Evo Morales has consolidated electoral hegemony through his third successful run for the presidency in October 2014. The insights of Romantic Marxism, if they are to contribute to a new research agenda in the study of contemporary conflict in the Andes, are best mediated through the specifically Mariáteguist lenses of colonialism and imperialism, uneven and combined development,

---

102 Felipe Quispe, "Las luchas de los *ayllus* kataristas hoy," in *Movimiento indígena en América Latina: resistencia y proyecto alternativo*, eds. Fabiola Escárzaga and Raquel Gutiérrez (Puebla: Universidad Autónoma de Puebla, 2005), 71–75.

racialized capitalism, and indigenous liberation. Far from an abstract or academic debate alien to the concrete struggles of subaltern actors on the ground in the Andes, the discussion of the life and activism of Felipe Quispe has demonstrated the living character of an anticolonial, Romantic Marxism in the region, whose logic necessarily confronts the competing logics of state, capital, and imperialism with an escalating intensity.

FIVE

Chile's New Left:
More Than a Student Movement

"Education is the mother of all battles, and we will win or lose our battle for the future in the educational sector."

Sebastián Piñera[1]

"This is not a students' movement or a workers' movement. It is a movement of students and workers."

Staughton Lynd[2]

The contours of a new left began to take shape in Chile in 2011. An explosive student rebellion linked arms with workers, bringing the far-right Chilean president Sebastián Piñera (2010–2014) every day into further disrepute. The neoliberal development model and the state that had enforced it felt threatened from below for the first time in decades. The subterranean rumblings of the

---

1 John Paul Rathbone and Jude Webber, "FT Interview: Sebastián Piñera," *Financial Times*, October 4, 2011.
2 Staughton Lynd, "Students and Workers in the Transition to Socialism: The Singer Model," *Monthly Review* 54, no. 10 (March 2003): 32–42.

student eruption began in May. They then evolved—albeit through peaks and valleys—into the roar of late 2011. The government said nothing is free, and that someone has to pay for the education system. The students said nationalize the copper industry and tax the rich, and we'll have funds for free, quality education and much else besides.[3]

By the end of August 2011, Piñera's approval ratings had reached a seventeen-month personal nadir of 26 percent, also a record low for any president since the end of the dictatorship in 1990.[4] This singular achievement was accomplished in the face of nearly uniform condemnation and defamation of the student movement and its allies by the Chilean mainstream media. By early October, Piñera's approval rating had plunged still further, to 22 percent, apparently the lowest recorded in Chilean history.[5]

A billionaire business mogul and leader of the Alliance for Chile coalition, Piñera assumed office in mid-January 2010 after having won the second round of elections with 52 percent of the popular vote. Shortly thereafter he manufactured an image as savior of the nation when, in February 2010, an earthquake of an astonishing 8.8 magnitude on the Richter scale struck the long, threadlike country that runs along the Pacific coastline of the Southern Cone and stretches eastward and upward into the Andes. It seemed as though even the most obscure of government-funded reconstruction efforts in subsequent weeks and months were accompanied by the immaculate portraiture or cultivated oratory of the media-savvy president.

This guardian mantle was requisitioned a second time by Piñera in September and October the same year, although now with millions of captivated eyes locked on developments in Chile. Thirty-three miners were trapped for more than two months 2,300 feet underground near the northern city of Copiapó until their rescue on October 13, for which Piñera claimed full credit. "President Sebastián Piñera," reported the *New York Times*, "presid[ed] over each rescue as a kind of master of ceremonies," as "the months of waiting boiled over every time the rescue capsule popped out of the ground."[6] He had

---

3 Francisco Herreros, "Recursos para financiar una educación pública, gratuita y de calidad," *Rebelión*, October 5, 2011; *Punto Final*, "¿Hasta cuándo abusan de la paciencia nuestra?" September 16–29, 2011.

4 Enrique Gutiérrez, " 'Preocupante', la condición de 5 estudiantes en ayuno: medicos," *La Jornada*, August 23, 2011.

5 Jonathan Franklin, "Camila Vallejo—Latin America's 23-Year-Old New Revolutionary Folk Hero," *Guardian*, October 8, 2011.

6 Alexei Barrionuevo and Simon Romero, "Freed Miners in Chile Tell of Ordeals and Plot New Lives," *New York Times*, October 13, 2010.

reached the pinnacle of his political career, with 63 percent approval ratings amongst the populace.

The pageantry of crisis, however, could not indefinitely hold at bay the underlying fissures in Chilean society. By mid-2011, Piñera's benevolent mask had been definitively torn off. The streets of Santiago and other cities began to witness the brutality of armed police repeatedly smashing peaceful student and worker demonstrations.

On October 6, 2011, for example, police assaulted a student march in the Chilean capital with tear gas and water cannons, detaining at least 130 protesters and possibly 250. Dozens of civilians were injured, including widely revered student leaders of the moment, such as Camila Vallejo, and various journalists and photojournalists. One expression of the indiscriminate repression meted out on that day was the injury of CNN reporter Nicolás Orarzún at the hands of state agents. Other journalists were summarily arrested. Meanwhile, defensive stands by protesters against the police reportedly left wounded twenty-five *carabineros*, as members of the police force—despised and feared in roughly equal measure—are known in Chile.[7]

A late August editorial that year in the left-wing Mexican daily *La Jornada* correctly suggested that what was happening in Chile amounted to much more than a student movement. The students were the spark that ignited a much more profound tinderbox of discontent, the complexities of which were not yet fully known at the time.

The demand for free and quality education at all levels remained a central focus of struggle. But the conflict between the popular classes and the state deepened and extended, first from high school and university students to teachers and university professors, and then outward to public sector workers, bus drivers, the Mapuche indigenous liberation struggle, barrio organizations in the urban shantytowns, women's groups, environmentalists, and diffuse layers of the working class and popular sectors of society.

Whereas Piñera wallowed in the paltry backing of roughly a quarter of the population, 80 percent of Chileans supported the students in the streets.[8] "We are

---

7 Enrique Gutiérrez, "Reprime el gobierno de Sebastián Piñera protesta de los estudiantes," *La Jornada*, October 7, 2011; Jonathan Franklin, "Camila Vallejo." Police repression also led to one death in the course of this struggle. Manuel Gutiérrez Reinoso, a sixteen-year-old youngster, was pushing his disabled brother in a wheelchair on August 25, the second day of a national strike and protest called by the Unified Workers Central (CUT), when, according to various witnesses, he was shot and killed by the police. See "Editorial: Otro crimen de Carabineros," *Punto Final*, September 2–15, 2011.

8 "Chile: movimiento más que estudiantil," *La Jornada*, August 24, 2011.

an auxiliary social movement to the principal social force of the workers," said Alfredo Vielma, a seventeen-year-old student activist, "that is to say, our parents."[9]

As the student movement gathered momentum it accumulated forces around it, and with those new forces the movement acquired new causes, new demands, and new sources for reflection on how different social sectors were in various ways pitted against a common enemy, expressed ultimately in the neoliberal state, established decades earlier during the dictatorship but never dismantled under electoral democracy.

On August 4, 2011, for example, thousands converged on the streets of Santiago banging pots and pans, "a form of protest last heard under the dictatorship of General Pinochet. This time the *cacerolazos*, as they are called, are being staged in the name of educational Utopia," reported the *Economist*, with near-audible disdain.[10] Another motivation, or even antidictatorial impulse, for August 4 was the ban on marches the government had introduced in an ill-conceived attempt to quell an earlier wave of demonstrations.

On August 21, 2011, 500,000 people marched through Santiago and occupied Parque O'Higgins in a day of protest for public education. At the end of August, the United Workers' Central (CUT)—weakened organizationally by the informalization of the world of work and politically by its historic association with the Concertación—orchestrated a two-day national strike, something it had not even attempted in two decades. On August 25, 400,000 marched again for free and quality access to education at all levels, but on this day new discourses and ideas began circulating, and additional banners were raised.[11]

The people now wanted to put an end to the system of private pensions, to have free and high-quality access to public health care, and a new labor code to protect workers' most basic rights. They demanded an end to precarious jobs and better salaries for workers. They figured they could finance the bulk of these aims quite easily by raising business taxes and nationalizing the copper mines.

They were fighting against the neoliberal state, the characteristics of which had been institutionalized through a constitution written and conceived under the dictatorial regime in the 1980s. Thus arose a novel, overarching proclamation—that the people demand a participatory Constituent Assembly to remake the Chilean state, society, and economy in the interests

---

9 "La educación es un derecho social," *Punto Final*, July 22–August 4, 2011.

10 "We Want to Change the World: A Trial of Strength between the Students and the Government," *Economist*, August 13, 2011.

11 Paul Walder, "¿Quién escuchará la voz del pueblo?" *Punto Final*, no. 741, September 2–15, 2011.

of the poor, working classes, and oppressed groups, a constitution embedded in social justice.

The Constituent Assembly demand—echoing those in Venezuela and Bolivia in the 2000s—emerged out of both the aggregated interests of the different sections of society's marginalized and oppressed that had been brought together through association in the streets, but also through an impulse to generalize, on a wider scale, the democracy that such an association implied—a new form of doing politics, where the grassroots are present in the streets, and where assemblist forms of democracy show the popular classes their potential social power.

Marx identified this process as "revolutionary practice." In their struggle to satisfy needs, the rank and file of the Chilean student youth and working classes increasingly recognized their common interests and became more conscious of their social power; through their self-activity they began to see themselves as subjects capable of altering the structures of Chilean society as well as changing themselves in the process through self-organization and self-activity from below.[12]

Revolutionary practice need not be a dull affair. Indeed, it almost requires a collective millenarian drive to overcome the daily alienation of capitalist society. A central component of the student rebellions under Piñera was the festivity of "tactical creativity," as one of the better analyses of the process suggests.[13] In addition to occupations, student walkouts, hunger strikes, marches, protests, workers' actions, and clashes with the security apparatuses of the state, the movement witnessed danceathons, kissing contests—*con pasión por la educación*—and an unadulterated embrace of the carnivalesque, as tens of thousands jubilantly coalesced in the thoroughfares and avenues of power in order to unveil its bankrupt hypocrisy.

"Before we recover the education system we want we have to build a participatory, integrative, and equitable political model" of organizing, Vielma argues, revealing the sort of intensified politicization of Chilean youth that was occurring on a wide scale. "Chile can be a more just society and this will come about through the installation of direct forms of democracy. The people have to decide for themselves what they are going to do with their governments and natural resources."

---

12 For a relevant discussion of Marx's conceptualization of "revolutionary practice," see Michael Lebowitz, *Build It Now! Twenty-First Century Socialism* (New York: Monthly Review Press, 2006), 19–20; and David McNally, *Another World Is Possible: Globalization and Anti-Capitalism*, 2nd ed. (Winnipeg: Arbeiter Ring Press), 375.

13 Manuel Larrabure and Carlos Torchia, "'Our Future is Not for Sale': The Chilean Student Movement Against Neoliberalism," *The Bullet*, no. 542, September 6, 2011.

Vielma went on to point out that the people in the streets were "demanding the recovery of education as a social right, an integral, pluricultural, anti-classist, anti-racist education. All schools must return to the hands of the state which has reneged on its role of subsidizing and guaranteeing a good, free education for all.... So long as we are not guaranteed a free, high-quality education we will not stop coming out in these mobilizations."[14]

Origins and Dynamics of the Chilean Moment

To locate precisely the neoliberalization of the education system at the root of today's student upsurge in Chile, one necessarily returns to the era of dictatorship. In 1980, the Pinochet regime introduced a decree that established a dualized public-private education system in the country, the same system that persists in essence to this day.

On an ideological and organizational level, teachers deemed sympathetic to Allende's legacy were purged from their jobs, while police surveillance, informant networks, and changes in the curriculum and content of textbooks reproduced those purges on a daily basis. Arts and humanities were punished as passé subjects, while those areas of inquiry functional to the productive structures of the new free-market Chile were duly rewarded.[15]

On a structural level, the responsibility for administering schools was decentralized to the scale of municipal governments. The state, adhering closely to the neoclassical fanaticism of University of Chicago economist Milton Friedman, would continue funding schools but only indirectly through a voucher system. Vouchers were provided to families such that parents would then select schools for their children to attend. Schools were put in a position whereby their financing depended directly on the number of students they attracted, "imparting a strict competition ethic into the education system."[16] Fully privatized schools were also allowed to compete in this overall scenario.

The disparities of access to education were even starker at the university level after the General Law of Universities was introduced in 1981. This legislation established a policy of privatization, and in its wake "resources destined for higher education underwent a 40 percent reduction between 1981 and 1990,"

14 "La educación es un derecho social."
15 Marcus Taylor, *From Pinochet to the 'Third Way': Neoliberalism and Social Transformation in Chile* (London: Pluto Press, 2006), 89.
16 Ibid., 90. "Social service decentralisation," Taylor further explains, had the added benefit of "disarticulat[ing] the national power of unions involved in the provision of services" (88).

while "all pretences of a free university system" were abandoned and the promise of "small private higher education institutions" offered instead. As sociologist Marcus Taylor notes, "such reforms transformed higher education into an entity of the capitalist marketplace, promoted entrepreneurial profit-minded investment and remodelled the content of post-secondary education to consolidate the reorganized productive structures of the economy."[17]

Two decades of Concertación administrations consolidated this model, while Piñera attempted to deepen and extend it through increases in privatization at the elementary and secondary school levels. The consequence has been that a tiny layer of the Chilean population now sends their children to elementary and secondary schools where there are exorbitant fees to attend.

Approximately 70 percent of students in such schools come from families with an average income of $US 2,700 per month, compared to an average family income of $US 330 for more than 80 percent of students attending fully subsidized municipal schools. The quality of education received in these different institutions is reflected in the fact that 93 percent of students attending municipal high schools fail to achieve sufficiently high grades in general, or on scores of standardized entrance tests, to enter traditional universities, and "only 10–20 percent of young Chileans belonging to the poorest 40 percent economic strata are currently enrolled in post-secondary education."[18] Of the meager 4.2 percent of GDP the state spends on education, only 0.7 percent is directed to the university level.[19]

The Rot of Neoliberalism-Lite

Just as one's tongue is a good indicator of general body health, the brokenness of the Chilean education system is an expressive symptom, a visible cue, of a wider, endemic disease of neoliberal capitalism in the country. There are precise limits to the metaphor, however, because sections of Chile's body politic were doing just fine, as others suffered painfully. Growth of GDP averaged 4.4 percent in Chile during the 2002 and 2008 copper commodities boom. That dipped to -1.7 percent in the recession of 2009, as the delayed reverberations of the global crisis in the core countries rippled through the southwestern edges

---

17 Ibid., 92.
18 Larrabure and Torchia, "'Our Future Is Not for Sale.'"
19 Jude Webber, "Education: Student Protests Tap into Wider Desire for Social Equality," *Financial Times*, October 4, 2011.

of Latin America. But growth picked up to 5.8 percent in 2010 and 2011.[20]

In gross terms, Chile's a relatively rich country. It is a member, for example, of that club of privileged societies known as the Organization for Economic Cooperation and Development (OECD). The top 10 percent of income earners enjoy average incomes on a par with Norway. But the masses below lead a much different life, with the lowest 10 percent living on an average income equivalent to the Ivory Coast.[21] The country is the most unequal of any in the OECD and suffers the highest rate of poverty (18.9 percent) in that group—an assortment of countries, it should be noted, which in general does not share an illustrious record on equality or care for the poor. Chile is also the fifth most unequal in Latin America and the Caribbean, the region of the world that scores worst on equality measures.[22]

Table 1, reflecting the distribution of national income between the five quintiles of Chilean society during the lead up to the student protests, provides us a further window into these dynamics—or, better, stasis—between 2000 and 2009. The poorest 20 percent of the population received a paltry 3.4 percent of national income in 2000, and this moved less than 1 percent upward by 2009, despite the social democratic proclamations issued forth regularly by Concertación governments over this period. Similar experiences were endured by the second and third quintiles, who each budged forward only 1 percent in their share. The fourth quintile also moved 1 percent forward, while the richest 20 percent of society lost a mere 3.6 percent of national income.

Table 1. Chilean Distribution of National Income

Year	1 Quintile Poorest	2 Quintile	3 Quintile	4 Quintile	5 Quintile Richest
2000	3.4	6.9	10.7	17.6	61.5
2009	4.2	7.9	11.7	18.4	57.9

Source: Derived from CEPAL, *Anuario estadístico de América Latina y el Caribe, 2010* (Santiago: CEPAL, 2011), 67.

Pause and reflect for a moment. In Chile, a country held up as a model for development in the Global South, despite years of relatively high growth—driven in large part by high copper prices—the richest 20 percent of society

20 ECLAC, *Preliminary Overview*, 59; EIU, *Chile: Country Report* (London: Economist Intelligence Unit, April 2011), 3.

21 Larrabure and Torchia, "'Our Future Is Not for Sale.'"

22 "Chile, el reino de la desigualdad," *Punto Final*, July 22–August 4, 2011.

continued to receive a whopping 58 percent of the nation's income, compared to 4 percent for the bottom 20 percent. These figures, moreover, are too generous, masking as they do the even more profound discrepancies that would appear if we had comparable figures for wealth (assets), rather than merely income. It is within this all-embracing context that the battle over education must be positioned.

Movement from Nowhere?

Just as the seeming spontaneity of the Arab Spring of 2011 hid a much longer and richer process of preceding struggles and organizational advances of the region's labor and social movements, the Chilean outbreak did not suddenly materialize from nothing. Between the end of April and mid-June 2006, radical high-school student protests against the deterioration of public education erupted in several cities. These actions by *los Pingüinos*—or penguins, as the students are known, because of their black-and-white uniforms—were violently repressed by police, stoking further radicalization and the wider participation of education workers and working-class parents throughout different parts of the country. These were the biggest demonstrations in the country since the popular struggles for democracy in the Pinochet era and represent the most immediate precursor to the 2011 revolts.[23]

The student and worker agitation against the privatization of education was indicative of a spreading disgust with many of the basic continuities in Chile's social structure and political economy between the time of Pinochet and Michelle Bachelet, head of the Socialist Party, and the last president of the long reign of Concertación. These demonstrations were followed in August and September of the same year by a successful miners' strike at Escondida, the world's largest copper mine, situated in the Atacama desert of Chile's far north. The battles in the mining zones then found their echo in May 2007 in the forest industry of the south, where a militant worker in a timber strike was shot dead after he tried to drive a tractor through a police barricade, stimulating wider community support for the forestry workers and their martyr. Also in 2007, subcontracted garbage workers engaged in a successful strike in Santiago. It is worth noting that these movements were illegal, and represented the first important strikes in industrial sectors where the workforce has been

---

23 Orlando Sepúlveda, "Chilean Students Launch Mass Protests," *International Socialist Review*, issue 49 (September–October 2006).

dispersed and fragmented through waves of subcontracting. The atomized, overworked, underpaid, and precarious labor force in these sectors is characteristic of the world of work more generally in Chile in the current period.[24]

"After seventeen years of a neostructuralist-inspired Concertación coalition," Fernando Ignacio Leiva suggests, "the case of Chile already foretells some of these nodal points around which such contradictions will emerge."[25] Leiva was referring to the fractures of the neoliberalism-lite practiced by center-left governments throughout the region. He argues that new articulations of an autonomous civil society will emerge as an antithesis to "an institutionalised and hegemonic form of participation that subordinate[s] civil society and the soc—-emotional component of social relationships to the requirements of globalisation and the capitalist profit rate." Leiva perceives in this expansion of social movement struggle the strengthening capacities of the popular classes for "building on their everyday sociability and historical memory to defend their rights and challenge capital and the state or the destruction of their social fabric, grassroots dynamics, and leaderships through state-designed and NGO-enforced social programmes and civil society-state alliances."[26]

For Leiva, the contradictions of the development model in Chile and elsewhere will continue to engender "struggles over whether the objectives of strengthening social solidarity should be to increase the power of the dispossessed and exploited or to provide an individualised and symbolic more than material sense of security so that citizens do not rebel against a daily existence made more precarious by the expansion of capitalism."[27] The activities in 2006 and 2007, of the students, timber workers, copper miners, and garbage collectors were meaningful signals of initial steps toward rebuilding rebellion against the expansion of capitalism. "Ultimately," Leiva contends, "the question is what purposes are being served by increasing coordination among the state, markets, and existing networks," central to the Concertación project. "Is it to raise profits and the self-expansion of capital, or is it to increase the satisfaction of human needs and human dignity?"[28]

In 2009, the incipient extraparliamentary struggles of the mid-2000s began to take a back seat to the electoral contest scheduled for the end of that year.

---

24 Manuel Riesco, "Is Pinochet Dead?" *New Left Review* 2, no. 45 (September–October 2007): 7–8.
25 Fernando Ignacio Leiva, *Latin American Neostructuralism: The Contradictions of Post-Neoliberal Development* (Minneapolis: University of Minnesota Press, 2008), 187.
26 Ibid.
27 Ibid.
28 Ibid.

However, in 2010, following the elections, cracks reopened on several fronts. One of the most crucial areas of growing combativeness in recent years has been the Mapuche indigenous struggle in Chile's southern regions. In the early months of 2010, there were several land occupations carried out by La Alianza Territorial Mapuche (Mapuche Territorial Alliance, ATM), and in mid-July thirty-two Mapuche political prisoners began what became an eighty-two-day hunger strike that galvanized social struggle and solidarity across different sections of Chilean popular society and won considerable levels of attention and support internationally.[29] Meanwhile, on the island of Pascua, the Rapa Nui indigenous peoples executed a series of land takeovers and occupations of public and private buildings in defense of their historic rights to the territory and claims for self-determination. In April 2010, they took over the government plaza on the island, and over the month of July alone carried out thirty-five different land squats.[30]

2010 also witnessed the spread and intensification of environmental battles over thermoelectric, hydroelectric, and mining developments throughout various parts of the country. As far as workers' struggles are concerned, four thousand subcontracted miners went on strike and set up road blockades around a private mine, Doña Inés de Collahuasi, owned by Swiss and South African multinationals. The workers demanded better working conditions and better pay. The strike and blockades were broken up after a few days, and eighty of the subcontracted workers involved in the protests were fired. However, when issues were still unresolved months later, a thirty-three-day strike was conducted in November. Because the multinationals were losing $US 9 million a day due to the work stoppage, they eventually were forced to partially cave in and acquiesce to a modest raise and other benefits for workers.

The same year also saw important strikes by bus drivers, postal workers, and dockworkers. Meanwhile, in another sector of the labor market, a novel workers' action unfolded. In the wake of the earthquake, unemployed, mainly female workers were provided with twelve thousand temporary, low-paying jobs to carry out reconstruction efforts funded by the government. When all but three thousand of these limited contracts came to an end, thirty-three women again facing the threat of unemployment occupied the Chiflón del Diablo mine and refused to come out until jobs were guaranteed. The action generated widespread public support, and a number of workers in the women's region won full-time jobs as a result in the municipality.

---

29 Mónica Iglesias Vázquez, "Chile 2010: *In Crescendo*. Informe de coyuntura sobre conflicto social," *OSAL*, no. 29 (May 2011): 46–50.
30 Ibid., 50–52.

Perhaps most important, though, were a series of strikes carried out by public sector workers over the course of 2010. It would be these strikes that most closely corresponded to the demands coming from student activists, and allowed the basis for the growing worker-student alliances that developed over the first half of 2011.[31] While the latest return of the high school penguins and university students would not begin in a massive way until May 2011, there were stirrings and minor episodes throughout 2010 that foreshadowed what was to come. In early April 2010, high school students took to the streets to protest a rise in bus fares, putting them in line with bus drivers who had struck earlier for unpaid back pay among other issues. By the end of April, university students had joined the fray.

On July 26, high school students hit the capital with a show of significant force once again, this time in coordination with a public sector strike. On November 10, they launched large mobilizations against the entire privatizing agenda of Piñera in the education system. High school students also organized various solidarity demonstrations with other popular sectors that were coming into conflict with the state, not least the thirty-five Mapuche prisoners on hunger strike. University students joined many of these struggles over 2010 and became a leading sector of revolt in 2011, as we have seen. All of this is simply to note that a relatively long period of gestation, of slow building and movement rearticulation, was the necessary backdrop for the spectacular events witnessed in 2011.

The Social and the Political

In his brilliant survey of the Chilean left since the 1990s, Fernando Ignacio Leiva identifies a panoply of developments and complexities up to the present.[32] In one camp, the Socialist Party (PS), Party for Democracy (PPD), and Radical Party (PRSD) have, in joining the Concertación coalition, completely submitted to the interests of transnational capital.

In another, a traditional left, composed of the Communist Party (PC), the Christian Left (IC), the Humanist Party (PH), and a split from the PS, the Allendista Socialists, is to be found. This group formed an electoral alliance in the 2009 elections called Juntos Podemos Mas-Frente Amplio. This left is debilitated by its inability to respond to the changing sociopolitical and class

---

31 Ibid., 56–61.
32 Fernando Ignacio Leiva, "The Chilean Left After 1990: An *Izquierda Permitida* Championing Transnational Capital, a *Historical Left* Ensnared in the Past, a *New Radical Left* in Gestation," in *The New Latin American Left: Cracks in the Empire*, eds. Jeffery R. Webber and Barry Carr (Lanham, MD: Rowman and Littlefield, 2013).

conditions of Chilean society in order to build a social base, or to overcome its top-down organizational culture and fastidious adhesion to electoral politics. An ossified rigidity predominates.

A third eclectic melange of the SurDa Movement, the Social and Democratic Force (FSD), Generation 80, and various small anticapitalist groupings (the most important being the Movement of Peoples and Workers (MPT), represents an incipient radical left politics. These "formations have sought to construct new forms of representation based on bottom-up organizing, social mobilization and autonomy from political parties and the state."[33] The SurDa movement, which operates with other groupings in a broadly autonomist-Marxist current, has been particularly successful at winning leaderships in various university student federations, and their influence can be seen in the politics unfolding in the streets.

Finally, a multifarious array of issue-specific, local antipoverty, and antidiscrimination organizations, environmental assemblies against toxic dumping and other eco-depravities in poor neighborhoods, and community health and youth cultural groups, has grown up at the barrio level in impoverished communities, taking on initiatives in the spirit of "solidarity, collective action, territorial organizing, and efforts to preserve the historical memory of past popular struggles."[34] Leiva calls this the social left, fighting to sustain collective memories of struggle against an all-pervasive mall culture and consumerism, weave a microfabric of resistance in marginalized zones, and "keep the utopian dream of social justice through self-reliant collective action alive, reaffirming the construction of a popular identity and dignity in the midst of vastly transformed society."[35]

If we take this portrait seriously, as we should, the left aligned with Concertación has clearly been delegitimated in the extreme, and offered no hope for student struggles and the wider popular movement in the making. The historical left is largely moribund, despite the fact that Camila Vallejo, the most prominent student leader of 2011, is the daughter of Communists, the niece of *miristas* (members of the Movement of the Revolutionary Left, MIR), and a member of the Communist youth. The incipient radical left currents of anticapitalist initiatives and social left seemed to be resonating most pervasively with the student-worker revolt, both in terms of ideological development and organizational tactics and strategy.

The strengths of this break with the Concertación and the ossified left, as

---

33 Ibid.
34 Ibid.
35 Ibid.

we have shown, are many. The biggest social movement against neoliberalism in Chilean history shook the pillars of the Piñera regime. Assemblist forms of democracy in the streets revealed to the popular classes and oppressed their potential social power, while their political consciousness made leaps forward with every development in the movement. Women and youth were front and center, from the grassroots to the highest echelons of the movement. The Mapuche and other indigenous liberation struggles, as well as the ecological component of the crisis of capitalism, were a part of the everyday awareness of activists in the movement. The carnivalesque character of the mass actions, the justice of their demands, and the audacity of the youth won over huge segments of the Chilean population to their cause.

The movement was democratic and participatory while also being quite disciplined and organized. There are good reasons to believe that many of the small breakaway acts of property violence—sensationalized at length in the local media—were instigated by agents provocateurs, undercover state forces seeking to provide a pretext for police violence, to undermine the legitimacy of the movement in the eyes of the wider public, and to generate internal fissures within the student and other popular organizations.[36]

It would be remiss, however, to avoid discussing the potential limits of the autonomist political expressions that dominated the student uprising. "The autonomists," writes Argentine political economist Claudio Katz, "eschew political affiliation and ideological definition. They share feelings, attitudes, and projects, but they do not support a common doctrine. They broadcast a moral critique of capitalism from an anti-authoritarian perspective, rejecting

---

36 Larrabure and Torchia, "'Our Future Is Not for Sale,'" muse on some of these possibilities, referencing statements from Camila Vallejo: "Another victory for the student movement was the growing support from broad sectors of the population. Parents, teachers,
and copper miners openly expressed their support, recognizing that all their grievances
against the neoliberal regime were being expressed in the student strike. However, the
government responded quickly by threatening to declare an early winter break to the
school year, and even its possible cancellation. In addition, the corporate media began
its demonization campaign against the students, using isolated incidents of violence
conducted by 'los encapuchados' (the 'black bloc') to delegitimize the whole movement.
   "Responding to these attacks, Camila Vallejo asserted that, although these violent
provocateurs do not represent the collectively agreed tactics of the student movement,
their actions are driven by their marginalization from the system and their rage should
be understood as a reaction to their future-less position at the bottom of the neoliberal ladder. At the same time, she added, government infiltration within some of these
groups cannot be ruled out. Indeed, adding to the suspicion, about one hundred 'encapuchados' were found attempting to torch the central offices of the National Teachers
Union, a staunch ally of the student movement."

all forms of leadership and state power. They use a libertarian language and defend *autoorganización* [self-organization], emphasizing values of solidarity and community. They question participation in mainstream institutions and encourage *autogestión* [self-management] in the economic sphere."[37]

Perhaps the most widely celebrated thinker to have expressed the ideas of the new Latin American autonomism is John Holloway, particularly in his book *Change the World without Taking Power*.[38] His thesis, distilled to its barest elements, is as follows: it may or may not be possible to change the world without taking power (we cannot know for sure); within this context of uncertainty, the best way to imagine revolutionary change is to seek the dissolution of power rather than the conquest of power; and it is particularly important to avoid a strategy focused on the conquest of *state* power, which was ruinous for the revolutionary left in the twentieth century. Many have pointed out important flaws in Holloway's perspective: oversimplification of a very complex history of competing theoretical and strategic debates in the international history of the workers' movement; too little account taken of a vast critical literature within the Marxist tradition on the state; lack of serious theoretical and analytical treatment of history and the role of the revolutionary left therein; mystification of the Zapatista experience in Mexico through an analysis rooted in discourse rather than the real contradictions of the political situation on the ground; and abandonment of the terrain of politics and strategic orientation, a vacuum that will inevitably be filled by capitalist or procapitalist forces if left empty.[39]

The ideas that Holloway has sought to clarify need to be taken seriously, and they continue to resonate in particular settings within the Latin American left, particularly as the contradictions of the electoral center-left become dramatized in the context of the global slump reaching Latin America in a strong way since 2012. Today, variations on the themes Holloway has taken up in the past are making themselves visible once again in the streets of Chile. Much of this, as noted, is to be welcomed and celebrated, but there are certain strategic limits to consider.

Particularly evident is the potential problem of generalizing the entirely sound critique of the Concertación and the traditional parties of the left, such as the PC, into a principled position against strategizing explicitly and openly around the necessary connections between the social and the political.

---

37 Claudio Katz, "Problems of Autonomism: Strategies for the Latin American Left," *International Socialist Review*, issue 44 (November–December 2005).

38 John Holloway, *Change the World without Taking Power* (London: Pluto Press, 2005).

39 Daniel Bensaïd, "On a Recent Book by John Holloway," in *Change the World without Taking Power?... or ... Take Power to Change the World?*, ed. IIRE (Amsterdam: International Institute for Research and Education, 2005).

◊

On October 1, 2011, at the Europe against Austerity gathering in London, I was privileged to hear Olivier Besancenot, the best-known spokesperson of the New Anti-Capitalist Party (NPA) in France, suggest the following. He was speaking of Europe, of course, but there is a universal element to his intervention:

> What type of movements and what type of alternative? We can no longer debate in the way we used to debate. Previously it was a thing we had big arguments about. Some people thought that it was only workers' mobilisations and nothing else which would allow us to establish a political alternative and there were others who thought that we had to recreate a credible political alternative in order to encourage workers mobilisations. Today there is a complementary, dialectical relationship which obliges us to try to create a synthesis between the left in the social movements and the political left in each of our countries. This needs a complementary relationship in which one strengthens the other, without a hierarchical relationship between them and which gives us both political responsibilities and responsibilities in the movements.[40]

"Movements and parties," writes Katz in an intervention in ongoing Latin American left debates, "constitute two modes of contemporary popular organization. Both are essential to the development of socialist convictions. They reinforce confidence in self-organization, and they develop the norms for the future exercise of people's power. Movements sustain the immediate social struggle, and parties fuel a more fully developed political activity. Both are necessary for facilitating direct action and electoral participation. But this complementarity is frequently questioned by exclusivist advocates of movement or party. Some movement-oriented theorists—who subscribe to autonomist points of view— believe that party organization is obsolete, useless, and pernicious."[41]

The mass Chilean social movement inevitably ran up against these questions again, particularly as elections approached and Piñera's period in office drew to a close. Sustaining and renewing the grassroots dynamism and self-activity of the protests of 2011 in lasting organizational forms, with a strategic political vision that prevented co-optation by the bourgeois state and fought new articulations of the old Concertación coalition, would be among the most pressing challenges they faced.

---

40 Fred Laplat and Olivier Besancenot, "Europe Against Austerity Conference Report," *International Viewpoint*, issue 441 (October 2011).
41 Claudio Katz, "Socialist Strategies in Latin America," *Monthly Review* 59, no. 4 (September 2007).

Chile's Passive Revolution?

The 2011–2012 student-worker revolts mark a before-and-after point in contemporary Chilean history. "Post-2011 society is no longer the same as that of 2010," sociologist Franck Gaudichaud observes, "because of the massive character of the process and the themes it was able to introduce into the common sense of society." Nonetheless, he continues, "the 'model' continues, and it continues to have many material and subjective resources at its disposition."[42]

Change in continuity captures the character of the first and second round of presidential and parliamentary Chilean elections in November and December of 2013, the parameters of which were in part determined by the strength of renewed popular militancy in society. Michelle Bachelet, leader of the PS and candidate for the Nueva Mayoría (New Majority, NM) coalition—effectively a rebranded Concertación, expanded to incorporate the Partido Comunista de Chile (Chilean Communist Party, PCC)—handily defeated the center-right's candidate, Evelyn Matthei. Bachelet captured 62 percent of the vote to Matthei's 38 percent. This was a huge margin of victory but soured for Bachelet by the fact that only 42 percent, or 5.7 million of the 13.5 million strong electorate, voted.[43]

The expansive abstention is indicative of contradictory elements of the current Chilean moment. "Cutting both ways," writes sociologist René Rojas, "such middling participation levels reflect the large chunks of Chilean society defeated by neoliberal exclusion as well as newly activated layers looking for options beyond current partisan offerings."[44] Bachelet's victory was assisted by the media's portrayal of her as a charismatic *mariana* figure, a leader somehow above all of the internal failings of the Concertación, despite her long-term role in the coalition and former term as president. She was portrayed as the "mother" of the nation, smiling, protective, and understanding.[45]

Equally important to the NM's solid victory was the relative internal dissolution of the right. The NM presented itself as a renewed coalition, with a new name, and now embracing PCC alongside Christian Democrats. The PCC had long been the principal force in the left outside the Concertación coalition. In the NM government the PCC boasts six members of parliament,

42 Franck Gaudichaud, *Las fisuras del neoliberalismo Maduro chileno: Trabajo, "democracia protegida" y conflict de clases* (Buenos Aires: CLACSO, 2015), 35. See also Carlos E. Ruiz Encina, *Conflicto social en el "neoliberalismo avanzado": Análisis de clase de la revuelta estudiantil* (Buenos Aires: CLACSO, 2013).
43 *Economist*, "Bachelet by a Mile: Chile's Presidential Election," December 16, 2013.
44 René Rojas, "Insurgency and Orthodoxy," *Jacobin*, April 2, 2015.
45 Gaudichaud, *Las fisuras del neoliberalismo*, 36.

one minister, and various members in prestigious state positions. Most importantly, of course, Vallejo was elected on their ticket in the Santiago district of Florida, winning her seat with 40 percent of the vote. Karol Cariola, secretary general of the PCC Youth and also a major student leader in the 2011–2012 rebellions, won a seat for the PCC.

Alongside these student spokespeople, two other high-profile student activists were elected to Congress: the nominally independent Giorgio Jackson of Revolución Democrática (Democratic Revolution, RD) won a seat with the support of the NM coalition, and Gabriel Boric, Vallejo's more militant and independent successor as president of the Confederation of Chilean Students, won a seat for Izquierda Autónoma (Autonomous Left, IA).[46]

Bachelet ran on a platform of tax reform to curb the profits of the biggest corporations in Chile, electoral reform to improve the unrepresentative binomial system, educational reform (ostensibly moving toward free university education over six years), and constitutional reform, in response to the demand for a Constituent Assembly. In this sense, the NM was remarkably adept at measuring the pulse of society and selectively incorporating elements of the new common sense established by the student-worker revolts into their electoral program. The system of accumulation first established under the Pinochet dictatorship and the political mode of postauthoritarian domination forged by the Concertación were facing a dual crisis of legitimacy. In this context, significant sections of the dominant classes recognized the imperative of partial reforms in order to restore stability. At one and the same time, NM was capable of incorporating the PCC and, crucially, its leading student cadres, and signalling to capital that fundamental aspects of the economic model would not be jeopardized. The confidence that capital placed in Bachelet can be seen in the flows of campaign money directed her way in 2013.[47]

The NM did introduce a series of democratizing reforms in its first term. There was a modest corporate tax increase, although with inbuilt loopholes. It limited mega hydroelectric projects, banned genetically modified seeds, and modified water regulation in response to the environmental movement. Bachelet also introduced timid reforms to the labor code, made changes to the binomial electoral system, and increased the budget for health and education. In a culturally conservative country, the government introduced a law on civil unions that did not discriminate on the basis of sexual orientation, introduced

46 Ibid.
47 Ibid., 37.

a bill around therapeutic abortion, and created a Ministry of Culture.[48] Vallejo was also made head of the Education Commission of the lower house. The initial response of the student movement was confused. It oscillated between integration in the moments of "participation" arranged by the government and the desire to mobilize their bases in the streets, but, at least in the first year, they were unable to actually carry out street actions on anything approximating the scale of the earlier protest wave.[49]

New and clearer battle lines seemed to be drawn once again in 2015, however. That January, the government introduced its much anticipated first steps to educational reform. There seemed to be little doubt that the government would not fulfill its commitment to seriously moving toward free university education accessible to all. The student movement kicked off once again. Late May 2015 saw over 100,000 take to the streets, and 200,000 nationwide two weeks later. They were joined by "teachers, unionists from strategic industries, direct-action environmentalists, Mapuche land-resisters, and welfare rights activists."[50] In mid-June 100,000 teachers struck and marched in Santiago. Subcontracted workers from the partially privatized transit system and precariously employed miners joined the teachers. The miners went on a couple of weeks later to block roads with a series of labor demands.

More recently, Bachelet's popularity has fallen as the NM has been drawn into a variety of corruption scandals, including one involving Bachelet's son, a low-ranking Concertación bureaucrat. Although not yet organized, as in Brazil, discontent from the right, cohering around anticorruption and responsible government, is in danger of eclipsing the real social polarization highlighted by student-worker and Mapuche led antineoliberalism.[51]

Gaudichaud describes the new government as a species of *progressive neoliberalism*, or *mature social liberalism*, enacting what Gramsci called *transformismo*.[52] The role of NM in this regard is to introduce reforms within the overarching logic of continuity, navigating both economic and political pressures from the right, and channelling and defanging to the extent possible pressures from below—the shantytown debtors movement, Mapuche struggle, class-struggle unions in the copper mines and the ports, the militant environmental movement, and the student unions.[53] During the first year Bachelet's ability to play this role seemed rel-

---

48 Ibid., 38.
49 Ibid., 37.
50 René Rojas, "Challenging Chile's Neoliberal Consensus," *Jacobin*, August 26, 2015.
51 Rojas, "Challenging Chile's Neoliberal Consensus."
52 Gaudichaud, *Las fisuras del neoliberalismo*, 38.
53 Ibid., 42.

atively clear. But the global crisis is beginning to bite in Chile as well, with GDP dropping from previous highs to 1.9 percent and 2.0 percent in 2014 and 2015, with a projection of 2.1 percent in 2016.[54] The student movement has rekindled some of its earlier momentum, and there are signs of intensifying class struggle.

The Latin American Conjuncture

Comparatively little has been said about the Chilean student revolt as it relates to the wider dialectics of Latin American social and political life over the twenty-first century, particularly the region's experience with the uneven and contradictory rise (and present travails) of the left. The timing of the student revolt in Chile was in some ways out of step with regional dynamics. Latin American popular classes began blocking roads, occupying lands, leading strikes, taking over factories, amassing in capital cities, and overthrowing presidents in the early part of this century, as the steepest recession since the early 1980s struck South America between 1998 and 2002. The legitimacy of neoliberalism had been struck a fierce blow. Heads of state were overthrown in Argentina, Ecuador, and Bolivia, and self-proclaimed left governments of different hues assumed office through elections in most countries.

The new regimes rode a commodities boom between 2003 and 2011 and delivered modest gains in poverty alleviation and reductions in poverty. But their failure to break thoroughly with neoliberalism, much less capitalism, led their economies up against a wall as the fallout of the world crisis began to strike home in 2009, and in particular since 2012, as the weight of the global crisis—and especially the slowing growth of China—struck South American economies squarely in the jaw.

Class contradictions came to the fore. On the one hand, working classes, peasantries, and indigenous peoples began to struggle against the policies of governments that spoke an eloquent discourse of change but practiced a more banal continuity in their everyday political-economic programs. This has been particularly true of Bolivia and Ecuador, where the promise of transformation seemed greatest, and where the limits of that transformation have thus been most difficult to absorb. On the other hand, as we saw in chapter 2, a new right, in extraparliamentary and parliamentary forms alike, has taken advantage of economic and political crises facing left governments since 2012 in countries as diverse as Argentina, Brazil, and Venezuela.

---

54 ECLAC, *Preliminary Overview*, 58.

Chile was effectively bypassed in the first tumultuous decade of uneven left turns in South America between 1998 and the onset of the global slump. With Salvador Allende's social democratic project brought violently to an end by a military coup, the dark nights of Augusto Pinochet reigned between 1973 and 1990. Chile is one paradigmatic case of historian Greg Grandin's insight that "state- and elite-orchestrated preventive and punitive terror was key to ushering in neoliberalism in Latin America."[55] Pinochet led a bloody, militarized assault on organized working-class life, and physically annihilated political left formations. Those leftists who escaped death, prison, or exile were, at best, driven into clandestine obscurity. Meanwhile, the Chicago Boys effectively transformed Chile's economy into Milton Friedman's free-market laboratory. The country became one of the most unequal in the world, thus positioning the government for wave after wave of effusive plaudits from the International Monetary Fund, World Bank, and financial savants across the globe.

Mass struggle for democracy eventually defeated Pinochet, but the left had not yet recovered organizationally or ideologically by the time a Christian Democratic-Socialist coalition known as Concertación (the full name being Concertación de Partidos por la Democracia, Coalition of Parties for Democracy) formed the first post-Pinochet government in 1990. Residual authoritarian practices codified under the dictatorship persisted under the elected regime, and the Concertación governments perfected Pinochet's neoliberal economy over their next two decades in power. Any and all reform, the Concertación insisted, "would involve change within a fourfold conjuncture of limits: namely, the limits of the stability of the democratic transition, the limits of the sanctity of private property, the limits of fiscal prudence, and, ultimately, the limits of sustained capital accumulation."[56] As sociologist Marcus Taylor has painstakingly pointed out, "In practice, this has translated into the maintenance of neo-liberal and technocratic solutions to socio-economic issues in an attempt to sustain rapid capital accumulation in the export sectors and to avoid antagonising powerful class forces."[57] The Concertación years were characterized by relative political quiescence at the base of society as a disoriented and disarticulated working class groped in the nightfall for new tools of resistance.

But if Chile in the early 2000s was out of alignment with a new cycle of protest occurring elsewhere in Latin America, it became tightly attuned to

---

55 Grandin, *The Last Colonial Massacre*, 14.
56 Marcus Taylor, "Evolutions of the Competition State in Latin America: Power, Contestation and Neo-Liberal Populism," *Policy Studies* 31, no. 1 (2010): 51.
57 Ibid.

international rhythms of resistance since the latest crisis of capitalism began fastening its grip over world events in 2008. While remaining attentive to the globe's great geographic and political variety, Chile's student rebellion of 2011 ought to be understood in the context of the undulating tide of combat internationally, from Tunisia to Egypt, Greece, Spain, Quebec, and so many other established or emergent locales of ferment and agitation in that period. Indeed, the Chilean revolt was one important expression within this decidedly eclectic gamut of the possibilities engendered by student-worker collaboration. "After two decades of strong economic growth, social progress and enviable political stability," the *Economist* magazine lamented at the time, "Chile has suddenly started behaving in a manner more akin to some of its neighbours."[58]

According to Gaudichaud, the key challenge two years into Bachelet's second administration is to build sociopolitical fronts capable of forging a genuine counterhegemonic popular bloc. This bloc needs to bring under its wing wide layers of wage workers, precarious workers, downwardly mobile middle-class sectors, subaltern youth, and others; needs to allow for an "articulating dialectic across distinct exploitations and oppressions (culture, patriarchy, ecology) with a converging dynamic in which, ultimately, capital is the animating target."[59] Obstacles standing in the way of such a project are structural and far-reaching. The unions are fragmented and their memberships thin. Atomized popular classes are mired in personal debt. The key critical and revolutionary left political groupings are small and often trapped by their associations and identities with heroic and painful pasts. As these fragmentary lefts lose their ability to connect to the everyday concerns of the popular urban classes and the rural dispossessed, inroads are being made instead by right-wing evangelical Protestantism, preaching the theology of the market and individualistic solutions to structural and shared problems. Still, 2011–2012 marked a before-and-after point in recent Chilean history. A new generation of militants with antisystemic desires and none of the fear of their elders is unlikely to go quietly into the night.

---

58 "The Dam Breaks: Pent-Up Frustration at the Flaws of a Successful Democracy," *Economist*, August 27, 2011.
59 Gaudichaud, *Las fisuras del neoliberalismo*, 42.

SIX

Evo Morales and the Political Economy of Passive Revolution in Bolivia, 2006–2016

In the opening salvos of Latin America's uneven lurch to the left in the early twenty-first century, Bolivia distinguished itself as the region's most radical socio-political terrain. Left-indigenous movements in the countryside and cityscapes alike threw the state into crisis and brought two successive neoliberal presidents to their knees—Gonzalo Sánchez de Lozada in 2003 and Carlos Mesa in 2005.[1] Evo Morales's party, the MAS (Movimiento al Socialismo), leapt into the power vacuum opened up by this series of revolts, and there has been serious debate on the left as to how best to button down the central political dynamic of the country ever since. Morales became the first indigenous president through the December 2005 elections with 54 percent of the popular vote, assuming office in January 2006. He repeated this extraordinary electoral success in December 2009, with 64 percent, and again in October 2014, with 61 percent.

---

1 For the best accounts in English of the 2000–2005 period, see Forrest Hylton and Sinclair Thomson, *Revolutionary Horizons: Past and Present in Bolivian Politics* (London and New York: Verso Books, 2007); Raquel Gutiérrez Aguilar, *Rhythms of the Pachakuti: Indigenous Uprising and State Power in Bolivia* (Durham, NC: Duke University Press, 2014). My own interpretation of the period is offered in *Red October: Left-Indigenous Struggles in Modern Bolivia* (Chicago: Haymarket Books, 2012).

In late October 2014, when the results of the general elections were in, Morales, looking out from the balcony of the Presidential Palace, addressed throngs of supporters gathered in the Plaza Murillo below: "This victory is dedicated to Fidel Castro, to Hugo Chávez, who rests in peace, to all of the anti-imperialist and anti-capitalist presidents and governments."[2] The divided opposition had been crushed, just as they had been in 2005 and 2009. Multimillionaire businessman Samuel Doria Medina of Unidad Demócrata (Democratic Unity, UD) placed a distant second with 24 percent. Jorge "Tuto" Quiroga, who briefly assumed the presidency in 2001 after the death of one-time dictator Hugo Banzer, garnered only nine percent for his Partido Demócrata Cristiano (Christian Democratic Party, PDC). Meanwhile, the center-left ex-mayor of La Paz, Juan del Granado, received a paltry 3 percent for his Movimiento Sin Miedo (Movement without Fear, MSM) party, an erstwhile ally of the MAS. Finally, the Partido Verde de Bolivia (Green Party of Bolivia, PVB), under the indigenous leadership of Fernando Vargas, also won only 3 percent.

The territorial dominance of the incumbents was impressive, with the MAS taking a majority in eight of the country's nine departments. In the western highlands and valleys the victory for Morales was decisive: La Paz, 69 percent; Oruro, 66 percent; Potosí, 69 percent; Cochabamba, 67 percent; and Chuquisaca, 63 percent. But perhaps most importantly, the MAS also won in three of the four so-called media luna lowland departments, longtime strongholds of the conservative and racist right: Santa Cruz, 47 percent; Tarija, 52 percent; and Pando, 52 percent. Beni proved to be the only bastion of the opposition, with the UD winning there with 51 percent of the popular vote.[3]

The opposition camp suffered notable fragmentation following the 2009 general elections. In that contest, the opposition had united around Plan Progreso Para Bolivia—Convergencia Nacional (National Convergence, PPB-CN). With ex–Cochabamba mayor Manfred Reyes Villa as their presidential candidate, they captured 26 percent of the popular vote. But by the time of the municipal and departmental elections in 2010, the PPB-CN had

2 "Evo celebra con anuncio de cumplir sus megaproyectos," *Página Siete*, October 13, 2014, www.paginasiete.bo/decision2014/2014/10/13/celebra-anuncio-cumplir -megaproyectos-35143.html.

3 "El TSE señala que Evo Morales venció con 60.04% de los votos," *La Razón*, October 19, 2014, www.la-razon.com/index.php?_url=/nacional/animal_electoral/TSE-senala -Evo-Morales-vencio_0_2146585372.html; "Candidatos presidenciales cierran campaña electoral en Bolivia," *Página Siete*, October 8, 2014, www.paginasiete.bo/nacional/ 2014/10/8/candidatos-presidenciales-cierran-campana-electoral-bolivia-34560.html.

fallen apart, and various regional expressions of the right ran independently.[4] Even after gathering forces of relative unity again for the presidential contest of 2014, backing in large part Doria Medina under the UD banner, the right fell short even of its weak 2009 results.

In late January 2015, the day before his third formal inauguration as president, Morales "turned up for an indigenous ceremonial inauguration at the pre-Inca ruins of Tiwanaku wearing an outfit engraved with the sun god, worthy of an emperor," reports Andres Schipani for the *Financial Times*. "The symbolism was fitting: Bolivia's longest-serving leader has not only championed indigenous rights but also managed to enrich one of Latin America's poorest countries."[5]

With the support of more than 60 percent of the popular vote, the symbolic weight of Evo Morales's third inauguration was heavy. The ceremonial images in Tiwanaku, and later in the National Congress, conveyed the pride of place occupied, at least symbolically, by indigenous peoples, peasants, miners, and workers in the MAS government. According to Brazilian-Bolivian sociologist Fernanda Wanderley, in recent years the predominance of symbolism has often cast a shadow over any coherent evaluation of the fit between the government's practice and its ostensible ideals and political commitments: "This is the symbolic and political force of this government. The question of whether it is actually committed to these ideals constitutes another register of analysis. And while the sensation of an economic bonanza and macroeconomic stability are maintained, this question will remain secondary."[6] "Indeed," Schipani notes elsewhere, "shopping centres and restaurants have sprawled in one of Latin America's poorest countries, and consumer companies appear happy. Supermarket sales rocketed from $71m, before Morales took office, to $444m last year, while restaurant sales grew 686 percent in the same period…. As a local economist known for his policy critiques says: 'This is the apex of consumerism. Call this model however you want. But please, do not call it socialism, or anti-capitalism, have some respect for Marx, please!'"[7]

Immediately following the electoral results vice president Álvaro García

4 Fernando Mayorga, "Campo y 'campito' de la oposición: Radiografía de partidos y actores," *El desacuerdo*, no. 1, issue 7, September 1, 2013.

5 Andres Schipani, "Bolivia: Lower Gas Prices and Andean Deities," *Financial Times*, January 22, 2015.

6 Fernanda Wanderley, "La dimensión simbólica del Gobierno de Evo Morales," *Página Siete*, February 11, 2015, www.paginasiete.bo/opinion/2015/1/29/dimension-simbolica -gobierno-morales-45579.html.

7 Andres Schipani, "Wealth Redistribution and Bolivia's Boom," *Financial Times*, October 10, 2014.

Linera published a communiqué in the major newspapers, drawing the central features of what he called the "new political map": "What has happened in Bolivia in the last decade, is the emergence and consolidation of a type of logical and moral integration of society, that is, an almost unanimous manner of understanding and acting in the world, characterized by the constitutional tripod of: a plural economy with a state axis, recognition of indigenous nations with a government of social movements, and a regime of territorial autonomies."[8] The establishment of a plural economy driven by state intervention, and indigenous liberation through territorial and political recognition, are said to have ushered in a democratic and cultural revolution, displacing the corruption and injustice of the preceding orthodox neoliberal order with a government of social movements. With an average growth rate of 5 percent since 2006, impressive drops in levels of poverty and extreme poverty, massive infrastructural projects like the new cable-car linking the sprawling shantytown of El Alto with the capital city of La Paz, and social achievements in areas such as illiteracy reduction, it is not difficult to see why Morales is popular.[9]

Much social democratic commentary, relying on sympathetic interpretations of changes in the constitutional order, agrarian reform, poverty reduction, education, health, economy, and the environment under Morales,[10] has tended to emphasize the process in Bolivia as one of "empowerment and social advance, not least in material well-being," despite some recognition of "inevitable frustrations and the inability to achieve all the advances that people naturally aspire to."[11] While alongside the social democratic analysis there is now an impressive literature on the critical left pointing to different contradictions within the Bolivian process, more emphasis has typically been placed in this critical subset of the literature on the socioecological features of the current model of extractivism, rather than on its class content or sociopolitical forms.[12]

---

8 Álvaro García Linera, *El Vicepresidente describe el nuevo campo político en Bolivia* (La Paz: Vicepresidencia del Estado Plurinacional de Bolivia, 2014).

9 Drina Ergueta, "La revolución pendiente," *Página Siete*, January 27, 2015, www .paginasiete.bo/opinion/2015/1/27/revolucion-pendiente-45331.html.

10 Linda Farthing and Benjamin Kohl, *Evo's Bolivia: Continuity and Change* (Austin: University of Texas Press, 2014), 145.

11 John Crabtree and Ann Chaplin, *Bolivia: Processes of Change* (London: Zed, 2013), vii.

12 For excellent examples of socioecological critique and analysis, see Nicole Fabricant, "Good Living for Whom? Bolivia's Climate Justice Movement and the Limitations of Indigenous Cosmovisions," *Latin American and Caribbean Ethnic Studies* 8, no. 2 (2013): 159–178; Nicole Fabricant and Bret Gustafson, eds., *Remapping Bolivia: Resources, Territory, and Indigeneity in a Plurinational State* (Santa Fe, NM: School for Advanced Research, 2011); Derrick Hindery, *From Enron to Evo: Pipeline Politics, Global Environ-*

In addressing these latter, relatively neglected themes through the lens of Marxian class analytics, the present chapter makes a four-part contribution to recent debates on the evolution of the Bolivian political economy since 2006. First, it delineates García Linera's influential theoretical framing of the "creative tensions" of the process of change and suggests as an alternative Antonio Gramsci's notion of passive revolution as a more compelling interpretive framework. The next three sections then shift away from notions of politics and ideology as relatively autonomous from the process of capital accumulation to focus instead on the dialectical unity of internal relations between economics and politics. That unity is captured through an emphasis on class struggle, and specifically the structural class dynamics of passive revolution in the Bolivian case, moving through: 1) the overarching lens of what I call "extractive distribution"; 2) then on to the class contradictions inherent to the "plural economy" promoted by the MAS; next to 3) the specific transformations of the urban labor market that have accompanied the framework of extractive distribution and passive revolution during the Morales epoch (2006–2015), and that call into question the social democratic defense of such a model of capitalist accumulation. The chapter concludes with some speculative comments on the likely limits on any easy reproduction of an extractive-distribution model of accumulation—even on its own terms—within an international context of declining commodity prices.

From Creative Tension to Passive Revolution?

The prolific writings of vice president Álvaro García Linera offer one window into the complexities of the political, ideological, and economic developments that have transpired since Morales first assumed office.[13] The defining feature of the revolutionary process since 2010, according to García Linera, is the emergence of what he calls "creative tensions" or contradictions.[14] In arguably his most important book since he became vice president, *Tensiones creativas de la revolución* (Creative Tensions of the Revolution), he describes five stages of what he sees as the Bolivian revolutionary process that began in 2000 with the Cochabamba Water War. In the fifth stage, beginning in 2010, earlier contradictions between two competing projects for society are resolved with the victory of the national-popular bloc aligned with the government over

mentalism, and Indigenous Rights in Bolivia (Tucson: University of Arizona Press, 2013).

13 For more information on García Linera, please see chapter 4, note 10.

14 Álvaro García Linera, *Tensiones creativas de la revolución: La Quinta fase del Proceso del Cambio* (La Paz: Vicepresidencia del Estado Plurinacional, 2011).

the autonomist-bourgeois bloc of the eastern lowlands, but tensions remain within the constitutive sectors of the national-popular bloc itself. In this optic, the creative tensions, if properly managed, can help push along the course of the revolution. They can positively reinforce one another and mutate into *productive subjective and objective forces* of the revolution.

Mao is García Linera's point of reference here, as he outlines what he takes to be the primary and secondary contradictions of the conjuncture. The fissures of the former divide the supporting elements of the national-popular project, on one side, and the array of imperial forces lined up against it, together with the remnants of the recalcitrant domestic right, on the other. The secondary contradictions are the creative tensions internal to the revolutionary process itself. These creative tensions can be transcended through democratic and revolutionary means by the "government of social movements." In summary form, according to García Linera, a revolutionary process opened up in 2000 and went through a variety of phases. It culminated in the election of Morales in 2005 and 2009, with its latest consolidation working its way through the October elections in 2014. Hegemony was achieved by 2010, after which tensions and contradictions of the process became creative, internal forces operating within the national-popular bloc supporting the government. The Bolivian people were thus united around plurinationality, indigenous territorial autonomy, and a plural economy—involving public, private, and social-communitarian forms of property, with the state presence in the economy subordinating the other forms of property. The process is in motion toward an integral state, understood as the state's ultimate dissolution into society, while the economy is moving—even with setbacks—to one dominated by the logic of use-value over exchange-value.[15]

From different angles a number of critical Latin American theorists are likewise returning to Gramsci but through his notion of passive revolution rather than the integral state, in an attempt to conceptualize the processes of containment occurring in many South American states presently occupied by left or center-left governments, including Bolivia's. As Peter Thomas has shown, Gramsci's concept of passive revolution was developed across three principal moments in the *Prison Notebooks*, which together comprise a "strategic or partial theory" of the "specific organizational form of bourgeois hegemony." The first refers to the process of Italian state formation in the Risorgimento. The second involves a comparative mode of analysis, incorporating Germany and other social formations, "which seemed to have gone through a

---

15 García Linera borrows the concept of the "integral state" from Gramsci but deploys it in distinct ways.

similar contradictory process of (economic) modernization without (political) modernization, lacking a radical Jacobin moment such as had accompanied the French Revolution." The third encompasses a wider conceptualization of passive revolution, in which the notion "could have an international and even epochal meaning, as a type of logic of bourgeois hegemony as such, with fascism in Italy as merely its 'current' form."[16]

Most relevant to our discussion here is the way in which passive revolution refers "to instances in which aspects of the social relations of capitalist development are either instituted and/or expanded, resulting in both 'revolutionary' rupture and a 'restitution' of social relations."[17] This is the sense in which, as Adam Morton notes, the concept captures "progressive aspects of historical change during revolutionary upheaval that become undermined resulting in the reconstitution of social relations but within *new forms* of capitalist order."[18] "One may apply to the concept of passive revolution," Gramsci writes with reference to the Italian Risorgimento, "the interpretive criterion of molecular changes which in fact progressively modify the pre-existing composition of forces, and hence become the matrix of new changes."[19] In the dynamic of revolution/restoration that Gramsci is referring to in the sections of the notebooks on the European processes of 1848, the dialectical relationship between political oppositions from above (thesis) and below (anti-thesis) do not result in the transcendence of the former through revolutionary rupture. "The thesis alone in fact develops to the full its potential for struggle," Gramsci writes, "up to the point where it absorbs even the so-called representatives of the antithesis: it is precisely in this that the passive revolution or revolution/restoration consists."[20] Radical popular forces in the 1848 conjuncture were unable to comprehend that "the role of the other side prevented them from being fully aware of their own role either; hence from weighing in the final balance of forces in proportion to their effective power of intervention; and hence from determining a more advanced result, on more progressive and modern lines."[21]

---

16 Peter Thomas, "Hegemony, Passive Revolution, and the Modern Prince," *Thesis Eleven* 117, no. 1 (2013): 20–39.

17 Adam David Morton, *Revolution and State in Modern Mexico: The Political Economy of Uneven Development* (Lanham, MD: Rowman and Littlefield, 2011), 18.

18 Morton, *Revolution and State in Modern Mexico*, 18.

19 Antonio Gramsci, *Selections from the Prison Notebooks of Antonio Gramsci*, ed. and trans. Quintin Hoare and Geoffrey Nowell Smith (New York: International Publishers, 1971), 109.

20 Gramsci, *Selections from the Prison Notebooks*, 110.

21 Gramsci, *Selections from the Prison Notebooks*, 113.

Again, the sense of passive revolution in Gramsci that is most important to us here is that which, according to Morton, seeks "to capture how a revolutionary form of political transformation is pressed into a conservative project of restoration while lacking a radical national-popular 'Jacobin' moment."[22] Particularly essential is Gramsci's treatment of transformism, understood "as one of the historical forms of 'revolution-restoration' or 'passive revolution.'" In an initial period of Italian transformism, between 1860 and 1900, Italy moved through a "'molecular' transformism; that is, individual political figures molded by the democratic opposition parties were incorporated one by one into the conservative-moderate 'political class' (characterized by its aversion to any intervention by the popular masses in state life...)." In a second period, from 1900 forward, transformism consists of "whole groups of extremists [ex-syndicalists and anarchists] who crossed over to the moderate camp." An intervening third period, stretching from 1890 to 1900, witnessed "a mass of intellectuals [join] the parties of the left—called socialist but in fact simply democratic."[23]

Transformism describes both processes of programmatic convergence of historically oppositional political forces on the right and left and the moderation of political contestation from below through absorption of its energies into the bureaucratic apparatuses of the state. "Indeed one might say," Gramsci notes,

> that the entire State life of Italy from 1848 onwards has been characterized by transformism—in other words by the formation of an ever more extensive ruling class.... The formation of this class involved the gradual but continuous absorption, achieved by methods which varied in their effectiveness, of the active elements produced by allied groups—and even of those which came from antagonistic groups and seemed irreconcilably hostile. In this sense political leadership became merely an aspect of the function of domination—in as much as the absorption of the enemies' elites means their decapitation, and annihilation for a very long time.[24]

For the Italian-Mexican theorist Massimo Modonesi, such a process of transformism in contemporary South America is more easily detected than the creative tensions alluded to by García Linera. For Modonesi, the South American passive revolution today involves a process of modernization pushed forward from above, which partially and carefully recognizes demands coming

---

22 Adam David Morton, "The Continuum of Passive Revolution," *Capital and Class* 34, no. 3 (2012): 318.

23 Antonio Gramsci, *Prison Notebooks*, vol. 3, ed. and trans. Joseph A. Buttigieg and Antonio Callari (New York: Columbia University Press, 2011), 257, Q8, §36.

24 Gramsci, *Selections from the Prison Notebooks*, 58–59.

from those positioned below; through this process, the state managers guarantee more the passivity and silence of the popular movements than their complicity.[25] In his recent book *El estado de derecho como tiranía* (The Rule of Law as Tyranny), Luis Tapia, one of the great interpreters of Bolivia's most influential twentieth-century Marxist René Zavaleta Mercado—and now a left-wing critic of the Morales government—provides a moving cartography of the series of overlapping and intertwined social cleavages that cut across Bolivian history and that continue to inform contemporary dynamics through a novel terrain of passive revolution.[26] These cleavages—national/colonial, uneven and combined development, and ideological/cultural—Tapia argues, are politicized in different combinations and with different intensities depending on the period in question. In complex ways a passive revolution has run through these three cleavages in recent times, taking the form of a process of containment and redirection of a radical left-indigenous insurrectionary process (2000–2005), which overthrew two neoliberal presidents through mass mobilization, into the consolidation of a state-capitalist process of modernization (2006–present) from above, built upon an alliance with multinational capital interested in extracting natural resources during a world commodities boom.[27]

Tapia's detailed reading of politics and ideology in contemporary Bolivia parallels the key theoretical features of Modonesi's most elaborate iteration of the theory of passive revolution in the twenty-first-century South American setting.[28] For Modonesi, passive revolution involves an unequal and dialectical combination of restorative and transformative tendencies simultaneously in the same political period. Ultimately, however, it is possible to discern which tendency dominates the character of a given epoch. The transformative dynamics of passive revolution mean that it involves changes in relation to the preceding period, but these changes are, in the end, limited to such a degree that the fundamental underlying relations of domination in society persist, even if their political expressions have been altered. At the same time, the specific

25 Massimo Modonesi, "El fin de la revolución pasiva en Brasil," *La Jornada*, June 22, 2013.

26 Luis Tapia, *El estado de derecho como tiranía* (La Paz: Autodeterminación, 2011).

27 For another recent contribution that advances a spatially inflected reading of passive revolution in contemporary Bolivia, see Chris Hesketh and Adam David Morton, "Spaces of Uneven Development and Class Struggle in Bolivia: Transformation or *Transformismo*," *Antipode* 46, no. 1 (2014): 149–169.

28 Massimo Modonesi, "Revoluciones pasivas en América Latina: Una aproximación gramsciana a la caracterización de los gobiernos progresistas de inicio del siglo," in *El Estado en América Latina: Continuidades y rupturas*, ed. Mabel Thwaites Rey (Santiago: CLACSO, 2012), 139–166.

class content of passive revolutions can vary within certain limits—that is to say, the different degrees to which particular components of popular demands are incorporated (the transformative tendency) within a matrix that ultimately sustains the fundamental relations of domination (the restorative tendency).[29] Passive revolutions involve neither total restoration of the old order, the full reenactment of the status quo ante, nor radical revolution. Instead, they involve a dialectic of revolution/restoration, transformation/preservation.[30]

Capacities for social mobilization from below in early stages are contained or co-opted—or selectively repressed—while the political initiative of sections of the dominant classes is restored. Passive revolutions involve the establishment of a form of domination capable of enacting conservative reforms masked in the language of earlier impulses emerging from below, achieving in this way a passive consensus of the dominated classes.[31] Rather than an instantaneous restoration, there is rather a molecular change in the balance of forces under passive revolution, gradually draining the capacities for self-organization and self-activity from below through co-optation, guaranteeing passivity to the new order and encouraging demobilization, or at least controlling what mobilization of the popular classes occurs.[32]

For Modonesi, five preliminary features of the passive revolution orchestrated by left and center-left governments can be identified in twenty-first-century Latin America. First, they tend to promote to different degrees a range of antineoliberal or post-neoliberal reforms, oscillating—depending on the case—between deep and substantial reform and moderate reformist conservatism. Brazil can stand in as a point of reference for the latter, while Venezuela best captures the former.[33] Second, while these passive revolutions were initiated by antagonistic and mobilized forces from below pitted against neoliberalism, the limits of these movements have gradually been expressed in part through their gradual, subordinated incorporation into the state, with processes of change now being led and carried out by sections of the dominant classes and the state from above. This is true even when certain demands formulated from below have been incorporated into the new project from above.[34] What is more, the pace and limits of reform in the new dynamic are strictly delimited by

---

29 Ibid., 142.
30 Ibid., 143.
31 Ibid.
32 Ibid., 149.
33 Ibid., 150.
34 Ibid., 151.

bourgeois state institutions and the law.[35] Third, the new political configurations that have assumed governmental power have promoted or taken advantage of the relative demobilization and political pacification—more or less pronounced across the distinct cases—of popular movements, allowing progressive governments more efficient and effective sociopolitical control of the popular layers of society.[36] Fourth, popular movements have been fully or partially co-opted and absorbed by conservative forces, alliances, and political projects now occupying the institutional terrain of the state apparatus. This has been achieved in part through the use of targeted redistribution and clientelistic arrangements between governments and movements (or movement layers). Fifth, progressive governments have often relied upon a popular, charismatic leader, reinforcing the pacifying and delegative characteristics of these passive revolutions.[37]

Modonesi's theoretical framing captures nicely the social, political, and ideological temporalities of Bolivia during the Morales period.[38] In both Modonesi and Tapia, however, the sociopolitical and the ideological are treated relatively autonomously from the process of capital accumulation involved in the Bolivian passive revolution. What we require, instead, is a clearer sense of the base/superstructure metaphor as a dialectical unity of internal relations, rather than succumbing to one determinism or another.[39] As Thomas demonstrates, Gramsci "fundamentally redefines the concept of 'superstructure' and strips it of the mechanistic and metaphysical encrustations that had been ascribed to it during the period of Marxism's diffusion and vulgarisation."[40] Gramsci understood superstructure and ideology "in a non-reductive sense—that is, he views the superstructures not as mechanically derived from an originary 'base,' but as constituting a dialectical unity or 'historical bloc' with the dominant relations of production, the means by which they were organised, guaranteed, and made to endure (or, just as importantly, challenged and transformed)."[41] As Thomas goes on to show, for Gramsci, the "superstructures are the terrains on which, or the forms in which, members of a social group come to 'know' in a particular, 'practical' way the determining conditions of their lives within a particular historical situation."[42]

---

35 Ibid.
36 Ibid.
37 Ibid., 152.
38 I have made this argument in more detail elsewhere. See Webber, "Managing Bolivian Capitalism."
39 On the philosophy of internal relations, see Ollman, *Alienation*.
40 Thomas, *The Gramscian Moment*, 96.
41 Ibid., 100.
42 Ibid., 100–101.

In this sense, Gramsci very much parallels Marx's own use of the base/superstructure metaphor. "Marx did not conceive social reality atomistically," as Derek Sayer so convincingly illustrates, "as made up of clearly bounded, separate, interacting entities…. He saw the world, rather, as a complex network of internal relations, within which any single element is what it is only by virtue of its relationship to others."[43] Base and superstructure cannot, therefore, be thought of as substantively distinct levels of a social formation, or as relatively autonomous from one another, or as separate entities that then interact in causal or functional processes.[44] In an effort, then, to shift the present emphasis in Modonesi, Tapia, and others in the ongoing discussions of passive revolution in the Latin American context from a relatively autonomous politics to an internally related base and superstructure, the next sections focus on extractive distribution, the class contradictions of the plural economy, and the novel characteristics of urban class transformations induced thus far by Bolivia's passive revolution; these processes are understood to be internally related to changes in Bolivia's state-form under Morales.

The approach here explicitly avoids responding to the overly "politicist" reading of passive revolution on offer in Modonesi and Tapia by returning to any crude economic reductionism or determinism. The contradictions of capitalist accumulation in contemporary Bolivia are not understood here as economic laws operating separately and then interacting with political class relations. Rather class struggle is conceptualized as inherently embedded in the accumulation process. The actions of the Bolivian state under Morales are not understood to flow "more or less directly from the 'requirements of capital,'" nor are the "forms, functions and limits of the political" separable from capital accumulation and its contradictions.[45] What is necessary theoretically, and shown here to be demonstrable empirically, is an adequate conceptualization "of the relation between the economic and the political as discrete forms of expression of social relations under capitalism," with the "specificity of the political and the development of political forms firmly [founded] in the analysis of capitalist production."[46] The actions of the state are not the mechanistic expression of an economic law of capital, but neither is the political under Morales properly understood except in relation to the disciplinary exigencies of capital accumulation.

---

43 Sayer, *The Violence of Abstraction.*
44 Ibid., 83.
45 Holloway and Picciotto, "Capital, Crisis, and the State," 104.
46 Ibid.

Extractive Distribution

Running through the formal development plans and official economic state-ments of the Morales government and the relevant ministries since 2006 has been an emphasis on the necessity of establishing productive transformation of the primary-export model of accumulation, a strengthening of the plural economy—with its public, private, and social-communitarian forms of prop-erty—and the generation of high-quality jobs.[47] These components of de-velopment have been articulated as fundamental prerequisites for improving poverty indicators and reducing social inequality in the country.[48] The various development plans offer together an extended diagnosis of the Bolivian econ-omy, reaching the conclusion that the deep and longstanding levels of social inequality in the country are linked to its history of primary-export develop-ment, rooted principally in the extraction of natural resources—natural gas, mining minerals, and agricultural products, with little value added.

Having reached this conclusion, the general objectives laid out in the plans turn on policy orientation designed to transcend extractive development and shift toward a development model based on integrated, productive, indus-trialized, and diversified development. Through the lens of the development plans, the MAS government has suggested that revenue generated through the extant strategic sectors of the economy—particularly hydrocarbons, min-ing, electricity, and natural resources—should be redirected through various mechanisms to the development of sectors that generate more income and employment (industrial manufacturing, tourism, agriculture, housing, com-merce, services, and transport).[49]

The state in this vision of development will play a central role in the transition between models of accumulation, managing natural resources extraction such that the wider strategic goals of development will ultimately prove attainable. Precisely

---

47 See, especially, *El Plan Nacional de Desarrollo: Bolivia Digna, Soberana, Productiva y Democrática para Vivir Bien, 2006–2011* (La Paz: Bolivia, 2006); *El Plan Nacional de Desarrollo: Bolivia Digna, Soberana, Productiva y Democrática para Vivir Bien: Linea-mientos Estratégicos, 2006–2011,* 2nd updated ed. (La Paz: Bolivia, 2007); Luis Alberto Arce Catacora, "El nuevo modelo económico, social, comunitario y productivo," *Economía Plural* (Monthly Publication of the Ministry of the Economy and Public Finance) 1, no. 1 (2011): 1–14.

48 Fernanda Wanderley, *¿Qué pasó con el proceso de cambio? Ideales acertados, medios equivocados, resultados trastrocados* (La Paz: CIDES-UMSA, 2013), 86.

49 Silvia Escobar de Pabón, Bruno Rojas Callejas, and Carlos Arze Vargas, *País sin indus-trias, país con empleos precarios: Situación de los derechos laborales en Bolivia, 2011–2012* (La Paz: CEDLA, 2014), 7.

because multinational capital has been central to the hydrocarbons and mining sectors since the transition to neoliberalism in the mid-1980s, it will be necessary, according to the MAS, to recover a protagonistic role for the state—issuing, for example, higher taxes and royalties on multinational companies, and stoking state involvement and investment in the natural resource sectors. State management and oversight will allow, in this view, internal savings and freedom from external debt without risk of running fiscal deficits. Redistribution of the social wealth will be possible through the priming of cash-transfer programs to vulnerable social sectors, and the use of revenue accrued by the state through natural resources to fund new national actors in the sought-after plural economy—private and public enterprises, cooperatives, and communities.[50] Through the development of a plural economy—with the key actor being the state—conditions will be laid for the generation of more and better employment, and through employment, a socially inclusive development model. Internal demand will play a greater role than external demand in the new, increasingly endogenous model of development, and therefore Bolivia will be less vulnerable to the vagaries of fluctuating commodity prices on the international market. Expanding and enhancing the internal productive apparatus of the country, while maintaining fiscal stability, will reduce the historic dependency on primary products and allow for the transition to a highly industrialized and diversified development model.[51]

In reality, little in the structural basis of the primary-export model of capital accumulation has been altered since 2006, although the economy from the crude perspective of GDP has been performing well in a favorable international environment. The inherent class contradictions within the model of development pursued by the MAS since 2006 have been partially concealed in this context of an external environment characterized by an extraordinary commodities boom, driven above all by China's rapid growth. Average expansion of the country's GDP under Morales has been 5 percent, with peaks of 6.1 percent and 6.8 percent in 2008 and 2013, respectively. In 2014, the pace of growth was maintained at 5.2 percent, putting Bolivia third in Latin America and the Caribbean for the year, behind Panama and the Dominican Republic. Foreign direct investment into Bolivia has risen dramatically over the Morales administrations, from $US 278 million in 2006, to $US 651 million in 2010, to $US 1.8 billion in 2013. Accumulation of international reserves has soared from $US 1.8 billion in 2005 to $US 15.4 billion in 2014.[52]

---

50 Escobar de Pabón, Rojas Callejas, and Arze Vargas, *País sin industrias*, 7.
51 Ibid., 7–8.
52 CEPAL, *Balance Preliminar de las Economías de América Latina y el Caribe 2014* (Santiago: CEPAL, 2013), 8, 56, 65, 70.

So the economy is growing, but there has been little variation in the dependency on primary products—indeed, relative to the recent past this dependency has worsened. Natural gas exports to Brazil and Argentina accounted for 54.7 percent of total exports in 2013, while mining exports were 25.4 percent of the total. Just over 80 percent of total exports that year were of primary materials (if primary materials include mining minerals, hydrocarbons, and agricultural products), a fact that obviously makes the country's economy vulnerable to volatility on international markets in the medium to long term but brought in bountiful revenue during the height of the commodities super-cycle (2003–2011).[53] Table 1, focusing more narrowly on the primary exports of mining minerals and hydrocarbons (leaving aside agriculture commodities for the moment), is suggestive of deep trends of continuity relative to the last five decades, and even a sharp recent uptick in the primacy of extractive resources as a share of total exports since the MAS assumed office relative to the immediately preceding period. Between 1995 and 2005 the figures show a diminution in the relative weight of extractive products and, since then, a sharp return.[54]

Table 1. Share of Exports of Extractive Sectors in Total Exports, 1952–2012

Period	Mining	Hydrocarbons	Extractive Sectors	Other Sectors	Total
1952–1960	69.70	N/A	69.70	30.30	100.00
1960–1965	76.40	N/A	76.40	23.60	100.00
1965–1970	66.10	10.20	76.30	23.70	100.00
1970–1975	62.80	20.50	83.30	16.70	100.00
1975–1979	56.80	12.20	69.00	31.00	100.00
1980–1985	48.60	42.70	91.30	8.70	100.00
1985–1990	40.00	39.20	79.20	20.80	100.00
1990–1995	43.50	17.20	60.70	39.40	100.00
1995–2000	34.90	9.50	44.40	55.10	100.00
2000–2005	15.30	29.60	44.90	55.10	100.00
2006–2009	22.80	46.20	69.00	31.00	100.00
2010–2012	45.90	23.60	69.50	30.50	100.00

Source: Fernanda Wanderley, *¿Qué pasó con el proceso de cambio? Ideales acertados, medios equivocados, resultados trastrocados* (La Paz: CIDES-UMSA, 2013), 69.

53 CEPB, *Bolivia en el contexto económico mundial—2013* (La Paz: Confederación de Empresarios Privados de Bolivia, 2014), 33–34.
54 Wanderley, *¿Qué pasó con el proceso de cambio?*, 69.

Over the last twenty years the underlying structure of the Bolivian economy has not changed dramatically. The extractive sector narrowly conceived (hydrocarbons and minerals) increased in relative importance in terms of its contribution to GDP, moving from 10.1 percent in 1999 to 13.7 percent in 2012.[55] Meanwhile, the share of industrial products in total exports has actually fallen under the MAS government, from 47.4 percent in 2001, to 26.3 percent in 2010.[56] It is also significant to note that approximately 50 percent of tax revenue collected by the Bolivian state is captured through the export of natural resources, reflecting continuities in the state's weak capacity to collect taxes in other areas in the Morales period compared to his predecessors. At the same time, as we will see in more detail below, the capital-intensive extractive sectors of mining and hydrocarbon extraction are not creating a significant number of jobs, even as they expand rapidly.[57]

Significant spending on public infrastructure in the boom years contributed to a spike in domestic demand, and together with rising incomes, remittances from abroad, and targeted cash-transfer programs, helped reduce poverty from 62.4 percent to 36.3 percent between 2002 and 2011, and extreme poverty from 37.1 percent to 18.7 percent over the same period.[58] This is undoubtedly one of the most important factors in explaining Morales's ongoing popularity, despite the fact that these figures are mirrored elsewhere in the region, which has seen overall declines in poverty rates during the commodities boom. Neighboring Peru, for instance, a paragon of market liberalism, has also witnessed falls in poverty from 48.7 percent in 2001 to 21.1 percent in 2013.[59]

The compensatory state, to draw on Gudynas again, might be thought of as the form of appearance of passive revolution in contemporary Bolivia, an expression of a conflict-ridden process of accumulation, rooted in the extraction of primary material exports and their partial redistribution to targeted, vulnerable layers of the population, or what I am calling here extractive distribution.

Plural Economy?

Parallel to the problems encountered in the planned transition away from primary-export-led accumulation, the notion of a plural economy advanced

---

55 Ibid., 70.
56 Escobar de Pabón, Rojas Callejas, and Arze Vargas, *País sin industrias*, 10.
57 Wanderley, *¿Qué pasó con el proceso de cambio?*, 74.
58 CEPAL, *Panorama Social de América Latina 2014* (Santiago: CEPAL, 2013), 95.
59 Ibid., 96.

by García Linera and others within the Morales administration cannot account for the tendencies of concentration and centralization within capitalist accumulation. As economists Carlos Arze and Javier Gómez have pointed out, the contradictory dynamic between large-scale capitalist enterprises in the extractive industries and forms of smaller-scale production for the market that are subsumed into capitalist accumulation causes an array of unstable developments across intermediary class sections in Bolivian society. Street vendors, petty extractivists, small-scale industrial producers, and medium-scale producers involved in commercial agriculture for export, all at incipient levels of accumulation, are increasingly making political demands on the Bolivian state to improve their competitive prospects on the market.[60] Much of the recent wave of scholarly investigation into sections of this "popular economy" tends to conceal a great deal of the exploitative class stratification it involves, despite offering rich empirical description, rooted in impressive ethnographic field research.[61]

In the absence of structural changes to social property relations under the Morales administrations, these kinds of demands have led the state toward policies of improving the profit margins of these petty sectors at the expense of waged labor: depression of salaries, further precariousness in labor relations, flexibilization of territorial rights to self-determination of rural indigenous communities, relaxation of environmental regulations, and loose implementation of the law vis-à-vis contraband import-export activities and the narcotics industry.[62] Furthermore, the favorable evolution of own-account workers over the last several years—through access to credit and subsidies, among other measures—has allowed some segments of this layer of the population to transform themselves into small-scale capitalists, who then accumulate profits through the exploitation of waged labor. Such phenomena are observable in mining, contraband trade, commercial agriculture, and urban transport sectors, among many other areas of the Bolivian economy.[63]

---

60 Carlos Arze and Javier Gómez, "Bolivia: ¿El 'proceso de cambio' nos conduce al vivir bien?" in *Promesas en su laberinto: Cambios y continuidades en los gobiernos progresistas de América Latina*, eds. Carlos Arze, Javier Gómez, Pablo Ospina, and Víctor Álvarez (La Paz: CEDLA, 2013), 164.

61 Nico Tassi, Alfonso Hinojosa, and Richard Canaviri, eds., *La economía popular en Bolivia: Tres miradas* (La Paz: Centro de Investigaciones Sociales, Vicepresidencia del Estado, 2015); Nico Tassi, Carmen Madeiros, Antonio Rodríguez-Carmona and Giovana Ferrufino, *"Hacer plata sin plata": El desborde de los comerciantes populares en Bolivia* (La Paz: Pieb), 2013.

62 Arze and Gómez, "Bolivia," 165.

63 Ibid., 166. On such processes of novel processes of class stratification in Bolivian society,

Some of these patterns can be explained with reference to trends in public and private investment. Official indicators suggest that total investment—public and private—increased from 2006 to 2011, rising to 17.3 percent of GDP from only 14.5 percent of GDP between 2000 and 2005. Foreign direct investment (FDI), mainly in the extractive resource sectors, increased after 2006, after a sustained fall that reached negative figures in 2005. Crucially, alongside increases in FDI, public investment—financed by natural resource rents rather than external borrowing—has also been increasing. From 6.1 percent of GDP in 2006, it rose to 11.4 percent in 2011. In absolute terms, this signified a spike to $US 8.3 billion between 2006 and 2012, more than 2.3 times higher than the six years prior to Morales.[64]

However, the increase in public investment has not necessarily been mirrored by a transcendence of earlier problems in its quality. Efficiency problems and corruption have been rampant, while the neoliberal antipathy to the state's involvement in productive economic activities largely persists under the Morales administration. As in earlier periods, MAS investment has concentrated on infrastructure and within this domain overwhelmingly on highways (79 percent). Public investment has been comparatively weak in areas that its development plans have indicated are strategic for the transition away from a primary-export model of accumulation. For example, between 2007 and 2011 industry received $US 16.8 million of public investment, or 1.2 percent of total public expenditure. Agriculture received $US 94.8 million, or 6.4 percent of the total. Part of the problem in public investment priorities, some analysts have argued, is related to the loss of central state control of spending to subnational entities (departments and municipalities) since changes to the law in 2005. Between 2002 and 2005, the central state controlled 47 percent of the budget of public investment, whereas in the subsequent six-year period this fell to 36 percent. Subnational spending has often prioritized immediate political payoffs, and public works of infrastructure—highways to nowhere, for example—meet the demand for visibility and ostensible progress.[65] (Table 2 highlights the sectional distribution of recent public investment patterns.)

see also William Neuman, "A Colorful Bolivian Bastion, Floating Above It All," *New York Times*, May 13, 2013, www.nytimes.com/2013/05/14/world/americas/a-colorful-bolivian-bastion-floating-above-it-all.html?pagewanted=all; Andres Schipani, "Bolivia's Indigenous People Flaunt Their New-Found Wealth," *Financial Times*, December 4, 2014; Miriam Shakow, *Along the Bolivian Highway: Social Mobility and Political Culture in a New Middle Class* (Philadelphia: University of Pennsylvania Press, 2014).

64 Escobar de Pabón, Rojas Callejas, and Arze Vargas, *País sin industrias*, 15.

65 Ibid., 16.

Table 2. Public Investment Patterns, 2000–2011

Sector	2000–2005	2006–2011
Multi-sector	7 percent	6 percent
Social	41 percent	30 percent
Infrastructure	42 percent	50 percent
Productive	11 percent	15 percent

Source: Silvia Escobar de Pabón, Bruno Rojas Callejas, and Carlos Arze Vargas, *País sin industrias, país con empleos precarios: Situación de los derechos laborales en Bolivia, 2011–2012* (La Paz: CEDLA, 2014), 167.

Attempts by the state to fulfill the objectives laid out in the development plan regarding public support for national economic agents across the plural economy have largely taken the form of the creation of trusts, which are administered by state financial entities. These trusts are designed to finance credit for private enterprises, microbusinesses, cooperatives, and small producers, alongside investment in public enterprises.[66] Meanwhile, regarding the seven state-led industrial manufacturing projects announced in 2007—in paper, sugar, and citrus fruit processing plants, among others—only three were in operation by 2012. Lack of technical capacity expressed itself in design errors and economic miscalculations, causing interminable delays in some cases, while planned activities have simply not been carried out in others, and opportunities and instances of corruption have amplified significantly.[67]

In such an environment, as Arze and Gómez point out, it is difficult to discern any movement toward communitarian socialism or *vivir bien* (living well). Instead, what is notable is a typical configuration of dependent capitalism, in which foreign capital dominates an extractive sector destined for export markets, while a layer of smaller domestic capitalists assumes a structurally subordinate position; both of these sectors, meanwhile, live off the exploitation of Bolivian laboring classes. The state is not "integral" here, at least in the manner envisioned by García Linera. Rather it is a typical capitalist state that ensures, as best it can, the reproduction of capitalist accumulation.

"To his credit," stresses John Paul Rathbone in the *Financial Times*, "Morales has run Bolivia's economy far better than most of his leftist peers. Crucially," Rathbone argues, "he understood that a solid macroeconomy brought him autonomy which allowed him to mouth off at capitalists and imperialists at will, but at no real cost. Such rhetoric brought him popular support at home.

---

66 Ibid., 17.
67 Ibid.

It also provided political cover for closer alliances with the country's private sector."[68] The *Economist* is likewise at pains to point out that García Linera believes that "creating socialism in a country like Bolivia first requires the state to build capitalism—echoing the Russian Mensheviks of a century ago, rather than Mr. Castro's Bolshevism. The government nationalised part of the oil and gas industry and reversed earlier privatisations, but went no further."[69]

The emergent layers of petty capitalists have been drawn in large part from Bolivia's indigenous population. And it is precisely these emergent social sectors, in alliance with older dominant sectors in Bolivian society—agroindustrialists, mining capital, and foreign oil corporations—that have consolidated themselves and articulated their interests in the influential circles of the government, as left-oppositionists and indigenous plurinationalists have been pushed out.[70] The logic of big capital runs alongside the legitimating function of indigenous bourgeois class formation.[71]

As anthropologist Sarela Paz points out, there have always been contradictions within the national-popular bloc, but these have risen decisively to the foreground since 2010. Cooperative miners (with links to transnational mining capital), coca growers (with interests in commercializing land and legalizing holdings as individual rather than collective titles), and commercial traders of El Alto and the western highlands (with links to Chinese capital) are among the most powerful players within the MAS today.[72]

Any demands from popular sectors that might move the process of change in a more radical direction—defense of collective property of land, territorial indigenous autonomies in the lowlands, socialized control of agroindustry, limits on the growth of genetically modified products, devel-

68 John Paul Rathbone, "Why Third Time Might Be Unlucky for Evo Morales," *Financial Times*, October 13, 2014.

69 "Bello: Bolivia's Rentier Republic," *Economist*, May 3, 2014.

70 Sarela Paz, "Elecciones providenciales en Bolivia y los rumbos del 'Proceso de Cambio,'" *Pueblos en Camino*, October 11, 2014.

71 Anthropologist Salvador Schavelzon offers the interesting hypothesis that it is precisely these layers, shifting away from rural indigenous identities, that may account for the precipitous decline in indigenous self-identification between the 2001 and 2012 censuses. In 2001, 62 percent of the Bolivian population self-identified as indigenous. In 2012, that number dropped to 42 percent. See Schavelzon, "El Censo y la nueva clase media como desafío a las naciones y pueblos indígena originario campesinos," *El desacuerdo*, no. 1, issue 6 (August 18, 2013). Schavelzon is author of the most comprehensive analysis of the Constituent Assembly process. See Schavelzon, *El nacimiento del Estado Plurinacional de Bolivia: Etnografía de una Asamblea Constituyente* (Buenos Aires: CLACSO, 2013).

72 Paz, "Elecciones providenciales en Bolivia."

opment of a state mining sector, trade policies that seek to limit trade liberalization and to strengthen national agriculture and manufacturing—do not sit comfortably with the aspirations of these new emergent sectors and their geometries of power.[73]

During the second administration of the Morales government (2010–2014), the early social foundations of the national-popular coalition ruptured, and ascendant social layers assumed important roles in the new configuration of power. At the epicenter of the governance formula underpinning the MAS administration today is an alliance between agro-industrial capital of the eastern lowlands and transnational capital in the hydrocarbons and mining sectors, on the one hand, and the incipient indigenous bourgeoisie in cooperative mining, commercial trading, contraband, and narcotics, on the other. Large capitals operating in Bolivia understand politically that older forms of exercising domination over society through explicit racism and conservative political parties are no longer tenable, and they are willing to share power with upwardly mobile indigenous capitalists. Meanwhile, these emergent indigenous layers are threatened by the objective interests of those indigenous workers and peasants below them in socializing wealth, natural resources, land, and the productive bases of the Bolivian economy, and are therefore willing to tactically align themselves with the most reactionary elements of the media luna business sectors.[74]

"The major achievement of Evo Morales is to be where he is, with the face that he has and with the level of education that he has," notes the eminent historical sociologist and activist Silvia Rivera Cuscicanqui, "because the majority of the indigenous people who felt inferiority and shame now say: I'm beautiful, I'm strong, I'm intelligent."[75] This was part of the reason for Rivera Cuscicanqui's critical support of the government over its first term (2006–2010). However, by 2014 she was stressing the contradictions of the present moment and what the MAS government has come to represent:

> It's clear that we are living through a stellar moment of growth and that this has made it possible to redistribute resources through the so-called nationalization, although this only changed the proportion of tributes that they [private capital] captured relative to that captured by the state. All of this has created conditions for an acute economic moment in which some people escape poverty and enjoy a certain empowerment through the fact of having

73 Ibid.
74 Ibid.
75 "El indianismo de este Gobierno es de caricatura," *Página Siete*, October 12, 2014, www
.paginasiete.bo/nacional/2014/10/12/indianismo-este-gobierno-caricatura-34976.html.

lost their shame. However, there is a certain kind of internationalization of colonialism happening, which also brings with it a capitalist project with an indigenous face, a project which implies the exploitation of one's neighbour. The capitalist coca grower, merchant, cooperativist, who have indigenous faces, have entered the game of accumulation. There are almost folkloric elements of redistribution, parties, and gifts, but in class terms we are in an extractivist capitalist project rooted in primary exports.[76]

Rivera Cusicanqui's remarks on the emergent patterns of primary-export accumulation under Morales are perceptive. In the next section, we link these overarching trends to the key changes that have occurred in the urban labor market alongside the country's commodities boom.

Urban Labor Markets: A Closer Look

Leading Bolivian economists and sociologists have now compiled considerable data and analysis of the urban labour markets of the country's key cities—La Paz, Cochabamba, Santa Cruz, and El Alto during the Morales era.[77] The results, in many ways, help to establish the determining tendency of the revolution/restoration dialectic of Bolivia's passive revolution of the twenty-first century as decidedly restorative. When the nonagrarian GDP is considered, the total contribution of productive urban activities—manufacturing, construction, energy, gas, and water) was 29 percent by 2011. This indicates that the bulk of GDP in the urban centers continues to rely on the growth of tertiary activities (commerce, public transport, banking and business services, and social and personal services), which do not contribute to the accumulation of capital, although they help establish the foundations for this to occur.[78] Also decisively important to the urban economy has been a 50 percent decline in the importance of industrial manufacturing to nonagricultural GDP, alongside an increase in commerce and transport, accounting for two-thirds of this section of GDP in 2011.[79] Table 3 indicates differentiated sectional growth within

---

76 Ibid.

77 The two most important studies to date are Silvia Escobar de Pabón and Bruno Rojas Callejas, *Más asalariados, menos salario: La realidad detrás del mito del país de independientes* (La Paz: CEDLA, 2011); and Silvia Escobar de Pabón, Bruno Rojas Callejas, and Carlos Arze Vargas, *País sin industrias, país con empleos precarios: Situación de los derechos laborales en Bolivia, 2011–2012* (La Paz: CEDLA, 2014).

78 Escobar de Pabón, Rojas Callejas, and Arze Vargas, *País sin industrias*, 21.

79 Ibid., 22.

nonagricultural GDP. What leaps out most immediately is the dynamism of the construction sector, from negative growth in 2007 to close to 10 percent in 2011. The expansion here is closely related to an increase in liquidity and speculative investment in real estate.[80]

Table 3. Nonagricultural GDP: Sectoral Growth, 2001–2011 (percent)

Economic Activity	Annual Growth, 2001–2007	Annual Growth, 2008–2011
Total	2.9	4.6
1. Mining and Hydrocarbons	0.2	1.0
2. Industrial Manufacturing	4.7	3.6
3. Electricity, Gas, and Water	3.1	6.9
4. Construction	-0.5	9.1
5. Commerce, Restaurants, and Hotels	3.0	7.4
6. Transport and Communications	3.9	6.6
7. Finance and Business Services	0.8	5.2
8. Services	3.1	1.9
Extractive (1)	0.2	1.0
Secondary (2,3,4)	4.0	4.5
Tertiary (5,6,7,8)	2.6	5.1

Source: Escobar de Pabón, Rojas Callejas, and Arze Vargas, *País sin industrias*, 24.

The structural reconfiguration of the nonagricultural economy in the axis cities of Bolivia, and above all the fall in industrial manufacturing, is reflected in patterns of the evolution of their labor force and occupational structures (see Tables 4 and 5). It is impressive to note that the rapid expansion of hydrocarbons extraction and mining has had very little discernible impact on job creation in Bolivian cities. Rather, the dynamic activities, in terms of a rate of job generation above average, were construction and transport.[81] In one expression of the weakness of advances in industrialization, despite government rhetoric to the contrary, job expansion in industrial manufacturing grew at a slower rate between 2008 and 2011 than it had in 2001–2007.[82] Tertiary activities continued to employ six of every ten workers in 2011.

---

80 Ibid., 23.
81 Ibid., 24.
82 Ibid.

Table 4. Axis Cities: Annual Growth of Employment by Economic Activity, 2001–2011 (percent)

Economic Activity	2001–2007	2008–2011
Total	3.6	3.5
1. Mining and Hydrocarbons	3.8	0.3
2. Industrial Manufacturing	4.6	3.1
3. Electricity, Gas, and Water	3.2	2.3
4. Construction	5.8	10.2
5. Commerce	-3.7	3.5
6. Transport and Communications	5.7	5.7
7. Finance and Business Services	3.9	-1.0
8. Services	9.1	1.9
Extractive (1)	3.8	0.3
Secondary (2,3,4)	4.9	4.9
Tertiary (5,6,7,8)	3.1	3.0

Source: Escobar de Pabón, Rojas Callejas, and Arze Vargas, *País sin industrias*, 25.

Table 5. Axis Cities: Employment by Economic Activity, 2001–2011 (percent)

Economic Activity	2001	2007	2008	2011
Total	100	100	100	100
1. Mining and Hydrocarbons	0.6	0.6	1.0	0.9
2. Industrial Manufacturing	17.0	18.0	20.7	20.5
3. Electricity, Gas, and Water	0.4	0.2	0.5	0.4
4. Construction	7.9	9.1	6.4	8.0
5. Commerce	35.6	28.2	35.0	34.5
6. Transport and Communications	8.0	9.2	9.6	10.4
7. Finance and Business Services	7.5	7.7	6.6	5.6
8. Services	23.0	26.9	20.3	19.7
Extractive (1)	0.6	0.6	1.0	0.9
Secondary (2,3,4)	25.3	27.4	27.6	28.9
Tertiary (5,6,7,8)	74.1	72.0	71.5	70.2

Source: Escobar de Pabón, Rojas Callejas, and Arze Vargas, *País sin industrias*, 25.

The rhythms of the urban labor market during a period of primary-export expansion under the MAS government have reconstituted some of the worst features of the preceding period of orthodox neoliberalism. Instances of this trend can be witnessed in the increase in part-time work alongside the extension and intensification of workdays for the employed, and the increase in less-skilled and more insecure jobs in the cities, with workers constantly transiting between employment situations, unemployment, and inactivity.[83] This insecurity operates politically as an invisible mechanism of control and discipline of the urban labor force.

Table 6 revealingly divides employment patterns into five sectors of the labor market. The business sector refers to typically capitalist enterprises, involving a clear differentiation between owners of capital and owners of labor, and in which the wage relation is operative. In a capitalist economy, depending on the property of the means of production, one can distinguish between state and private segments of this sector. The semi-business sector is distinct from the business sector insofar as the owners of the means of production also participate in production together with their small number of employees. That is to say, semi-business enterprises operate under simple forms of cooperation, and without as clear a separation between capital and labor as the business sector. The family sector, meanwhile, is constituted by independent workers who work alone or with the assistance of their unpaid family members. Finally, there is the domestic service sector, an almost exclusively female domain of employment, which groups together those employed in individual homes.[84]

Since 2001, jobs have been concentrated in the semi-business sector, in part through the neoliberal process of subcontracting and the externalization of the labor process of the business sector. By 2011, as Table 7 suggests, this sector had risen to 22.4 percent of employment in the major cities. The business sector remained, in contrast, relatively constant in terms of job creation. The family sector declined modestly, and the domestic service sector diminished importantly. If we were to take the state and business sector as a proxy for the formal sector and semi-business and family with the informal sector, 63 percent of employed labor—70 percent of women and 60 percent of men—can be located in the informal sector, in which a higher proportion of occupants were waged laborers in 2011 than in 2001. Yet there are limits to the formal–informal divide insofar as it does not always help us to determine levels of precarity. If the waged workers in Bolivia's semi-business sector are the worst off in terms of income and labor stability, 50 percent of workers in

---

83 Ibid., 30–31.
84 Escobar de Pabón and Rojas Callejas, *Más asalariados, menos salario*, 5.

the business sector and 40 percent of workers in the state sector shared a precarious wage situation. As in the experience of unemployment, results are also gendered. In 2011, women were more likely than men to be unemployed or suffer low wages and precarious employment stability due to their relative segregation in less qualified, precarious jobs.[85] Again, the determining tendency of neoliberal restoration is apparent in these general trends.

Table 6. Axis Cities: Employment by Sector of Labor Market, 2001–2011 (percent)

Sector of Labor Market	2001	2011
State	10.1	8.3
Business	25.1	25.4
Semi-Business	13.8	22.4
Family	45.5	40.6
Domestic Service	5.5	3.3

Source: Adapted from Escobar de Pabón, Rojas Callejas, and Arze Vargas, *País sin industrias*, 33.

Critical Bolivian economists have also categorized quality of work along the axes of nonprecarious, precarious, and extremely precarious, considering income, access to social security, and job stability.[86] Their principal findings on this measure are reflected in Table 7. In 2001, in the axis cities, only 22.1 percent of workers had a nonprecarious job, with the majority being employed in moderately precarious jobs and 22.5 percent having extremely precarious jobs. Nonprecarious forms of labour between 2001 and 2011 have diminished slightly, while moderately precarious labor has fallen significantly. Most regressively, extremely precarious labor has spiked from 22.5 percent in 2001 to 51.6 percent in 2011.

---

85 Escobar de Pabón, Rojas Callejas, and Arze Vargas, *País sin industrias*, 34.
86 Ibid., 35.

Table 7. Axis Cities: Quality of Work by Labor Market Sector, 2001–2011*

Labor Market Sector	2001			2011		
	Non-precarious	Moderately precarious	Extremely precarious	Non-precarious	Moderately precarious	Extremely precarious
Total	22.1	55.4	22.5	20.9	27.5	51.6
State	50.7	46.5	2.8	40.8	52.0	7.2
Business	28.7	54.8	16.5	20.4	50.8	28.8
Semi-Business	9.9	59.8	30.3	10.5	51.1	38.3
Family	18.4	51.1	30.5	22.7	1.8	75.5
Domestic Service	–	–	100	1.2	1.7	97.1

Source: Escobar de Pabón, Rojas Callejas, and Arze Vargas, *País sin industrias*, 36.

* Does not include quality of work employers

Again, precarity transcended the formal/informal divide in the labor market, with 60 percent of those employed in state sectors and roughly 80 percent of those working in other sectors experiencing some form of precarious employment.[87] Also, while precarity was an attribute of labour for a majority of workers, it characterizes female labor particularly. Above all, there has been an accelerated shift of women toward extremely precarious labor. In 2011, only 27 percent of men and 14 percent of women had a nonprecarious job, while 40 percent of men and 65 percent of women had an extremely precarious job. Overall, it is notable that the primary-export boom experienced in the Bolivian economy in recent years has not been accompanied by a dramatic improvement in the situation of the country's laboring classes. Indeed, by one estimate, labor's share of national income relative to capital continues to deteriorate. Their share falling continuously since 2000, laborers received 26 percent of national income in 2011, while capital's share grew to 53.3 percent.[88]

---

87 Ibid., 36.
88 Ibid., 34.

Concluding Remarks: Dawn of Austerity?

The social landscape of contemporary Bolivia is perhaps more privy to misunderstanding than any other country in Latin America. Amid the revelry surrounding the first indigenous president in republican history assuming office, a bonanza of consumerism unparalleled in recent Bolivian history, and enormous public modernization projects of highways and satellites, all introduced under the rubrics of indigenous liberation and communitarian socialism, disquieting new forms of class rule and domination have been easy to downplay or ignore altogether.

The often sizable chasm between this government's rhetorical flourish and its routine politics has not been lost on the international voices of global capital. "While speaking like his left-wing allies in Argentina and Venezuela," writes John Otis in the *Wall Street Journal*, "Economy Minister Luis Alberto Arce has avoided the pitfalls that have led them down a path of spiralling inflation, falling currencies and recessions… business-friendly policies have produced vigorous economic growth and fervent support." Otis observes that "Mr. Arce, who spent 19 years at Bolivia's Central Bank under fiscally conservative presidents, has often followed their orthodox playbook. He has maintained balanced budgets. Bolivia has squirreled away $14 billion in international reserves, one of the highest levels in the world given the size of the economy." Otis also quotes Baudouin Duquesne, who spent five years as director of the Inter-American Development Bank and now has the same job in Venezuela: "Arce has been a very careful economic manager.… He is one of the main reasons why Bolivia is in the position it is today."[89]

Schipani, of the *Financial Times*, likewise juxtaposes Morales's "anti-capitalist rhetoric" and his "prudent macroeconomic and fiscal policies, and mostly improved relations with the country's diffident private sector."[90] "Even with the rhetoric, today's Bolivia is a country that is totally open, with a market economy that is thriving thanks to an almost Thatcherite handling of public finances," states Humberto Zogbi, until recently Coca-Cola's general manager for Bolivia.[91] "Mr. Morales's… success," the *Economist* essentially concurs, "has recently owed less to 'anti-capitalism' and much more to his accommodation with

---

89 John Otis, "Bolivian Economic Gains Could Boost Morales' Election Odds," *Wall Street Journal*, October 9, 2014, http://blogs.wsj.com/frontiers/2014/10/09/bolivian -economic-gains-could-boost-moraless-election-odds/.

90 Andres Schipani, "Morales Says 'Evo For Ever' Is Not in the Cards," *Financial Times*, October 15, 2014.

91 Quoted in Andres Schipani, "Evo Morales Heads for Third Term in Bolivia," *Financial Times*, October 10, 2014.

economic orthodoxy and local capitalists. After a turbulent early period… he has presided over several years of political stability and economic growth. And he has made his peace with private business."[92] Daniel Lansberg-Rodríguez, again in the *Financial Times*, celebrates the way that Bolivia, together with Ecuador under Rafael Correa, publicly denounces "the global 'imperialist' system—therefore remaining eligible for Venezuelan oil and cash handouts—… while avoiding the more disastrous interventionist policies that have hamstrung economic stability in Venezuela and Argentina."[93]

This chapter has sought to understand some of the seemingly paradoxical features of the contemporary political economy in Bolivia through the theoretical lens of passive revolution. Rather than a political process of creative tensions, à la García Linera, I have suggested patterns of political and ideological containment, co-optation, and pacification. In the revolutionary/restorative dialectic of passive revolution, I have demonstrated on multiple levels the determining tendency of restoration, of preservation over transformation. But, above all, I have sought to provide an economic account of passive revolution in twenty-first-century Bolivia, through a Marxian class-analytic lens. This has meant discerning the broad trends of extractive distribution, the contradictions of the plural economy, and the transformations of the urban labor markets of the country's major cities.

Although the register has been one mainly of critique, I have also sought to demonstrate the conjunctural conditions of economic expansion that Bolivia experienced in the midst of the commodities boom of the early part of this century. The question now is whether or not these conjunctural conditions are coming to an end. "Mr. Morales's tenure has coincided with an economic bonanza," the *Economist* reports. "If the end of the commodities boom augurs tougher times, Bolivians have yet to feel it…. Public expenditure has risen from 8 billion bolivianos ($1 billion) in 2005 to 21 billion bolivianos in 2013, with much of it going on social programmes and bonuses. Abundance has stoked demand. The Torre Multicine, a new mall in La Paz, swarms with shoppers laden with clothes, perfumes, and fast food. In the posh neighbourhood of Calacoto a restaurant set up by Claus Meyer, one of Europe's better-known chefs, serves modern interpretations of Bolivian classics for prices that would have been unimaginable a few years ago."[94]

92 "Bello: The Travails of ALBA," *Economist*, October 18, 2014.
93 Daniel Landsberg-Rodríguez, "Latin America Swaps Its Populists for Apparatchiks," *Financial Times*, August 19, 2014.
94 "Bolivia's Election: Happy Evo After," *Economist*, October 11, 2014.

But the media representatives of global capital doubt the sustainability of this trend in the context of the end of the super-cycle commodity boom. "In the past 10 years," writes John Paul Rathbone in the *Financial Times*, "South America never had it so good. The continent surfed a global commodity price boom, helped by abundant global capital…. Growth is already slowing fast, to just 1.2 percent for the region this year. As the World Bank warns in its most recent regional outlook: 'It is not clear whether the slowdown is bottoming out.' Levels of investment that had reached heights comparable to those in Asia, spurred by the 'commodity supercycle', are falling."[95] All of this is compounded by the extraordinary downturn in oil prices in recent months. "The [Bolivian] government's budget for 2015 is based on projections that the average price of oil will be $80 a barrel," the *Economist* reports, "well above the $50–60 most forecasters expect. That will affect Bolivia's revenue from natural gas, which is the main export and provides nearly half of government revenue. The price of minerals, another economic mainstay, has also fallen."[96]

The fragility of the current regime of accumulation in Bolivia is precisely related to deteriorating external conditions and the deepening of the primary export model within the country over the Morales period.[97] Household spending continues to be the key driver of growth in Bolivia in an immediate sense, but household demand itself has been contingent on the spin-off dynamism of wider sectors of the economy as a result of natural gas and mining mineral extraction, allowing for bigger incomes and cash transfers as well as significant spikes in public spending on infrastructure and construction.[98] In 2013, 40 percent of public spending was targeted in infrastructure—in transport, especially, followed by energy and communications. After infrastructure, 27 percent of public investment was directed toward the productive sector (first hydrocarbons, followed by mining and agriculture). Social investment in a broad sense amounted to 29 percent of public spending that year, which was 46 percent more than it had been in 2012—not least because of the approaching general elections. Spending on health and social security was still quite minimal as a proportion of the overall spending, at only 4 percent, while

---

95 John Paul Rathbone, "The Party Is Ending for Latin America," *Financial Times*, October 30, 2014.
96 "Third Time Unlucky: Evo Morales's Next Term as President May Not Run as Smoothly as His First Two," *Economist*, January 26, 2015.
97 CEPB, *Bolivia en el contexto económico mundial—2013* (La Paz: Confederación de Empresarios Privados de Bolivia, 2014), 14.
98 Ibid., 38.

education and healthcare received 8.7 percent, basic sanitation 5.4 percent, and urbanization and housing projects 10.8 percent.[99]

The economic minister, Luis Arce, insists that the Bolivian economy can continue to grow in 2015 at rate of 5 percent, even if the price of oil drops to $US 30 per barrel, because of the $15 billion in international reserves which can be drawn on if it proves necessary to re-prime domestic activity.[100] However, Gonzalo Chávez, an economist at the Catholic University in La Paz, estimates that export earnings from gas will plummet by at least $US 1.3 billion in 2015, equivalent to 4 percent of GDP, assuming an average oil barrel at $US 60. For Chávez, 5 percent growth is achievable with oil at between $US 90 and $US 100 a barrel, whereas the maximum rate of growth at $US 50 to $US 60 a barrel would be between 3.4 percent and 4 percent.[101]

99 Ibid., 22–23.

100 "Arce: Bolivia crecerá más de 5% incluso si el crudo baja a $US 30," *Página Siete*, January 28, 2015, www.paginasiete.bo/economia/2015/1/28/arce-bolivia-crecera -incluso-crudo-baja-45481.html. See also *La Razón*, "Luis Arce: Bolivia está mejor preparada que todos los países de la región para enfrentar caída de precios del petróleo," February 8, 2015, www.la-razon.com/economia/Luis-Arce-Bolivia-preparada -enfrentar_0_2213778607.html.

101 Andres Schipani, "Bolivia: Lower Gas Prices and Andean Deities," *Financial Times*, January 22, 2015. See also "Expresidente del BCB estima más baja del precio del crudo y menos ingresos al país," *Página Siete*, October 15, 2014, www.paginasiete.bo/economia /2014/10/15/expresidente-estima-baja-precio-crudo-menos-ingresos-pais-35390.html.

SEVEN

The Long March East: Evo Morales and the Consolidation of Agrarian Capitalism in Bolivia[1]

With the support of more than 60 percent of the popular vote, the symbolic weight of Evo Morales's third inauguration was heavy. The ceremonial images in Tiwanaku, and later in the National Congress, conveyed the pride of place occupied, at least symbolically, by indigenous peoples, peasants, miners, and workers in the MAS government. According to Bolivian sociologist Fernanda Wanderley, in recent years the predominance of symbolism has often cast a shadow over any coherent evaluation of the fit between the government's practice and its ostensible ideals and political commitments: "This is the symbolic and political force of this government. The question of whether it is actually committed to these ideals constitutes another register of analysis. And while the sensation of an economic bonanza and macroeconomic stability are maintained, this question will remain secondary."[2]

---

1 Many thanks to Enrique Castañón Ballivián for providing me with leads, suggestions, and sources that helped in the research for this chapter. Thanks as well to Leandro Vergara-Camus and Cristóbal Kay for their helpful, extensive commentary on early iterations of this chapter.
2 Fernanda Wanderley, "La dimensión simbólica del Gobierno de Evo Morales," *Página Siete*, February 11, 2015.

The establishment of a plural economy driven by state intervention, and indigenous liberation through territorial and political recognition, are said to have ushered in a democratic and cultural revolution, displacing the corruption and injustice of the preceding orthodox neoliberal order with a government of social movements.

With an average growth rate of 5 percent since 2006, impressive drops in levels of poverty and extreme poverty, massive infrastructural projects like the new gondola linking the sprawling shantytown of El Alto with the capital city of La Paz and the Tupac Katari satellite, and social achievements in areas such as illiteracy reduction, it is not difficult to see why Morales is popular. But in what sense does the new political economy introduced by Morales since 2006 offer a radical alternative to neoliberalism, much less a revolutionary transformation of Bolivian society, economy, and state?

This chapter explores this question in relation to Bolivia's evolving agrarian class structure over the Morales era of contested neodevelopmentalism (2006–2016), in historical comparison with the eras of nationalist import-substitution industrialization (1952–1985), and orthodox neoliberalism (1985–2005). According to the Bolivian government, there has been a dramatic and egalitarian transformation of land tenure between the country's two long periods of agrarian reform, 1953–1992 and 1996–2014, with the post-2006 governments of Morales achieving the bulk of reform carried out in the latter period. At the close of the 1953–1992 period, 39.24 million hectares, or 68 percent of land, was in the hands of large and medium property owners, this narrative suggests. Their share dropped to 9 percent by 2014, with only 6.3 million hectares under their control. Meanwhile, the latter period saw a dramatic expansion of state property (24.5 million hectares, or 34 percent), indigenous Tierras Comunitarias de Origen (Communitarian Lands of Origin, TCOs) (23.7 million hectares, or 33 percent), and peasants and interculturals (Andean indigenous-peasant migrants from the highlands to the lowlands) (17.8 million hectares, or 24 percent).[3] By 2010, the Ministry of Rural Development and Land claimed that the distribution of rural properties undertaken to that point had already achieved a "communitarian renewal of agrarian reform" and in a short while would achieve "an equitable and inclusive structure for all economic actors," which would result in "practically two thirds of the national territory being in the hands of the country's majority, with the state having control of a half of the remaining third part of the national territory, and the sector of individual property owners linked to agro-industrial

---

3 INRA, *Estado de saneamiento* (La Paz: Instituto Nacional de Reforma Agraria, 2015).

activity having access to the other half of the last third."[4] For the Morales government, this trajectory represents a radical rupture with the inherited agrarian class structure in Bolivia, which was characterized by a fundamental dualism of concentrated large capitalist properties on one side, and a majority rural population of land-poor or landless indigenous peasants on the other.

This chapter challenges the notion that there has been extensive, egalitarian reform in Bolivia under Morales. Its argument hinges on the changing balance of agrarian class forces in Bolivian society and the related changes in the class composition of the ruling MAS bloc over time. Initially, there was a period under Morales's rule, between 2006 and 2009, in which the indigenous-peasant social movement alliance, the Unity Pact, fought from below for a genuine transformation of the Bolivian rural class structure, and in which the agro-industrial elite fought openly against the central government through an autonomist and regionalist destabilization campaign, headquartered in Santa Cruz and radiating outward through the rest of the lowland departments of the country. The main institutional terrain of struggle in these opening years of the Morales regime was the Constituent Assembly process, and there was a possibility during this period of deep structural reform to the countryside. However, by 2010 the Morales government had defeated the political project of autonomy in the lowlands, and this laid the basis for a class realignment in the ruling bloc. Between 2010 and 2016, a novel agro-capital-state alliance emerged, with subordinate support from rich peasants in the coca, soy, and quinoa commercial export sectors, among others. The Unity Pact fragmented, and the lowland indigenous movements were expelled from their early participation in the governing alliance between 2006 and 2009. The result of these changes in class composition for agrarian reform has been dramatic. Fundamentally, the strategic zones of productive land in the country have been concentrated in the hands of national and transnational agro-industrial capital devoted to soy production and its derivatives for export. The marginal, least productive land in the country, meanwhile, contains the most densely populated zones of the majority of landless and land-poor indigenous peasants. There has been very little redistribution through the expropriation of private landholdings, and what relatively little redistribution of state property has been carried out has tended to be of marginal land of little to zero agricultural potential. In between the agro-industrial capitalists, who capture most of the country's agricultural rent, and the landless and land-poor peasants, sits a layer of rich peasants, or small-

---

4 As quoted in Control Ciudadano, *Reconducción comunitaria de la reforma agraria y producción agícola: evaluación agrícola* (La Paz: CEDLA, 2012), 12.

scale agricultural capitalists who are subordinately incorporated economically into wider, transnationally controlled commercial crop value chains, and politically into the ruling bloc agrarian coalition between the state and industrial agricultural capital. Paradoxically, the Morales regime is more successfully carrying out the project of industrial agrarian capitalist expansion in the east that was first attempted by the Bolivian state in the post-revolutionary 1950s.

After a brief survey of Bolivia's rural sociospatial dynamics, the chapter is divided into three major parts. First, it explores the dynamic of the 1952–1985 period of nationalist import-substitution industrialization. Second, it focuses on the period of orthodox neoliberal restructuring between 1985 and 2000. Third, and finally, it examines more thoroughly the evolving agrarian class structure and agrarian policies under the Morales administrations between 2006 and 2016. This last section is separated into two further subdivisions. In the first the period of insurgent contestation of 2006–2009 is explored, and in the second, the shift to a novel configuration of agro-capital-state alliance is explained.

There are some limitations of data facing any attempt at comprehensively analyzing agrarian reform in contemporary Bolivia. At the time of publication, the results of the last National Agricultural Census (CNA), carried out between October and November 2013, had still not yet been made public in full, disaggregated detail. The last census of this kind was carried out in 1984. The figures employed in the following analysis, therefore, draw from official information on the process of land registration and agrarian property from the National Institute of Agrarian Reform (INRA), statistics on the agrarian sector from the National Statistical Institute (INE), the Vice-Ministry of Land, the Ministry of Rural Development and Land, and the secondary analyses of the most important research institute on agrarian affairs in Bolivia, Fundación Tierra.

Sociospatial Demographics of the Bolivian Countryside

In a first social, ecological, and geographic approximation, the Bolivian countryside can be divided into the overarching categories of the highlands and the lowlands. The former includes the densely populated, indigenous-peasant high plateau (altiplano) and valleys of the central, western, and southwestern departments of Cochabamba, La Paz, Oruro, Potosí, and Chuquisaca. The lowlands, meanwhile, take the shape of a crescent moon, arching from northwestern Pando to southeastern Tarija, and pass through Beni and Santa Cruz in between. Santa Cruz contains the most fertile land in the country and is the epicenter of Bolivia's industrial capitalist agriculture, while Beni's expanses are home to the bulk of the country's cattle ranching industry. The highlands represent 37 percent of the national territory in terms of surface area and contain 70 percent of Bolivia's rural and urban population. The rural areas of the highlands are inhabited by 2,681,000 people, or 82 percent of the country's rural population. The lowlands, by comparison, encompass 63 percent of Bolivian national territory, 30 percent of the total Bolivian population, and 18 percent of the national rural population.[5] In the lowlands, between 1980 and 2000, more than 11 million hectares were concentrated in only 7,000 properties, each in excess of 5,000 hectares, while over the same period in the Andes 200,000 hectares were occupied by some 250,000 agricultural producers with plots of fewer than 20 hectares.[6]

Table 1. Population by Geographic Area (2001–2012)

	Year	High Plateau	Valleys	Lowlands	Total
Number of Municipalities	2001	80	172	75	327
	2012	86	178	75	339
Total Population	2001	1,523,266	4,421,016	2,330,043	8,274,325
	2012	1,908,528	5,123,316	3,028,012	10,059,856
	Variation	25.3%	15.9%	30.0%	21.6%
Urban Population	2001	942,202	2,423,469	1,799,559	5,165,230
	2012	1,287,594	3,063,272	2,438,096	6,788,962
	Variation	36.7%	26.4%	35.5%	31.4%
Rural Population	2001	581,064	1,997,574	530,484	3,109,095
	2012	620,934	2,060,044	589,916	3,270,894
	Variation	6.9%	3.1%	11.2%	5.2%
Proportion of Rural Population	2001	18.7%	64.2%	17.1%	100.0%
	2012	19.0%	62.9%	18.1%	100.0%

Source: Colque, Urioste, and Eyzaguirre, *Marginalización de la agricultura campesina e indígena*, 21.

5 Gonzalo Colque, Miguel Urioste and Jose Luis Eyzaguirre, *Marginalización de la agricultura campesina e indígena: Dinámicas locales, seguridad y soberanía alimentaria* (La Paz: Fundación Tierra, 2015), 20–21.
6 Gonzalo Colque, Efraín Tinta, and Esteban Sanjinés, *Segunda Reforma Agraria: Una historia que incomoda* (La Paz: Fundación Tierra, 2016), 77.

As Table 1 suggests, there have been minimal demographic changes across the high plateau, valleys, and lowlands in the recent period despite dramatic socioeconomic transformations. For 2012, the high plateau represented 19 percent of the rural population, scarcely a 0.3 percent change relative to 2001. The valleys were home to 62.9 percent of the rural population, 1.3 percentage points less than 2001. The lowlands grew slowly from 17.1 percent to 18.1 percent. The most important demographic change across all the regions was the growth of small, intermediate urban areas.[7]

More than 30 distinct indigenous peoples, with a population of under 200,000, are scattered across the lowlands of the east and the Amazon. Systematically ignored in earlier iterations of agrarian public policy, they have emerged as a significant sociopolitical force since the early 1990s, demanding exclusive rights to self-governance of their communitarian territories and the natural resources often found within their parameters.[8] In the highlands and valleys, the population is majority Quechua and Aymara, organized socioeconomically as impoverished smallholders organized in peasant unions, rural semiproletarians, or members of indigenous ayllus (independent indigenous communities).[9] The lowlands also contain smallholding peasant colonizers (now often called "interculturals"). This migrant population of Quechua and Aymara Andean origin are now living in various state-planned and spontaneous human settlements that first emerged in the 1960s and 1970s, in tropical zones in Cochabamba, the agricultural frontier in Santa Cruz, and the lowlands of northern La Paz.[10]

Capitalist agriculture is located mainly in the Bolivian east, in the department of Santa Cruz, and is devoted principally to the production of soy for export, and to a lesser extent sugarcane and cotton.[11] In recent years, agricultural activities have expanded on an aggregate scale due to the spike in international soy prices, but peasant and indigenous agricultural activities have lost ground relative to agroindustry, and many former peasants are abandoning the countryside as a result.[12] There has been a recent increase in the peasant cultivation of quinoa in the high plateau between 2008 and 2013,[13] but the

---

7 Colque, Urioste, and Eyzaguirre, *Marginalización de la agricultura campesina e indígena*, 21.
8 Colque, Tinta, and Sanjinés, *Segunda Reforma Agraria*, 85.
9 Ibid.
10 Ibid.
11 Ibid.
12 Colque, Urioste, and Eyzaguirre, *Marginalización de la agricultura campesina e indígena*, 15.
13 Tanya Kerssen, "Food Sovereignty and the Quinoa Boom: Challenges to Sustainable Re-Peasantisation in the Southern Altiplano of Bolivia," *Third World Quarterly* 36, no. 3

peasant sector has not exhibited more general tendencies of growth. In the last two decades, peasant cultivation of nonindustrial agricultural products has been a marginal contributor to GDP, averaging 2 percent, with a high of 2.9 percent in 1997, and a low of 1.7 percent in 2011.[14] Food demand in internal markets is increasingly met with import products from Peru, Chile, and Argentina.[15] Indeed, Bolivia has never before imported as much food as in the years 2006–2010, with the total value over these years estimated to be over $US 1.1 billion.[16]

While the national reduction in poverty levels in recent years has been justly celebrated, rural Bolivia is still predominantly poor. According to figures from the National Institute of Statistics (INE), between 2001 and 2012, the national proportion of Bolivians living in poverty fell from 58.6 percent to 44.9 percent. However, in 2012, 71.5 percent of the rural population remained poor, compared to 32.1 percent in urban areas. As Table 2 indicates, the most impoverished rural areas are located in the high plateau (79.4 percent), followed by the valleys (71.8 percent), with the lowlands (62.1 percent) considerably better off. Unsurprisingly, given the intense history of racism in the country, INE figures also suggest a strong correlation between indigenous ethnicity and poverty, with 70 percent of the indigenous population categorized as poor.[17]

(2015): 489–507.

14 Colque, Urioste, and Eyzaguirre, *Marginalización de la agricultura campesina e indígena*, 15.

15 Ibid., 16.

16 Miguel Urioste, "Concentration and 'Foreignisation' of Land in Bolivia," *Canadian Journal of Development Studies* 33, no. 4 (2012): 441.

17 Colque, Urioste, and Eyzaguirre, *Marginalización de la agricultura campesina e indígena*, 24.

Table 2. Profile of Urban and Rural Poverty, 2001–2012

Year	Description	High Plateau	Valleys	Lowlands	Total
2001	Bolivian Population	1,523,266	4,421,016	2,330,043	8,274,325
	Population of Bolivian Poor	1,156,485	2,735,441	1,016,219	4,908,144
	Percentage	75.9	61.9	43.6	58.6
	Urban Population	942,202	2,423,469	1,799,559	5,165,230
	Population of Urban Poor	608,439	1,055,999	627,922	2,292,360
	Percentage	64.6	43.6	34.9	44.4
	Rural Population	581,064	1,997,547	530,484	3,109,095
	Population of Rural Poor	548,046	1,679,442	388,297	2,615,784
	Percentage	94.3	84.1	73.2	84.1
2012	Bolivian Population	1,908,528	5,123,316	3,028,012	10,059,856
	Population of Bolivian Poor	974,233	2,385,387	1,160,503	4,520,123
	Percentage	51.0	46.6	38.3	44.9
	Urban Population	1,287,594	3,063,272	2,438,096	6,788,962
	Population of Urban Poor	481,435	906,409	794,047	2,181,892
	Percentage	37.4	29.6	32.6	32.1
	Rural Population	620,934	2,060,044	589,916	3,270,894
	Population of Rural Poor	492,798	1,478,977	366,455	2,338,231
	Percentage	79.4	71.8	62.1	71.5

Source: Colque, Urioste, and Eyzaguirre, *Marginalización de la agricultura campesina e indí-gena*, 23. Derived from National Institute of Statistics (INE).

The latest housing and population census indicates that rural population growth between 2001 and 2012 was a mere 5 percent, relative to a 31 percent increase in urban areas.[18] This is suggestive of structural problems endemic to

18 Ibid., 19.

indigenous and peasant livelihood strategies in the highland and valley areas, with few employment opportunities, fragmented tiny plots of land (*minifundios*), and low agricultural productivity.[19]

Rural society in Bolivia in the period before the first Agrarian Reform of 1953 was characterized by a mix of medium and large landowners reliant on varieties of coerced indigenous labor, relatively autonomous indigenous communities with predominantly noncapitalist social relations, relatively richer smallholders-in-transition, who produced for the market and occasionally employed day laborers, and small units of agrarian capitalist production in the valleys and the east, rooted in systemic use of wage labor.[20] From the late nineteenth to mid-twentieth century, capitalist mining enclaves in silver and then tin drove the national economy, but these embryonic capitalist developments overlapped with often quasi-feudal labor relations of indentured servitude in the rural areas.[21] Thin industrial development, alongside extractive capitalist mining with scarce articulation to the rest of the Bolivian economy, meant that in 1950 the urban population was only 26.2 percent of the Bolivian total. Peasant community production for subsistence in autonomous indigenous communities, together with low productivity on the haciendas, meant that the population in the cities and mining centers relied mainly on imported agricultural products.[22]

Phase I—Nationalist Import-Substitution Industrialization (1952–1985)

The 1952 National Revolution witnessed the nationalization of the mines and the construction of state capitalism, rooted in state property in the strategic mining zones and thinly developed industrial bases elsewhere in the economy, with heavy state intervention and the expansion of state-owned enterprises. While the nationalization of the mines was relatively easy, however, the same was not true of agrarian reform.[23] Pre-revolutionary Bolivia was notable for the

---

19 Ibid., 20.
20 Enrique Ormachea Saavedra, "Pequeña y gran producción agrícola capitalista y trabajo asalariado en Bolivia," in *Asalariados Rurales en América Latina*, eds. Alberto Riella and Paola Mascheroni (Buenos Aires: CLACSO), 165.
21 Carlos Toranzo, "El agro en el modelo de desarrollo boliviano: La continuidad del Estado anticampesino," in *Recientes transformaciones agrarias en Bolivia*, ed. Fundación Tierra (La Paz: Fundación Tierra, 2015), 31.
22 Ormachea Saavedra, "Pequeña y gran producción agrícola capitalista y trabajo asalariado en Bolivia," 167.
23 Toranzo, "El agro en el modelo de desarrollo boliviano," 32.

highest inequality of land concentration in all of Latin America, with 82 percent of land in the possession of 4 percent of landowners.[24] In the wake of the National Revolution of 1952, however, radicalized peasants seized large landholdings through wide-scale direct action in Cochabamba, La Paz, Oruro, Potosí, and Chuquisaca, challenging the pre-revolutionary rural class structure.[25]

While the radicalized peasantry of the highlands pushed forward the egalitarian elements of the Agrarian Reform of 1953, other bases of the ruling Movimiento Nacionalista Revolucionario (Revolutionary Nationalist Movement, MNR) pursued a radically different vision. The result was a mixed reform, reflecting the dual character of the MNR's approach to agrarian reform: small-scale redistribution in the highlands, on the one hand, and propulsion of large landed properties in the east, on the other.[26] The smallholding peasantry of the highlands was not strategically important to the MNR's overarching economic vision—despite the fact that this highland peasantry constituted the ruling party's strongest and most reliable base of political support in the coming decades. The peasantry was rather expected to slowly disappear, providing a future source of labor for expanding industrial capitalism. With this in mind, the MNR used the resources of the state to pursue what it hoped would be the creation of two wings of an industrial bourgeoisie. In the west, import-substitution industrialization policies were pursued in an effort to foster the conditions for the development of a mature national bourgeoisie, capable of producing the industrial goods hitherto imported, while in the east efforts were made to develop an agricultural bourgeoisie, which theoretically would devote itself to meeting the demands of the domestic market, as well as producing a surplus for export.[27]

Also in pursuit of this development model, the postrevolutionary state supported the "colonization" of the lowlands of the country, which until then had been scarcely populated, by Quechua and Aymara Andean peasants, as well as Japanese and Mennonite immigrants (once the preferred plan, rooted in racist assumptions, of large-scale European immigration proved impossible to realize).[28] More importantly, however, the Agrarian Reform of 1953

---

24 Susan Eckstein, "Transformation of a 'Revolution from Below': Bolivia and International Capital," *Comparative Studies in Society and History* 25, no. 1 (1983): 108.

25 James Dunkerley, *Rebellion in the Veins: Political Struggle in Bolivia, 1952–1982* (London: Verso Books, 1984), 67.

26 Toranzo, "El agro en el modelo de desarrollo boliviano," 32.

27 Colque, Tinta, and Sanjinés, *Segunda Reforma Agraria*, 73; Toranzo, "El agro en el modelo de desarrollo boliviano," 32–33.

28 Ormachea Saavedra, "Pequeña y gran producción agrícola capitalista y trabajo asalariado en Bolivia," 168.

encouraged the transformation of preexisting agricultural haciendas in Santa Cruz into medium and large capitalist enterprises. Free title was granted to what had been state property in many instances, a highway was built connecting the western and eastern sections of the country (from Cochabamba to Santa Cruz), as well as a road network linking Santa Cruz to the neighbouring countries of Brazil and Argentina. Until the mid-1950s, Santa Cruz did not have a single highway tying it to other regions of the country, or to neighboring countries. The highway between Cochabamba and Santa Cruz was a principal component of Plan Bohan, a development program planned and financed by the United States, with a vision oriented toward the development of agrarian capitalism in the eastern lowlands. Plan Bohan was later refashioned as the "March Toward the East."[29] The state of 1952 also provided agricultural machinery for private farmers to rent, erected tariff barriers, provided subsidies, fixed prices, and developed experimental farms for the investigation of novel agricultural techniques, cheap lines of credit, and public refineries for sugar and rice.[30]

Between 1953 and 1993, the National Council of Agrarian Reform (CNRA) granted legal title to 97,000 properties, extending over 13.5 million hectares in Santa Cruz. Fifty-five percent of these properties (7.5 million hectares) were large properties of over 10,000 hectares.[31] During the 1970s and early 1980s—especially during the dictatorships of Hugo Banzer (1971–1978) and Luis García Meza (1980–81)—the process of land distribution was marked by grave levels of corruption that allowed for the legalization of large agrarian properties in the lowlands of the east.[32] Alongside sugarcane and rice, cotton flourished among this nascent agro-bourgeois development.

Capitalist agriculture in Santa Cruz during the nationalist ISI period (1952–1984) was characterized by low levels of technology, and as a consequence depended heavily on seasonal wage labor, concentrated in the harvest periods of rice, sugarcane, and cotton.[33] Despite state-backed and spontaneous "colonization" from the Andean highlands, Santa Cruz lacked a sufficient local

---

29 Gonzalo Colque, *Expansión de la frontera agrícola: Luchas por el control y apropiación de la tierra en el oriente boliviano* (La Paz: Fundación Tierra, 2014), 33.
30 Ormachea Saavedra, "Pequeña y gran producción agrícola capitalista y trabajo asalariado en Bolivia," 168–170.
31 Colque, *Expansión de la frontera agrícola*, 39.
32 Colque, Tinta, and Sanjinés, *Segunda Reforma Agraria*, 77.
33 Ormachea Saavedra, "Pequeña y gran producción agrícola capitalista y trabajo asalariado en Bolivia," 171.

labor supply to meet expanding demand. In 1980, for example, 69.4 percent of the seasonal workforce for cotton and sugar cane came from the highlands—mainly the valleys—and only 30.6 percent from within the department of Santa Cruz itself.[34] Of the temporary laborers in these crops there were two principal types. First, a layer of semiproletarians existed that combined wage work in sugarcane and cotton with independent agricultural activity elsewhere for the remainder of the year. Second, there were agrarian proletarians, who when they were not working in the sugarcane and cotton harvests were selling their labor power to the cultivators of other crops. There were also seasonal workers who were otherwise unemployed—either they were young workers looking for work for the first time, or they were workers unable to find work outside of the harvest seasons.[35] As early as 1980, a slim majority of the temporary harvest workforce (52.2 percent) were proletarians, while the rest (47.8 percent) were semiproletarians. In the case of sugarcane, the proletarian proportion of the labor force was larger due to the longer duration of harvest, necessitating a workforce available to sell their labor power consistently for longer periods.[36]

In the decades following the National Revolution, Santa Cruz became the most dynamic center of capitalist accumulation in the Bolivian countryside, producing cotton, coffee, sugar and timber for export.[37] The agro-industrial dominance of Santa Cruz was then solidified and extended further with the implementation of neoliberalism since the mid-1980s.[38] Meanwhile, in the highlands, the minifundios continued to fragment under the weight of demographic expansion—smaller and smaller plots were divided among the children across generations of growing families. The subsistence peasant economy began to decompose by the 1970s, and with the debt crisis of the early 1980s, together with the drought of 1982–1984, this early decomposition would mature rapidly.[39]

---

34 Ibid.

35 Ibid.

36 Ibid., 172.

37 Lesley Gill, *Peasants, Entrepreneurs, and Social Change: Frontier Development in Lowland Bolivia* (Boulder, CO: Westview, 1987); Allyn MacLean Stearman, *Camba and Kolla: Migration and Development in Santa Cruz, Bolivia* (Gainesville, FL: University Press of Florida, 1985).

38 Honor Brabazon and Jeffery R. Webber, "Evo Morales and the MST in Bolivia: Continuities and Discontinuities in Agrarian Reform," *Journal of Agrarian Change* 14, no. 3 (2014): 435–465.

39 Mamerto Pérez Luna, "El proceso de descomposición de la economía campesina boliviana," *Cuestión Agraria* 2 (November 2015): 39–63.

Phase II—Orthodox Neoliberalism (1985–2005)

As elsewhere, Bolivian neoliberalism stressed an export-orientation in agriculture. Over the fifteen years of neoliberal orthodoxy in the country (1985–2005), transnational corporations and large domestic agricultural enterprises in Santa Cruz came to dominate this accelerated insertion into the global economy. While the traditional peasant economy of the highlands deteriorated, agro-industrial enterprises in the lowlands concentrated their domination in a few select crops, soy above all. While in 1986, 77 percent of the total cultivated surface area of the country was host to cereals, fruit, vegetables, and tubers, in which small peasant production was predominant, by 2004 such crops had diminished to 48.2 percent of the national total. In another metric, peasant production in 1963 amounted to roughly 82 percent of the total value of agricultural production in Bolivia, whereas by 2002 this figure had fallen to only 39.7 percent, and industrial capitalist agriculture hit 60.3 percent.[40]

In the mid-1980s, agricultural trade liberalization was introduced alongside the general implementation of neoliberal economic restructuring.[41] Bolivia established trade agreements with Chile and Mercosur, alongside the Tariff Union of the Andean Community of Nations (CAN), all of which ended protection of domestic peasant production and undercut peasant competitiveness in traditional crops such as potatoes, onions, and barley. Between 1985 and 1988, farm income was slashed in half as a result. Combined with the drought associated with El Niño that struck Bolivia relentlessly between 1982 and 1984, the decline of the peasant economy accelerated and there was extensive out-migration from the rural highlands.[42] Between 1976 and 1996, the rural population fell from 59 percent to 39 percent of the total population.[43]

With trade liberalization, the Bolivian peasant economy was exposed to the superior technological levels of international agrarian capitalism, and food imports quickly substituted for domestically produced goods.[44] Internal processes of peasant differentiation intensified, moreover, as richer peasants took on new technologies and expanded their plot sizes to remain competitive,

40 Enrique Ormachea Saavedra, ¿Revolución agraria o consolidación de la vía terrateniente? El gobierno del MAS y las políticas de tierras (La Paz: CEDLA, 2007), 29–32.
41 Webber, From Rebellion to Reform in Bolivia; Webber, Red October.
42 Kerssen, "Food Sovereignty and the Quinoa Boom," 493.
43 Pablo Pacheco Balanza and Enrique Ormachea Saavedra, Campesinos, patrones y obreros agrícolas: una aproximación a las tendencias del empleo y los ingresos Rurales en Bolivia (La Paz: CEDLA, 2000), 9.
44 Pérez Luna, "El proceso de descomposición de la economía campesina boliviana," 57.

while poorer peasants were driven increasingly into proletarian status. Meanwhile, the strata of medium peasants, capable of guaranteeing their family's reproduction through the mobilization of their own resources, shrank further.[45] According to one survey, already by 1988, 76 percent of the peasantry were poor peasants, understood as peasants lacking the means to reproduce their family on the basis of the income generated from their land and thus obligated to sell their labor power elsewhere on a temporary basis. In the same survey data, medium peasants constituted 11 percent of the peasantry, when we understand medium peasants to be those rural production units based fundamentally on family labor, with the ability to reproduce that labor without selling labor power elsewhere. Rich peasants, meanwhile, made up 13 percent of the peasantry, if we understand rich peasants to be those who regularly made a profit after reproducing their family and re-investing in the means of production, and who purchased the labor power of poorer peasants, and utilized modern technology in the production process.[46]

Highly mechanized production techniques were introduced to the novel crops of soy, sorghum, sesame, and hard yellow corn in the lowlands, while the production techniques of older lowland commercial crops such as rice and sugarcane were modernized. These changes to agricultural production processes brought with them further alterations in the magnitude and character of agricultural wage labor. The first decade of neoliberalism witnessed, in particular, a lower global demand for rural wage labor, given the reduced requirements of labor per hectare of production. There was also a specific reduction in temporary periods of seasonal labor for harvest periods. A growing social layer of unskilled "permanent temporary workers" emerged, floating from job to job and living in locations of dense agribusiness. At the same time, there was an expansion at the highest end of skilled employment, with a surge in demand for agricultural engineers and the like.[47] Table 3 documents the evolution of demand for labor power across selected crops in this period.

---

45 Pérez Luna, "El proceso de descomposición de la economía campesina boliviana," 58.
46 Ormachea Saavedra, *¿Revolución agraria o consolidación de la vía terrateniente?*, 27–28.
47 Ormachea Saavedra, "Pequeña y gran producción agrícola capitalista y trabajo asalariado en Bolivia," 176.

Table 3. Department of Santa Cruz—Evolution of Demand for Labor in Selected Crops

Crops	1976	%	1980	%	1992	%	% Change, 1980–1992
Soy	153,660	1.1	455,000	3.4	395,040	5.9	15.4
Cotton	2,459,146	16.8	1,992,498	14.9	947,794	14.1	52.4
Corn	2,596,186	17.8	3,545,760	26.5	1,200,625	17.9	66.1
Rice	3,201,100	21.9	2,450,000	18.3	2,208,751	33.0	9.9
Wheat	62,850	0.4	72,000	0.6	63,917	1.0	11.2
Sunflower	0	0.0	0	0.0	29,194	0.4	-
Sorghum	80,613	0.6	78,000	0.6	41,250	0.6	47.1
Beans	0	0.0	0	0.0	161,300	2.4	-
Ratoon Sugarcane	3,580,529	24.5	4,392,428	32.8	1,156,176	17.2	73.7
Sugarcane leaf	2,465,578	16.9	390,525	2.9	502,041	7.5	28.6
Total	14,599,662	100.0	13,376,211	100.0	6,702,088	100.0	50.0

Source: Ormachea Saavedra, "Pequeña y gran producción agrícola capitalista y trabajo asalariado en Bolivia," 177.

The magnitude and character of wage labor continued to evolve through different phases of Bolivian neoliberalism, however. Alongside capital-intensive mechanization of agricultural production in the lowlands and concomitant drops in demand for labor in that region, capitalist social relations gradually penetrated more deeply the peasant economies of the highlands and valleys and accelerated processes of internal peasant differentiation as neoliberalism advanced. A layer of rich peasants emerged whose small-scale production required higher levels of wage labor. As a result of these twin dynamics, statistical evidence suggests an initial decline in the aggregate number of agricultural laborers in Bolivia between 1976 and 1996, followed by a growth in agricultural wage labor between 1996 and 2012.[48] This increase came principally from medium-scale, nonmechanized capitalist enterprises throughout the country and, above all, through the temporary contracting of the labor of poor peasants by small agricultural capitalists, or rich peasants, in the valleys and high plateau.[49]

---

48 Ormachea Saavedra, "Pequeña y gran producción agrícola capitalista y trabajo asalariado en Bolivia," 178–181.

49 Ibid., 181, 184. Here we follow Ormachea Saavedra in distinguishing between rich peasants, or small capitalist agricultural producers, and capitalists in a strict sense, because of their distinct positions within the social division of labor. In the case of rich

As was common with neoliberal experiments elsewhere in Latin America, the ideology of a minimal state and maximized free market mechanisms in Bolivia contrasted with the reality of the state's fierce interventions on behalf of capital. Indeed, Bolivian neoliberals rescued a central element of the 1952 agricultural vision. In particular, under neoliberalism, the state continued to support the agricultural bourgeoisie of the east. This orientation of state support for industrial agriculture in the lowlands was redoubled through international leverage from an array of like-minded institutions, most importantly the World Bank and the Inter-American Development Bank.[50] In 1991, the World Bank initiated its Eastern Lowlands Natural Resource Management and Agricultural Production Project, with the stated objectives of developing the eastern lowlands through zoning, mapping and soil studies, increasing profitable production of agricultural commodities, developing technology and credit systems to spike agricultural productivity, enhancing existing road infrastructure, and improving the living conditions of local indigenous populations.[51] Its principal objective in practice was the expansion of commercial and profitable agriculture through the increase of soy production by approximately 200,000 tons per year. In pursuing this strategic objective, the bank played a key role in expanding and consolidating the soy sector in Bolivia.[52]

In the mid-1980s, the first experimentation in soy production in Bolivia took place through the pioneering work of Mennonite and Japanese producers as commercial opportunities were opened up through agricultural liberalization. Between 1986 and 1992, soy cultivation grew from 63,000 to 217,000 hectares, and the value of exports from $US 19 million to $US 57 million.[53] Between 1986 and 1992, a rapidly extending agricultural frontier in Santa Cruz was incorporated into soy production. The presence and authority of the Bolivian state, and its ability to police this frontier and enforce its hegemony over state property, had long been contested, but there was

---

peasants or small capitalist agricultural producers, capitalist production—production for profit on the market through the use of wage labor—is organically combined with the direct labor of the small capitalist alongside the hired labor. In the case of the capitalist agricultural producer, in the strict sense, he or she does not work as a direct producer but exclusively extracts surplus value from the agricultural proletarians who live from the sale of their labor power.

50 Toranzo, "El agro en el modelo de desarrollo boliviano," 34.

51 World Bank, *Eastern Lowlands: Natural Resource Management and Agricultural Production Project.* Implementation Completion Report. Credit 2119-BO. Report No. 17866 (Washington, DC: World Bank, 1998).

52 Colque, *Expansión de la frontera agrícola*, 47.

53 Ibid.

now a rush of deforestation, private appropriation of land, and the escalating production of soy.[54]

A second phase of soy expansion between 1994 and 2004 witnessed the first serious incursions of foreign capital into the agrarian sector in Santa Cruz—mainly Brazilian, and secondarily Argentinian, and Colombian—focusing first on the direct production of soy. Later, the entirety of the agro-industrial value chains of harvesting, processing, storing, and exporting would enter the radar of a wider array of major foreign investors.[55] Large-scale soy agriculture emerged in the late 1990s and early 2000s, based on intensive use of advanced machinery, techniques of mono-cropping, and various agricultural inputs.[56] The 1990s also witnessed the abandonment by many Andean peasant migrants based in the lowlands of their subsistence crops to adapt in various ways to the production of agricultural goods for export. The 2000s then consolidated this general trajectory as soy prices soared.

The hasty extension of the agricultural frontier in the 1990s proceeded with little regulation or state mediation of land tenure. State land was being given away almost for free, with prices of $US 30 per hectare in the expansion zone. These same lands today are valued at between $US 2,000 and $US 5,000 per hectare.[57] One of the few intensive studies of the expansionary zones of the agricultural frontier in Santa Cruz concluded that 70 percent of land dedicated to agriculture and ranching in the area was concentrated in the hands of large-scale agroindustrialists by the mid-2000s, compared to the 8 percent held by medium-sized Mennonite and Japanese producers, and the 14 percent held by small Andean peasant colonizers.[58] In other words, between 1993 and 2004, the most powerful agrarian actors in the area gained control of the most valuable frontier property.[59]

---

54 Ibid., 49.

55 Ibid., 35–37.

56 Ibid., 48.

57 Ben McKay and Gonzalo Colque, "Bolivia's Soy Complex: The Development of 'Productive Exclusion,'" *Journal of Peasant Studies* 43, issue 2 (2016): 5, doi: 10.1080/03 066150.2015.1053875.

58 Colque, *Expansión de la frontera agrícola*, 53. The Mennonite and Japanese soy producers are naturalized Bolivian citizens, but analytical commentary and databases on the agrarian situation in the country continue to employ these terms as separate categories. Insofar as it is difficult to avoid the reproduction of such characterizations on ethnic terms, it is at least useful to note additionally that the categories of Mennonite and Japanese soy producers in this case can be thought of as a close proxy for medium-scale capitalist producers.

59 Ibid., 54.

Although there are severe limits to the data available on landholdings in the agricultural frontier of Santa Cruz, some informed estimates have been developed, suggesting that by 2010 Brazilian investors owned roughly half a million of the best land within the 1 million hectares devoted to the cultivation of soy in the region.[60] By the mid-2000s, there were probably no more than 100 Brazilian landholders, but each one controlled between 3,500 and 8,000 hectares.[61] The juridical security of their land possessions, however, is highly uncertain as the vast majority of land purchased by Brazilians has not been administered by INRA through the land registration process, and thus there are no official land titles for their properties.[62] Brazilian investment into Bolivian land for the purposes of soy production began slowly in the 1980s, accelerated in the 1990s, and has expanded still further into ranching interests since the mid-2000s. According to Bolivian law, for Brazilians to own land in Bolivia they have to prove permanent residence in the country. One way Brazilian investors have bypassed the bureaucratic hurdles to establish such proof has been through the establishment by their bank attorneys of fictitious front companies on their behalf, which exist only on paper, but which are ostensibly made up of Bolivian associates. Another way has been through marriages of convenience with Bolivian citizens, through which the immediate granting of citizenship to the investor is facilitated.[63]

Between 1990 and 2007, the cultivated surface area in the lowlands expanded from 413,320 hectares to 1,821,631, or by 4.4 times. More than a million of these hectares were devoted to oilseed plants, and overwhelmingly to soy among them.[64] Between 1990 and 2010, soy production in Santa Cruz increased by 8 times.[65] The annual value of agricultural production in Santa Cruz doubled between 1992 and 2004, and as a proportion of national agricultural GDP, Santa Cruz's share grew from 33 percent to 44 percent over the same period.[66] In the wider South American soy complex, Bolivian soy production is a marginal contribution to total cultivation figures. Between 1970 and 2013, cultivation of soy in South America grew from 1.44 to 52 million hectares.

60 Urioste, "Concentration and 'Foreignisation' of Land in Bolivia," 449.
61 Mamerto Pérez Luna, *No todo grano que brilla es oro: Un análisis de la soya en Bolivia* (La Paz: CEDLA, 2007), 93.
62 Urioste, "Concentration and 'Foreignisation' of Land in Bolivia," 442.
63 Ibid.
64 Colque, *Expansión de la frontera agrícola*, 37–38; Enrique Castañón Ballivián, "Discurso empresarial vs. realidad campesina: la ecología política de la producción de soya en Santa Cruz, Bolivia," *Cuestión Agraria* 2 (November 2015): 66.
65 Colque, *Expansión de la frontera agrícola*, 7.
66 Pérez Luna, *No todo grano que brilla es oro*, 19.

Approximately 90 percent of this production is accounted for by Brazil (53 percent) and Argentina (37 percent) together, with the remaining 10 percent divided between Paraguay, Uruguay, and Bolivia.[67] However, in the Bolivian domestic context the acceleration of soy cultivation has dramatically transformed the agrarian structure of society. Whereas in the mid-1980s roughly 9 percent of cultivated surface area in the country was devoted to industrial agricultural commodities like soy, by 2012 this figure was 48 percent.[68]

Environmental fallout—deforestation, soil degradation, and water contamination—from this agricultural transformation toward soy production has been severe.[69] Agroindustrialists engaged in soy farming are responsible for more deforestation in contemporary Bolivia than any other actor.[70] Partially as a consequence of these shifts in agricultural production in Santa Cruz, this department has suffered some of the greatest ecological symptoms of climate change in Bolivia—rising temperature, reduced precipitation, growing desertification, and increased patterns of obligatory land use changes from agriculture to ranching due to declining soil productivity. There are also more floods in the region than in the past, affecting indigenous and peasant communities located adjacent to soy production zones as a result of agricultural practices that reduce native forest cover, fail to integrate fallow periods, and do not engage in crop rotation. Because of low precipitation rates, water sources are becoming scarcer, and there are frequent disputes between indigenous and peasant communities and large-scale private ranchers who have dammed brooks and streams in order to monopolize water sources for their cattle.[71]

INRA and Neoliberal Multiculturalism

It was almost a decade into neoliberal restructuring and the transition to soy in agriculture that the first MNR government of Gonzalo Sánchez de Lozada (1993–1997) ushered in major legislation, the Law of the National Agrarian Reform Institute (INRA), transforming the approach to agrarian reform adopted in 1953. The Sánchez de Lozada government fundamentally deepened

---

67 Castañón Ballivián, "Discurso empresarial vs. realidad campesina," 66.

68 Ibid.

69 Susanna B. Hecht, "Soybeans, Development and Conservation on the Amazon Frontier," *Development and Change* 36, no. 2 (2005): 375–404; Daniel Redo, Andrew C. Millington, and Derrick Hindery, "Deforestation Dynamics and Policy Changes in Bolivia's Post-Neoliberal Era," *Land Use Policy* 28, no. 1 (2011): 227–241; Hindery, *From Enron to Evo.*

70 Urioste, "Concentration and 'Foreignisation' of Land in Bolivia," 443.

71 Ibid., 443–444.

the process of neoliberal restructuring first introduced in 1985, but together with his Aymara vice president, Víctor Hugo Cárdenas, he framed this second generation of neoliberal reforms in the rhetoric of social solidarity with the poor and a multicultural sensibility toward the indigenous majority of the country.[72] The linchpin of the new government's program was the Plan de Todos (Plan for Everyone), which was supposed to offer a social-market solution to the enduring problems of unemployment, low wages, and the ostensible inefficiencies of the remaining state-owned enterprises.[73] The MNR in this period wedded itself to the notion of a new Bolivia, in which the culturally integrationist nationalism of the post-1952 revolutionary period would be replaced by constitutional recognition of the pluricultural and ethnically heterogeneous nature of Bolivia.[74] This quintessentially neoliberal multiculturalism, however, paired cultural recognition of Bolivia as multiethnic and pluricultural in the constitution, educational reform, and decentralization of authority to new municipalities, with the entrenchment of an orthodox allegiance to financial and trade liberalization, privatization, reduction of the public sector, and fiscal austerity.[75]

In 1992, as a response to the ongoing and untenable rate of subdivision of small parcels of land in the highlands due to demographic growth, as well as the public exposure of corruption by the CNRA (related to the legalization of land illegitimately distributed by the Banzer and García Meza dictatorships), an intervention by a government commission into the activities of CNRA

---

72 Brabazon and Webber, "Evo Morales and the MST in Bolivia," 441.
73 Merilee Grindle, *Audacious Reforms: Institutional Innovation and Democracy in Latin America* (Baltimore, MD: Johns Hopkins University Press, 2000), 113.
74 Carmen Medeiros, "Civilizing the Popular? The Law of Popular Participation and the Design of a New Civil Society in 1990s Bolivia," *Critique of Anthropology* 21, no. 4 (2001): 401–425; Kevin Healy and Susan Paulson, "Political Economies of Identity in Bolivia, 1952–1998," *Journal of Latin American Anthropology* 5, no. 2 (2000): 2–5.
75 Healy and Paulson, "Political Economies of Identity in Bolivia," 11; Charles R. Hale, "Does Multiculturalism Menace? Governance, Cultural Rights and the Politics of Identity in Guatemala," *Journal of Latin American Studies* 34 (2002): 485–524; Charles R. Hale, "Rethinking Indigenous Politics in the Era of the 'Indio Permitido,'" *NACLA Report on the Americas* 38, no. 2 (2004): 16–21; Benjamin Kohl, "Restructuring Citizenship in Bolivia: El Plan de Todos," *International Journal of Urban and Regional Research* 27, no. 2 (2003): 341; Xavier Albó, "And from Kataristas to MNRistas? The Surprising and Bold Alliance between Aymaras and Neoliberals in Bolivia," in *Resistance, Rebellion, and Consciousness in the Andean Peasant World, 18th to 20th Centuries*, ed. Steve J. Stern (Madison: The University of Wisconsin Press, 1995); Bret Gustafson, "Paradoxes of Liberal Indigenism: Indigenous Movements, State Processes, and Intercultural Reform in Bolivia," in *The Politics of Ethnicity: Indigenous Peoples in Latin American States*, ed. David Maybury-Lewis (Cambridge, MA: Harvard University Press and The David Rockefeller Center for Latin American Studies, 2002).

and INC was initiated, an ongoing national dialogue and debate on agrarian reform was launched, and four years later the INRA Law was passed. An institute of the same name, INRA, was also established to carry out land registration processes.[76] As a signal of the World Bank's continued presence in Bolivian agrarian reform policymaking, the process of national dialogue in the early 1990s was financed and overseen by the bank through its National Project for Land Administration (PNAT).[77]

In this sense and others, the context in which the INRA Law was approved was in many senses the apogee of neoliberalism in the country. Nonetheless, the law itself contained internal contradictions that expressed in part the renewed strength of lowland indigenous resistance and defense of their territories and ways of life. As a result, the law embraced, on the one hand, the overarching extension of market mechanisms into the adjudication of land tenure, the security of individual property rights, and a general orientation away from the redistributive components of the 1953 agrarian reform. On the other hand, lawmakers, in the wake of lowland indigenous mobilizations like the March for Territory, Development, and Political Participation of Indigenous Peoples in 1990, organized by the Confederación de Pueblos Indígenas de Bolivia (Confederation of Indigenous Peoples of Bolivia, CIDOB), were forced to recognize communal indigenous territorial rights in the lowlands in a more substantive way than ever before in the history of the republic.[78] Internationally, CIDOB and the lowland indigenous mobilizations more generally also legitimated their struggles with reference to the 1989 indigenous rights Convention 169 of the International Labour Organization (ILO), which the Bolivian government ratified in 1991.[79] Locally, lowland indigenous mobilizations were spurred by growing incursions into their territories in the late 1980s by multinational corporations in the hydrocarbon and forestry sectors, among other extractive activities.[80]

Undoubtedly, the most novel feature of the INRA Law was its legal recognition of lowland indigenous territories through the new juridical category

---

76 Colque, Tinta, and Sanjinés, *Segunda Reforma Agraria*, 78.

77 Penelope Anthias and Sarah A. Radcliffe, "The Ethno-Environmental Fix and Its Limits: Indigenous Land Titling and the Production of Not-Quite-Neoliberal Natures in Bolivia," *Geoforum* 64 (2015): 262.

78 Alejandro Almaraz, "Luchas políticas y legales por la tierra en Bolivia: La luchas indígenas y campesinas en los dos ciclos de la Reforma Agraria," in *Recientes transformaciones agrarias en Bolivia*, ed. Fundación Tierra (La Paz: Fundación Tierra, 2015), 52–53.

79 Lorenza Belinda Fontana, "Indigenous Peoples vs. Peasant Unions: Land Conflicts and Rural Movements in Plurinational Bolivia," *Journal of Peasant Studies* 41, no. 3 (2014): 301.

80 Anthias and Radcliffe, "The Ethno-Environmental Fix and Its Limits," 261.

of TCOs, which were considered to be communally held, tax-free, inalienable, and indivisible territories, and thus impervious to market forces that might otherwise undermine what the law considered to be indigenous collective patrimony.[81] At the same time, there were inbuilt features of the same law that systematically undermined the ostensible indigenous exclusive control over their original territories. For a start, the state retained the rights to subsoil resources within TCO territory. Because many TCOs are located in areas with ample hydrocarbon and mineral deposits, as well as forests, potentially marketable as timber, loopholes in the process of creating the law, allowing for capitalist extraction by multinational corporations, were pursued in the interests of many powerful players in contention over the law's letter and intent.

"As state officials, World Bank employees and indigenous leaders laboured over the text of the INRA Law," Penelope Anthias and Sarah Radcliffe point out, "transnational companies, other government ministries—and indeed other Bank staff—were busy drawing other maps of these territories, zoning them into sites of gas, mineral, and timber extraction. By 2008, 20 of Bolivia's 84 TCOs were subject to contracts for hydrocarbon exploration or exploitation."[82] It is also true that because the INRA Law allowed for private landowners' claims to be made within the territory of TCOs, many TCOs are not "continuous areas of collectively-owned land, but patchworks of collective, private and undefined property rights—particularly in the Chaco region."[83] Finally, while the INRA Law included provisions for the state expropriation of fallow large landholdings that did not serve a socioeconomic function, with the idea that these would then be redistributed to landless or land-poor indigenous peasants, in practice the powerful confederations acting in the interests of agro-industrial capital— Cámara Agropecuaria del Oriente (Agricultural Chamber of the East, CAO), the Asociación de Productores de Oleaginosas y Trigo (Association of Wheat and Oilseed Producers, ANAPO), Cámara de Industria, Comercio, Servicios y Turismo de Santa Cruz (Chamber of Industry, Commerce, Services and Tourism of Santa Cruz, CAINCO), Federación de Ganaderos de Santa Cruz (Santa Cruz Federation of Ranchers, FEGASACRUZ)—mobilized their considerable influence on the state to prevent even basic land registration from being carried out by INRA in the agricultural frontier, much less the expropriation and redistribution of land.[84] Moreover, political representatives working on behalf of

---

81 Fontana, "Indigenous Peoples vs. Peasant Unions," 301.
82 Anthias and Radcliffe, "The Ethno-Environmental Fix and Its Limits," 264.
83 Ibid., 265.
84 McKay and Colque, "Bolivia's Soy Complex," 14; Gabriela Valdivia, "Agrarian Cap-

agroindustry were repeatedly able to alter the mechanisms of the INRA Law's implementation to relativize what they saw to be potentially negative implications for their landholdings. One example was their successful fight for the right to appeal all processes on any INRA resolutions before the National Agrarian Tribunal, which was set up for this purpose.[85]

Two other features of the implementation process of the law also weighed against both its redistributive potential and theoretical recognition of indigenous territory. First, INRA (the institution responsible for carrying out the land registration process) was not properly financed by the Bolivian state and was thus dependent upon the conditional aid of organizations like the World Bank and Danish and Dutch development aid programs. The autonomy of INRA was compromised in this sense from the outset.[86] Between 1996 and 2005, for example, INRA had a budget of $US 78.7 million, of which a paltry $US 8.8 million was covered by the National Treasury. The remaining $US 69.9 million was financed through international aid and external loans.[87] Second, during the first decade of INRA's existence, the actual land registration process was contracted out to a number of national and transnational private land registry corporations, leading to a series of distortions linked to poor implementation of the law, an abandonment of the political principle of aiming for redistributive outcomes to the land registration process, and a concomitant redirection of implementation procedures toward a merely technical registration of private property, a failure to fulfill INRA's mandate, and a misuse of funds.[88] For example, in 1997, the Dutch firm Kadaster was contracted to register 3.1 million hectares with a budget of $US 9.6 million. Years later, the company had surveyed only 14 percent of the land with a budget in excess of the agreed payment.[89]

With the introduction of the INRA Law, the state had a mandate to intervene in and define property rights for 106,751,723 hectares, virtually the entire Bolivian national territory.[90] This was to be completed between 1996 and 2006. It is important to stress, however, that only a very small proportion of these 107 million hectares scheduled for land registration processes is cultivated agricultural land (2.7 million hectares) or land with such agricultural or ranching

italism and Struggles Over Hegemony in the Bolivian Lowlands," *Latin American Perspectives* 37, no. 4 (2010): 67–87.

85 Colque, Tinta, and Sanjinés, *Segunda Reforma Agraria*, 93.

86 Ibid., 89.

87 Ibid., 143.

88 Ibid., 90.

89 Ibid., 146–147.

90 Ibid., 132.

potential (33:8 million hectares with both cultivated and potentially cultivable land taken together).[91] Once this fact is highlighted, it becomes clear that any serious study of the hectares distributed through the INRA reform process, as well as the subsequent agrarian reform modifications under the MAS governments, needs to assess their productive quality in addition to crude quantity.

By 2006, a decade after the introduction of the INRA Law, of the 107 million hectares scheduled for land registration, 12.4 million had been granted titles, several million more had been adjudicated and were awaiting only the signature of the president for final title, and another 15.9 million were somewhere within the "process of registration."[92] In percentage terms, 11.7 percent of the territory to be processed had been titled, 14.9 percent was in the process of being titled, and 73.3 percent had not yet been subject to any INRA process.[93] The state of the INRA land registration process over its first decade is depicted precisely in Table 4.

Table 4. Process of Land Registration and Title, 1996–2006

	No. of Titles	Surface Area in Hectares	Percentage
1. Surface Area Subject to Land Registration		106,751,722	100.0
2. Surface Area Titled	22,178	12,476,740	11.7
2.1 Small property	19,793	677,840	5.4
2.2 Medium property	821	381,688	3.1
2.3 Agricultural Enterprise	882	1,323,857	10.6
2.4 Communitarian Property	550	2,017,080	16.2
2.5 Communitarian Lands of Origin (TCOs)	132	8,076,275	64.7
3. State Property		106,886	0.1
4. Surface Area in the Process of Registration		15,915,920	14.9
5. Surface Area without Any Intervention		78,252,176	73.3

Source: Colque, Tinta, and Sanjinés, *Segunda Reforma Agraria*, 155.

In assessing Table 4, it is important to clarify that the number of titles is not equivalent to the number of beneficiaries. Thus, of the titles granted to communitarian properties, there were 8,005 beneficiaries. In the category of small property, there were 45,072 beneficiaries. For medium properties, there

---

91 Ibid., 133–134.
92 Ibid., 154.
93 Ibid., 158.

were 724 beneficiaries, and for agricultural enterprises, 486 beneficiaries (actual persons, or corporations legally recognized as persons). These indicative figures suggest that medium properties titled in the first decade of the INRA process were on average 24 times bigger than small properties, and the properties of agricultural enterprises 99 times bigger than small properties.[94]

It is clear that, over time, INRA's land registration process became increasingly vulnerable to pressures from both the World Bank and large landholding lobbyists.[95] In spite of the much celebrated social-market hybridity of the law, in fact it provided large landowners with a basic protection of their properties so long as they did not "abandon" them. Under INRA guidelines, the state only considered land to have been abandoned when the owner failed to pay taxes on that property at a self-assessed market value. Effectively, this meant that "absentee landowners [were able] to protect their holdings by paying annual taxes of 1 percent of the value that they themselves establish[ed]."[96] By 2006, it was evident that the INRA land registration process had proved bureaucratically incompetent insofar as only a tiny portion of the total allotted area had been registered and titled, and politically incapable of altering the unequal structure of Bolivian land tenure, despite contradictory advances in the novel legal category of TCOs.

In summary, the neoliberal period introduced dramatic liberalization of agricultural markets, which led to the acceleration of internal differentiation among the highland peasantry. In violation of the free market ideology of neoliberalism, the Bolivian state over this period, together with the World Bank, continued to provide extensive subsidization of the agricultural bourgeoisie in the east. The major transformation of this bourgeoisie in the neoliberal period was a turn to soy, first by Mennonite and Japanese experimental middle-sized producers, and later by Brazilian, and to a lesser extent Argentinian and Colombian investors. Finally, the second decade of the neoliberal period witnessed the emergence of a multicultural state ideology, but one in which indigenous recognition was only possible insofar as it did not violate the precepts of neoliberal orthodoxy in economics. The multicultural ideological turn of state officials was in part a reflection of renewed energies in lowland indigenous social movements, and efforts to contain these energies from above. These contradictory forces were then embedded in the INRA law,

94 Ibid., 158.
95 Webber, *From Rebellion to Reform in Bolivia*, 169; John Crabtree, *Patterns of Protest: Politics and Social Movements in Bolivia* (London: Latin America Bureau, 2005), 79.
96 Kohl, "Restructuring Citizenship in Bolivia," 342.

although it leaned ultimately toward protection of private landholdings and a market-oriented vision of agricultural development. By 2006, a new political era in the country had been introduced, with Morales's rise to the presidency, and, at least briefly, a renewed intensity of class struggle over alternative agrarian futures seemed to open up the possibility of substantive reform.

Phase III—Neodevelopmental Agrarian Reform, 2006–2016

(i) Insurgent Contestation (2006–2009)

When Evo Morales was elected in December 2005, following five years of rural and urban social movement mobilization on a level unparalleled elsewhere in Latin America, the issue of agrarian reform was thrust once again into the center of political debate in Bolivia. The agro-industrial elite of the lowlands responded vociferously to the new government's overtures to the popular rural classes, threatening insurrection against the state and initiating what would become a four-year campaign of regionalist/autonomist destabilization against the central government, rooted in the media luna departments of Pando, Beni, Santa Cruz, and Tarija.[97] Articulating the particular agrarian modalities of the government's more general defense of a "plural economy," Morales quickly committed state support toward three key rural sectors, which were seen as mutually beneficial to one another rather than intrinsically conflictual: large-scale, agro-industrial exporters; small-scale family peasant production; and communal indigenous landholdings.[98]

In an early indication of coming confrontation between the government and large landowners in the east, Morales appointed Alejandro Almaraz, a longstanding militant for far-reaching agrarian reform and one of the founding members of the leadership of the MAS in the 1990s, to be Vice Minister of Land. Almaraz became one of the most instrumental ideologues of, and symbolic forces behind, the first legislation on agrarian reform introduced by the Morales government, Law 3545 or the Law of Communitarian Renewal of Agrarian Reform (LRCRA) in November 2006.[99] The social mobilizations of 2000–2005 required that the MAS at least appear to respond to the fundamental demands of social justice in the countryside. Likewise, the loom-

---

97 Webber, *From Rebellion to Reform in Bolivia*, 67–101.
98 "El Estado promoverá desarrollo de tres 'plataformas' agrarias," *La Prensa*, May 17, 2006.
99 "De leal al MAS a disidente," *La Razón*, November 4, 2012.

ing expiration date on the INRA land registration process (1996–2006) also necessitated a new law on agrarian reform. The significant extent to which LRCRA modified the principles of the INRA Law was justified by the government with reference to INRA's poor record of bureaucracy, inertia, lack of transparency, and the corrupt redistribution of land to the powerful, as well as the general trajectory of the 1996–2006 period of agrarian reform, which reinforced rather than overturned the power of the large landowners.[100]

The most novel characteristics of the Communitarian Renewal legislation were its modification of the INRA Law's mechanisms of land registration and title, such that they more closely corresponded to the spirit of redistributive reform. The concept of large properties having to fulfill a specific socioeconomic function in order to avoid expropriation and redistribution was made more precise, and the procedures to expropriate and redistribute were clarified to enable greater ease of applicability. The distribution of state property to landless and land-poor indigenous peasants and communities was prioritized in the law, and novel amendments to legal procedures were introduced to expedite the process of land registration.[101] According to Almaraz himself, the LRCRA had at its core the notions that land should be redistributed from the land-rich minority to the landless and land-poor indigenous majority.[102] For Almaraz, the content of the law reflected the demands of twenty years of indigenous peasant struggle, retaining the redistributive ideas found within parts of the 1953 agrarian reform but transcending that earlier paradigm in many ways through the explicit recognition of indigenous communal territorial rights in the lowlands.[103]

Following on from the early introduction of the new agrarian reform law, the principal terrain of class struggle over the future of Bolivian agrarian social relations shifted to the simultaneously institutional and extraparliamentary conflicts over the content and trajectory of the Constituent Assembly between 2006 and 2007.[104] Allied with the MAS inside the Constituent Assembly, but often taking independent positions to the left of the party's executive, was the Unity Pact. This social movement alliance was composed of an array of lowland and highland indigenous-peasant popular organizations, including

---

100 Colque, Tinta, and Sanjinés, *Segunda Reforma Agraria*, 162.

101 Ibid., 163.

102 Almaraz, "Luchas políticas y legales por la tierra en Bolivia," 50.

103 Ibid., 53.

104 Pablo Regalsky, "Las paradojas del proceso constituyente boliviano," *Herramienta* Web 2, September 2009, www.herramienta.com.ar/herramienta-web-2/las-paradojas -del-proceso-constituyente-boliviano.

CIDOB, the Consejo Nacional de Ayllus and Markas of Qullasuyu (National Council of Ayllus and Markas of Qullasuyu, CONAMAQ), the Confederación Sindical Única de Trabajadores Campesinos de Bolivia (Unified Syndical Confederation of Rural Workers of Bolivia, CSUTCB), Confederación Nacional de Mujeres Campesinas Indígenas Originarias de Bolivia "Bartolina Sisa" (Bartolina Sisa National Confederation of Peasant, Indigenous, and Aboriginal Women of Bolivia, CNMCIOB-BS), and the Confederación Sindical de Comunidades Interculturales de Bolivia (Syndicalist Confederation of Intercultural Communities of Bolivia, CSCIB).[105] These organizations together sought to take advantage of the assembly process to refound Bolivian state–society relations on new grounds, understanding as they did that the Morales government owed its existence to the movements' extraordinary effervescence between 2000 and 2005. The Unity Pact was central in the domain of the assembly, as well as in the Bolivian political contest more generally, to articulating notions of geographic space and territory that went well beyond the productive potentialities of land. The notion of indigenous territory articulated by the indigenous peasant alliance was one that linked integral cultural and symbolic forms of indigenous modes of life to the material appropriation of land and territory. Territory is understood, in this sense, as the multidimensional material foundation that allows for the reproduction of distinct indigenous modes of life and self-determination, including their cultural and symbolic dimensions. Land was thus not reduced merely to a means of economic support, or a basis of subsistence—although it was understood to involve this—but was also conceived as the prerequisite for further reaching conceptualizations of indigenous self-determination and forms of rule.[106]

Famously, for René Zavaleta, one of Bolivia's most important twentieth-century radical social theorists, the country is best conceived as a *sociedad abigarrada*, or motley society, in which one finds a coexistence of various historical times, modes of production, conceptions of the world, and structures of authority.[107] One way of conceiving of the indigenous struggle of the Unity Pact within the Constituent Assembly process is to think of it as a method of recovering those indigenous historical times, modes of production, conceptions of the world, and structures of authority that had been subordinated

---

105 Jorge Viaña, "Estado plurinacional y nueva fase del proceso boliviano," in *El Estado en América Latina: Continuidades y rupturas*, ed. Mabel Thwaites (Buenos Aires: CLACSO, 2012), 382.

106 Colque, Tinta, and Sanjinés, *Segunda Reforma Agraria*, 44.

107 René Zavaleta, *Lo nacional popular en Bolivia* (Mexico: Siglo XXI, 1986).

historically to the monocultural republican state since the early nineteenth century, and the subsequent combination of the republican state's racist logic with the logic of capital accumulation, since the first embryonic stages of capitalist transition in the late nineteenth century. The idea embedded in the Unity Pact's struggle for territory was, in this way, an effort to call into question the basic contradiction of the Bolivian nation-state and the form of its organization of national territory, premised as it is on colonial conquest and the interests of capital, both of which combined historically in an effort to make invisible, through violent imposition, the indigenous territories and modes of self-governance that struggled to persist in subaltern ways.[108]

The autonomist right of the lowlands, meanwhile, was attempting to subvert the functioning of the Constituent Assembly through both formal opposition from inside its institutional structures and extraparliamentary mass destabilization directed at undermining the central government. In August 2008, the government was strengthened after a recall referendum organized by the opposition to oust the government led instead to the ratification of the president and vice president with an impressive 67 percent of the national vote. The opposition prefects of the departments of La Paz and Cochabamba were also revoked and replaced with government supporters. As expected, the referendum also saw the ratification of oppositional prefects in Santa Cruz, Tarija, Beni, and Pando.[109] After losing ground in the electoral domain, the autonomist right of the lowlands opted for extraparliamentary destabilization in the form of a civic-coup attempt at the departmental level. From September 9 to September 16, 2008, major right-wing mobilizations were launched, and seventy-five government institutions were occupied across the media luna departments, including the offices of the state's agrarian reform institution (INRA) and its telephone company (ENTEL). Airports were seized, and Morales was prevented from entering the territory of large swathes of the country. Rubén Costas, the governor of Santa Cruz, was launching what he thought would be the final assault on the Morales government. He called the president an assassin, and said the patience of the people of Santa Cruz had run out and that Morales had to go. The Civic Committee of Santa Cruz coordinated the actions from on high, while their violent shock troops in the

108 Pilar Lizárraga Aranibar and Carlos Vacaflores Rivero, "La descolonización del territorio: luchas y resistencias campesinas e indígenas en Bolivia," in *Capitalismo: Tierra y poder en América Latina (1982–2012)—Bolivia, Colombia, Ecuador, Perú, Venezuela*, vol. II, eds. Guillermo Almeyra, Luciano Concheiro Bórquez, João Márcio Mendes Pereira, and Carlos Walter Porto-Gonçalves (Buenos Aires: CLACSO, 2014), 36.
109 Viaña, "Estado plurinacional y nueva fase del proceso boliviano," 376–377.

Unión Juveñil Cruceñista (Union of Cruceño Youth, UJC) carried out the necessary thug violence in the street.[110]

However, events in Porvenir, in the department of Pando, took a turn that eventually ground the opposition's momentum to a halt. Dozens of peasant and student supporters of the government were murdered by right-wing oppositionists linked to the Pando prefect Leopoldo Fernández. In response the Morales government took over Pando militarily, and peasant and indigenous organizations loyal to the party began to organize a massive march, threatening to surround Santa Cruz. Organized indigenous youth from the shantytown of Plan 3000 in Santa Cruz also engaged in increasingly successful street battles with UJC hooligans. The fundamental outcome of this dynamic led ultimately to a concerted spike in support for the government and the near disappearance of an organized oppositional bloc, with decisive consequences for the rhythm of politics in Bolivia thereafter.[111]

The Constituent Assembly had agreed on the text for the new constitution back in December 2007. However, in the context of persistent political instability in the country, a modified and moderated version of the text was only ratified by the Bolivian Congress in late October 2008, after negotiations brokered by the Union of South American Nations (UNASUR) led to a temporary settlement between the government and regional opposition. The text was subsequently ratified by two-thirds of the Bolivian electorate through a direct referendum in January 2009. In terms of content, the constitution has been accurately described as a "patchwork of overlapping and often conflicting claims involving indigenous peoples and nonindigenous propertied citizens," rather than "a unified set of rules for governing the national territory."[112] It promises, on the one hand, protection for indigenous rights to self-determination and autonomy (Article 2), while, on the other, it reinforces private property rights (Article 315).[113] While Article 38 sets a maximum land-size ceiling of five thousand hectares, Article 315.11 allows for agro-industrial groups to be constituted by an unlimited number of business associates, who are each permitted to have that maximum five thou-

---

110 Boris Miranda, "El fin de las logias y el último autonomista," *El desacuerdo*, September 29, 2013.

111 Viaña, "Estado plurinacional y nueva fase del proceso boliviano," 377.

112 Pablo Regalsky, "Political Processes and the Reconfiguration of the State in Bolivia," *Latin American Perspectives* 37, no. 3 (2010): 36.

113 Regalsky, "Political Processes and the Reconfiguration of the State in Bolivia," 36; Nam Kwon Mun, "La problemática transición boliviana hacia la época postneoliberal: el caso de la economía comunitaria," *Revista de Estudios Sociales* 54 (October–December 2015): 28.

sand hectares.[114] The five-thousand-hectare ceiling, moreover, is not retroactively binding on preexisting large properties. Further, the constitution declares Bolivia to be a "plurinational state," while simultaneously legalizing large landholdings and subordinating claims of indigenous territorial autonomy to existing departmental boundaries.[115] "The constitution," Willem Assies argues, "guarantees the right to private property (in rural areas on the condition that it complies with a socio-economic function) alongside communal and state property."[116]

What were some of the early results in land registration and titling ushered in by the new agrarian reform law and in the context of the new constitution? In short, there was a dramatic uptick in the efficiency of registration and titling, but these efficiency gains did not counteract deep continuities with INRA insofar as the structural inequality of Bolivia's rural class structure remained largely intact. In the 2006–2009 period there was little advance in registering and titling medium and large agro-industrial properties in Santa Cruz both because the government's priorities were elsewhere, but also because of the fierce political opposition initially mounted by large landowning producers in the lowlands to the Law of Communitarian Renewal of Agrarian Reform.[117] The pace of land registration and land titling on an aggregate level over this period was remarkably high by comparative standards, however. Recall that during the 1996–2006 period on INRA land registration, 12.4 million hectares were formally granted title. In the much shorter span of time between 2007 and 2009, 11.7 million hectares were granted title. The sum of these two periods reaches 24.1 million hectares, 22 percent of the total surface area scheduled to be registered.[118] The fact that the number of titles granted in the first three years of the Morales administration is almost equal to that achieved in a decade under the INRA Law is testament to the efficiency, by this metric, of the new procedures and legal dispositions introduced by the Law of Communitarian Renewal. The details of the progress of land registration and title between 2007 and 2009 are shown in Table 5.

114 McKay and Colque, "Bolivia's Soy Complex," 15.
115 Regalsky, "Political Processes and the Reconfiguration of the State in Bolivia," 37; Pablo Regalsky, "Acerca de las paradojas de la crisis hegemónica, del nacionalismo de Evo y de la confusion en los movimientos indígenas," *Herramienta* 46 (March 2011), www.herramienta.com.ar/revista-herramienta-n-46/ acerca-de-las-paradojas-de-la -crisis-hegemonica-del-nacionalismo-de-evo-y-d.
116 Willem Assies, "Bolivia's New Constitution and Its Implications," in *Evo Morales and the Movimiento al Socialismo in Bolivia*, ed. Adrian J. Pearce (London: Institute for the Study of the Americas, University of London, 2011), 115.
117 Urioste, "Concentration and 'Foreignisation' of Land in Bolivia," 443.
118 Colque, Tinta, and Sanjinés, *Segunda Reforma Agraria*, 163–164.

Table 5. State of Land Registration and Title, 2007–2009

	No. of Titles	Surface Area in Hectares	Percentage
1. Surface Area Subject to Land Registration		106,751,722	100.0
2. Surface Area Titled	80,525	11,799,221	11.1
2.1 Small property	77,907	846,865	7.2
2.2 Medium property	504	322,376	2.7
2.3 Agricultural Enterprise	136	427,701	3.6
2.4 Communitarian property	1,848	2,659,576	22.5
2.5 Communitarian Lands of Origin (TCOs)	130	7,542,703	63.9
3. State Property Registered		15,239,784	14.3
4. Surface Area in the Process of Registration		14,258,859	13.4
5. Surface Area without Any Intervention		52,870,232	49.5
6. Accumulation from Previous Period	22,178	12,583,626	11.8
6.1 Surface Area Titled	22,178	12,476,740	11.7
6.2 State Property Registered		106,886	0.1

Source: Gonzalo Colque, Efraín Tinta, and Esteban Sanjinés, *Segunda Reforma Agraria*, 164.

While the figure of 11.7 million hectares titled is impressive relative to the 1996–2006 period, it is far lower than the 31.1 million hectares INRA claims to have titled between January 2006 and December 2009.[119] The first distortion in the INRA figures is that because they begin their timeline in January 2006, 3.4 million hectares of land titled between January and October 2006, under the INRA Law, is misleadingly calculated as a product of new legislation under Morales. Second, and more significantly, the figure of 31.1 million hectares referred to by INRA officials during the first Morales administration refers to both "titled" and "registered" properties. This exaggerates the work done under Morales's reign because 18.6 million hectares of the "registered" land in question here had already been registered in the 1996–2006 period.[120]

The main novelty of the 2006–2009 period, apart from the expediting of the process of registering and titling, was an extension of TCOs to the Andean highlands, and in particular the departments of Oruro and Potosí. But the 2006–2009 era was not marked by any radical redistribution of land.[121] A

---

119 INRA, *La tierra vuelve a manos indígenas y campesinas* (La Paz: Instituto Nacional de Reforma Agraria, 2010).
120 Colque, Tinta, and Sanjinés, *Segunda Reforma Agraria*, 165.
121 Ibid., 170.

solution to the problems of landlessness and land poverty in the most densely populated agrarian countryside in Bolivia was not on offer.[122] Most of the limited redistrubtion of land that did take place through the granting of title to TCOs was not a consequence of the expropriation of large landholdings and their subsequent redistribution. According to INRA, the MAS government had redistributed 3.9 million hectares of land by 2010. But this figure included 499,000 hectares in Oruro and 492,000 hectares in Potosí that were merely changes in title from *proindiviso* (community land that is collectively titled and not formally divided into individual plots) to the category of TCO—that is, a juridical distinction between two communal forms of title to land.[123] These apparent land transfers, then, amounted to little more than an alteration in legal status. Excluding these figures, redistribution through the process of registering TCOs had by 2010 reached the figure of 2.9 million hectares. Of this total, the vast majority of these redistributed lands (72.8 percent) were transfers from state-owned property to TCOs. Only 27.2 percent of lands distributed to TCOs, then, were the result of expropriation or partial expropriation.[124]

Indeed, despite the initial political confrontation with the agro-industrial elite of the lowlands, the dynamism of the soy economy continued apace in the opening years of the Morales government, while peasant production continued its decomposition. In one indication of this trend, industrial crops accounted for 70.1 percent of agricultural production in 2005–2006 and 80.4 percent in 2010–2011. Crucially, 76 percent of the total growth in the volume of agricultural production between 2005 and 2011 was soy (40 percent) and sugar cane (36 percent) taken together.[125] While 78 percent of soy producers are classified as small producers, this figure contrasts dramatically with the miniscule proportion of cultivated soy land over which they have control (9 percent).[126]

Growing out of the initial incursions of Brazilian, and to a lesser extent Argentinian and Colombian, foreign capital into the soy sector, new forms of transnational investment were advanced that focused less on direct production of land and more on control over later stages in the soy commodity value chain, such as harvesting, processing, commercialization, storage, and export.[127] Across this "soy complex," five companies came to control 90 percent of the

---

122 Ibid., 172.
123 Control Ciudadano, *Reconducción comunitaria de la reforma agraria y producción agrícola*, 6–7.
124 Ibid., 10.
125 Ibid., 5.
126 Colque, *Expansión de la frontera agrícola*, 61.
127 Ibid., 56.

production of soy and its derivatives for export.[128] These were Gaveltal Bolivia, Industria de Aceites, Archer Daniels Midland SAO (ADM), Industrias Ole-aginosas, Cargill Bolivia, and Bunge (Global Company). Transnational inves-tors operating through these companies have captured vast shares of Bolivia's storage, processing, and export markets, including some of the world's biggest agro-industrial corporations: ADM, Bunge, Cargill, and Louis Dreyfus.[129]

Transnational capital established its presence throughout the value chain initially through the acquisition of already existing Santa Cruz agro-enterprises. They often did so by purchasing these domestic enterprises under the names of Brazilian and Argentinian subsidiaries of the transnational firms.[130] Because of the incomplete land registration process in the most dynamic sector of the Bolivian agricultural economy—the agricultural frontier of soy expansion—precise data on the relationship between these new transnational firms and di-rect production of soy and land ownership is not available, but their activities seem mainly to consist of "grain purchases, storage, processing facilities, mar-keting and export."[131] By the end of the first Morales term in office, most small-scale soy producers were selling their products directly or indirectly to these transnational enterprises further up the soy value chain.[132]

(ii) Agro-Capital-State Alliance (2010–2016)

If in the phase of insurgent contestation (2006–2009) the possibility, in Gramscian terms, of the transformative character of the epoch being domi-nant had seemed high at moments, the accent shifted decisively toward res-toration in the post-2010 period. According to vice president Álvaro García Linera, a revolutionary process opened up in 2000 and went through a variety of phases. It culminated in the election of Morales in 2005 and 2009, with its latest consolidation working its way through the elections in October 2014. Hegemony was achieved by 2010, after which tensions and contradictions of the "process of change" became creative, internal forces operating within the national-popular bloc supporting the government. The Bolivian people were thus united around plurinationality, indigenous territorial autonomy, and a plural economy—involving public, private, and social-communitarian forms of property, with the state presence in the economy subordinating the other forms of property. The process is in motion toward an integral state, under-

128 Ibid.
129 McKay and Colque, "Bolivia's Soy Complex," 16.
130 Colque, Expansión de la frontera agrícola, 59.
131 McKay and Colque, "Bolivia's Soy Complex," 16.
132 Colque, Expansión de la frontera agrícola, 62.

stood as the state's ultimate dissolution into society, while the economy is moving—even with setbacks—to one dominated by the logic of use-value over exchange-value.[133]

The sociologist Jorge Viaña tells a somewhat different story about the character of the process from 2010 forward. The defeat of the organized oppositional bloc allowed for the hardening of the most conservative layers within the government, while simultaneously providing a space for the internal divisions within the popular bloc to deepen and expand. Internal dissidents in the ruling party were increasingly depicted as enemies of the process itself, particularly the lowland indigenous organizations, which continued to struggle for meaningful territorial self-determination of indigenous peoples in the parts of the country under their domain.[134]

What is very clear is that while the relationship between the agro-industrial elite of the lowlands and the Morales regime was one of antagonism between 2006 and 2009, from 2010 forward the situation has been dramatically different. After the political defeat of the autonomist movement of the lowlands, the agro-industrial elite changed tactics and opted for a close working relationship with the Morales government.[135] They were in return embraced by officialdom. Recall that in August 2008 Rubén Costas was plotting Morales's ouster from office. By 2013, he was regularly lunching with Morales and joining García Linera for formal government ceremonial acts in Santa Cruz. The president is also now entirely at home in his regular consultations with CAO, ANAPO, CAINCO, and the Confederación de Empresarios Privados de Bolivia (Confederation of Private Employers of Bolivia, CEPB)—that is, precisely those business organizations that backed the civic-coup attempt of 2008.[136]

One of the greatest strengths of the leadership of Evo Morales, according to the sympathetic reading of journalist and former advisor to the government Walter Chávez, is his ability to move at a rhythm adequate to the pace of the process that the country has been living through over the last two decades, never pushing the pace of change beyond what is possible in the particular conjuncture. He could have entered into a pact with the elite of Santa Cruz

---

133 Álvaro García Linera, *Tensiones creativas de la revolución: La Quinta fase del Proceso del Cambio* (La Paz: Vicepresidencia del Estado Plurinacional, 2011).

134 Viaña, "Estado plurinacional y nueva fase del proceso boliviano."

135 Castañón Ballivián, "Discurso empresarial vs. realidad campesina," 73.

136 Miranda, "El fin de las logias y el último autonomista"; Boris Miranda, "Santa Cruz, el objeto del deseo: ¿El proceso de cambio tiene rostro camba?," *El desacuerdo*, June 23, 2013; Gisela López Rivas, "El presidente en Santa Cruz," *El desacuerdo*, September 29, 2013.

early in his first administration, but instead he rejected the demands of the bourgeois-autonomist bloc and entered into a long struggle against them across all political fields. Without this decision by Morales, the future of the process of change would be quite different today. For Chávez, the path of the democratic and cultural revolution introduced by Morales has been one of struggle–victory–inclusion–expansion. The incorporation of a politically defeated but economically dynamic business sector in Santa Cruz is simply the latest exemplar of this successful road to transformation. By bringing business elites formerly on board, Morales achieved cultural hegemony, avoided costly polarization of society, and prolonged the process of revolutionary change. According to Chávez, the Santa Cruz elite now accepts the statesmanship of Morales, recognizing in him a moral and political leader at the head of an historic process which is, among other things, bringing economic development to Bolivia.[137] "Santa Cruz has opened itself up to the process of change," García Linera suggests, "and the national-popular project of the indigenous, peasant, and workers movement has irradiated territorially and widened the bases of the intellectual and moral leadership of this process."[138] "Gabriel Dabdoub, who heads the Santa Cruz Federation of Private Business and opposed Mr. Morales during his first term," notes Andres Schipani in the *Financial Times*, "says the private and public sector are now working together."[139]

If, on the one hand, the agro-industrial elite and the post-2010 Morales government forged a new agro-capital-state alliance, this corresponded with the rupture in the relationship between the government and lowland indigenous organizations. A realignment in the class composition of the ruling party was set in motion. An initial indication of the new divisions was the government's conflict with CIDOB in June 2010. In late June, an indigenous march led by CIDOB departed Trinidad, the capital of the department of Beni, in protest against the Organic Plurinational Electoral Law and the Framework Law for Autonomies, which the government had just introduced as a means of implementing different components of the new constitution. The marchers were supported by seven indigenous MAS members of congress from the lowlands, who went on hunger strike in solidarity. The protesters saw the new laws as falling short of historic demands for designated seats in congress for

---

137 Walter Chávez, "Evo, Santa Cruz y la Revolución: El largo camino hacia la conquista de la hegemonía," *El desacuerdo*, September 29, 2013.

138 As quoted in "García Linera afirma que Santa Cruz se abrió al Proceso de Cambio," *Página Siete*, October 9, 2014.

139 Andrés Schipani, "Bolivia's Evo Morales Secures Redistributionist Mandate," *Financial Times*, October 13, 2014.

indigenous self-representation; they also argued that the new legislation did not sufficiently encompass respect for consultation with indigenous communities before any development projects are initiated in their territories, and minimized the integrity of indigenous territorial autonomy and therefore self-determination in the lowlands. Specifically, they wanted the immediate approval of mechanisms that would better protect the recognition of TCOs.[140]

The CIDOB activists were dismissed by government officials as "dividers" (*fraccionalistas*) of the national-popular bloc, playing into the hands of imperialism and the domestic right. The government proved increasingly incapable of distinguishing between indigenous lowland activists and the right-wing governors of the media luna departments that had attempted the civic coup in 2008. Even if it was true that conservative political forces and liberal NGOs were attempting to steer the dynamics within lowland indigenous protests— as they inevitably were, and as they have done throughout the recent past—the rejection of CIDOB's basic claims in the protest was an extraordinary miscalculation on the part of the government. The political error, as Viaña points out, was to deny the fundamental legitimacy of the lowland indigenous struggle, and therefore to move from negotiation toward directing all of the resources of the state against the movement. If the government is actually committed to plurinationality, Viaña contends, a fundamental requisite in the lowlands is respect for the territorial integrity of the 26 million hectares of TCOs such that the lowland indigenous peoples can, in material and cultural terms, continue to reproduce themselves.[141]

By mid-2011, the emergent divisions within the national-popular bloc escalated when Morales gave a green light to a decades-old plan to build a highway connecting Villa Tunari (in the department of Cochabamba), north to San Ignacio de Moxos (in the department of Beni) through Isiboro-Sécure Indigenous Territory and National Park (TIPNIS).[142] The TIPNIS highway conflict set off indigenous marches by those lowland indigenous groups asserting their right to self-government and prior consultation before any development project is planned and executed. The government in turn sponsored counterdemonstrations and sent in police to repress the marches. The indigenous protests were, the government argued, manipulated, even led, by foreign NGOs and the domestic right. While there is evidence that American interests and the Bolivian

---

140 Viaña, "Estado plurinacional y nueva fase del proceso boliviano," 378.

141 Ibid., 380, 386.

142 Jeffery R. Webber, "Revolution against 'Progress': Neo-Extractivism, the Compensatory State, and the TIPNIS Conflict in Bolivia," in *Crisis and Contradiction*.

right have sought to intervene in the TIPNIS crisis to their own ends—as they will always do, given the opportunity—the organic character of the movement's core is difficult to dismiss even by the most blinkered government loyalists. It is worthwhile to note, too, the presence of voices within the TIPNIS indigenous marches that have been critical of their organizations' leaderships for being insufficiently attuned to the right's attempts to co-opt their struggle. The TIPNIS crisis led to the first major formal ruptures within the rural bases of the national-popular bloc that had until then lent critical support to the government. In late 2011, CIDOB, together with CONAMAQ, split from the Unity Pact.[143]

Once CIDOB and CONAMAQ had formally left the Unity Pact, the MAS initiated a concerted effort to undermine their capacities to independently represent lowland indigenous groups—in 2012, dissident supporters of the government within CIDOB disclaimed the elected authorities and called for "an extended commission" through which new ones would be elected. More dramatically, in December 2013, minority affiliates of the MAS within CONAMAQ occupied the organization's headquarters in La Paz, beating and expelling the legitimate authorities. They did so with the support of the police, who guarded the headquarters and prevented the return of CONAMAQ's elected representatives.[144] Together, the CIDOB conflict of June 2010 and the TIPNIS conflict of 2011, as well as the splits in the Unity Pact later that year, represented a new consolidation of the most conservative layers of the governing party and the identification of internal dissidents as enemies of the "process of change."

This tendency was compounded further by the expulsion or desertion from the party of a series of high-profile left-wing intellectuals and activists who had supported the government between 2006 and 2010—Lino Villca, Román Loayza, Félix Patzi, Alejandro Almaraz, Alex Contreras, Raúl Prada, Gustavo Guzmán, and Pablo Solón.[145] Many of these were signatories, alongside other left-indigenous oppositionists, of the *Manifiesto de la Coordinadora Plurinacional de la Reconducción: Por la recuperación del proceso de cambio para el pueblo y con el pueblo* (Manifesto of the Plurinational Coordinator for Renewal: For the Recovery of the Process of Change for the People and with the People), published in June 2011.[146] This document famously elicited Álvaro

143 Viaña, "Estado plurinacional y nueva fase del proceso boliviano," 382.

144 Raúl Zibechi, "Developmentalism and Social Movements in Bolivia." *Americas Program*, December 9, 2014.

145 Paola Sóliz Chávez, "¿Qué será lo que quiere el negro? Lo que todavía no se había dicho del affaire Rebeca Delgado," *El desacuerdo*, June 23, 2013.

146 *Manifiesto de la coordinadora plurinacional de la reconducción: Por la recuperación del proceso de cambio para el pueblo y con el pueblo*, June 2011.

García Linera's acerbic "Leninist" pamphlet, denouncing what he took to be an emergent infantile ultra-left.[147] Such was the evolving political context in which agrarian class struggle unfolded between 2010 and 2016.

Within this dynamic, what were the results of the land registration and titling process? As Table 6 indicates, in the 2010–2014 period, 16.5 million hectares were granted title, divided between state property (9.1 million), TCOs (7.4 million), a new category of peasant communitarian property (6.5 million), large agricultural enterprises (1.3 million), medium agricultural enterprises (964,000), and small holdings (2.3 million). By the end of this period there were also 26.8 million hectares in the process of registration, and 14.5 million hectares in which no registration process had yet been initiated.[148]

Table 6. State of Land Registration and Title, 2010–2014

	No. of Titles	Surface Area in Hectares	Percentage
1. Surface Area Subject to Registration		106,751,722	100.0
2. Surface Area Titled	288,982	16,510,514	15.5
2.1 Small property	280,102	2,327,345	14.1
2.2 Medium property	1,823	963,587	5.8
2.3 Agricultural enterprise	356	1,339,972	8.1
2.4 Communitarian property	6,523	4,500,315	27.3
2.5 Communitarian Lands of Origin (TCOs)	178	7,379,295	44.7
3. State Property Registered		9,195,850	8.6
4. Surface Area in the Process of Registration		26,867,679	25.2
5. Surface Area without Any Intervention		14,555,048	13.6
6. Accumulation from Previous	102,703	39,622,631	37.1
6.1 Surface Area Titled (1996–2006)	22,178	12,476	11.7
6.2 State Property Registered (1996–2006)		106,886	0.1
6.3 Surface Area Titled (2007–2009)	80,525	11,799,221	11.1
6.4 State Property Registered (2007–2009)		15,239,784	14.3

Source: Colque, Tinta, and Sanjinés, *Segunda Reforma Agraria*, 175.

The titling of 16.5 million hectares in this period represents a significant degree of acceleration in the process of land titling relative to earlier phases. Of

---

147 Álvaro García Linera, *El "ONGismo", Enfermedad infantil del derechismo: (O cómo la reconducción del Proceso de Cambio es la restauración neoliberal)* (La Paz: Vicepresidencia del Estado Plurinacional de Bolivia, 2011).
148 Colque, Tinta, and Sanjinés, *Segunda Reforma Agraria*, 175.

this titled land, TCOs accounted for just under half, with peasant communitarian property amounting to 27.2 percent of the total. This latter development was novel, with more than half of peasant communitarian property being titled in the highlands but with significant consolidation in the lowlands as well.[149] Fourteen percent of titled properties were granted to smallholders, much of this in colonization settlements and coca grower settlements in the Chapare region of Cochabamba. Finally, medium and large properties accounted for 13.9 percent of titles, including 56 titles granted in excess of 5,000 hectares each.

Table 7 breaks down the number of titles into the number of beneficiaries, an important next step in a comprehensive view of the land registration and titling process. What is evident in this snapshot is that in the categories of medium and business properties each beneficiary has title to an average of 995 hectares, in TCOs 48 hectares, and in peasant and intercultural properties, 17 hectares.[150]

Table 7. Beneficiaries of Registration and Title According to Types of Property

Types of Property	No. of Titles	No. of Beneficiaries	Surface Area Registered and Titled by Hectare	Hectares per Title	Hectares per Beneficiary
Peasant and Intercultural (Small Property, Communitarian Property)	444,880	1,135,283	17,800,000	40	16
Medium and Large Agribusinesses (Medium Property and Agricultural Enterprise)	3,293	6,328	6,300,000	1,913	996
Communitarian Lands of Origin (TCOs)	1,283	494,414	23,900,000	18,628	48
Total	449,456	1,636,025	48,000,000*	107	29

*This total does not correspond to the number of hectares titled between 1996 and 2014. This is because the figure here includes not only titled land but registered land. Because of

---

149 Colque, Tinta, and Sanjinés, *Segunda Reforma Agraria,* 179.
150 Ibid., 195.

limits to available data, it is not possible to elaborate the relevant figure with reference only to titled land. In any case, this is a limitation that does not damage the qualitative value of these figures.

Source: Colque, Tinta, and Sanjinés, *Segunda Reforma Agraria*, 194.

Predictably, these agribusiness properties were located mainly in Santa Cruz and Beni, and to a lesser extent in Tarija, Chuquisaca, and the north of La Paz.[151] In the 2010–2014 period there has been a bigger number of titled hectares distributed to the agribusiness sector, and a larger average size to title processes—up to 3,763 hectares per agribusiness title on average, compared to 1,500 between 1996 and 2006.[152]

The titles granted to large and medium enterprises are not as large in surface area as TCOs or peasant communitarian properties, but are qualitatively distinct. And it is this attention to quality that needs to be stressed in any meaningful assessment of agrarian reform during the Morales epoch to date. The strategic zones of the most productive agricultural, ranching, and forestry land in the country are concentrated in the lowlands, precisely in those areas in which titles for medium and large enterprises have been concentrated.[153] A characteristic feature of TCOs, by contrast, is that they tend to be situated on the margins of agro-industrial centres and economic corridors (highway and road networks) and are largely of poor or null agricultural potential.[154] The recurring pattern of distribution and registration is one of marginal lands to the rural majority and potentially productive lands to the agribusiness sector.[155]

As Table 8 indicates, the substance of this pattern can be sharply demonstrated through a closer look at the results of land registration in the zone of expansion of Santa Cruz, where 75 percent of cultivated land in the country is located. These figures indicate that in terms of productive agricultural land in this area, the indigenous-peasant sector has title to less than a third, while medium and large enterprises concentrate the rest in their hands.[156]

---

151 Ibid., 180.
152 Ibid., 191.
153 Ibid., 184.
154 Ibid.
155 Ibid., 196.
156 Ibid., 201.

Table 8. Land Registration in "Zone of Expansion" in Santa Cruz, 1996–2014

Type of Property	Surface Area Registered and Titled in Hectares	Percentage	No. of Titles	Percentage	Surface Area Per Title (Average)
Small Property	618,350	16.9	17,593	82.9	67.4
Medium Property	544,743	14.9	1,672	7.9	325.8
Agricultural Enterprise	1,711,014	46.7	888	4.2	1,926.8
Communitarian Property	323,924	8.8	376	1.8	861.5
Communitarian Lands of Origin (TCOs)	138,899	3.8	87	0.4	1,596.5
Unknown	329,419	9.0	622	2.9	529.6
Total	3,666,349	100.0	21,238	100.0	5,307.6

Source: Colque, Tinta, and Sanjinés, *Segunda Reforma Agraria*, 201.

What is more, official government projections suggest that at the conclusion of the land registration process, the medium and large agribusiness sector will have title to between 15 and 17 million hectares, mainly in Beni and Santa Cruz. The expedited process of land registration in the post-2010 Morales administration has led to the titling of 2 to 3 million hectares to the agribusiness sector per year. The path dependency of this patterned set of state priorities is that the most valuable land in the country will continue to be held by a small group of agro-industrial capitalists at the expense of the landless and the land-poor majority.[157]

As part of its so-called Patriotic Agenda 2025, the government has proposed that agro-industrialists in Santa Cruz substantially increase their exports in the coming years through the extension of cultivated surface area by one million hectares annually over the next decade.[158] This would mean an extension from the 3.5 million hectares in cultivation in 2015 to 13.6 million hectares by 2025. In concordance with the government's vision, the agro-industrial sector in Santa Cruz has projected a tripling of the volume of their production from 15 to 45 million metric tons over the same timeline.[159] To support this dynamic,

---

157 Ibid., 202.
158 Castañón Ballivián, "Discurso empresarial vs. realidad campesina," 67.
159 Nilton Ramírez Funes, "La 'nueva fase' del 'Proceso de Cambio' reproduce el proyecto neoliberal de apoyo a la agroindustria," *Boletín Agrario* 1 (April 2015): 1.

the government has promised more public investment into infrastructure for production and transport, as well as guarantees of subsidized energy inputs and exchange rate stability.[160] If past patterns of industry growth are any indication, and if the reverberations of the global economic slump continue to propel commodity prices downward, these projected figures may very well prove fantastical. However, they are indicative all the same of the advanced concretization of an agro-capital-state alliance in Bolivia since 2010.

The results of this alliance have been an extension of the soy agricultural frontier in Santa Cruz and a concomitant decline in peasant agriculture in the highlands. Through its depiction of surface area devoted to distinct types of crop between 1989 and 2013, Table 9 provides a panoramic indication of this overarching trend.

Table 9. Surface Area Cultivated and Type of Agricultural Production 1989–1990 and 2012–2013

Crops	Cultivated Surface Area				Rate of Growth
	1989–1990		2012–2013		1989–1990 to 2012–2013 (p)
	Hectares	Percentage	Hectares	Percentage	
Rice	112,372	9.0	157,503	4.8	1.48
Corn	225,687	18.0	328,646	9.9	1.65
Sorghum	25,302	2.0	201,630	6.1	9.44
Wheat	86,867	6.9	158,020	4.7	2.64
Sugarcane	63,396	5.1	159,032	4.8	4.08
Sunflower	3,725	0.3	280,864	8.5	20.68
Sesame	0	0.0	15,000	0.5	–
Soy	178,306	14.3	1,176,268	35.5	8.55
Subtotal	695,655	55.6	2,476,962	74.8	5.68
Others*	555,846	44.4	836,896	25.2	1.80
Total	1,251,501	100.0	3,313,859	100.0	4.32

Source: Ormachea Saavedra, "Pequeña y gran producción agrícola capitalista y trabajo asalariado en Bolivia," 174.

(p) preliminary

* Includes: barley, quinoa, cacao, coffee, bananas, peaches, mandarins, oranges, pineapples, plantains, grapes, garlic, peas, celery, beans, broad beans, tomatoes, cotton, peanuts, potatoes, yucca, alfalfa, cabbage.

---

160 Ramírez Funes, "La 'nueva fase' del 'Proceso de Cambio,'" 1.

In 2006, Santa Cruz accounted for 71.9 percent of total agricultural production in the country. By 2013 this figure had expanded to 76.3 percent. There was a related drop in the relative participation of the valleys and high plateau, which, as we have shown, contain the majority of the country's peasant producers.[161] Over the last twenty-five years, there has been growth in the surface area dedicated to industrial crops such as sugarcane and rice, and, most importantly, oilseed plants, including sunflower and sesame, but dominated by soy. The latter reached 1,176,263 hectares of cultivated surface area by 2013.[162] The decline in peasant productivity accounts in part for the expanding reliance on food imports. The value of food imports experienced a 219 percent increase between 2005 and 2014, from $US 227 million to $US 723 million. In 2014, 9 percent of the country's total imports were food imports.[163] Despite a pronounced rhetoric around food security by the Morales government in the post-2010 period, the state has in practice supported the expansion of a transnationally controlled export sector, while peasant and communitarian production has declined. In contrast to the promises of various development plans of the Morales government, the communitarian economy has not been able to transform itself into an important provider of food, nor a generator of employment, nor a source of improved income for peasants. What is instead increasingly clear is the continuity in agrarian structure rooted in primary exports, foreign investment, the sanctity of large private properties in the most productive agricultural zones, and limited redistribution of state property in areas of low agricultural potential.[164]

Within the soy sector, the 'semi-proletarianization and petty bourgeois rentierism' of small landholders is rapidly unfolding.[165] The exorbitant cost of agro-capital inputs—seeds, fertilizers, herbicides, pesticides, and machinery—as well as storage and processing costs, have priced many small producers out of producing on their own lands. Increasingly, they rent their small parcels of land to medium and large enterprises and devote themselves to pursuing various forms of agricultural or urban wage labor.[166] Growing stratification in the soy sector has ensured that the material base of the industry—land, industrial inputs, and processing and storage facilities—remains in the hands

---

161 Ormachea Saavedra, "Pequeña y gran producción agrícola capitalista y trabajo asalariado en Bolivia," 173.
162 Ibid.
163 Colque, Urioste, and Eyzaguirre, *Marginalización de la agricultura campesina e indígena,* 40.
164 Nam Kwon Mun, "La problemática transición boliviana hacia la época postneoliberal," 33–35.
165 McKay and Colque, "Bolivia's Soy Complex," 2.
166 Ibid.

of a concentrated group of agribusinesses.[167] There are now capital costs of roughly $US 406 per hectare to cultivate soy competitively. This requires both access to land on a scale sufficiently large to allow for profitability and access to financing to cover the cost of the requisite technology and inputs.[168]

In one of the most thoroughgoing case studies available thus far on the agricultural soy frontier in Santa Cruz, Enrique Castañón Ballivián investigated fifty peasant families in the settlement of Cuatro Cañadas and found extensive evidence of heightened internal peasant stratification.[169] A third of the fifty families have no land, while the remaining families have an average plot size of fifty hectares. Even for those with land, investment in the necessary agro-capital inputs is beyond the reach of a majority of them.[170] Poor peasants, in this settlement, constitute approximately 30 percent of the fifty families studied. They tend to be recent migrants from the Andes or the children of families that migrated to the zone in the 1970s. Poor peasants have no land or tiny portions of family plots that do not allow for the peasants' self-reproduction. They thus regularly sell their labor power, usually either to agribusinesses or to rich peasants.[171] Middle peasants are a majority (58 percent) of the families in the settlement study. A majority of middle peasants arrived in the Cuatro Cañadas in the 1970s as part of the early colonization projects. Although they tend to have access to plots of land of fifty hectares, they lack sufficient capital to purchase the inputs necessary to put the land into competitive production. While some middle peasants take out loans to finance the self-production of their land, the majority prefer to rent their land to other producers.[172] In exchange for renting their land, these families usually receive 25 percent of net profits from cultivation. They often then combine this income with the sale of their own labor power elsewhere in order to survive. Rich peasants represent 10 percent of the families, and tend to have settled in the area for at least fifteen years. They own on average sixty-seven hectares of land, but control between one hundred and two hundred hectares each because their monopoly on the ownership of machinery in the peasant settlement makes them necessary to productive processes. These rich peasants are able to invest in the renewal and expansion of means of production and to pay for the employment of wage laborers. Nonetheless, in the soy complex as a whole, they are situated in

---

167 Castañón Ballivián, "Discurso empresarial vs. realidad campesina," 75.
168 Ibid., 78.
169 Ibid.
170 Ibid.
171 Ibid., 79.
172 Ibid., 80.

a deeply subordinate position vis-à-vis larger agro-industrial firms.[173]

This particular class dynamic in one settlement maps onto wider trends in agrarian class structure during the ten years of MAS governments thus far. Public institutions involved in the agrarian reforms of the MAS government since 2010 have concerned themselves principally with expediting the process of land registration and titling, but without attention to expropriation and redistribution of large landholdings this has not led to an overturning or serious modification of the extant class structure in the countryside.[174] The biggest gain for the indigenous-peasant sector of all agrarian reform initiatives since 1996 has been the introduction of the category of TCOs and the legal recognition of indigenous territories in the highlands and lowlands. This partial achievement of the lowland indigenous struggle is nonetheless full of contradictions, as our discussion above of the patchwork mixed-property character of TCOs, incursions of multinational extractive capital, and ongoing state sovereignty over subsoil rights has indicated. Land registration has also helped to facilitate the legal rights of a layer of small-scale capitalized peasants in different areas of the country. In particular, the intercultural sector, those migrant Quechua and Aymara peasants from the highlands to the lowlands, has consolidated rights to smallholder titles. These are the producers of coca, soy, quinoa, and other commercial export crops on a small scale; these are not independent small producers, but are rather deeply integrated into larger value chains of agro-industrial development in the country.[175] Some of these capitalized small producers have become rich peasants, relying on the purchase of the labor power of semi-proletarianized poor peasants, and sometimes using sophisticated machinery and technological inputs for their production processes. Politically, this section of the peasantry has been a backbone of popular support for the governments of Morales.

If rich peasants are employing more wage labor in the valleys and highlands, the medium and large agribusiness sector, by contrast, has reduced its global demand for labor through increasingly capital-intensive methods of production.[176] As the most comprehensive study of agrarian reform available in the country suggests, the result of land registration in the Morales era has not been to modify the fundamentally dual agrarian structure of concentrated agribusiness landholdings alongside land-poor or landless peasants, but rather has complicated this dual structure's organization, socioeconomic relations,

---

173 Ibid., 81.
174 Colque, Tinta, and Sanjinés, *Segunda Reforma Agraria*, 211.
175 Ibid., 218.
176 Ibid., 219.

and the political alliances that exist between agro-capital and the state, and also agro-capital and capitalized small producers.[177]

This new complexity takes the form of three unstable and related sectors. First, there is a nucleus that controls the bulk of land rent. Second, there is a semiperipheral sector whose viability is ensured through subordinated relations with the nucleus. Third, and finally, there is a sector that is either functional to the first two in the form of wage labor or a reserve army of potential labor, or a surplus rural population excluded altogether from the requirements of capital accumulation in the countryside. By one estimate, the nucleus and semiperipheral sector, based primarily in the lowlands, constitute 18 percent of agricultural units but control 66 percent of productive land in the country. The excluded sector, meanwhile, represents 82 percent of agricultural units but controls only 34 percent of productive land.[178] Politically, the agribusiness nucleus was in a tight alliance with the state between 1996 and 2006. This broke down into an openly antagonistic period of the first administration of Evo Morales (2006–2009). After the defeat of the civic-coup attempt, however, the agro-industrial nucleus forged a renewed alliance with the post-2010 Morales government, together with the semiperiphery of capitalized small producers. Together they now constitute the agrarian class composition of the government's support base.[179]

The semiperipheral actors here are the rich peasants of the high plateau, valleys, and lowlands, including the migrant intercultural sector. They are the leading layer within the CSUTCB, which has been deeply integrated into the state under Morales. They had direct or indirect authority over an array of public institutions, including SNRA, INRA, CAN, and Ministerio de Desarrollo Rural y Tierras (Ministry of Rural and Land Development, MDRYT).[180] However, the benefits to this sector that flow from their subordinate incorporation into the state are premised on the reproduction of higher levels of agrarian power, namely the ongoing state-sanctioned and subsidized expansion of agro-industrial capital in the agricultural frontier of Santa Cruz.[181] The absorption of layers of the peasantry into these apparatuses of the state, as in Gramsci's framing of transformism, led to the decapitation of peasant movements, the containment of independent peasant militancy, rather than a fundamental transformation of the state apparatuses and political economy of the Bolivian countryside. Meanwhile, a solution through

---

177 Ibid., 220.
178 Ibid., 221.
179 Ibid., 222.
180 Ibid., 223.
181 Ibid., 224.

agrarian reform for the landless and land-poor majority remains pending and in structural contradiction with the priorities of the agrarian class composition of the Morales government's rural allies. For Alejandro Almaraz, the former Vice Minister of Land, who was fired from his position in 2011 for openly contesting the conservative turn of the MAS leadership, the post-2010 period has been one of defeat for the indigenous-peasant majority in the countryside. What he took to be the indigenous-peasant project and potential of the Constituent Assembly process and the early years of the Law of Communitarian Renewal of Agrarian Reform—of the redistribution of land through communitarian and territorial re-appropriation, and the uprooting of the fundamental structures of agrarian life in Bolivia—have been undermined. The agrarian oligarchs of Santa Cruz, in alliance with transnational agribusiness, have been reinstalled in power through a novel agro-capital-state configuration.[182] Ironically, the most regressive aspect of the nationalist ideology of the 1952 revolution, premised on the march to the east, has found its most mature expression in the second decade of the twenty-first century, under the national leadership of a former *cocalero* of indigenous origin, Evo Morales.

Conclusion

This chapter has tried to explain the changing dynamics of class struggle, the composition of the agrarian ruling bloc, the core policies of agrarian reform, and their most important concrete results across the Morales era from 2006 to the present. It has also attempted to contextualize agrarian reform under Morales, with the previous periods of nationalist import-substitution industrialization (1952–1985) and orthodox neoliberalism (1985–2005). The core argument advanced was that by the second period of the MAS administration (2010–2016) a new configuration of agro-capital-state power had been consolidated, and that this ensured that the main beneficiaries of the Morales regime's agrarian policy would be the national and transnational agricultural capitals in the country's soy export sector, while the main losers would be the landless and land-poor indigenous peasant majority. A middling section of rich peasants, or small agricultural capitalist producers, represents a subordinate layer of beneficiaries, economically integrated into the wider agro-industrial value chains controlled by foreign capital. This social layer is incorporated politically into the ruling bloc as well, albeit in a subordinate fashion premised on

---

182 Almaraz, "Luchas políticas y legales por la tierra en Bolivia," 54.

the ultimate reproduction of concentrated agro-industrial power. Historically, the consolidation of industrial agrarian capitalism in the east under Morales realizes, if in unforeseen ways, one of the twin projects of the 1952 National Revolution's underlying commitment to capitalist development.

Between 1952 and 1985 the country witnessed the extension in the east of labor-intensive, low-tech, and state-financed development of capitalist agriculture in cotton, sugarcane, and rice. The period allowed for an extreme concentration of land through a series of corrupt state handouts to large landowners, particularly under the dictatorships of Banzer and García Meza. Between 1985 and 2005, with the support of the World Bank, state subsidization of agrarian capitalist development in the eastern lowlands continued, but now alongside dramatic liberalization of agricultural markets, which much more rapidly eroded the peasant economy of the highlands. Cotton, rice, and sugarcane production ceded leading positions to soy and other oilseed plants, produced for export. After experimental inroads made by Mennonite and Japanese settlements, first Brazilian, and to a lesser extent Argentinian and Colombian, investors brought foreign investment into the soy sector during the neoliberal period. Within this context of rapidly expanding soy production, the Sánchez de Lozada government introduced its contradictory INRA Law, which expressed the social-market ideas of neoliberal multiculturalism.

In the first period of the Morales government (2006–2009) there seemed to be a resolute break with neoliberal policy in agrarian matters. The Law of Communitarian Renewal of Agrarian Reform was introduced in 2006, the Unity Pact fought for wide-scale transformations in the agrarian class structure both inside and outside the halls of the Constituent Assembly, and the new constitution of 2009 seemed to embody some of the aims of the indigenous peasant movement, even if it was expressly contradictory in several areas of concern. The agro-industrial elite of the lowlands had squared off against the Morales government in this period, mobilizing its considerable material resources for an autonomist and regionalist battle to destabilize the regime and subvert the Constituent Assembly, including even a civic-coup attempt in September 2008.

Once this autonomist right had been defeated politically, however, there was a realignment in the class composition of the ruling bloc, expressed in the thesis of an agro-capital-state alliance between 2006 and 2010. The results, as we have shown, have consolidated agro-industrial capital, both national and foreign, in the soy sector, while subordinately integrating rich peasants and exploiting wage labor of the landless or land-poor, or excluding them altogether as part of the surplus population irrelevant to capitalist accumulation.

EIGHT

Dual Powers, Class Compositions, and the Venezuelan People: Reflections on *We Created Chávez*

George Ciccariello-Maher is an American scholar-activist formed in the anarchist tradition, broadly conceived. Currently a political theorist at Drexel University in Philadelphia, he taught in the past at San Quentin State Prison in California and the Venezuelan School of Planning in Caracas. His doctoral dissertation, from the University of California–Berkeley, explores the problems of identity-production across the oeuvres of French syndicalist Georges Sorel, the Martinique-born Afro-French revolutionary Frantz Fanon, and the Argentine-Mexican theoretician of Marxism and liberation theology, Enrique Dussel.[1] While researching the dissertation, Ciccariello-Maher moved to Venezuela

---

1 See George Ciccariello-Maher, "Identity against Totality: The Counterdiscourse of Separation beyond the Decolonial Turn," (PhD diss., UC Berkeley, 2010). In a series of articles, he has developed the theoretical concerns that are finally taken up in his dissertation. See, for example, Ciccariello-Maher, "To Lose Oneself in the Absolute: Revolutionary Subjectivity in Sorel and Fanon," *Human Architecture: Journal of the Sociology of Self-Knowledge* 5, no. 3 (2007): 101–111; Ciccariello-Maher, "Dussel's *20 Theses* and Anti-Hegemonic Praxis," *Listening: Journal of Religion and Culture* 43, no. 1 (2008): 37–49; Ciccariello-Maher, "Constituent Moments, Constitutional Processes: Social Movements and the New Latin American Left," *Latin American Perspectives* 40, no. 3 (2013): 126–145; Ciccariello-Maher, "Decolonial Realism: Ethics, Politics and

to follow on the ground the political awakening of the popular classes unfolding in that country in the era of Hugo Chávez's rule (1999–2013). *We Created Chávez*, his first book, emerged in part from his experiences living in the country. Drawing on years of embedded engagement with Venezuelan social movements and relationships of trust built up over time with many of their preeminent organic intellectuals, Ciccariello-Maher has become perhaps the most high-profile and incisive left-wing commentator on Venezuelan politics in the United States today. Deploying some kind of militant ambidexterity, he writes, with one hand, a steady stream of articles of critical solidarity with the Bolivarian process in the popular press,[2] and, with the other, defends Venezuela against US imperialism on American mainstream news programs and in the newspapers.[3]

We Created Chávez offers a people's history of three periods in recent Venezuelan political development. The first begins in 1958 and ends in 1989, and is known as the era of *puntofijismo*, after the power-sharing pact, Punto Fijo (Fixed Point), agreed between three centrist political parties: the Comité de Organización Política Electoral Independiente (Independent Electoral Political Organization Committee, COPEI), the Unión Republicana Democrática (Democratic Republican Union, URD), and Acción Democrática (Democratic Action, AD). Under the arrangement, exalted in conservative and liberal historiography alike for the relative political stability it achieved, the Partido Comunista de Venezuela (Communist Party of Venezuela, PCV) was outlawed, and the presidential office alternated between COPEI and AD. Ciccariello-Maher takes apart the common mythologies of democratic harmony associated with this period, revealing instead both authoritarian repression on the part of the state and myriad forms of popular resistance that sprung up against the pacted regime.[4] The second historical period featured in the book stretches from the 1989 urban riots against neoliberal austerity—known as

---

Dialectics in Fanon and Dussel," *Contemporary Political Theory* 13, no. 1 (2014): 2–22.

2 See, for example, George Ciccariello-Maher, "Collective Panic in Venezuela," *Jacobin*, June 18, 2014; Ciccariello-Maher, "Venezuelan Jacobins," *Jacobin*, March 13, 2014; Ciccariello-Maher, "#LaSalida? Venezuela at a Crossroads," *Nation*, February 22, 2014.

3 Ciccariello-Maher has made recent television appearances on Fox News, Fox News Latino, CNN, CNN en Español, and Al-Jazeera, and is regularly quoted in the *Philadelphia Inquirer*, *Time*, and the *Christian Science Monitor*, among other mainstream outlets.

4 For an important parallel critique of the mainstream "exceptionalism" thesis, which stresses Venezuela's ostensible separation from the class conflict, authoritarianism, violence, and war characteristic of other Latin American countries during the Cold War, see Steve Ellner, *Rethinking Venezuelan Politics: Class, Conflict, and the Chávez Phenomenon* (Boulder, CO: Lynne Rienner Publishers, 2009).

the Caracazo—through the left-populist coup attempts of 1992, to the election of Hugo Chávez to the presidency for the first time in 1998. These three events constitute the immediate prelude, in a sense, to the third and most important period explored, the "Bolivarian Revolution," which begins in earnest with Chávez's ascension to office in 1999 and continues after his death in March 2013. According to Ciccariello-Maher, the alteration of Venezuelan society in the last of these three periods has been profound. "Since Chávez's election in 1998... Venezuela has become a radically different place, and the 'Bolivarian Revolution' that he inaugurated (in name, at least) has seen power wrested from old elites and unprecedented social improvements and is poised to transform even the state itself" (p. 6).

We Created Chávez is the single most important book available in English advancing an explicitly anticapitalist framework for understanding the historical, social, and political conditions underlying the rise of Hugo Chávez and the character of the Bolivarian process to date. For this reason alone, it deserves sustained theoretical and empirical engagement by Marxists. But the book is also unusual in the level of political and historical sophistication it brings to bear on contemporary Venezuela. In many ways, *We Created Chávez* sets a new standard for scholarship on the Bolivarian process, and one hopes that with its pedagogic and engaging prose style it will reach an audience well beyond the confines of academia. Our engagement and critique is divided into two major parts. First, I examine the concepts that form the book's theoretical edifice—in particular the mutually determining dialectic between social movements and Chávez, the concept of "the people," and the notion of dual power. The second part shifts from the abstract to the concrete, tracing the historical and political sociology of the text through the rural guerrilla movements of the 1960s, the urban guerrillas of the 1970s, the new urban sociopolitical formations that emerge in the 1980s and erupt in the Caracazo of 1989, Afro-indigenous struggles and the legacies of racism, and the debates around social and political transformations of the formal and informal working classes in contemporary Venezuela, and Latin America more generally.

Conceptual Apparatus

Revolutionary Paradox
Ciccariello-Maher believes that the contemporary context in Venezuela is a revolutionary one, although it is characterized by an apparent paradox. On the

one hand, "revolutionary militants" operating within autonomous, anticapitalist, and antistate urban collectives of the self-organized poor are entirely cognizant of the continuities in the current state form under Chávez's rule—"with its bloated bureaucracy, sordid corruption, violent police, and chaotic prisons" (p. 5)—with the state form dominant under his predecessors. On the other hand, these revolutionaries "nevertheless pledge their loyalty, however temporarily and contingently, to the man currently sitting atop that state" (pp. 5–6). What is significant for such anticapitalist collectives and groupings "is not what happens in the gilded halls of official power," nor ultimately the president himself, but rather the process, "the deepening, radicalization, and autonomy of the revolutionary movements that constitute the 'base' of the Bolivarian Revolution" (p. 6). Fidelity to Chávez, even in the face of deep continuities in Venezuela's state-form, then, is only paradoxical on its surface; from the vantage point of radical popular movements, it reflects a sophisticated adaptation to a complicated scenario, perpetually in flux: "there… exists a complex and dynamic interplay and mutual determination between the two: movements and the state, 'the people' and Chávez" (p. 6).

This thesis, pivoting on the existence of a mutually determining dialectic between the people and the state in contemporary Venezuela, is one Ciccariello-Maher shares with many other commentators on the left. The British historian D. L. Raby, for example, refers to the defining role of "the people themselves at grass-roots level" in the shaping of the Bolivarian process, and points to "that dialectical interaction between Chávez and the popular classes which has been the hallmark of the entire process."[5] This perspective also finds an echo in the work of Michael Lebowitz, a Canadian economist and former advisor to the Chávez government, who argues, "the relationship between Chávez and the masses is a dialectical one: you can see the electricity flow in both directions when Chávez speaks in public to the poor."[6] Sociologist Dario Azzellini, meanwhile, calls it Venezuela's "two-track approach, combining bottom-up and top-down strategies."[7] "The relationship between society and the state is reciprocal," one can similarly read in Sujatha Fernandes's important

5 D. L. Raby, *Democracy and Revolution: Latin America and Socialism Today* (London: Pluto Press, 2006), 165–166.

6 Michael Lebowitz ,"The Bolivarian Process in Venezuela: A Left Forum," eds. Susan Spronk and Jeffery R. Webber, *Historical Materialism* 19, no. 1 (2011): 241. Also see Lebowitz, *Build It Now!* and Michael Lebowitz, *The Socialist Alternative: Real Human Development* (New York: Monthly Review Press, 2010).

7 Dario Azzellini, "Constituent Power in Motion: Ten Years of Transformation in Venezuela," *Socialism and Democracy* 24, no. 2 (2010): 9.

urban ethnography of social movements in Caracas, "just as the strong figure of Chávez has given impetus and unity to popular organizing, so the creative movements fashioned in the barrios help determine the form and content of official politics."[8] If the ostensible dialectic between Chávez and the people has by now become something close to cliché, Ciccariello-Maher still offers one of its more refined interrogations.[9]

Drawing on the method of C. L. R. James in *The Black Jacobins*, Ciccariello-Maher is wary of making Chávez the center of his narrative.[10] In other words, *We Created Chávez* is not Richard Gott's *Hugo Chávez and the Bolivarian Revolution*, which pays inordinate attention to the president himself.[11] Just as it was the slave revolution that made Toussaint L'Ouverture, it was the popular movements of contemporary Venezuela that created Chávez, and not the other way round. "By refusing to center our analysis on the Venezuelan president from the get-go," Ciccariello-Maher writes, "by resisting the constant historiographic temptation that James scornfully dismissed as 'the personification of social forces,' by averting our eyes from the dazzling brilliance of the commanding heights of political power—whose light is blinding in more ways than one—a whole new world comes into view" (p. 7).

The People

And what steps in to replace the Big Man as subject of history? Is it the working class of E. P. Thompson?[12] The peasantry of Eric Wolf?[13] Some combination? For Ciccariello-Maher, such a class-analytic alternative would seem to amount to the same kind of reductionism as methodological individualism, albeit in a different register: "Or, is the very concept of a historical subject—a single

---

8 Sujatha Fernandes, *Who Can Stop the Drums? Urban Social Movements in Chávez's Venezuela* (Durham, NC: Duke University Press, 2010), 5.

9 Ciccariello-Maher's recent attempt to expand his theoretical framework in different ways in order to interpret social movement–state relations in Ecuador and Bolivia has been much less successful. The extent to which the respective governments of Rafael Correa and Evo Morales represent transformative projects is much exaggerated. See Ciccariello-Maher, "Constituent Moments." My own, more critical perspective on both Bolivia and Ecuador has been offered in earlier chapters of this book.

10 C. L. R. James, *The Black Jacobins: Toussaint L'Ouverture and the San Domingo Revolution* (New York: Vintage, [1938] 1989).

11 Richard Gott, *Hugo Chávez and the Bolivarian Revolution in Venezuela* (London: Verso Books, 2005).

12 E. P. Thompson, *The Making of the English Working Class* (New York: Vintage, 1966).

13 Eric R. Wolf, *Peasant Wars of the Twentieth Century* (Norman: University of Oklahoma Press, [1969] 1999).

bearer of future history, be it an individual or a class—far too unitary and homogenizing to accurately explain contemporary Venezuelan dynamics" (p. 7)? Instead of the frequent caricature of Chávez directing things from on high, or the neglected possibility of a popular bloc led by a particular class doing it from below, Ciccariello-Maher finds more persuasive the concept of "the people," particularly as it has been developed in the theoretical work of Dussel.[14].

In Ciccariello-Maher's reading of Dussel, the people is "a *category of both rupture and struggle*, a moment of combat in which those oppressed *within* the prevailing political order and those excluded *from* it intervene to transform the system, in which a victimized *part* of the community speaks for and attempts to radically change the *whole*" (p. 8). Crucially, "the external division that the *pueblo* [the people] marks through its struggle is, according to Dussel, reflected in its internal multiplicity, in which dialogue and translation between its component movements serve to provide a common identity in the course of struggle" (p. 8). A key argument of *We Created Chávez*, then, is that the people, as a collective protagonist in Venezuela, has been forged through shared experiences of conflict in recent decades—a line has been repeatedly drawn, and they have found their interests aligned on the same side. Complex and unstable bases of unity have been soldered together out of this protagonist's multiple parts. A fragmented and heterogeneous array of oppressed, exploited, and marginalized subjects have come to identify, albeit critically, with chavismo and Chávez. The class dynamics of the "internal multiplicity" constituting "the people" is never sufficiently explained in *We Created Chávez*, a subject to which we will return. Nonetheless, Ciccariello-Maher's selective borrowing from James and Dussel nicely establishes a frame for the different analytical angles taken up in the central chapters, many of which fruitfully shed light on Venezuela's manifold history of urban and rural guerrillas, women, students, the formal working class, the peasantry, informal proletarians, and Afro-indigenous communities.

Dual Power

A final element in the theoretical framework advanced in *We Created Chávez* turns on questions of revolutionary strategy and state power in contempo-

---

14 See Enrique Dussel, *Twenty Theses on Politics*, trans. George Ciccariello-Maher (Durham, NC: Duke University Press, 2008). To a lesser but nonetheless important extent, "the people" here corresponds with its usage in the work of Ernesto Laclau. See, particularly, Ernesto Laclau, *On Populist Reason* (London: Verso Books, 2007). For favorable reference by Ciccariello-Maher to this component in Laclau's theory of populism, see p. 236 of *We Created Chávez*.

rary Latin America.[15] Ciccariello-Maher identifies a set of twin dangers that he claims "plague contemporary discussion of revolutionary change in Latin America in particular: the tendency to fetishize the state, official power, and its institutions and the opposing tendency to fetishize anti-power" (p. 16). Put another way, this is a debate between state-centric historical and political perspectives coming "from above,"[16] or from constituted power, and horizontalist vantage points "from below,"[17] or from constituent power. These "twin fetishes" fall short on this account "by establishing too firm a distinction between what they support and what they oppose," when what is required is a re-establishment of "a relationship between the horizontal and the vertical more generally" (p. 18).

If Dussel's conception of "the people" offers a way around the identification of any singular revolutionary subject in contemporary Venezuela, an unorthodox reading of Lenin's "dual power" is, it would seem, the alternative on offer to the twin fetishes of state-centricism and horizontalism. Ciccariello-Maher's conceptualization of dual power is worth quoting at length:

> I propose to speak of this reservoir of rebellious energy that exists outside, beyond, and against the state according to Lenin's concept of "dual power." Writing in *Pravda* in early 1917 from the unprecedented and previously unforeseeable political crossroads of the brief interregnum separating the February and October revolutions, Lenin spoke of the emergence of "an entirely different kind of power": alongside the Provisional Government of Kerensky, an alternative government had emerged, a "dual power" (*dvoevlastie*) consisting of workers' councils (notably alongside armed peasants) positioned outside and against the existing state structure. Here, dual power refers not only to the unstable *situation* of tense equilibrium between this alternative structure and the traditional state but also to the second, nonstate, dual power

---

15 The question of the party would seem to flow naturally into such a discussion, but the Partido Socialista Unido de Venezuela (United Socialist Party of Venezuela, PSUV) does not feature in the book.

16 Examples of this perspective in the historiography of the Bolivarian process criticized by Ciccariello-Maher include Gott, *Hugo Chávez*; Gregory Wilpert, *Changing Venezuela by Taking Power: The History and Policies of the Chávez Government* (London: Verso Books, 2007); Hugo Chávez and Marta Harnecker, *Understanding the Venezuelan Revolution: Hugo Chávez Talks to Marta Harnecker* (New York: Monthly Review Press, 2005); Luis Bonilla-Molina and Haiman El Troudi, *Historia de la Revolución Bolivariana: Pequeña Crónica, 1948–2004* (Caracas: Universidad Bolivariana, 2004).

17 Here Ciccariello-Maher focuses on John Holloway, *Change the World Without Taking Power* (London: Pluto Press, 2002); Marina Sitrin, *Horizontalism: Voices of Popular Power in Argentina* (Oakland, CA: AK Press, 2006); and Raúl Zibechi, *Dispersing Power: Social Movements as Anti-State Forces* (Oakland, CA: AK Press, 2010).

itself. It is the condensation of popular power from below into a radical pole that stands in antagonistic opposition to the state but functions not as a vehicle to seize the state (unlike Lenin's initial formulation), but instead as a fulcrum to radically transform and deconstruct it. This alternative power is irrevocably marked by its situation, its dual-*ness*, and this is what makes it "entirely different": it is not and cannot be merely another power, but is instead fundamentally a power-against-the-state. Dual power is, therefore, not a state of affairs but a political *orientation* and the transformative institutions that uphold that orientation, and the question in contemporary Venezuela is whether this orientation will expand or recede. (pp. 239–240)

The use of this provocative interpretation of dual power in the descriptive, historical sections of *We Created Chávez* is often insightful, especially insofar is it directs our attention to configurations of popular power and forms of self-organization which are frequently evoked in passing in the extant critical historiography of Venezuela, but seldom studied with the rigor or sophistication on display in the book under consideration. At the same time, the theoretical conceptualization of dual power as merely an orientation rather than a state of affairs lowers the bar considerably in terms of determining which historical moments have actually witnessed its presence. This becomes important because the low bar set on what constitutes dual power, I want to argue, is related to undertheorized and underspecified notions of revolution, the state, and, critically, capitalism that pervade the book as a whole.

What is most problematic in Ciccariello-Maher's relatively subjectivist rendering of dual power as an institutionally bounded political orientation is the way it evades the objective instability of such moments historically, and the necessity that one side, be it revolutionary or counterrevolutionary, must ultimately topple the other for any sustained resolution to play itself out. In concrete historical situations, a scenario of dual power cannot continue indefinitely—nor, for that matter, can revolutionary processes (it has now been fifteen years since Chávez was first elected). In a passage that continues to resonate, Trotsky, in *History of the Russian Revolution*, notes that a situation of dual power

arises where the hostile classes are already each relying upon essentially incompatible governmental organizations—the one outlived, the other in process of formation—which jostle against each other at every step in the sphere of government. The amount of power which falls to each of these struggling classes in such a situation is determined by the correlation of forces in the course of struggle. *By its very nature such a state of affairs cannot be stable.* Society needs a concentration of power, and in the person of the ruling class—or, in the situation we are discussing, the two half-ruling classes—irresistibly strives to get it. The splitting of sovereignty foretells nothing less than civil war…. Each of the powers, having created its own fortified drill ground, fights for possession of the rest of the territory, which often has to endure the double sovereignty in the form of successive invasions by the two fighting powers, until one of them decisively installs itself.[18]

Unsustainable instability, shifting balances in the forces of struggle, and fiercely resolute contestation between two fighting powers until one proves victorious are all notions that sit uneasily with the idea of a positively reinforcing—if tension-ridden—dialectic between progressive managers of a capitalist state and the gradual extension of an institutionally bounded dual power bent on that state's destruction, decentering, or radical transformation.

Ciccariello-Maher's deepest theoretical sympathies and political instincts appear to lie with the antipower horizontalists. But he is too subtle a thinker to imagine the state can be wished away or ignored. Drawing on Dussel, and reinterpreting Lenin, he tries to resolve the problem of the state by foreseeing its potential transformation by way of "the people" adopting a political orientation of dual power:

> I will speak neither of power from above nor entirely from below, but instead of a "dual power" that exists in ongoing, tense, and antagonistic opposition to the state, straining insistently upward from the bases to generate a dialectical motion allowing the revolutionary transformation of the state and its institutions, with the ultimate goal of deconstructing, decentralizing, and rendering it a nonstate. (p. 19)

The temporality of the state's transformation envisioned here and elsewhere in *We Created Chávez*, however, is quite evasive of any decisive moments of rupture with state power during the Chávez era; by decisive, I mean moments of rupture after which we might be able to say which side came out on top. Instead, there is a tendency to see the very gradual expansion of an orientation to dual power on the part of the people as evidence that a revolutionary process in Venezuela, set in motion before Chávez's election, continues to unfold with forward momentum. This, I think, is connected to an exaggerated sense of the malleability of the capitalist state once it has been captured by reformist politicians, so long as those politicians are pressured from below by the collective, radical organization of their political base. For example, Ciccariello-Maher re-

---

18 Leon Trotsky, *History of the Russian Revolution* (New York: Pathfinder, [1932] 2005), 225.

peatedly encourages us to understand "the state (and Chávez) as produced by human hands and therefore subject to radical transformation" (p. 16).

The question of which social class comes out on top from a situation of dual power has obviously long been a theoretical concern of Marxist theory and a political problem for socialist revolutionaries. In relation to our discussion of contemporary Venezuela, and specifically Ciccariello-Maher's relatively loose conceptualization of revolution in *We Created Chávez*, it makes sense to note briefly that the question of how a situation of dual power is resolved—who comes out on top—brings us fairly inevitably at some point to distinguishing between political and social revolutions as a first step toward conceptual clarification. Theda Skocpol has offered a classically restrictive definition of social revolution that I think remains pertinent:

> Social revolutions are rapid, basic transformations of a society's state and class structures; and they are accompanied and in part carried through by class-based revolts from below. Social revolutions are set apart from other sorts of conflicts and transformative processes above all by the combination of two coincidences: the coincidence of societal structural change with class upheaval; and the coincidence of political with social transformation. In contrast, rebellions, even when successful, may involve the revolt of subordinate classes—but they do not eventuate in structural change. Political revolutions transform state structures but not social structures, and they are not necessarily accomplished through class conflict.[19]

In a complementary, if not completely coincidental, mode of analysis on a variation of this question Neil Davidson offers the following distinction between political and social revolutions, as well as their possible relationship to one another:

> Political revolutions are struggles within society for control of the state, involving factions of the existing ruling class, which leave fundamental social and economic structures intact.... Political revolutions may involve more or less popular participation, may result in more or less improvement in the condition of the majority, can introduce democracy where it has previously been absent; but ultimately the ruling class that was in control of the means of production at the beginning will remain so at the end (although individuals and political organizations may have been replaced on the way), and the classes that were exploited within the productive process at the beginning will also remain so at the end (although concessions may have been made by

---

19 Theda Skocpol, *States and Social Revolutions: A Comparative Analysis of France, Russia, and China* (Cambridge: Cambridge University Press, 1979), 4.

the winning faction to secure their acquiescence or participation).... Social revolutions, however, are not merely struggles for control of the state, but struggles to transform it, either in response to changes that have already taken place in the mode of production, or in order to bring such changes about.... The relationship between political and social revolutions is complex. Some political revolutions have social implications and all social revolutions have political implications. Some revolutions, taken by themselves, appear to be merely political revolutions, [but] are in fact the opening or concluding episode of a more extended social revolution.... More importantly in the context of this discussion, some revolutions conclude as political revolutions because they fail as social revolutions.[20]

When investigating potential revolutionary processes still in motion—such as, say, Bolivia since 2000 or Venezuela since 1999—definitional clarity becomes both more difficult and more important. "One way out of the quandaries of process and consequence that arise in defining revolution," I have suggested elsewhere, "is to separate the notion of *revolutionary epoch* from *social revolution*. The concept of revolutionary epoch provides us with a way of understanding that revolutionary transformative change is possible but not predetermined in a certain period, stressing the uncertainty—and yet not wide openness—of alternative outcomes."[21]

The centrality of all of this becomes important when one considers whether or not it makes sense to follow chavista activists in our theoretical work—as distinct from our colloquial use, or in our political propaganda—in naming the process unfolding in Venezuela the "Bolivarian Revolution." Does any of the evidence in *We Created Chávez* suggest that there has been a revolution in Venezuela, or that what is happening can be characterized as a revolutionary process? Although it is beyond the scope of this reflective chapter to defend the position I am about to advance, I would suggest that, at a minimum, it is plausible to contend that Venezuela has not even entered a *revolutionary epoch* at any time since 1989, much less achieved a *political* or *social revolution*; instead, Venezuela has witnessed a series of *rebellions* from below with wide-scale popular participation, and other actions from above with lesser popular participation, which have forced significant concessions from factions of the ruling class, produced significant changes in the personnel of state management, led to the transformation of some old political organizations as well as the creation of

---

20 Neil Davidson, *How Revolutionary Were the Bourgeois Revolutions?* (Chicago: Haymarket Books, 2012), 494–495.
21 Webber, *From Rebellion to Reform in Bolivia*, 46.

new ones, and allowed for major social improvements through the distribution of a greater share of the oil rent to the popular classes in a context of high oil prices on the world market. By comparison, the left-indigenous insurrectionary process that unfolded in Bolivia in 2000–2005 arguably constituted a genuine *revolutionary epoch* that overthrew two heads of state through mass mobilization. This surge from below has been partially contained by the government of Evo Morales since 2006, and has thus far looked therefore like a *political revolution* emerging as a consequence of an aborted *social revolution*. To be convincing, this hypothesis would require a lengthy defense, but its plausibility alone suggests the need for greater specification of terms like dual power and revolution than exhibited in *We Created Chávez*.

Compare, by way of further elaboration, the view of dual power as institutionally bounded political orientation advanced by Ciccariello-Maher to that proposed in the following passage from the work of the late French Marxist Daniel Bensaïd:

> For Lenin—as for Trotsky—the revolutionary crisis is formed and begins in the national arena, which at the time constitutes the framework of the struggle for hegemony, and goes on to take its place in the context of the world revolution. The crisis in which dual power arises is therefore not reduced to an economic crisis or an immediate conflict between wage labour and capital in the process of production. The Leninist question—who will come out on top?—is that of political leadership: which class will be capable of resolving the contradictions which are stifling society, capable of imposing an alternative logic to that of the accumulation of capital, capable of transcending the existing relations of production and opening up a new field of possibilities. The revolutionary crisis is therefore not a simple social crisis but also a national crisis: in Russia as in Germany, in Spain as in China. The question today is doubtless more complex to the extent that capitalist globalisation has reinforced the overlapping of national, continental and world spaces.... It nonetheless remains an illusion to believe we can evade this difficulty by eliminating the question of the conquest of political power (on the pretext that power today is divorced from territory and scattered everywhere and nowhere) in favour of a rhetoric of 'counterpowers'. Economic, military and cultural powers are perhaps more widely scattered, but they are also more concentrated than ever. You can pretend to ignore power, but it will not ignore you. You can act superior by refusing to take it, but from Catalonia 1937 to Chiapas, via Chile, experience shows right up to this very day that it will not hesitate to take you in the most brutal fashion. In a word, a strategy of counter-power only

has any meaning in the perspective of dual power and its resolution. Who will come out on top?[22]

In these few words, Bensaïd brings to bear at least three fundamental layers of complexity to the concept of dual power in the twenty-first century. First, he raises the centrality of political economy to the dispute at the heart of the situation of dual power—a struggle of the exploited to impose an alternative to the laws of capitalist accumulation, a struggle of transition, for the opening up of new horizons through the transcendence of existing relations of production. A second theme is the complexity of scale—national, continental, and worldwide—as well as the mediation of the logic of capital accumulation across these scales in an era of capitalist globalization. The third is the continuing necessity, even in the face of capitalist globalization, of the conquest of territorially bounded state power, in order to provide any meaning to a strategy of counterpower.

Discussion of dual power tends by nature to focus principally on politics, contingency, will, and the subjective element. But Bensaïd, in a clearer fashion than Ciccariello-Maher, bounds this subjectivity in the structural realities of the rules of reproduction and the laws of motion that characterize capitalism's uneven development as a world system. He also signals here, if only in gesture, the structural role of the capitalist state in the reproduction of capital accumulation across national, continental, and world scales. By contrast, in *We Created Chávez*, a subjectivist understanding of dual power tends to be accompanied by a conceptualization of the capitalist state as more malleable than it is, and an underdeveloped—indeed, almost entirely implicit—understanding of capitalism and its class dynamics across different scales.[23]

So far, this intervention has laid out the key theoretical arguments that frame the book and offered some preliminary critique. The next logical step is to examine the historical narrative developed in the body of the work, and to unpack some of the strengths that emerge in spite of theoretical limitations, and some of the weaknesses that arise as a consequence of those limitations.

---

22 Daniel Bensaïd, "Leaps! Leaps! Leaps!" *International Socialism* 2, no. 95 (2002), www.marxists.org/archive/bensaid/2002/07/leaps.htm.

23 Gabriel Hetland and Jeff Goodwin have commented usefully on the more general disappearance of capitalism from social movement studies. See Hetland and Goodwin, "The Strange Disappearance of Capitalism from Social Movement Studies," in *Marxism and Social Movements*, eds. Colin Barker, John Krinsky, Laurence Cox, and Alf Gunvald Nilsen (Chicago: Haymarket Books, 2013). This suggests that the relative neglect of political economy in *We Created Chávez* is symptomatic of a wider trend in the research culture of contemporary social movements, which evidently extends even into the terrain of the radical left.

Theory as History

First Wave Rural Guerrillas

Ciccariello-Maher's historical departure begins with the first wave of guerrilla movements that emerged in Venezuela in the early 1960s. This initial group of guerrilla fronts was pitted against the AD government of Rómulo Betancourt. Betancourt had first held the presidency between 1945 and 1948, as leader of the AD and chief of the ruling military-civilian junta. The AD consistently polled above 70 percent among eligible voters in this period, not least because Betancourt introduced a series of social and economic reforms—particularly in the domains of labor, education, and oil—more extensive than in any previous period of Venezuelan history. He was overthrown in a military coup in 1948, which laid the groundwork over the next several years for the eventual establishment of the Marcos Pérez Jiménez dictatorship (1950–1958). The AD, together with the PCV and radicalized youth in the capital city, fought the dictatorship alongside one another, forcing Pérez Jiménez to flee the country in January 1958. In the radicalized interregnum—reaching a revolutionary pitch in Caracas—between the dictator's ousting and the democratic assumption to the presidency of Betancourt after his return from forced exile in 1959, the interim government of Wolfgang Larrazábal instituted widespread social spending for the unemployed of Caracas through the popular program, Plan de Emergencia (Emergency Plan).[24]

In the 1959 elections, Betancourt took 49 percent of the national vote to win the presidency, but received the backing of only 12 percent of the capital city, the lower layers of which were now operating well to its left. In a context of falling oil prices internationally, escalating foreign debts, and the intensifying flight of foreign capital, Betancourt adopted a two-pronged economic and political strategy—one part accommodation, one part coercion. On the one hand, he sought to appease the peasantry through the most thoroughgoing program of agrarian reform outside of a revolutionary context to have been implemented in Latin American history to that date. This involved land redistribution and a redirection of social spending from the cities to the countryside, where the AD had long had its most significant political base. Also in the mode of appeasement, he shifted the AD well to the right ideologically and forged the basis for the Punto Fijo agreement with other establishment

---

24 This paragraph and the next draw in part on Timothy Wickham-Crowley, *Guerrillas and Revolution in Latin America: A Comparative Study of Insurgents and Regimes Since 1956* (Princeton, NJ: Princeton University Press, 1992), 44–45.

parties. On the other hand, he singled out the PCV for exclusion from power-sharing (and later made the party illegal), repressed leftist opponents of different stripes, and introduced harsh austerity measures that targeted the working class and unemployed of the capital, where his political base was weakest. The youth of the AD and the PCV—who had been radicalized in the struggle against the Pérez Jiménez dictatorship and the interim government of Larrazábal, and who looked to the recently successful Cuban Revolution as an example to emulate—broke with the rigged rules of the pacted democratic regime. Youth in the AD, declaring their allegiance to the *foquista* strategy of the Cuban Revolution, established the Movimiento de la Izquierda Revolucionaria (Movement of the Revolutionary Left, MIR), while the PCV sponsored the formation of the Fuerzas Armadas de Liberación Nacional (Armed Forces of National Liberation, FALN). The rural guerrilla strategy proved to be disastrous in Venezuela, with all movements physically liquidated by the end of the 1960s, and quelled politically much earlier.

Ciccariello-Maher frames much of his account of this story through a brilliant interview with the "guerrilla commander-turned-Chávez critic Douglas Bravo" (p. 25), passages from which are weaved in and out of wider narratives that draw from the rich memoirs and analyses of other guerrilla leaders from that era. In his late seventies at the time of the interview, Bravo is amusingly described as a "short man with dark hair, and angular face, and broad shoulders accentuated by a blazer with padded shoulders reminiscent of *Miami Vice*" (p. 25). Born in 1932, Bravo joined the PCV at the age of thirteen and led the FALN before being expelled by the majority leadership of the Communists in 1966. He had insisted in the late 1960s that armed struggle must continue, which put him up against the majority of the party's executive, which had returned to a perspective of above-ground, civilian mass organizing. Cast out of the PCV, Bravo established the Partido de la Revolución Venezolana (Party of the Venezuelan Revolution, PRV), and continued to wage a losing battle in the countryside.

The factor most emphasized by Ciccariello-Maher in his explanation for the emergence of the guerrillas in this period is the repressive and exclusionary character of the regime. Against mainstream historiography's celebration of puntofijismo as an epoch of class compromise and stability, *We Created Chávez* is convincing in its account of PCV activists being "bludgeoned... daily" (p. 29), the torture and execution of activists (p. 36), and the state of targeted repression against the militants of parties to the left of AD (p. 28). It is also correct to argue that this era was characterized by a "straitjacketed and heavily mediated democracy" (p. 25), even if it is probably an exaggeration to say that the regime was "increasingly alienated from the vast majority" (p. 25). That view, at best insufficiently substantiated,[25] is connected to a recurring voluntarism in other sections of the coverage of the 1960s. Ciccariello-Maher perceives several missed revolutionary situations, where the subjective factor of the PCV "fail[ing] to act" or "to make up its mind" is highlighted as the key variable for failure (pp. 28–29).

The political analysis of the complex internal factions of the guerrillas in this period, and the tracing of their origins and relationships to parties of the left and their infinite splits is detailed and elucidating. But these sections call out for an accompanying sociology of the guerrillas and the wider rural and urban class structure of Venezuela in this period. How were these guerrilla formations related to different *social forces* on the ground? What was the structural composition of the peasantry—for example, the proportion of sharecroppers?—in those few areas where the guerrillas enjoyed moderate successes, and how did it compare to the composition of the peasantry in those areas of resolute guerrilla failure? Ciccariello-Maher's search for a source of failure in revolutionary strategy is too readily circumscribed to poor decisions made internally to far-left organizations, with too little attention paid to formidable structural obstacles, as well as the forceful co-optive capacities of a constitutionally democratic system, however thinly democratic in practice.

In some ways, *We Created Chávez* offers convincing conclusions as to the failed guerrilla campaigns of the 1960s, particularly the way it links these failures theoretically to "vanguardism," understood as the separation of guerrilla leaders from any wider base: "What, then, were the lessons of failure of the Venezuelan guerrilla struggle?… vanguardism, the assumption that an enlightened leadership had but to show the way and the people would follow, and that if the masses did not support the struggle, so much the worse for the masses" (p. 43). But the class composition of any actually existing potential base of supporters for guerrilla action in Venezuela in the 1960s needs closer sociological analysis than the nebulous categories of "the people" or "the masses" will allow. There is mention of a "stubborn" peasantry (p. 33), "local *campesinos*" (p. 42), the "popular masses" (p. 35), "isola[tion] from any serious mass support" (p. 44), and later, with reference to the urban context, "the rebellious masses as a class" (p. 76), but we are left wanting to know much more about the specific content of these categories.[26]

---

25 Nine pages later, Ciccariello-Maher is clearer on how the vast majority was not consistently alienated from puntofijismo, when he writes of the guerrillas in the late 1960s facing "a repressive state that enjoyed ever-increasing legitimacy" (p. 44).

26 At another point, later in the book, we do learn something of basic urban-rural socio-

Yet it is not because of their critique of capitalism or investigation of rural class dynamics that these sections of the text excite our attention. The sociological limitations of the account are real, and better class-compositional portraits of Venezuelan guerrilla movements and the social structure of the countryside can easily be found elsewhere.[27] What impresses are Ciccariello-Maher's textured oral histories of guerrilla participants and his attention to the contemporary published memoirs and analyses of militants. Important, too, is his novel attention to the frequently neglected Afro-indigenous leadership of specific regional guerrilla fronts (p. 32), as well as the role of women in the guerrilla struggle (pp. 38–40). Perhaps the most incisive addition to historical record in this section of *We Created Chávez*, though, comes in its evisceration of Régis Debray's *Revolution in the Revolution*.[28] Through the Bravo interview, Ciccariello-Maher discusses Debray's clandestine visit to the Chirino guerrilla front in 1963 and summarizes Bravo's critique of "Debray's exaggerated emphasis on mobility, the privileging of the military over the political, and the rejection of urban combat" (p. 40). "In other words," Ciccariello-Maher writes, "Debray's Cuba-inspired doctrine would emphasize those very elements that the Venezuelan guerrillas had already been forced to abandon in practice, but despite this, the remaining traces of vanguardism

demographic trends—that the country was already 60 percent urban at the outset of the 1960s rural guerrilla campaigns and was already accelerating quickly on its way to today's 90 percent (p. 46)—but still little about specific class dynamics.

27 See Luigi Valsalice, *Guerrilla y política: Curso de acción en Venezuela, 1962–1969* (Buenos Aires: Editorial Pleamar, 1975); Richard Gott, *Guerrilla Movements in Latin America*, rev. ed. (Chicago: University of Chicago Press, [1970] 2008); Timothy Wickham-Crowley, "Two 'Waves' of Guerrilla-Movement Organizing in Latin America, 1956–1990," *Comparative Studies in Society and History* 56, no. 1 (2014): 215–242; Wickham-Crowley, "Winners, Losers, and Also-Rans: Toward a Comparative Sociology of Latin American Guerrilla Movements," in *Power and Popular Protest: Latin American Social Movements*, ed. Susan Eckstein, rev. ed. (Berkeley and Los Angeles: University of California Press, 2001); Wickham-Crowley, *Exploring Revolution: Essays on Latin American Insurgency and Revolutionary Theory* (Armonk, NY: M. E. Sharpe, 1991); John Duncan Powell, *Political Mobilization of the Venezuelan Peasant* (Cambridge, MA: Harvard University Press, 1971); James Petras, "Revolution and Guerrilla Movements in Latin America: Venezuela, Colombia, and Peru," in *Latin America: Reform or Revolution?*, eds. James Petras and Maurice Zeitlin (Greenwich, CO: Fawcett, 1968).

28 Regis Debray, *Revolution in the Revolution? Armed Struggle and Political Struggle in Latin America* (New York: Grove Press, [1967] 2000). For an earlier set of critiques that has largely fallen out of scholarly consciousness, see Leo Huberman and Paul Sweezy, eds., *Régis Debray and the Latin American Revolution* (New York Monthly Review Press, 1981). Ciccariello-Maher elaborates and extends the critique of Debray later in the text in the context of a discussion of new urban social movements that emerged in the 1980s (p. 82).

and *foquismo* would come to be the Achilles' heel of the later armed struggle as well" (p. 41).

Second Wave Urban Guerrillas

From the rural guerrilla campaigns of the early 1960s, the analysis deftly shifts direction in the next sections of the book to the centrifugal waves of new urban left formations over the course of the 1970s. The meticulous mapping of different political fragments emerging from the decomposition of older configurations of the left—their internal ideological ruptures, theoretical experimentations, and trial-and-error learning from ever-shifting tactics, linked to evolving strategies for building a base in the new urban terrain—makes this one of the more fascinating historical components of *We Created Chávez*.

Faced with a series of interrelated crises of the rural guerrilla form by the end of the 1960s, militants entered into "a slow and painful process of self-examination in an attempt to figure out what had gone so terribly wrong and why the people had failed to respond to their clarion call to topple the young democracy" (p. 46). The 1970s were, more than anything else, a season of innovation: "parties were formed for electoral participation, open fronts were formed for mass work, and even those who continued the clandestine struggle were breaking with old schemas and attempting to reformulate the guerrilla experience in a new context and with an eye to the failures of the past" (p. 47). A renewed PRV, out from the countryside and into the city, was one lodestone for older activists looking for a new home—prominent founding members of the PCV, for example, who had been expelled in the past joined the PRV in the 1970s—and a variety of younger militants, including sizeable sections of the PCV youth, and a collection of artistic and revolutionary intellectual collectives. The PRV's quest for new intellectual and historical resources to revive the Venezuelan revolutionary tradition involved a complicated reconciliation of myriad—often contradictory—engagements: the reclamation of the histories of rebellion of the country's indigenous and enslaved African populations, the appropriation of aspects of Maoism, engagement with the Peruvian communist theory of José Carlos Mariátegui, and readings of Gramsci, Luxemburg, Italian autonomism, and Che Guevara. "From recovering the 'three roots' [Simón Bolívar, Simón Rodríguez, and Ezequiel Zamora] to thinking about spiritualism and materialism," Ciccariello-Maher points out, "to emphasizing the cultural and interrogating the party form, to questions of ecology and the oil economy, in these years the PRV was, above all, a crucible of theoretical experimentation" (p. 51). Through its members' collective study and praxis over the course of the 1970s, the PRV eventually arrived at a conclusive critique of the Leninist party form, and ultimately dissolved itself in the early 1980s, but its legacy lived on through the dispersal of its former cadre into new organizations and movements, as the material carriers and evangelists of its eclectic traditions. Both the living individuals and some of the genuine political and theoretical discoveries made in this period in the PRV would eventually play a role in the Bolivarian process of the twenty-first century.

Another current established in the early 1970s arose out of a split from the PCV over the Soviet invasion of Czechoslovakia. Teodoro Petkoff, later in life a fierce critic of Chávez, led this split and helped to form the Movimento al Socialismo (Movement Toward Socialism, MAS) in the late 1970s. Ostensibly, the MAS "sought to infuse socialism with the spirit of the new left, with its internal democracy and rejection of vanguardism and two-stage theories of revolution" (p. 53), but rather than a horizontal radicalism, in practice the new formation's heterodoxy produced a lurch to the right over the next decade. Whereas in its founding documents the party called for "Socialism Now!," socialism barely featured in the party's 1978 and 1983 presidential campaign materials (p. 54). The party became fundamentally an (unsuccessful) electoral platform, abandoning even a pretense of grassroots organizing and participation. Marking its continued trajectory across the political spectrum, the party condemned Chávez's coup attempt of 1992 and aligned itself in the following elections with the COPEI with the candidacy of Rafael Caldera.

Perhaps a more genuine expression of the critique of traditional left parties than the MAS was La Causa Radical (Radical Cause, CR), which found its initial expression in 1971 in a loose network of radicals called Venezuela 83. With a strongly movementist orientation, this grouping sought to "rewrite the script in favour of a bottom-up, more directly democratic organization that would work within and alongside social movements" (p. 55). Venezuela 83 organized its political activity around the triad of "the student movement at the Central University in Caracas..., the sprawling Sidor steelworkers in the steamy Venezuelan East, and the historically combative *barrio* of Catia in western Caracas" (p. 55). By 1979, Venezuela 83 had transformed into the LCR, signaling in part a new effort to combine political work in municipal campaigns with its involvement in strategically positioned social movements. The party enjoyed a round of initial successes following quickly on the heels of neoliberalism's inauguration in the country. The leader of LCR, Andrés Velásquez, was elected governor of the state of Bolívar in 1989, and Aristóbulo Istúriz as mayor of Caracas in 1992. Key LCR figures publicly sympathized with Chávez's failed coup attempt of 1992, and "instead critiqued the political system and neoliberal policies that had generated it" (p. 56). Nonetheless, the majority in the party wanted to sustain a distance from Chávez. This subterranean tension inside the party became visible in the 1998 presidential elections, when the LCR split, with the left supporting Chávez and the right majority forming Patria Para Todos (Fatherland for All, PPT).

Simultaneous to the evolving political development of the MAS and the LCR, a checkered landscape of urban guerrilla groupings emerged from the splintering of the MIR, following its turn away from armed struggle in the late 1960s. In favor of above-ground, legal operations, one grouping called itself the "authentic" MIR and was led by Américo Martin. Two other groupings chose to continue armed operations, an older generation sticking to the eastern rural fronts under the moniker Bandera Roja (Red Flag, BR), and a younger generation bent on forming urban guerrillas under the name Organización de Revolucionarios (Organization of Revolutionaries, OR). A lasting legacy of the original venom of many of the political divisions occurring at the end of the 1960s, the plethora of small leftist formations in the 1970s—clandestine guerrilla operations and above-ground political fronts alike—persisted in a self-destructive sectarianism, "without even a minimal degree of coordination between fronts" (58). An environment that bred squabbling was also conducive to adventurism. The most emblematic moment of the latter curse of the 1970s left was perhaps the kidnapping of the American businessman William Niehous, carried out by a group later known as the Grupos de Comandos Revolucionarios (Revolutionary Commando Groups, GCR), including Carlos Lanz, who would later become Vice Minister of Education under Chávez. In an enlightening interview with Ciccariello-Maher, Lanz describes the decisive influence of the Italian Red Brigades on the GCR's decision to kidnap Niehous. "But if the Niehous kidnapping was a tactical success in some respects," Ciccariello-Maher concludes, "few would argue that it was worth the backlash it provoked: some four hundred revolutionary leaders were arrested and many killed as a direct result" (p. 61). The twin weaknesses of sectarianism and adventurism also made it difficult for other formations in the mid-1970s that sought to chart an intermediate course in the "vast space between clandestinity and electoralism" (p. 64). The decade ended as had the one before:

> Toward the end of the 1970s, the Venezuelan guerrilla movement faced a situation of long, drawn-out defeat, a slow death. Repression had forced them into clandestinity, thereby contributing to their isolation from the masses, and these dwindling urban guerrilla organizations found themselves as isolated from the masses as their rural counterparts had been a decade earlier. (p. 63)

Neoliberalism and the Caracazo

Ciccariello-Maher finds his surest footing in the next series of analytical developments, which take him ultimately to the 1989 Caracazo and the formation of the sociopolitical subjects at the heart of the rebellion over the course of the 1980s. A new shade and depth is given to the bright light of earlier arguments through sustained examination of concrete specificities. As in previous sections, the narrative here congeals around an extended interview, this time with Juan Contreras, a founding member of the "broad front of militant groupings" Simón Bolívar Coordinator, situated in arguably the most rebellious Caracas neighborhood, 23 de Enero, in the barrio of Catia in the western reaches of the capital. Attentive descriptions of the Caracas landscape provide geographic outlines to a wide array of urban organizing initiatives that unfolded over the 1980s. "Originally intended to accommodate sixty thousand residents in some nine thousand apartments, Pérez Jiménez's delusion of tranquil modernity," Ciccariello-Maher points out, "has since been replaced with the reality of urbanization: the wide open spaces between apartment blocks have been packed tightly with standard Venezuelan shantytown housing, humble brick-and-tin *ranchos* squeezed between and stacked one on top of the other" (p. 70). At a population of perhaps five hundred thousand today, 23 de Enero is a "choppy and turbulent sea of *ranchitos*, the undulating surface of which is broken only by the surreal jutting cliffs of the bulky multicolored superblocks [apartment complexes] which twice gave the area its name" (p. 70).

We are urged in these pages to shift our attention from the standard chronology of the origins of the Bolivarian process. Instead of the failed coup attempt of 1992 and the election of Chávez in 1998, the concentrated moments of interest are the 1989 Caracazo and the defeat of the April 2002 coup attempt through a popular uprising:

> The Caracazo (known colloquially as "27-F") and the reversal of the 2002 coup (similarly dubbed "13-A") can, therefore, be understood as *constituent* moments, those rare and explosive instances in which the force of the people appears as *the* decisive actor. The importance of such moments therefore eclipses the importance of Chávez's 1998 election and even his failed 1992 coup (known as "4-F"), both of which, although undeniably important, represented but muted echoes and reverberations in the halls of constituted power of that constituent roar that made them possible in the first place. (p. 90)

Even if it is difficult to agree that the Caracazo constituted "a full-scale insurrection" or that its "participants stared revolution in the face" (p. 89), the focus on these moments as foundational surges of collective power from below which fundamentally shaped and defined the Bolivarian process is utterly convincing.

Arguably, though, the actions of oil workers to overcome the 2002–2003 management lockout in the industry constitutes a third such constituent moment, a hypothesis that, if true, would make necessary a caveat to Ciccariello-Maher's claims in these passages about the leadership of informal workers in each of the definitive constituent moments of the Bolivarian process to date. (I will return to the question of the oil workers.) The analytical questions in operation here are relevant beyond the Venezuelan context. In *Red October: Left-Indigenous Struggles in Modern Bolivia*, I develop an assessment of the class composition and organizational infrastructure of the October 2003 uprising in Bolivia, known as the Gas War, which parallels Ciccariello-Maher's emphasis on the leadership of a racialized informal working class and spontaneity-organization dialectic but attempts to bring into focus the other social classes that worked with the informal working class, if in a subordinate position, in the constitution of a popular bloc, without which the overthrow of the president would never have been possible:

> The central argument of this chapter is that, during the October Gas-War, the largely informal indigenous working classes of El Alto utilized a dense infrastructure of class struggle to facilitate their leading role in the events. A dialectical relationship emerged between the rank and file of neighbourhood councils and the formal infrastructure and leadership of the Federación de Juntas Vecinales de El Alto (Federation of Neighbourhood Councils of El Alto, FEJUVE-El Alto) and the Central Obrera Regional de El Alto (Regional Workers' Central of El Alto, COR-El Alto). Without the formal structures, the rank and file base would have been unable to coordinate their actions at a higher scale than their local neighbourhoods, while without the self-activity, self-organization and radical push from the grassroots, the executive leadership of both El Alto organizations would have been more likely to engage in the normal processes of negotiation with the state, moderation of demands, and eventual fracturing and demobilisation of the rebellious movements.... The working classes of El Alto constituted the most important social force in the insurrection, but depended on alliances with the indigenous peasantry organized through its own infrastructure of rural class struggle..., the formal working class, and, to a lesser but important extent, sections of the middle class.[29]

An earlier reticence by Ciccariello-Maher to further qualify a revolutionary subject beyond the category of "the people" retreats backstage at one

---

29 Webber, *Red October*, 185–186.

critical moment in the analysis of the Caracazo and the period immediately leading up to it:

> But who was the subject of such revolutionary demands? From what location were they enunciated? It was not the working class at its point of production or the peasant in her *fundo* that sparked this insurrection, and it was certainly not the traditional leftist parties who led it. Moreover, while students played a key role, it was not the student-as-student who was the subject of the rebellion, just as the university was not its locus. Rather, it was informal workers (see also chapter 9) who provided both the driving force and the battleground for this revolutionary moment. (p. 93)

Accompanying the argument around urban informal proletarian leadership is one that turns on this class fraction's political organization over the course of the 1980s. Without such organization, the features of spontaneity within the Caracazo would have ultimately proved a weakness rather than a strength:

> The influence of organized militants was not limited to prior example or tactical innovation; instead it emerged in the process of transitioning from rioting to rebellion to full-scale insurrection, a function only possible through a deep and organic relationship between militants and *barrio* residents, something earlier generations of guerrillas had notably lacked. (p. 95)

If by the close of the 1960s rural guerrillas fell prey to the limits of the Cuban model exported to Venezuela's radically distinct social structure, and if by the end of the next decade the urban mirror to rural foquismo had also invited debilitating state repression upon themselves and other social movements, the 1980s saw a strategic shift in political organizing of the urban poor in Caracas, which coincided with Venezuela's specific experience of economic recession within a wider debt crisis playing itself out in Latin America more generally. Tactically, the new militant organizations operating in the barrios of Caracas began to respond, in the first instance, to the most immediate pressing needs of neighborhood residents—a proliferation of violence at the hands of drug traffickers and the police—through the formation of armed self-defense militias, and at the same time to link immediate needs with political assessments of the socioeconomic travails stemming from a steep economic recession. Organizations such as the Social-Historic Current—a laboratory of theoretical and practical experimentation which brought together ex-members of the PRV, unorthodox Marxist activists, adherents of liberation theology, and Afro-indigenous militants—walked "a fine line between openness and clandestinity," seeking to "resurface as a public current, a groundbreaking effort at constructing a locally rooted, bottom-up method of organizing the masses" (p. 74). Other key groupings deploying similar changes in strategic and tactical orientation included Desobediencia Popular (Popular Disobedience) and the Alexis Vive Collective. The police attempted to denigrate such organizations as a homogenous, violent, undifferentiated collective entity of "Tupamaros," but this had the contradictory result of militants appropriating the name for themselves "to symbolically unify their many struggles into one" (p. 80). In 1993, many of the myriad organizations that had lived through the Caracazo and the 1992 coup attempt united under the name Simón Bolívar Coordinator. In addition to sustaining the popular contestation of the violence of drug traffickers and the police, the Simón Bolívar Coordinator also pursued "above ground cultural work aimed at pre-emptively undercutting the basis for social violence: they painted murals, rehabilitated sports fields, and reclaimed music and culture, all in an effort to mobilize local youth toward more positive pursuits than drug peddling" (p. 78).

Afro-Indigenous Struggle

The midsection of the book falters, particularly chapters 4 and 5, which cover the student and women's movements, respectively. Likely a result in part of attempting to build on the weak edifice of comparatively sparse existing secondary sources, these histories of students and women in rebellion are often thinly stretched and inaptly integrated into the central lines of argumentation developed elsewhere in the book. Thankfully, the earlier nimble pace and analytic depth are recovered by chapter 6, as the lens turns its focus to the autonomies and entanglements at the center of Afro-indigenous struggle within the Bolivarian process. "How to balance autonomous demands for one's own community," Ciccariello-Maher asks, "with the broader demands of national liberation, of socialism, of a Bolivarian Revolution with a record toward such struggles that is patchy at best?" (p. 150). Afro-Venezuelan and indigenous community participation in the contested shaping of the Bolivarian Constitution through the 1999 Constituent Assembly takes up the initial sections, followed by incisive commentary on the importance of racism in Venezuelan society and politics, whatever the national mythology of *mestizaje*—a myth of harmonious racial mixing—would have us believe. Against a backdrop of long histories of racist subjugation, and the complicated connections of this oppression to class exploitation as capitalism developed in Venezuela, the Afro-Venezuelan and indigenous movements have entered into supportive alliances with the Bolivarian government while simultaneously defending their autonomy:

The overwhelming support that Afro and indigenous organizations provided for the briefly deposed Chávez government during the 2002 coup is a partial testament to the benefits that their communities have received, and hope to receive in the future, from the Bolivarian Process. But if this support and these benefits are inarguable, both sectors nevertheless view the Venezuelan state—and the government currently in charge of that state—with a healthy dose of suspicion that doubtless is the result of a long history of betrayal and genocide....The leaders of the Afro-Venezuelan movement learned long ago, during the waning guerrilla struggle and as members of the PRV during its period of self-reflection, that the best way to advance was by forceful but comradely blows. (pp. 160, 162)

Ciccariello-Maher usefully connects the ideological currents within the Afro-Venezuelan and indigenous movements to the theoretical terrain charted out by heterodox Peruvian Marxist José Carlos Mariátegui in the 1920s. Just as "Mariátegui advocated the cultivation of an 'Indo-American socialism,' which would draw upon indigenous communal traditions as the basis for the development of a non-Eurocentric socialist society" (p. 163), Afro and indigenous organizers in Venezuela today look to forms of struggle taken up by indigenous communities since the Spanish Conquest as contributions to a forward-looking socialism, as well as "Afro-Caribbean traditions, some of which are rooted in Africa itself and some of which emerged as a strategic response to the demands of escaping and combating slavery in the Americas" (p. 164). This means, in short, remembering the *cumbes* that housed runaway slaves, alongside the Paris Commune (p. 164).[30]

Formal and Informal Proletarians

The most important chapters in the latter third of the book are 7 and 9, in which the roles of the formal and informal working classes within the Bolivarian process are dissected in detail. Discussion of the formal working class in Venezuela is framed initially through snippets of a conversation with a key figure in the revitalization of the Venezuelan labor movement in the early 2000s, Orlando Chirino. The conversation pivots on the 2003 rank-and-file oil workers' rebellion against both the bureaucracy of the national labor federation, the CTV, and the management of the state oil company, Petróleos de Venezuela, S.A. (PDVSA), which together locked out workers and shut down the industry for several months beginning in late 2002—an

---

30 See Vanden and Becker, *José Carlos Mariátegui*; Löwy, "The Romantic and the Marxist Critique of Modern Civilization"; Löwy, "Marxism and Romanticism in the Work of José Carlos Mariátegui."

effort straightforwardly designed to destabilize the Chávez government after the unsuccessful right-wing coup attempt in April 2002. The workers, with the support of community allies and workers from different sectors across the country, managed to seize control of the industry, put it temporarily under workers' management, and thwart the destabilization plot.

Chirino's words evoke the dynamism of this workers' revolt, as well as the weight of its political consequences, and Ciccariello-Maher offers little critical commentary to directly undermine them. But in the course of the analysis that follows, it is evident that Ciccariello-Maher harbors more scepticism about the formal working class than any other segment of "the people" at the base of his analysis of the Bolivarian process. "As the millennium drew to a close," he writes, "amid the grinding pain of generalized pauperization and the shining hope for radical change, some estimates placed the manual formal working class in Venezuela at scarcely one-quarter of the working population" (p. 185). Without further ado, this number seems to call its strategic potential into question: "It is, therefore, perhaps unsurprising that the relationship of both this formal working class and its institutions to a broader 'people's history' was to be a deeply ambiguous one" (p. 185). Little more is offered in terms of information on the structural characteristics of this formal working class, the density of its location within different sectors of the economy, or how its structure specifically relates to Venezuela's reality as a rentier capitalist economy based on oil, above all.

There is no engagement in the chapter with the extant Marxist sociology of the working class and its transformations under neoliberalism, or earlier phases of capitalist development in the Global South generally, or in Latin America more specifically.[31] If we were to consider here G. E. M. de Ste. Croix's famous distinction between the *mode of surplus extraction* and the

---

31 See, for select examples of general developments in recent Marxist historical sociology of the working class, Jan Breman, *Footloose Labour: Working in India's Informal Economy* (Cambridge: Cambridge University Press, 1996); Breman, "A Bogus Concept?," *New Left Review* II, no. 84 (2013): 130–138; Breman, *At Work in the Informal Economy of India: A Perspective from the Bottom Up* (Oxford: Oxford University Press, 2013); Mike Davis, *Planet of Slums* (London: Verso Books, 2006); and Marcel Van der Linden, *Workers of the World: Essays Toward a Global Labor History* (Leiden: Brill Academic Publishers, 2008). On Latin America, see Ricardo Antunes, "La nueva morfología del trabajo en Brasil: Reestructuración y precariedad," *Nueva Sociedad* 232 (2011): 103–118; Susan Spronk, "Neoliberal Class Formation(s): The Informal Proletariat and 'New' Workers' Organizations in Latin America," in *The New Latin American Left: Cracks in the Empire*, eds. Jeffery R. Webber and Barry Carr (Lanham, MD: Rowman and Littlefield, 2013).

mode of production, we would remember that although a relatively small proportion of the workforce in ancient Rome were slaves, it was nonetheless a slave society for de Ste. Croix because the surplus extracted to reproduce the ruling class was acquired precisely through that minority slave population.[32] With such a framework in mind, oil workers in Venezuela's rentier capitalist economy, however small in number, become now, as before, somewhat more strategically significant than Ciccariello-Maher's passing number count of formal laborers would suggest.

The structural centrality—and not infrequent political militancy—of workers (in small numbers) located in strategic export sectors in the Latin American historical context (including a case study of Venezuelan oil as an example of radicalism) has been most judiciously theorized by Charles Bergquist, who remarks in the opening passage of his classic book *Labor in Latin America* (still relevant, on this point at least, after almost three decades),

> Twentieth-century Latin American historiography suffers from two very grave deficiencies. It has failed to recognize the decisive historical role of organized labor and the labor movement in the evolution of the societies of the region. And it has failed to account for the very different ideological and political trajectories of the various Latin American labor movements— Marxist in some countries; neo-fascist in at least one; liberal, until now, in several others.[33]

In the case I am most familiar with, tin miners in Bolivia amounted to roughly 10 percent of the economically active population for much of the second half of the twentieth century, but were by far and away the most radical sector of the popular classes. With their ability to shut down the country's principal source of foreign exchange, they proved immensely powerful on behalf of the interests of the working class as a whole (not just their sector) until their crucial political defeat in the mid-1980s during the country's experimentation with neoliberal shock therapy, which weakened the political capacities of the popular classes in all of their complexity for the next fifteen years. The contingency of the political formation of such a section of the working class is emphasized by Bergquist and underplayed by Ciccariello-Maher. It is significant that the 2003 rank-and-file oil workers' rebellion in Venezuela does not amount to one of his definitive constituent moments from below—1989, 2002—within the Bolivar-

---

32 G. E. M. de Ste. Croix, *The Class Struggle in the Ancient World: From the Archaic Age to the Arab Conquests* (Ithaca, NY: Cornell University Press, 1989).

33 Charles Bergquist, *Labor in Latin America: Comparative Essays on Chile, Argentina, Venezuela, and Colombia* (Stanford, CA: Stanford University Press, 1986), 1.

ian process. While recognizing historical moments of radicalization among the Venezuelan organized working class, he nonetheless stresses the

> danger of labor aristocracy, especially with respect to the broader Venezuelan class constellation. While *all* workers saw increased instability as economic crisis set in and neoliberalism took hold, this merely served to underline the privilege that formal employment promised and the imperative of maintaining that employment at all costs, thereby encouraging passivity and further alienating the formal from the growing informal sector. (pp. 292–293, note 54)

It is undoubtedly true that the CTV, while never a monolithic entity, was dominated by the AD throughout the course of pacted democracy, and indeed into the Chávez era. Its business unionism served much more as a channel for workers' co-optation than an infrastructure for their resistance. Ciccariello-Maher's account of this institutional subordination is nicely executed, as is his summary of dissident experiments in "new unionism" in the nationalized steel plant, SIDOR, in the 1970s. By far the strongest part of his treatment of the formal working class, however, is the deft appraisal he offers of the formation of the Unión Nacional de Trabajadores de Venezuela (National Union of Venezuelan Workers, UNT) in 2003, designed to replace the CTV. The promise of this move for the labour movement, as well as the incessant in-fighting that would perpetually undermine the UNT in practice, are conveyed with precision and insight. Battles between organized workers in SIDOR and the Chávez government are also tackled without mincing words, and the problems and potential of initiatives of industrial comanagement and workers' cooperatives are lucidly surveyed, rounding out the chapter.

The penultimate chapter of *We Created Chávez* dances between subtle, geographically sensitive reflections on the political dynamics of Venezuelan informal proletarians and crude caricatures of "old Marxist dogmas" (p. 233). Ciccariello-Maher gives himself too easy a time of taking down an ostensibly living Marxist orthodoxy, dismissive or worse of informal workers, by avoiding reference to any specific Marxists making such claims. No doubt one could find crude dismissals of "the lumpen" in specific contemporary Marxist texts, but it is a basic requirement of critique to identify those specificities and individual authors and investigate how representative they are of a living tradition. A quotation from *The Communist Manifesto* (p. 221) will not suffice, particularly when the great bulk of recent scholarship by Latin American Marxists on transformations of the working class is ignored.[34] The bogeyman of Marxist

---

34 Representative references are made to "orthodox and mechanical theories" (pp.

orthodoxy could not easily survive any journey through the contents of journals such as *Herramienta* or the *Observatorio Social de América Latina* over the last decade, not to mention the catalogue of books published by the Consejo Latinoamericano de Ciencias Sociales (CLACSO) over the same period, with Marxist contributions documenting theoretically and empirically the structural transformations of the Latin American working classes in all of their heterogeneous complexity, as well as new forms of consciousness and novel repertoires of collective action.[35] Ciccariello-Maher's emphasis on unnamed reproducers of stale orthodoxy elides the considerable evidence of a lively reinvigoration of Marxist theory and historical sociology in Latin America over the last fifteen years, correspondent to the uptick in popular movements in much of the region.

Mining theoretical sources for alternative ways of framing the informalization of the world of work in contemporary Venezuela Ciccariello-Maher finds inspiration in a melange of Frantz Fanon's writings on colonial Algeria, André Gunder Frank's dependency theory, and the neo-Weberian class analysis of Alejandro Portes and Kelly Hoffman.[36] These are odd choices in many ways. Rather than careful mediation of Fanon's concepts to twenty-first-century Venezuela, we encounter something closer to forceful assertion: "the residents of Venezuela's sprawling shantytowns emerged in many ways from the very same forces Fanon identified in colonial Algeria, namely, dependent development and the resulting exodus from the rural areas and concentration in the capital in search of opportunity" (p. 222). Similarly, none of the many criticisms of Frank's theory of "lumpendevelopment," or his contributions to

---

219–220), "old Marxist dogmas" (233), and the "moralistic Marxist dismissal of the so-called lumpen" (p. 226) without exemplary citations, apart from the above mentioned reference to *The Communist Manifesto*. It is argued that "the comforts of power have led some Chavistas to reassert Marxist orthodoxy in a way that echoes elite denigration of the 'horde' and the 'scum'" (p. 220), without evidence or citation of how this is "Marxist" rhetoric or state policy. For a good analysis of Marx's conceptualization of the laboring classes over time, which puts the selective quotations from *The Communist Manifesto* into perspective, see Benjamin Selwyn, "Karl Marx, Class Struggle and Labour-Centred Development," *Global Labour Journal* 4, no. 1 (2013): 48–70; and Selwyn, *The Global Development Crisis*.

35 For a volume in English that takes up some of these themes, see Spronk and Webber, *Crisis and Contradiction*.

36 Frantz Fanon, *The Wretched of the Earth* (New York: Grove Press, [1961] 2005); Andre Gunder Frank, *Lumpen-Bourgeoisie and Lumpen-Development: Dependency, Class and Politics in Latin America* (New York: Monthly Review Press, 1972); and Alejandro Portes and Kelly Hoffman, "Latin American Class Structures: Their Composition and Change During the Neoliberal Era," *Latin American Research Review* 38, no. 1 (2003): 41–82.

Latin American dependency theory more generally, as perhaps the most maladroit variations on that tradition, are taken into account.[37]

Imprecision in the theoretical frame is accompanied by a series of contentious claims that require, at a minimum, much further empirical substantiation. Reference is made, for example, to the "economic exclusion of *barrio* residents and informal laborers from the sphere of production" (p. 220), and the suggestion is made that "we might say in a similar way that it is only the quasi-lumpen *barrio* dweller who can grasp the totality of Venezuela's lumpen-capitalism. Thus if this 'lumpen' is frequently (although not entirely) absent from the sphere of production, this absence is more than compensated for by its contributions to the remaining spheres of circulation... and reproduction..., which are, after all, prerequisites to capital accumulation" (p. 223). It is also quite unclear what is meant by "the relative homogeneity of economic condition" of the "urban informal sector" (p. 224). The ambiguity arises from the fact that very little empirical information is offered on any of the three mentioned spheres, but particularly that of production.

Only twice in the chapter is an effort made to provide specific empirical detail of this kind. In the first, more generally descriptive instance, Ciccariello-Maher notes that "some *barrio* residents are now established in formal employment or have even themselves built small capitalist fiefdoms that respond—at a profit, of course—to the demand of local residents for everything from basic foodstuffs to cellphones and bootlegged DVDs. But the vast majority simply survive, eking out a living with informal labor and odd jobs, all the while dodging the *malandros* whose attempts to do the same by other means make the *barrios* some of the deadliest patches of soil on earth" (p. 219). These are evocative, anecdotal observations, but they are never paired with the sort of detail that might give us more solid command of the class structure and internal stratification within the barrios, and the possible connections between the binaries of informal and formal sectors of the capitalist economy. In the second instance, we learn that the proportion of informal workers rose to 53 percent in 1999 before dropping to 43.5 percent in the period of high economic growth after the 2003 oil lockout. When the informal sector is combined with "the formally unemployed," the collective figure "reaches well over half of the active population, with fewer than 20 percent of the population [earlier cited as 17 percent, specifically] as a whole employed in the formal sector. These informal laborers are overwhelmingly women and include a size-

37 For one survey of the relevant debates and a very extensive bibliography, see Kay [1989] 2013.

able segment of downwardly mobile former middle class" (p. 224).[38] From this empirical basis it is not possible to sustain the claims of overwhelming exclusion from the sphere of production and an associated dominance of the spheres of circulation and reproduction within the informal economy, nor is it possible to substantiate the relative homogeneity of economic condition of workers caught up in the informal economy. These are, at best, hypotheses, and, from what we know of the comparative political economy of informal class formation elsewhere in the Global South, probably poor ones.[39]

By some distance the most persuasive sections of this treatment of informal proletarian subjectivity are those dealing with the role of the urban territorial community in the historical formation of their identities in Venezuela:

> Regardless of where people worked and in what capacity, they needed to come home, needed to walk the streets safely, needed running water and spaces for sports and cultural activities, and these shared needs and the struggles they generated gave rise to a sort of *barrio* consciousness and *barrio* culture.... Class consciousness and culture thus emerge in a spatial and geographic aspect and are transformed in the process, sometimes intermingling with and sometimes plainly overruled by geographical concentration. But *barrio* culture also explains in part the peculiar way in which these actors have expressed themselves in action; class demands have been subsumed to territorial, neighbourhood demands that manifest, above all, *politically*. (pp. 226, 227)[40]

The assertion of the importance of such textured territorial infrastructures of class struggle captured in this treatment of barrio culture is rich and compelling. I would only suggest that appreciation of this domain need not cast out quite so strongly the sphere of production. David Camfield's theoretical formulation of *working classes as historical formations* is apposite here.[41] Build-

---

38 The sources for these contentious figures are less than ideal. The first is an article by Marta Harnecker from 2004, which offers no source from which she derived her figures on informal and formal employment. Marta Harnecker, "After the Referendum: Venezuela Faces New Challenges," *Monthly Review* 56, no. 6 (2004), http://monthlyreview .org/2004/11/01/after-the-referendum-venezuela-faces-new-challenges/. The second is a conjunctural news story from *Venezuela Analysis* in 2007. Venezuela Analysis, "Venezuela Employment at New Low, GDP Continues Strong," *Venezuela Analysis*, February 28, 2007, http://venezuelanalysis.com/news/2246.

39 See Breman, *Footloose Labour*; Breman, "A Bogus Concept?"; and Breman, *At Work in the Informal Economy*.

40 Elsewhere, I have written about the concepts of *lo vecinal*, *vecino*, and oppositional consciousness of race and class in the Bolivian context in complementary ways. Webber, *Red October*, 263–268.

41 David Camfield, "Re-Orienting Class Analysis: Working Classes as Historical Forma-

ing on the tradition of social history mapped out by E. P. Thompson, Camfield conceptualizes class "as a structural social process and relationship that takes place in historical time and specific cultural contexts."[42] Such a conceptualization, for Camfield, "must consciously incorporate social relations other than class, such as gender and race. Class formations in this theory flow from the historical relations people experience with the relations of production and other antagonistic social classes."[43] Such an historical approach to understanding class formations reveals that, while class "is ultimately anchored and sustained" at the point of production, "class relations pervade all aspects of social life."[44] Because "people do not stop belonging to classes when they leave their workplaces," a useful theory of class formation has to examine class in households and communities, as well as in workplaces.[45]

Fundamentally, it is never quite clear what the distinction is between formal and informal sectors in Ciccariello-Maher's work. Is it the organized and unorganized? The unionized and nonunionized? The legal and the illegal? Complicating this binary further, oftentimes the category of informal worker seems to be collapsed into lumpen, which is itself a subjective-political category in *We Created Chávez* rather than a social-relational one.[46] Whereas Marx, understanding class as a social relationship, never conceptualized the lumpen in terms of formality or informality, but rather by location in social production, for Ciccariello-Maher this dissolves into subjectivity and the political.

Life after Chávez

None of this should be read as a smug dismissal of Ciccariello-Maher's analytical framework, or a suggestion that somehow Latin American Marxism already had all of this figured out. Whether or not we ultimately find the category of "the people" sufficiently precise, for example, *We Created Chávez* offers rare and wonderful illumination of its unity in diversity: "a multiplicity of movements and struggles developed autonomously across Venezuelan society, in factories, *barrios*, schools, homes, parties, and a multitude of revolutionary organizations and political formations" (p. 234). This multiplicity of actors was

---

tions," *Science and Society* 68, no. 4 (2004): 421–446.
42 Ibid., 421.
43 Ibid., 424.
44 Ibid., 424.
45 Ibid., 424.
46 Thanks to Rob Knox for clarity on this point.

"eventually bound together in an explosive chain of events: the Caracazo, the pair of failed coups in 1992, and Chávez's election" (p. 235).

Likewise, Ciccariello-Maher's conception of dual power is much more theoretically ambitious than the existing English language literature on the mutually determining relationship between Chávez and "the people," or social movements and the state. He offers, via Venezuelan history, "a dialectical twist *internal* to Lenin's concept of direct seizure of power from below... not only is power built and consolidated from below in an orientation toward 'seizure,' but that seizure itself becomes a process in which Chávez is thrown forth as the result and partial expression of energies surging up from below and in which he thereafter contributes to a top-bottom dialectic that transforms, decentralizes, and begins to 'disperse' state power" (p. 242). The key evidence for such dispersal is located for Ciccariello-Maher in the "explosion of communal power" he sees unfolding, particularly through barrio assemblies, communal councils, and popular militias. In one of his bolder formulations, he suggests "the communal councils embody one of Lenin's central criteria for dual power, seeking to subject the official bureaucracy to the will of the people through direct participation at the local level (and ultimately to replace that bureaucracy entirely)" (p. 244). He argues this even while acknowledging some six pages later that recognition of "the institutionalization of communal power as being on par with other public powers... certainly does not [mean]—for the moment, at least—... [that] popular organs of power [are] in a position of supremacy" (p. 250).

Unfortunately, in a context of quite severe economic crisis and a newly belligerent domestic right, the pace of bureaucratization and rightward movement internal to the Bolivarian process since the death of Chávez in late 2013 suggests to me that even the last hedging quotation above sees too much forward momentum in the advance of "communal power" in contemporary Venezuela.[47] Perhaps Ciccariello-Maher would respond that I, like too many other Marxist and anarchist thinkers, am "prioritizing [my] ultimate aims in the present... lead[ing] to a blindness to how it is that revolutionary change occurs and how it has been occurring in Venezuela. Rather than the revolution under way in Venezuela, then, some see merely the continuity of the state, of corrupt institutions, of charismatic leaders" (p. 235). But I see neither continuity nor revolution.

A central problem running throughout *We Created Chávez* is its erasure of

---

47 See Webber, "Managing Bolivian Capitalism"; Susan Spronk and Jeffery R. Webber, "Sabaneta to Miraflores: The Afterlives of Hugo Chávez in Venezuela," *New Politics* 14, no. 4: 97–109; Webber and Spronk, "February Traumas: The Third Insurrectionary Moment of the Venezuelan Right," *New Politics*, February 25, 2014.

the political economy of capitalism, and its attendant social relations. Proper consideration of these themes—including scaling up to the international, and Venezuela's position within the international division of labor—would bring more forcefully to light the objective limits of the Bolivarian process in the present conjuncture. The failures of Venezuelan guerrilla movements in the 1960s and 1970s, because they are abstracted from social relations, are reduced to a trail of bad decisions. Dual power, transformed from a particular expression of an unstable balance of social forces within a revolutionary situation, becomes a subjective—if institutionally bounded—political orientation. State power is made excessively malleable in the absence of due consideration for capitalist laws of motion and rules of social reproduction. Problems of will and subjectivity override the capitalist economy in this analysis, as the autonomy of the political instead finds privilege of place. These are the theoretical weak links in an otherwise exceptional meditation on Venezuelan politics, and they ultimately allow for the analytical fumble of naming this a revolution.

NINE

Conclusion: From Hegemony to Impasse

Denial is one response to the recent fading of center-left hegemony in Latin America. Broadly speaking, there are two versions of this position. The first is social-democratic. From this perspective, the electoral victory of right-wing presidential candidate Mauricio Macri in Argentina in November 2015, the congressional electoral victory of the right-wing opposition in Venezuela in December 2015, the February 2016 referendum defeat of Evo Morales in his bid to run for a third consecutive time in the next presidential elections, Rafael Correa's decision not to run again in the next presidential elections in Ecuador, and the parliamentary coup in April 2016 in Brazil are relatively superficial setbacks.

"For the past 15 years," Mark Weisbrot writes in an emblematic intervention of this kind, "Washington has sought to get rid of Latin America's left governments; but its efforts have really succeeded, so far, only in the poorest and weakest countries: Haiti (2004 and 2011), Honduras (2009), and Paraguay (2012)." The region is more independent than ever and the poor are better off than at any time in recent decades. The Latin American left, Weisbrot argues, has overseen the overturning of economic and political relations with the behemoth to the north, constituting a "second independence" in the present century, after freedom from Spain and Portugal was secured in the early nineteenth. Riding on this legacy, Weisbrot predicts that the region's progressives are "likely to remain the dominant force in the region for a long time to come."[1]

---

1 Mark Weisbrot, "Has the Left Run Its Course in Latin America?" *Nation*, May 10, 2016.

Social democrats never considered revolutionary change in the region to be possible or desirable in the twenty-first century, and thus have interpreted the move toward the center of the political spectrum by left and center-left governments over the last several years as merely an adaptation to reality—a prudent course of moderation. The key here is to accept the inevitable and make a virtue of necessity, following the lead of Lula and Rousseff in Brazil. The only viable alternative ever available in the recent period was a regulated, humane capitalism—other desires were nefarious or naïve.[2]

A second track of denial claims a certain Marxist pedigree. It emphasizes the centrality of the state as an agent in social change and aligns closely to the governments of Bolivia, Cuba, and Venezuela, and sometimes also to those of Argentina, Brazil, Uruguay, and Nicaragua. The apparent setbacks for the left are, from this point of view, merely symptoms of the natural ebbs and flows of revolutionary processes—part of the anticipated dynamics of advance and retreat, and unsurprising unless one holds to an innocent expectation of linear revolutionary ascent. Growing tensions between social movements and left governments are understood to be creative and revolutionary impulses, ultimately working in favor of the maturation of transformative processes—as long as the social movements stay within acceptable parameters of alignment with governmental objectives. Sociopolitical expressions of independent opposition from the left, or from indigenous organizations, to these administrations tend to be implicitly or explicitly reduced, by state managers and loyalist intellectuals of this current, to machinations of imperialism or the domestic right; left-indigenous oppositions are seen as little more than the willing allies or useful idiots of empire. Despite periodic hiccups and policy reversals, governments of the left are understood to be building advanced, industrial capitalism in the region, and in so doing are laying the basis for a slow transition to socialism. Such change does not drop from the sky, nor is it achieved overnight.[3] The transitional phase will last decades, perhaps centuries.

---

2 For a perceptive, critical characterization of the social democratic perspective, see Pablo Ospina Peralta, "El agotamiento del progresismo," *Nueva Sociedad*, April 2016.

3 For an internally varied sampling of this statist vision of socialist transition in contemporary Latin America, see Álvaro García Linera, *Socialismo comunitario: Un horizonte de época* (La Paz: Vicepresidencia del Estado Plurinacional de Bolivia, 2015); Emir Sader, *The New Mole: Paths of the Latin American Left* (London: Verso Books, 2011); Atilio Borón, *Socialismo Siglo XXI: ¿Hay vida después del neoliberalismo?*, 2nd ed. (Buenos Aires: Luxemburg ediciones, 2009); Marta Harnecker, *A World to Build: New Paths Toward Twenty-First Century Socialism* (New York: Monthly Review Press, 2015); Ángel Guerra Cabrera, "El presunto 'fin del ciclo progresista," *La Jornada*, August 20, 2015; Katu Arkonada, "¿Fin del ciclo progresista o reflujo del cambio de época en América

The Argument So Far

This book has demonstrated why both of these denialist narratives are mistaken. It has proposed an alternative Marxist framework, which explicitly incorporates insights from feminist, antiracist, autonomist, and environmentalist theories and praxes. I have argued that the global economic crisis has made its delayed landing in Latin America, and that in this context the hegemony of the center-left is in sustained and protracted retreat, even while various new rights remain incapable of offering an alternative hegemonic project.[4] This is a novel period of political impasse, characterized by deep neoliberal economic continuities in underlying patterns of regional accumulation and insertion into the international division of labor. A serious and balanced assessment of the limitations of the period of progressive governments, and the cycle of social movement revolt that preceded them and made them possible, cannot therefore be restricted to unidimensional criticisms of US intervention and belligerent rights, even when these are crucial components of the story.

This book began by tracing the trajectory of the Latin American left since the early 1990s, paying particular attention to the shifting balance of forces between popular classes and oppressed groups, dominant domestic classes, and imperialism across the last two and half decades. From a nadir in the early 1990s, it was shown how the neoliberal economic crisis between 1998 and 2002 evolved into a political crisis that helped to produce an unexpected renewal of an extra-parliamentary left. The radicalism of this movement left—particularly in Argentina, Bolivia, and Ecuador—was subsequently moderated in various ways through increasing participation of movement actors in elections and state apparatuses, the rise to office of center-left and left governments, and a worldwide commodity boom driven by China's dynamic accumulation. The compensatory state was consolidated by progressive governments, through which distribution to the poor was made possible without changing the underlying class structure of society—a model contingent on commodity prices holding firm.

Latina? 7 tesis para el debate," *Rebelión*, September 8, 2015; Emir Sader, "¿El final del ciclo (que no hubo)?," *América Latina en Movimiento*, September 15, 2015; Marta Harnecker, "Movimientos sociales y gobiernos progresistas: construyendo una nueva relación," *Rebelión*, October 30, 2015.

4 In this sense, the book aims to contribute to the eclectic critical literature emerging on the current conjuncture, from activists and intellectuals like Silvia Rivera Cusicanqui, Raúl Prada and Luis Tapia in Bolivia, Alberto Acosta and Mario Unda in Ecuador, Roland Denis and Edgardo Lander in Venezuela, Eduardo Gudynas and Raúl Zibechi in Uruguay, Maristella Svampa in Argentina, Francisco de Oliveira in Brazil, Hugo Blanco in Peru, and Massimo Modonesi in Mexico, among others.

The initial impact of the global economic crisis on the region was relatively weak, particularly in South America. But by 2012, the tide shifted and crisis rolled through the region. With a downturn in commodity prices, easy rent for redistribution disappeared, and center-left governments were transformed into managers of austerity, alienating at one and the same time sections of capital that had reconciled themselves to center-left rule, as well as the traditional social bases of these regimes in the popular classes. This dual retraction of support has provoked a decline in center-left hegemony and the uneven appearance of new social and political movements of the right. Ecuador, Argentina, Brazil, and Venezuela are prominent exemplars of the new setting.

Against this backdrop, the book has also addressed the theoretical and empirical question of Latin American inequality. It was argued that the rise of the left in Latin America rejuvenated mainstream social scientific discussion of problems of inequality in the region. While clearly something to celebrate, the renewed attention to inequality has tended to be dominated by analytical approaches rooted in Weberian historical sociology and liberal democratic theory, and has thus been impoverished by thin conceptualizations of democracy and idealized treatments of capitalism, class, and social relations of oppression. Because liberal ideology conceives capitalist markets as fundamentally spheres of opportunity, it is incapable of comprehending the market as a field of coercion; liberalism is thus unable to understand movements for *freedom from* rather than *within* the market. The invulnerability of the economic sphere to democratic power is sanctified in liberal conceptions of democracy, and consequently severely restricts the horizons of human emancipation. This book has shown how inept the liberal framework is at tackling the fundamental concerns that the social movements and parties of the region's left have forced onto the agenda over the last two decades.

In light of the failings of dominant schemas, I offered a distinct approach to inequality. The stress here was on the totalizing power of capital and a processual and relational conceptualization of class relations and other internally related social oppressions—gender, sexuality, and race—within contemporary Latin American capitalism. If class is understood as a living, relational phenomenon, than it is necessarily conceived as also being multiply determined in and through gender, race, and sexuality in present-day Latin American societies. From this vantage point, the latter social oppressions are not dismissed as mere epiphenomena of the class structure, nor are they reduced to symptoms of class exploitation. Yet, the way in which these multiple forms of social oppression constitute capitalist society alongside class can only be fully comprehended when they are conceptualized as being internally related to class. Class, gender, and race are, then, a dialectical unity of multiple determinations rather than a series of separate spheres. They are discrete phenomena, but only comprehensible when shown to be in interaction with one another in concrete, historically specific settings. The way these dynamics are played out in contemporary Latin American capitalism was examined through the intensification of extractive capitalism in the Andes and the attendant rise of sharp socioecological struggles around dispossession of land and racist incursions of capital and the state into indigenous territories. An exploration of the life and activism of Ecuadorian indigenous dissident Luis Macas also captured the way in which emergent political subjectivities within this context of extractivism have been informed by a utopian-revolutionary dialectic, in which elements of the precapitalist past are drawn upon in order to better look forward to an anticolonial and socialist future.

From the utopian-revolutionary dialectic of Macas, the book bridged to an exploration of the relationship between Marxism and Romanticism in the work of early twentieth-century Peruvian Marxist José Carlos Mariátegui. What can Mariátegui teach us about the limits of the regional left turn and its dominant ideological currents? The preoccupation here was an investigation of select ideas in the Mariáteguist framework that can be drawn upon to counter the development within sections of the new left of an economistic and evolutionist dogma, presented in a specific Marxist idiom, which stresses the inevitability—even desirability—of extractive capitalism in the short to medium term. The clearest enunciations of the new gospel are located in the late writings and practice of Bolivian vice president Álvaro García Linera, and, in particular, his ideological and programmatic defense of extractive capitalism as a progressive intermediary stage toward industrialization, and, eventually, transition toward a postcapitalist horizon. Against the evolutionism of García Linera, I posed the utopian-revolutionary dialectic of Mariátegui—especially through his treatments of imperialism, uneven and combined development, and racism and indigenous liberation in colonial and republican Peru. Mariátegui, like Macas, looks backward to elements of a precapitalist past and points forward simultaneously to a socialist future.

From an interrogation of extractive capitalism and its attendant socioecological battles, the focus of the book shifted to another front in twenty-first-century Latin American social movement dynamics—the 2011–2012 student-worker revolts in Chile. It was argued that these revolts marked a before-and-after point in contemporary Chilean history, as exemplified by the incorporation of many of the central ideas and demands originating in the movement into the new common sense of society. Nonetheless, the Chilean state continues to enjoy a number of material and subjective resources with which to appropriate and bureaucratize claims and practices emanating from below.

The Nueva Mayoría (New Majority, NM) government of Michelle Bachelet, in office since 2014, promised to curb the profits of the biggest corporations in the country, introduce electoral and educational reform, and transform the constitution. In the mode of Gramsci's *transformismo*, however, the NM government has thus far introduced strictly limited reforms within an overarching logic of continuity, balancing economic and political pressures from the right, while channeling and modifying social movement pressures emerging from below—whether it be from students, shantytown debtors, Mapuche indigenous militants, radical environmentalists, or rank-and-file labor activists in the copper mines and ports. While movements on many fronts are visible in contemporary Chile, the formation of a genuine counterhegemonic popular bloc is hindered by important objective and subjective obstacles. Unions are fragmented and have declining memberships. The revolutionary left is divided and trapped in sectarian debates with long histories and deep foundations. These inchoate lefts are consequently less able to respond to the everyday concerns of the popular urban classes and rural dispossessed. Without such organic ties, the organized far left is not in a position to link the complex fray of localized immediate battles of impoverished communities to broader sociopolitical projects with transformative horizons. Into this political void, right-wing evangelical Protestantism is making advances, preaching a theology of the market and a starkly neoliberal individualism. Nonetheless, the revolts of 2011–2012 were a turning point. A new generation of radicalized working-class youth is unlikely to renege on its yearning for a new order or quietly accept Bachelet's passive revolution.

Following the examination of Chile's social movement–state relations, the book addressed the case of Bolivia, focusing first on urban structures and relations, before turning to the countryside. On a theoretical level the intervention on Bolivia develops a critique of García Linera's influential thesis of "creative tensions" within the "process of change," which he argues are leading—albeit with contradictions and setbacks—toward a structural transformation of the Bolivian state, society, and economy. As an alternative to "creative tensions," I argued for Antonio Gramsci's notion of "passive revolution" as a more compelling interpretive framework—in particular, a reading of passive revolution capable of capturing the dialectical unity of internal relations between economics and politics in the Bolivian process, as distinct from notions of politics and ideology as relatively autonomous from processes of capital accumulation.

Passive revolution was explored concretely through the dynamics of what I labeled "extractive distribution" within Bolivia's political economy, the class contradictions of what the Bolivian government calls the "plural economy," and the specific transformations of the urban labor market that have flowed from extractive distribution and passive revolution across the epoch of Evo Morales (2006–2016). Over time, the Bolivian process has witnessed the emergence of a layer of petty capitalists, drawn in large part from the country's indigenous majority. It is precisely this emergent layer, across various sectors of the economy, that has entered into alliance with older dominant sectors in Bolivian society—agro-industrial, mining, and oil capital—to underpin the Morales administration, particularly over the last six years. The logic of big capital (foreign and domestic), in this scenario, runs alongside the legitimating function of indigenous petit-bourgeois class formation.

Regarding the Bolivian countryside, I challenged the prevalent view that there has been dramatic and egalitarian agrarian reform in Bolivia under Morales. My argument rooted itself in an examination of the changing balance of agrarian class forces in Bolivian society, and the related changes in the class composition of the ruling bloc over time under the Movimiento al Socialismo (Movement Toward Socialism, MAS). Between 2006 and 2009, the indigenous peasant social movement alliance, the Unity Pact, was able to apply genuine pressure from below as it sought a transformation of the Bolivian rural class structure, and in that context the agro-industrial elite fought openly against the central government through an autonomist and regionalist destabilization campaign, headquartered in Santa Cruz and radiating outward through the rest of the lowland departments of the country. In this initial phase of the Morales government, the main institutional terrain of struggle was the Constituent Assembly process. Because of the intensity of rural mobilization from below, and the depth of organizational popular pressure, there was a fairly open-ended possibility during this period of deep structural reform to the countryside.

By 2010, the balance of forces had been altered. The Morales government defeated the political project of autonomy in the lowlands and this laid the groundwork for a class realignment in the ruling bloc. Over the next six years, a new agro-capital-state alliance emerged, with subordinate support from rich peasants in the coca, soy, and quinoa commercial export sectors, among others. The Unity Pact fragmented, and lowland indigenous social movements were expelled from the governing alliance. These changes in class composition had dramatic negative consequences for the possibilities of agrarian reform. In essence, the strategic zones of productive land in the country have been locked in the grips of national and transnational agro-industrial capital devoted to soy production and its derivatives for export, while the majority of landless and land-poor indigenous peasants remain relegated to marginal areas of low productivity. The promised expropriation of private landholdings has been abandoned, and what relatively little redistribution of state property has been carried out has tended to be of marginal land of little to zero agricultural potential. In terms of agrarian policy, the Morales regime has paradoxically proved more successful at carrying out the project of industrial agrarian capitalist expansion in the east than the original nationalist advocates of such a developmental vision in the post-revolutionary 1950s. But government talk of a slow transition to socialist communitarianism is pure fantasy.

After its Bolivian investigations, the book turned toward the Venezuelan conjuncture through a critical dialogue with George Ciccariello-Maher's *We Created Chávez*. Throughout, I situated the Bolivarian process under Hugo Chávez within Venezuela's deeper history since 1958—the rural guerrillas of the 1960s, the urban guerrillas of the 1970s, the new urban sociopolitical formations of the 1980s, Afro-indigenous struggles in the Bolivarian process, and changing compositions of the formal and informal working classes since the onset of neoliberalism and its current contestation in Venezuela. Theoretically, I interrogated the widespread view of a mutually determining dialectic between Chávez and social movements, and the concepts of "the people" and "dual power." I argued for more precise conceptualizations of revolution, capitalism, and the state in order to better understand the impasse in Venezuela today under Chávez's successor, Nicolás Maduro.

End of a Cycle?

There were myriad social gains achieved during the period of center-left hegemony. There were some advances toward alternative regional integration projects to counter US dominance in the region.[5] Laws granting impunity to leading figures of the Argentine dictatorship were overturned as unconstitutional, and constituent assemblies in Venezuela, Bolivia, and Ecuador re-

---

5 Carlos Eduardo Martins, "La Integración regional en América Latina y sus desafíos contemporáneos," *Cuadernos del pensamiento crítico latinoamericano*, no. 12 (May 2014); Daniele Benzi, "El exitoso ocaso del ALBA: Réquiem para el ultimo vals tercermundista," *Nueva Sociedad* 261 (January–February 2016): 77–91.

sulted in some transformative elements in the new constitutions established as a result.[6] Politically, the contrast with repressive conservative regimes in countries such as Colombia, Peru, Paraguay, Honduras, and Mexico is acute. In the sphere of ideology, there was a regional revival of anti-imperialism and, in some countries, proliferation of strategic debates in society over socialism and paths of transition to a post-capitalist mode of production.[7]

The bonanza of export rent was used by progressive governments to fund targeted social policies for pauperized strata, increase and sustain employment rates (albeit typically in insecure and low-paid jobs), and spike domestic consumption. There were measurable improvements in living conditions for popular sectors of society.[8] There was a reduction in poverty, and income inequality was slightly reduced (although this was also true of some countries in the region led by right-wing governments, as a cursory comparison of International Monetary Fund figures for Colombia and Brazil reveals, and the region remains the most unequal in the world). The pace of privatizations slowed and was even reversed in some economic sectors in a few countries. There was an uptick in spending on basic social services and infrastructure in poor urban neighborhoods and marginalized rural areas. Access to basic free education was expanded, and in some cases access to university was democratized. In the words of Ecuadorian sociologist Pablo Ospina Peralta, Latin American progressivism offered "something," however minimal, in the face of the "nothing" that dominated the decades of neoliberal reaction that preceded it.[9] But even these slight gains were slowed or reversed in the last few years, as the global economic crisis seriously began to pinch state revenues. The "social, political, and economic cycle of medium duration," sociologist Franck Gaudichaud observes, "seems to be slowly exhausting itself, although in multiform and nonlinear ways. With their real (but relative) advances, their difficulties and important limitations, the different experiences of very distinct progressive governments of the region… appear to be running up against significant endogenous problems, robust conservative powers (national as well as global), and lack of direction and unresolved strategic dilemmas."[10]

---

6 Salvador Schavelzon, "El fin del relato progresista en América Latina," *La Razón*, June 22, 2015.

7 Claudio Katz, "Desenlaces del ciclo progresivista," *Electronic Bulletin*, January 25, 2016.

8 Mabel Thwaites Rey, "The Cycle of Impugnation to Neoliberalism in Latin America and Its Critics," *Dynamo*, no. 1 (May 9, 2016): 9.

9 Pablo Ospina Peralta, "El reformismo progresista," *Nueva Sociedad*, May 2016.

10 Franck Gaudichaud, "¿Fin de ciclo en América del Sur? Los movimientos populares, la crisis de los 'progresismos' gubernamentales y las alternativas ecosocialistas," *Memoria*, October 13, 2015.

The decline of center-left hegemony is opening up a new period, likely to be marked by more intense forms of new right rule, lacking societal consent, and more reliant, therefore, on militarized and repressive domination. But the right will be unable to solve the structural problems underlying the region's economics. The new period is likely to be one of economic, social, and political instability, of renewed interventionism by the United States, and deteriorating living conditions for the majority of Latin American populations.[11]   Progressive governments in the region are increasingly wedged between growing popular demands for the sustenance of recent social gains, on one side, and the intensifying discontent of foreign and domestic capitals that had learned to live with center-left hegemony when there seemed to be no other option. In the present scenario, none of the progressive governments are ideologically, organizationally, or politically prepared to take the audacious steps against capital—nationalization of banks, monopolization of trade, agrarian reform, mass employment schemes, environmental regulations, boosts to popular consumption, and control of money laundering—that might realign them with popular bases of support. These "governments fear popular mobilization of their own bases of support," Guillermo Almeyra notes, "more than being toppled by the right, which is on the offensive."[12]

The cycle of progressivism in Latin America has demonstrated that mass mobilizations against neoliberalism in the early part of this century, and the subsequent occupation of state apparatuses by progressive governments of different shades, are insufficient on their own to structurally transform society, the state, and the economy in the current context of global capitalism. Indeed, the occupation of the state can often domesticate social movements and tame their desires through partial incorporation of their demands within an underlying framework of continuity. This observation, though, is hardly vindication of the radical autonomist view of changing the world without taking power, of ignoring state power and buckling down in defensive islands while the sea is governed by the right.[13] The new situation demands a sober assessment of the period, interrogation of established revolutionary truths, and ongoing, open-ended discussion of the strategic lessons to be drawn. "When major historical processes come to an end, and in turn major political defeats transpire," Raúl Zibechi explains, "confusion and despondency set in, desire intermingles with reality, and the most

---

11 Raúl Zibechi, "Las tormentas que vienen," *La Jornada*, December 27, 2015.
12 Guillermo Almeyra, "Fin de un ciclo," *La Jornada*, August 9, 2015.
13 Holloway, *Change the World Without Taking Power*.

coherent analytical frameworks blur."[14] Building on the basis of the arguments already advanced in this book, the rest of this chapter contributes such an initial, bird's-eye measuring of the conjuncture—gradations of change and continuity, complexities of economics and politics, and puzzles of socialist strategy.

Patterns of Accumulation and the International Division of Labor

A quarter of a century ago, Robert Brenner and Mark Glick published a seminal article in *New Left Review*, which, among other things, established the importance of the disciplining impact of the world economy on local, regional, and national institutional configurations.[15] They stressed the participation of every part of the capitalist world—if to uneven degrees—in the expansion before World War I, the interwar depression, the post–World War II boom, and the structural crisis since the late 1960s.[16] "Despite the heterogeneous modes of regulation of its constituent parts," Brenner and Glick contend, "the world economy as a whole [since at least 1900] has possessed a certain homogeneity, indeed unity, in terms of its succession of phases of development. The world economy has, it seems, been able to impose *its* general logic, if not to precisely the same extent, on all of its component elements, despite their very particular modes of regulation."[17] They called into question the notion of a willing compromise between capital and labor in particular national settings, in which capitalists would submit to wage increases and elemental features of a welfare state in pace with and in exchange for productivity increases on the part of workers. In reality, in the face of international competition, "capitalists, facing continuing pressure on their profits, could not, even if they wished to, viably promise workers, in exchange for involvement, secure employment and enriched jobs, or even a share of the returns from productivity growth."[18] Working classes could only lose ground by entering into false compromises and giving up their independence by identifying with their employers.

This formulation nicely reflects the nature of capitalism as operating on

---

14 Raúl Zibechi, "Progressive Fatigue? Coming to Terms with the Latin American Left's New 'Coyuntura,'" *NACLA Report on the Americas* 48, no. 1 (2016): 22.

15 Robert Brenner and Mark Glick, "The Regulation Approach: Theory and History," *New Left Review* 1, no. 188 (July–August 1991): 45–119.

16 However, for a compelling case against the long downturn thesis of the post-1960s period, see David McNally, *Global Slump: The Economics and Politics of Crisis and Resistance* (Oakland, CA: PM Press, 2010).

17 Brenner and Glick, "The Regulation Approach," 112.

18 Ibid., 116.

a world scale, a system in which global interdependence, rather than national independence, becomes a necessary starting point for comprehending the specific trajectory of different societies. It stresses the disciplining impact of capitalist competition. Brenner and Glick also capture the discontinuity of patterns of global capital accumulation over time, punctuated as they are by recurring crises. However, their framework misses the "constitutive heterogeneity of each phase," according to Fouad Makki.[19] Makki writes:

> It presumes a degree of uniformity that subsumes social and historical unevenness in a diachronic succession of temporal phases. But if we proceed from a more differentiated conception of historical temporality in which time is not simply a uniform medium, it becomes possible to appreciate plural, uneven, and interwoven processes of social change. Capitalist development so conceived does not move according to a single uniform beat, but operates through the complex contemporaneity of its unevenly combined social forms.[20]

The abstract, homogeneous time of capital on a global scale is captured effectively by Brenner and Glick, but they are less attentive to the concrete, heterogeneous temporality of capitalist development in specific social formations, determined by the timing and nature of the transition to capitalism and insertion into the world market of specific countries and regions, relative to others. It matters whether they were "early" or "late" developers in world-historical time—which never stands still—or whether they transitioned to the top of the world hierarchy of states, or were inserted at the bottom. The dynamic conditions of the uneven world market are constantly in flux and condition the form of development in particular countries and regions depending, among other things, on the timing of their development. This is the dialectic of the universal and the particular, the abstract and the concrete, which informs the uneven and combined development of capitalism in specific social formations.[21]

To this concrete temporal complexity of capitalist development on a global scale the additional issue of hierarchy in the world system also requires close consideration. Hae-Yung Song has recently complemented analyses such as Brenner and Glick's by adding to their emphasis on the global totality of capitalist social relations an attentiveness not only to the "generic aspects of the dynamics of (global) capital across nation-states," but also to "the ways in which the totality itself is constituted not merely differentially but hierarchi-

---

19 Fouad Makki, "Reframing Development Theory: The Significance of the Idea of Uneven and Combined Development," *Theory and Society* 44, no. 5 (2015): 489.
20 Ibid.
21 Ibid.

cally."[22] Song points to the necessity of understanding how hierarchy and un-evenness in world capitalism produces distinct political dynamics in societies situated at the lower echelons of the global system, or so-called late develop-ers. She stresses how their specific position within the world system and the timing of their capitalist development condition the patterns of class struggle and mediate the ways in which these struggles are expressed in the politics of "catch-up" development.[23] According to Song, the hierarchical world system of states, processes of state-building, and geopolitical conflicts are the political side of the operations of the capitalist mode of production on a global scale, rather than an independent sphere of politics and geopolitics with its own separate logic. Capitalist development in one geographic zone of the world system—including its political and geopolitical side—is necessarily related to, the cause or result of, the development of other zones.[24]

In the context of late, catch-up development, states often play the role of "enforc-ing capitalist development from above." In this sense, "the particular conditions of capitalist development within the hierarchically unfolding dynamics of capitalism" compel states to "act as the main agent[s] trying to overcome backwardness under conditions of 'catch-up' development."[25] However, even though the developmental state *appears* to be the principal actor and determinant of national developmental outcomes, in fact "the particular positioning and timing of development within the world system actually condition failure or success of capitalist development."[26] The developmental state in a catch-up situation presents itself as class-neutral, as the institutional representative of the nation. In reality, the character and role of the late-developer state "primarily involves… an apparatus to protect the national bourgeoisie from competition from more advanced bourgeoisie and to grant the national bourgeoisie the freedom to exploit domestic labour, typically by 'super-exploitation,' for example, long working hours and low wages in the conditions of 'catch-up' development in the hierarchical world economy."[27] In the context of the latest cycle of left governments in Latin America, we witnessed varied (failed) attempts to establish new forms of developmental capitalist states in the neolib-eral epoch of global capitalism. Governments of different ideological hues within the new left presented these state projects from above as precisely class-neutral

---

22 Hae-Yung Song, "Marxist Critiques of the Developmental State and the Fetishism of National Development," *Antipode* 45, no. 5 (2013): 1265.
23 Ibid.
24 Ibid., 1267.
25 Ibid., 1269.
26 Ibid., 1270.
27 Ibid.

programs of progress, as representative of the national interest of each specific society. Opponents on the left or right were similarly tarred as traitors of the nation.

The forms of interconnectedness of national states within the international system of states and the world market are doubly determined. From one side, they are conditioned by the historical cycles of accumulation on a global scale, which impel the production, distribution, and consumption of specific goods and services, in specific geographic zones and regions, for the world market—that is, the role of the international division of labor. From the other side, the form of insertion of national states into the international system of states and the world market is determined by the balance of forces between the core classes operating within the national territory of specific states. From the first direction, then, this interconnectedness has to do with the productive role of particular states within the world market (the principal productive activities of its economy, its export capacity, its level of indebtedness, and so on). From the second direction, the form of interdependence is determined by both the interests and perceptions of the fundamental antagonistic classes within national territories, but also across the scales of the nation, region, and world, reverberating back upon and conditioning the historical cycle of accumulation on a global scale.[28] The strength of the laboring classes vis-à-vis capital is measurable across these different scales and their internal relations with one another.

Taking into consideration the various elements conditioning the state-form and national outcomes of capitalist development, the historical specificity of the state in Latin America can be understood to derive from its subordinate historical incorporation into the world market, while the multiplicity of national state forms within the region flows out of the concrete processes of particular historical class formations in the concrete conditions of particular countries, the shape of the antagonistic interests, politics, and ideologies of the key classes, and how these again rebound back upon and exist in tension with each state's insertion into the historical cycles of accumulation on a global scale.[29]

Despite the political variation between different left governments in contemporary Latin America, and between all left governments and their conservative counterparts in the region, the starkest and most consistent areas of continuity between the orthodox neoliberal era of the 1980s and 1990s and

---

28 Mabel Thwaites Rey and Hernán Ouviña, "La estatalidad latinoamericana revisitada: Reflexiones e hipótesis alrededor del problema del poder politico y las transiciones," in *El Estado en América Latina: Continuidades y rupturas*, ed. Mabel Thwaites Rey (Buenos Aires: CLACSO, 2012), 61.

29 Ibid., 71.

the most recent era of progressivism are the principal bases of the region's insertion into the international division of labor and fundamental domestic patterns of capitalist accumulation. The antineoliberal uprisings of the early 2000s, followed by the rise of left and center-left governments in the mid-2000s, did not alter Latin America's insertion into the international division of labor. More than this, in the context of high primary commodity prices, all countries strengthened their existing profile as basic primary exporters.

On the right side of the political spectrum, Sebastián Piñera in Chile, Álvaro Uribe and Juan Manuel Santos in Colombia, Vicente Fox and Enrique Peña Nieto in Mexico, and Alan García and Ollanta Humala in Peru employed the resources acquired through the commodity bonanza to consolidate orthodox policies of trade liberalization and privatization. On the center-left and left—in Argentina, Brazil, Uruguay, Ecuador, Bolivia, Venezuela, and elsewhere—the new state revenues enabled the expansion of internal consumption, the subsidization of local businesses, and the targeted welfare programs of compensatory states.[30]

Advocates of neoliberal restructuring in the 1980s and 1990s stressed Latin America's export specialization in primary products for export to the world market after the era of import-substitution industrialization (1930s–1970s) was exhausted, in some senses inaugurating a return to the region's embrace of the free market in the late nineteenth century. The latter transition to neoliberalism involved a strong reorientation of agricultural production toward exports and the acceleration of mining and natural gas and oil extraction.[31] Rather than reversing it, the latest cycle of progressive governments consolidated this turn. While the contribution of primary commodities to Latin America's GDP rose, the contribution of the industrial sector declined from 12.7 percent in 1970–1974 to 6.4 percent in 2002–2006. Simultaneously, Latin America's productivity, technological innovation, pace of patent registrations, and levels of investment and development in industry weakened relative to accelerations across these areas in East Asia.[32]

The Argentine sociologist Maristella Svampa has characterized this regional trajectory as a shift from the *Washington Consensus* of neoliberalism to the *Commodities Consensus* of late.[33] The renewed focus on primary commod-

30 Claudio Katz, "Desenlaces del ciclo progresivista."
31 William I. Robinson, *Latin America and Global Capitalism: A Critical Globalization Perspective* (Baltimore, MD: Johns Hopkins University Press, 2008).
32 Claudio Katz, "Dualities of Latin America," *Latin American Perspectives* 42, no. 4 (2015): 12.
33 Maristella Svampa, "'Consenso de los Commodities' y lenguajes de valoración en

ity exports witnessed the expansion of mega-projects designed to extract and export natural resources with little value added. The extension of the mining, agro-industrial, and natural gas and oil frontiers has involved "a deepening dynamic of dispossession or plunder of lands, resources, and territories, and produces new forms of dependency and domination."[34]

A fetishistic productivism under the extractive model of accumulation is the shared worldview of progressive and conservative governments, despite their important political differences. Embedded in their ideological commitment to productively utilizing natural resources in a scenario of high global commodity prices, "there is a disqualification of other logics of valorizing territories," territories that are considered by state managers and private investors to be "socially empty" until they have been made "useful" by the metrics of exchange-value, or profit.[35]

Unsurprisingly, as discussed in previous chapters, the intensification of the exploitation of natural resources under extractive capitalism has generated a proliferation of socioecological value struggles over the use of resources, land, and territory. Left-indigenous oppositions have been met with ferocious repression in countries ruled by right-wing governments, but have also generated serious conflicts—and repression, if to a significantly lesser degree—in countries ruled by center-left and left administrations committed to extractivism.[36]

At the political-ideological level, the Commodities Consensus stresses the irresistible character of the extractivist inflection in Latin America's recent capitalist development. It sets the parameters for "realistic" visions of change and tends to close off the very possibility of debate. The ideological underpinnings of extractive capitalism, including under progressive governments, have encouraged popular resignation in the seeming absence of alternatives, the preordained destiny of Latin America's role in the international division of labour as supplier of primary materials to the world market. Those indigenous, peasant, and environmentalist movements that oppose the acceleration of the

---

América Latina," *Nueva Sociedad* 244 (March–April 2013): 30–46. Although her notion of re-primarizaton of Latin American economies exaggerates the extent of industrial decline—industry remains important, if reduced—Svampa captures important features of the current political-economic conjuncture and their attendant political and ideological expressions. For a thoughtful critique of Svampa, see Juan Grigera, "La insoportable levedad de la industrialización," *Batalla de ideas* 4 (2013): 46–57.

34 Ibid., 32.

35 Ibid., 34.

36 For a fuller discussion of these matters, see Todd Gordon and Jeffery R. Webber, *Blood of Extraction: Canadian Imperialism in Latin America* (Halifax: Fernwood, 2016).

model of accumulation are presented merely as expressions of antimodernity, the negation of progress, irrationality, and ecological fundamentalism, when they are not being targeted by progressive governments as dangerous allies of imperialism and the domestic right.[37]

The extractive model generates socioeconomic polarization, conflict over communal resources, and environmental destruction. It generates violence, criminalizes poverty, and militarizes conflict in societies over the use of territory, resources, and land.[38] Rather than generating a reversal of this model of accumulation, the steep decline in commodity prices in the last few years has witnessed extraction's intensification under progressive regimes and a desperate search for still more foreign investment by multinationals in deteriorating conditions. The end result is continued ferocity of socioecological conflict, violence, and dispossession without the high state revenues for compensatory redistribution of years past.

Since the mid-2000s, progressive governments in the region have proved incapable of altering the underlying patterns of capital accumulation that they inherited. There has been nothing approaching the import-substitution industrialization policies of the 1930s to 1970s, nor any redistribution of productive possibilities through agrarian reform. While countries like Bolivia and Ecuador have designed numerous development plans and initiatives around the use of the rent from natural resource exploitation to generate industrialization, all of these have been implicitly or explicitly abandoned in practice.[39] In Venezuela, too, by the close of the Chávez period, dependence on oil had accelerated to such a degree that oil accounted for 95 percent of total exports. In Latin America's most industrialized country, Brazil, the raw exports of soy and iron ore to China, as well as the expansion of deep-sea oil exploitation, have contributed to a national decline in industrial production.

By some accounts, Brazilian industry is roughly half what it was thirty years ago. In Argentina, 28 million hectares of arable land have been devoted to capital-intensive agricultural production of soy, corn, and cotton. The country made a modest industrial recovery over the Kirchner period, but industry is still at only 17 percent of GDP, compared to 23 percent in the 1980s. In Mexico, the traditional areas of industry built up during the period of ISI for the domestic market has largely been replaced by the rise of the maquila free-trade zones on the northern border with the United States, directed toward external markets,

---

37 Svampa, "'Consenso de los Commodities,'" 36.
38 Zibechi, "Las tormentas que vienen."
39 Ospina Peralta, "El reformismo progresista."

while in Central America and the Caribbean new forms of precariousness and severe labor discipline reign supreme, as manufacturing productivity is under fierce competitive pressure from Asian enterprises. Region-wide, according to figures from the Economic Commission for Latin America and the Caribbean, primary materials represented 73 percent of exports to China, with the sale of manufactured goods accounting for only 6 percent.[40]

Regional Integration

Regional integration projects during the progressive era were more of a cocktail of change and continuity, although even here the latter ingredient was the more concentrated of the two. The century began on a high note, with the popular defeat of the US-led initiative to establish a Free Trade Area of the Americas (FTAA) from Alaska to Tierra del Fuego, excluding Cuba.[41] Relatively more geopolitical autonomy from US and Canadian power was also achieved through the establishment of the Unión de Naciones Suramericanos (Union of South American Nations) in 2008, and the Comunidad de Estados Latinoamericanos y Caribeños (Community of Latin American and Caribbean States, CELAC) in 2011. The explicit exclusion from CELAC of the United States and Canada, as well as the inclusion of Cuba (and Cuba's assumption of the organization's rotational presidency in 2013), were signals of cooperative Latin American attempts to downgrade the role of the Organization of American States (OAS), which had long been seen as merely an offshore department of the American state.

CELAC includes thirty-three member countries and has facilitated an unprecedented number of meetings between Latin American state leaders, free of direct imperial interference. Nonetheless, it remains mainly a symbolic counterweight to North American dominance. Likewise, because UNASUR envelops all South American states, its basis of unity is as thin as the political eclecticism of its members allows. Close allies of the United States, such as Colombia, are able to channel US interests within the organization. Still, UNASUR has shown moments of independence, such as the suspension of Paraguay from the organization following the parliamentary coup that ousted Fernando Lugo in 2012.

---

40 Zibechi, "Progressive Fatigue?" 24; Katz, "Dualities of Latin America," 12.
41 Claudio Katz, *El rediseño de América Latina: ALCA, MERCOSUR y ALBA* (Buenos Aires: Ediciones Luxemburg, 2006).

Mercado Común del Sur (Southern Common Market, Mercosur), by contrast, was established in 1991 as a typical multilateral trade agreement, at the height of the neoliberal period. Its core members include Argentina, Brazil, Paraguay, Uruguay, and, most recently, Venezuela, with associate membership status extended to Bolivia, Chile, Colombia, Ecuador, Peru, and Suriname. With Brazil and Argentina as its central players, Mercosur was from the start designed to work as a free-trade area with a key role for foreign investors, but with shared tariff structures and a common bloc for negotiations with external parties to boost the bargaining power of the individual member nations. Halfway through the second decade of this century, Mercosur is in stasis. "It has not taken any steps toward macroeconomic coordination," Claudio Katz points out, while the "differences in currency, types of exchange, and fiscal policies among its members are enormous. Proposals to reduce the asymmetries between countries do not exist, and as industry declines there are no plans for manufacturing coordination or shared use of export profits."[42]

The sole project of an unambiguously anti-imperialist character, the Alianza Bolivariana para los Pueblos de Nuestra América (Bolivarian Alliance for the Peoples of Our America, ALBA), depended on the unmitigated commitment of the Venezuelan regime at the height of Chávez's rule, as well as high oil prices, to sustain Venezuelan ambitions of integration with weaker, poorer states.[43] Chávez is dead and the price of oil is in the doldrums. Together with Venezuela, ALBA eventually came to encompass Bolivia, Cuba, Nicaragua, Ecuador, Antigua, San Vicente, and Grenada. Various cooperative trade arrangements that violated the principles of the free market were encouraged between member states. Perhaps most emblematic was the exchange of Venezuelan oil for education and health services from Cuba.

The conception of ALBA since its inception has been openly hostile to US dominance of the region, and the organization has been expressly anti-imperialist in the shared diplomatic initiatives of its members. Because of its more overtly radical political character, ALBA is much more likely to suffer immediate negative consequences in the context of the decline of the progressive cycle, as left governments recede from the Latin American political scene. One early signal in this direction was the withdrawal of Argentina from participation in ALBA's subsidized television alternative to CNN en español, Telesur, almost immediately upon Macri's assumption to office. Trade within

---

42 Katz, "Dualities of Latin America," 25.
43 On the origins and character of ALBA, see Claudio Katz, *El rediseño de América Latina: ALCA, MERCOSUR Y ALBA* (Buenos Aires: Ediciones Luxemburg, 2006).

ALBA countries remains a tiny proportion of its members' total commercial exchange, and, without exception, the core transformative projects have remained ideas on paper—the Bank of the South, a common currency, and so on. Apart from the individual problems facing left governments in its leading member countries, ALBA's "immediate consolidation is limited by the severe underdevelopment of the economies that are participating in this initiative," Katz notes. "There is only one country with significant resources (Venezuela), and having oil wealth is not the same as having a medium-sized economy or an industrial base. There is an abyss between it and the economies of the central powers and an enormous gap between it and those of Mexico, Brazil, and Argentina."[44] This problem has only become greater with the fall in oil prices.

Much more integral to processes of regional integration than Venezuela and ALBA has been the dual role assumed by the region's main geopolitical power, Brazil. Under Lula and Rousseff, large Brazilian firms were backed by the state, and state managers became their ambassadors abroad. Brazilian foreign investment proliferated throughout the region, and the geopolitical role of the Brazilian state assumed a typically subimperial position in the region, promoting an independent project of its own in Latin America, sometimes in competition with US and other imperialisms, but subordinating itself simultaneously to the greater power of the United States when necessary. Brazil has projected its power through the Integration of Regional Infrastructure of South America (IIRSA) initiative, and the country's state development bank that backs it, BNDES. Brazilian energies behind BNDES very quickly eclipsed any previous notions of a robust, region-wide Bank of the South.[45] The loan portfolio of BNDES has increased by 3,000 percent since Lula first took office in 2003. IIRSA's infrastructure projects, underwritten by BNDES, continue to have as their priority "the export of commodities, rather than any sort of productive complementarity" across unevenly developed Latin American states.[46]

Together with South America's shift in principal trading partners from the United States to China during the commodity boom, the new Asian power also began to play a more competitive economic role in the region vis-à-vis American capital. China absorbs 40 percent of Latin American raw material exports. Chinese investment in the region grew remarkably quickly, from $US 15 billion in 2000 to $US 200 billion in 2012. As a creditor, China has eclipsed the World Bank in Latin America and the Caribbean. It lent in ex-

---

44 Katz, "Dualities of Latin America," 36.
45 Ibid., 24.
46 Zibechi, "Progressive Fatigue?," 26.

cess of $US 75 billion to the region between 2005 and 2011. These loans were granted with better conditions than the World Bank, IMF, and commercial loans to the region in the 1990s, but they remain directed toward extractivist projects of mining, oil and natural gas, and other raw materials—i.e., primary sources for meeting strategic Chinese needs.[47]

All of the various projects of South American association proved incapable of transcending nationalist pursuits and intercapitalist competition between capitals rooted in different countries. Each state prioritized its own comparative advantages in primary commodity exports, with no coordination across states or efforts to build cooperative industrial scales beyond national territories. This kind of fracturing across the region was evident in trade and credit relations with China. Each Latin American government entered into unilateral negotiations and agreements with the Asian country which were necessarily asymmetrical, and worked systematically to the disadvantage of the weaker Latin American players. There was no collective bargaining established between any South American bloc and China, which might have brokered more favorable trade and credit relations for Latin American states with the Asian power, and might also have allowed for a better counterweight from US dominance as a result. Instead, US dominance persists, but accompanied now by new dependent relations with China. China buys primary goods from Latin America and extends lines of credit for infrastructural projects to enable the further extraction of such commodities. Meanwhile it sells manufactured goods to Latin America and collects interest on its loans. The depth of subordination of Latin America to China in these senses is only rivaled by Chinese-African relations.[48]

As efforts at independent regional integration projects stall or recede, the Trans-Pacific Alliance, a principal mechanism for the rearticulation of US power in the region, is gaining momentum. After the defeat of the FTAA, the United States prioritized bilateral free trade agreements with its remaining Latin American allies. These are now being organized into the collective free-trade initiative of the Trans-Pacific Alliance, which in turn is part of the grander international strategy of the Trans-Pacific Partnership (TPP) and the Transatlantic Trade and Investment Partnership (TTIP). Thus far, the Latin American members of the Trans-Pacific Alliance include Chile, Colombia, Mexico, and Peru, with Costa Rica in the process of integration. On taking office, Macri's government expressed Argentina's interest in joining, and the United States is

---

47 Katz, "Dualities of Latin America," 20.
48 This paragraph draws on Katz, "Desenlaces del ciclo progresivista."

courting Uruguay, Paraguay, and Panama with the lure of observer status.[49]

To recap our survey of continuities in the international division of labor and regional integration, the capitalist world economy has been able to impose its logic, if in heterogeneous and uneven forms, across the globe through its successive phases of development in the last century or so. The period we are living through is no exception. Neoliberalism characterizes the current epoch, and in the last two decades, despite a turn to the left, Latin America has been unable to impose a postneoliberal order in the region at odds with the overarching global logic of the world economy. The starkest continuity in this respect has been the continuous deepening of the region's insertion into the international division of labor as a primary commodity exporter—the shift, in Svampa's formulation, from the Washington Consensus to the Commodities Consensus.

While there is a general abstract logic to the world economy across successive phases, there is also a constitutive, concrete heterogeneity and hierarchy that condition the state-forms and rhythms of class struggle in countries that are "late" developers and are situated on the bottom rungs of the world system of states. The specificity of the Latin American state form has to do with its historically subordinate insertion into the world market. During the last cycle of progressivism, there was a series of failed attempts to establish developmental capitalist states in Latin America, using the momentum of extraparliamentary social movements of the early part of the century to forge new left electoral governments. But once in office, state managers ruled from above through nationalist ideologies of productive fetishism, which pretended these new state forms were class-neutral, and that the new left governments were representatives of the national interest, the people as a whole.

This disguised their actual functionality to domestic and multinational sections of capital—particularly those involved in the various extractive zones of contemporary capitalism in present day Latin America. The continuities in the international division of labor, in this respect, together with the domestic continuities of individual countries governed by the left or center-left in terms of their patterns of capital accumulation, paralleled the failure of regional integration projects to consolidate relative autonomy for the region in the realm of geopolitics or competition between states. Crucially, the United States has retained its fundamental power in the region and is again on the offensive. The stasis of autonomous regional integration projects has allowed China, as well, to impose an asymmetrical trade and credit relationship on Latin America.

---

49 Katz, "Dualities of Latin America," 20.

Passive Revolution

The economics of the recent decade in Latin America are best understood, I have argued, in dialectical relation with the region's politics—avoiding both economistic reductionism and politicist voluntarism. By some distance the most perceptive political theorization of the current conjuncture in Latin America is Massimo Modonesi's work on passive revolution. Modonesi begins from the foundation of conceiving the Latin American progressive cycle in its totality as differentiated versions of passive revolution. This totality encompasses a series of important but strictly limited structural transformations of Latin American societies under left rule, which have, however, taken on conservative overtones, and have with time been catalyzed increasingly from above, relying ever more on demobilizing and subordinating subaltern political practices from below. These processes have emptied out, from top to bottom, channels of popular organization, participation, and protagonism that had been developed and refined during the extraparliamentary cycle of revolt in the early years of the present century.[50]

While commodity prices were high, progressive governments were able to consolidate their hegemony, but in the last few years this hegemony has entered into decline. The phase of hegemonic consolidation

> was forged fundamentally through the effective exercise of a series of state- and party-mediations, displacing the right from strategic institutional lymph nodes and ideological apparatuses of the state, and installing in their place a series of idea-forces, slogans, and political values of a national-popular character, such as sovereignty, nationalism, progress, development, social justice, redistribution, and plebeian dignity, among others…. This phase seems to have definitively ended. At least since 2013, a point of inflection is perceptible, with certain temporal and formal variations across different countries, a shift from a more progressive profile to one tendentially more regressive.[51]

It is not just that new right forces have appeared unevenly across much of Latin America, but that the progressive governments themselves have been reconfiguring their social bases and shifting their programs of governance to the right. In class terms, they have been shifting the cost of austerity in post-boom Latin America onto their former social bases of support through reductions in public spending and cuts to services, rather than more vociferously confronting the owners of capital in their societies and socializing more of the pro-

---

50 Massimo Modonesi, "Fin de la hemonía progresista y giro regresiva en América Latina: Una contribución gramsciana al debate sobre el fin de ciclo," *Viento Sur* 142 (2015).
51 Modonesi, "Fin de la hegemonía progresista."

ductive sources of societies' wealth. In Ecuador and Bolivia, governments are increasingly confronting—discursively and materially—left-indigenous social movements that are mobilizing around the key conflict areas of extractive capitalism. Mining, above all. In Argentina, in the lead-up to the 2014 elections, Kirchnerism accepted the right-wing Peronist Daniel Scioli as the party's presidential candidate—Scioli was exceedingly difficult to distinguish from Macri, and marked a sharp rightward turn within Peronism, reminiscent of the 1990s under Carlos Menem, when Scioli began his start in politics. In Brazil, the PT shifted hard to neoliberal austerity in Rousseff's second term, after she had campaigned on an anti-austerity agenda. In Venezuela, Maduro has moved steadily to the right and has relied on loyal state bureaucrats rather than facilitating and encouraging independent mobilizing capacities from the grassroots.

While since 2013 there has been a steady growth of newly independent social movements and popular organizations in countries governed by the left and center-left, these movements remain relatively underdeveloped—"due to their newness, and the absence of organizational consistency and political articulation, there does not appear to be a scenario in which Latin American politics could shift to the left in the immediate horizon."[52]

In some ways, this is a residual effect of the slowdown in social movement activity following the height of the protest cycle between 2000 and 2005, and the subsequent coming to office of left and center-left governments. These governments prioritized electoral cycles, guaranteeing governability free of social conflict. With these aims in place, they were relatively antagonistic toward autonomous popular organizing from below and neglected the construction of participatory channels of independent grassroots action and forms of self-governance and determination. Rather than helping to foment an increase in the capacities of self-organization and self-activity of the subaltern classes, progressive governments focused on improving a passive capacity for consumption, drawing on rents captured from high commodity prices to secure governability and consent. Without improving capacities for struggle from below, transformative potentials became increasingly dim. The turn was instead toward conservatizing moderation and popular inactivity imposed from above. In Modonesi's words,

> This weakness, or absence of empowerment, suggests that the pacifying intention which operated as a counterpart to the structural transformations and redistributive policies… provoked a decade of loss in terms of the accu-

---

52 Ibid.

mulation of political force from below, seen from the vantage point of the autonomous capacity of popular forces, in contradistinction to their ascendancy that marked the 1990s and that broke neoliberal hegemony, opening up the current historical scenario.

If popular movements laid the foundations for center-left hegemony, center-left hegemony channeled their energies into bureaucratic state management, targeted redistribution of commodity rents, and the avoidance of conflict with the propertied classes. This consensus was relatively stable during an epoch of high commodity prices, but the lubricant of high state revenues has disappeared, and the rusty gears of open class conflict are once again sounding their alarm. Unfortunately, the internal rightward shift of progressive governments, and the rearticulation of new right forces, is occurring in a context of diminished subaltern capacities to mobilize on their own behalf.

Big Men and Bureaucrats

One of the clearest political patterns to have emerged over the progressive cycle is the bureaucratization of social movement actors through their entry into bourgeois state apparatuses. Rather than transforming state institutions, the institutions have systematically transformed the movements. The logic of elections and polling, and the calculus of public opinion, came to predominate.[53]

The problem of bureaucracy is not merely one of the inherited structures of the old state moving against the grain of progressive government policy, or residual civil servants from the old order who are recalcitrant in the face of change. There is also the issue of representatives of subaltern movements being themselves transformed into impediments to change once they enter the institutionality of the capitalist state, even at its lowest echelons. This bureaucratic layer of subaltern movement representatives begins to live off the state they are ostensibly fighting to transform. Their own material reproduction comes to depend on the preservation of the status quo. Subaltern bureaucrats are also opened up to an unfathomable array of opportunities to enrich themselves through corruption. The inherent instability that would come with any audacious deepening of transformative processes, and the continual transference of power to independent, self-organized popular organizations from below that this would necessitate, often becomes in these situations a threat to the bureaucratic layer, the material conditions of their reproduction, and the sustain-

---

53 Schavelzon, "El fin del relato progresista."

ability of their privileged social status. Bureaucratic traps of this kind remain a tremendous obstacle to anticapitalist projects—indeed, even to projects for deep structural reform within capitalism.[54]

Pervasive in the ideological development of the progressive cycle has been a deepening cult of bureaucracy and leadership. This is attached to the idea that history is made by leaders with extraordinary abilities and capacities. Grassroots popular protagonism—which, of course, made these governments possible—recedes backstage. Bolivia is one striking example. A few days after the 2016 referendum defeat of Morales's bid to amend the constitution to run for the presidency for a third consecutive time, vice president Álvaro García Linera addressed an Aymara indigenous community meeting in the department of Oruro. "If he goes," García Linera said of Morales, "who is going to protect us? Who is going to care for us? We are going to be left as orphans if Evo goes. Without father, without mother, we are going to be left like that if Evo goes."[55] The paternalism on display in words of García Linera is all the more striking in a country that hosted the most militant and widespread movements from below of anywhere in Latin America between 2000 and 2005, laying the basis for Morales's ascent to office. "The problem with caudillismo," Zibechi points out, "is that it is a culture of the right, functional to those who want to substitute the protagonism of those from below with those from above…. It is a political and cultural operation of legitimation, at the cost of emptying out the content of collective actors. It is a conservative, elitist politics that reproduces oppression instead of superseding it."[56]

Accompanying the cult of bureaucracy and caudillismo is a defensive hostility on the part of state managers in the face of left oppositions and criticisms. State managers lose their ability to differentiate between creative left opposition and opposition from the domestic right and imperialism. Legitimate popular opposition to reactionary measures instituted by progressive governments is quickly and thoughtlessly treated as merely an expression of imperial machinations and manipulations. Social movements of left and indigenous origin have been tarred as traitors of the nation in Argentina under Cristina Fernández de Kirchner, Rafael Correa in Ecuador, Evo Morales in Bolivia, and Nicolás Maduro in Venezuela. The cult of bureaucracy and infal-

---

54 Thwaites Rey and Ouviña, "La estatalidad latinoamericana revisitada," 81; Raúl Zibechi, "Una izquierda para el siglo XXI," *La Jornada*, January 22, 2016.
55 Quotes in Raúl Zibechi, "El caudillismo es cultura de derecha," *La Jornada*, March 4, 2016.
56 Zibechi, "El caudillismo."

lible leadership of left governments encourages a sensibility of "not bothering the driver," to praise without cessation the wise decisions of the executive.[57] The result over time is the alienation of the government from legitimate left critics, the fomentation of right oppositions, and the consolidation of conservative tendencies internal to progressive administrations.

Renewal

Latin American social movement struggles in the beginning of the twenty-first century were characterized by direct action, grassroots participatory democracy, and the instantiation of politics as nonprofessional activity. The assembly form as a space of deliberative decision-making became a privileged mode of doing politics. Social movements combined antagonistic confrontation with the state and experimentations with new forms of autonomous prefiguration of the postneoliberal, and in some cases postcapitalist, societies they hoped to forge.[58]

When progressive parties assumed the mantle of state leadership, however, the tendency was toward a social movement practice of *subaltern participation*—the pacifying incorporation of popular sectors into the gears of the capitalist state—rather than an *autonomous and antagonistic participation*, in which the ongoing capacity to disrupt and to lay the groundwork for emancipatory and prefigurative inspiration is maintained. The necessary struggle *against, within, and beyond* the state became instead a muted and moderated struggle captured by the state.[59] Social movements lost the necessary strategic orientation of sustaining, at each phase and moment of the class struggle, a tight connection between specific social movement struggles and a revolutionary horizon of transforming capitalist society in its totality. Modest reforms and increases in consumptive capacities became ends in themselves, rather than laying the basis for ever greater contradictions and ever greater, and more audacious, structural ruptures with the existing order.[60] The new left regimes channeled and captured the momentum of social change from below rather than sparking and incentivizing

---

57 Guillermo Almeyra, "Venezuela y el indispensable golpe de timón," *La Jornada*, January 10, 2016.

58 Massimo Modonesi and Mónica Iglesias, "Perspectivas teóricas para el estudio de los movimientos sociopolíticos en América Latina: ¿Cambio de época o década perdida?," *De Raíz Diversa* 3, no. 5 (January–June 2016): 107.

59 Thwaites Rey and Ouviña, "La estatalidad latinoamericana revisitada," 85.

60 Ibid., 75.

ongoing alterations in the balance of class forces in favor of subaltern sectors.

Actually existing apparatuses of the capitalist states cannot be captured by left governments and straightforwardly retooled for purposes other than the reproduction of capitalist society. But neither is the state merely an instrument of the bourgeoisie. Within a specific national territory, and within the limits of capitalist reproduction, the state represents the material condensation of the balance of class forces. Those positive aspects of state delivery—public education, health care, and so on—are the accumulated legacy of past popular struggle, always unevenly achieved in capitalist states, and permanently under threat of reversal. Ultimately, there can be no self-transformation of the state from within its apparatuses, given the fundamental role of the state in reproducing dominant class relations and the mode of capitalist exploitation.

It may be that there is a revolutionary road to postcapitalism that begins through the electoral assumption of office by left forces. But any revolutionary deepening of such a process would quickly lead to an organic crisis of the state and fierce counterattack by bourgeois forces. What began with elections would then become something else altogether. Revolutionary transformation of capitalism will always require the purposeful extension of new forms of solidarity, self-management, the institutionalization of new social and political forms of struggle, and extended modalities of popular power from below, outside of, and against the bourgeois state, even if left parties and social movements do not forgo, in the first instance, the electoral terrain of competition.[61]

With the exhaustion of the progressive cycle, the political moment in Latin America is likely to become much darker before it gets brighter. But if the social movements combating the parliamentary coup in Brazil, or the popular antagonisms aligned against the authoritarian regime in Honduras, are harbingers of struggles to come elsewhere in the medium term, the tide will eventually turn again, creating conditions more favorable to the struggles of Latin America.

---

61 Panagiotis Sotiris, "Rethinking Political Power and Revolutionary Strategy," *Viewpoint*, issue 4, September 8, 2014.

Acknowledgments

I relied on the support and insight of many people in the research and writing of this book. Todd Gordon, Rob Knox, Juan Grigera, Luciana Zorzoli, Adam Hanieh, and Susan Spronk provided insight and advice in relation to different parts of this book. Given the geographic scope of the study, I leaned heavily on the scholarship of others, particularly the painstaking, concrete investigations undertaken by Latin American intellectuals with precise expertise in the individual countries discussed, either in passing or in more depth. I've acknowledged these sources in the footnotes, but I would like to add additional appreciation here.

My immediate and extended family have been a bedrock of support. Thanks to my parents, Roger and Elaine Webber, and my sisters, Elizabeth, Ruth, and Theresa, as well as Olga Shustyk, Gerry Dykstra, and Rebecca Dykstra.

Thanks most of all to Tieneke Dykstra, to whom this book is dedicated.

I am indebted to the entire team at Haymarket for their ongoing interest in my work and for their rigor and commitment. Sincere thanks to Caroline Luft, Anthony Arnove, Dao X. Tran, Nisha Bolsey, Rachel Cohen, Julie Fain, Rory Fanning, Jason Farbman, Eric Kerl, Jon Kurinsky, Jim Plank, John McDonald, Jesus Ramos, and Ahmed Shawki.

My ideas on contemporary Latin American political economy and social struggle have been sharpened through conversations with all of the dedicated members of the London Latin American Marxist Reading Group. Likewise, sections of the book take up themes that have been studied collectively in the Historical Materialism and World Development Research Group with which I am affiliated in London. Many thanks to all of the participants in those discussions. At Queen Mary University of London, I have learned a great deal from each of my PhD students—Angus McNelly, Kristin Ciupa, and Sue Iamamoto.

I also want to mention those individuals who read parts of this manuscript or otherwise contributed in specific ways to its completion.

Pedro Mendes Loureiro provided me with expertise on Brazilian sources for the relevant discussion in chapter 2. Sean Purdy, Juan Grigera, and Adam Hanieh provided me with penetrating feedback on the same section.

An earlier version of chapter 3 appeared in *Latin American Research Review*. It was also presented at the Latin American Studies Association annual conference in San Juan, Puerto Rico, in 2015. Many thanks to Phil Oxhorn and José Jouve Martín for their comments.

A version of chapter 4 was previously published in *Theory and Society*. It began life in a radically different form, as a comparative study of Romantic Marxism in the work of E. P. Thompson and José Carlos Mariátegui. I presented it in this initial manner at the Global E. P. Thompson Conference, hosted by the Program on the Study of Capitalism, at Harvard University in 2013. Thanks to the organizers of the conference—Rudi Batzell, Sven Beckert, Andrew Gordon, Gabriel Winant, and Jessica Barnard—for the invitation to participate. I benefited from the commentary on multiple subsequent drafts by Rob Knox, Forrest Hylton, Madeleine Davis, and Lucas Martín Poy Piñeiro.

A version of chapter 6 was previously published in *Third World Quarterly*, as part of a special issue on social class and development organized by members of the Historical Materialism and World Development Research Group. Thanks to Ben Selwyn, Jon Pattenden, Liam Campling, and Adam Morton for their comments on earlier drafts. Thanks as well to Massimo Modonesi for rich discussion on the concept of passive revolution, and its relevance in contemporary Latin America, during his visit in 2015 to Queen Mary University of London.

A significantly shorter version of chapter 7 was published in the *Journal of Agrarian Change*. Thanks to Enrique Castañón Ballivián for providing me with leads, suggestions, and sources that helped in the research for the chapter. Thanks as well to Leandro Vergara-Camus and Cristóbal Kay for their extensive commentary on early iterations. This chapter was also presented at the Latin American Studies Association annual conference in New York City in 2016.

Finally, a version of chapter 8 was previously published in *Historical Materialism*. This chapter emerged initially from the notes of a workshop at the

Historical Materialism New York Conference at New York University, April 26–28, 2013. In the workshop, George Ciccariello-Maher and I discussed and debated each other's recent books on Venezuela and Bolivia. Thanks to Christy Thornton for chairing the session and to Geo for his close and careful attention to my work, and for his spirit of comradely debate. Many thanks also to Rob Knox for his comments on an earlier draft.

Index

About the Author

Jeffery R. Webber is a senior lecturer at the School of Politics and International Relations, Queen Mary University of London. He is the author of *Red October* and *From Rebellion to Reform in Bolivia*. With Todd Gordon, he is coauthor of *Blood of Extraction: Canadian Imperialism in Latin America*.